THE
GRIMKÉ
SISTERS
from
South Carolina

Studies in the Life of Women

THE
GRIMKÉ
SISTERS
from
South Carolina

**PIONEERS FOR
WOMAN'S RIGHTS
AND
ABOLITION**

BY
GERDA LERNER

SCHOCKEN BOOKS · NEW YORK

To Carl

ACKNOWLEDGMENTS

I AM deeply indebted to the following institutions for giving me access to their excellent collections of manuscripts and for permission to use excerpts from many of the unpublished letters and documents pertaining to the Grimké sisters.

Howard H. Peckham, Director; William S. Ewing, Curator of Manuscripts; and Robert W. Keyes, Assistant Curator of Manuscripts, The William L. Clements Library, University of Michigan. Their many knowledgeable suggestions greatly lightened my task;

John Alden, Keeper of Rare Books, and Miss Ellen Oldham, Curator of Classical Literature, Rare Book Department, Boston Public Library, accorded me every courtesy;

James Rawle, Curator, Manuscript Division, Historical Society of Pennsylvania, and the librarians in charge of the various collections offered me every facility for research and helped me greatly to acquire an understanding of nineteenth-century Philadelphia by giving me access to their superb collection of pictures and local history;

The librarians of the Society of Friends, Arch Street Center, Philadelphia, kindly afforded me an opportunity to study their extensive records of the various Meetings of the Society of Friends;

Mrs. Margaret S. Grierson, Director, and Miss Elizabeth Duval, Bibliographer, The Sophia Smith Collection, Smith

College, far exceeded professional courtesy during my stay. Their gracious hospitality and the generous way in which they opened to me the rich resources of their superb collection on the woman's rights movement will be long remembered;

David C. Mearns, Chief, Manuscript Division, The Library of Congress afforded me every facility for research at that great institution;

Mrs. Dorothy Porter and Mrs. E. Ellis, Moorland Foundation, Howard University, were patient and helpful in allowing me to study the Grimké Family papers;

The New York Public Library and its superb staff not only gave me access to manuscript sources and genealogical records, but provided me for many months with a place to work and every facility to make research easier. The rich resources of the Schomburg Collection of the New York Public Library were indispensable to my work;

The collection of nineteenth-century newspapers at the New York Historical Society was a valuable source of information on local history. Wilmer R. Leech, Curator of Manuscripts, was generous with his time and offered many helpful suggestions;

The Charleston County Free Library provided me with the wills of John Faucheraud and Mary Grimké;

Miss Ellen Peterson, Hyde Park Branch, Boston Public Library, was most helpful in culling facts pertinent to my research from the Henry A. Rich Collection;

The Women's Archives, Radcliffe College; The Philadelphia Public Library; the Library of the University of North Carolina, Chapel Hill, N. C. were valuable sources of research.

I have greatly benefited over the past three years by the

opportunity of working at the Libraries of Columbia University, whose rich resources make any research easier and pleasanter.

To Mrs. Arthur Cort Holden of New York City I owe a special debt of gratitude for her generosity in making available to me the full facilities of her fine private library on the history of women. Her loan of rare books from her collection greatly facilitated my work. Her knowledge, her generous friendship and her enthusiasm for this project were most encouraging.

I have benefited greatly from the guidance and criticism of Professors Eric L. McKitrick and Robert D. Cross of Columbia University, who have seen this work in its various stages. Their understanding of my goals and their confidence in me and in this work have been an inspiration of lasting value.

Professor Carl Degler of Vassar College has read this manuscript and contributed greatly to its improvement by his keen critical judgment. The suggestions offered generously by Professor James P. Shenton of Columbia University were most helpful.

I am most grateful to Mrs. Anne N. Barrett of Houghton Mifflin Company, whose editorial advice and gentle guidance helped shape this book in its final stages. My thanks also to Mr. Philip Rich and Miss Linda Glick for their helpful contributions. To Edith Margolies I owe a special debt of gratitude for her unflagging confidence and support. I appreciate the professional competence and personal interest of Mrs. Shirley Lerman and Mrs. Sarah Hope, who typed the manuscript.

To Virginia Brodine, who first aroused my interest in the contribution of women to American history and who inspired the writing of this book, public expressions of gratitude will be less meaningful than our many years of close friendship. I do, however, wish to record my indebtedness to her.

Through all the years spent on this work my husband, Carl Lerner, has been a helpful partner in research, an enthusiastic admirer of Sarah and Angelina Grimké, an incisive and sharp critic and, as always, a tower of strength.

As for my children, Stephanie and Daniel, without their tolerant understanding, their patient cooperation and their abiding confidence in the outcome, this work would not have been possible.

In quoting from the Grimké sisters' letters and diaries, original spellings and italics have been retained, including frequently ungrammatical constructions, misspellings and faulty punctuation. The only changes made were the substitution of "and" for "&," the addition of punctuation marks where clarity required it, and the transcribing of dates from the Quaker system to the usual calendar.

CONTENTS

CHAPTER
ONE

We Abolition Women are turning the world upside down.
Angelina E. Grimké,
February 25, 1838

O N WEDNESDAY, February 21, 1838, starting about noon,
people from all over Boston began arriving at the State
House in carriages, by horseback and on foot. By one o'clock
the crowd was so great that guards were posted inside the
Hall of Representatives to reserve seats for the members of
the Legislative Committee scheduled to meet at two.[1] It
was what the newspapers then called a "mixed" audience,
which meant mostly men with a sprinkling of ladies who in
their ruffled skirts, their frothy bonnets and gaily colored
shawls brightened the galleries. One could recognize many
of the more prominent citizens in the hall, while the inevitable ruffian element clustered around the entrance, undecided
whether the coming spectacle merited giving up a few
hours in the tavern. Here and there, a few respectable colored people could be seen in the crowd. The attendance of
so many people at a legislative hearing was quite out of the
ordinary, especially since no advance public notice had been
given, but news of this kind could be trusted to travel speed-
ily by word of mouth. Today, a *woman* would address a
Committee of the Legislature of the State of Massachusetts.

Groups of abolitionists had come early from Lynn, Lowell, Worcester, Shrewsbury and several other of the surrounding townships. A good many of them had previously heard the speaker on her recent tour through New England. They could testify to the scoffers and doubters that she was perfectly capable of sustaining oratory and refuting objections by logical argument. However, they had to admit that for a woman to speak before a friendly small-town crowd was quite a different matter from speaking before a legislative body. Questions from the legislators in the presence of such a large crowd might well overawe the young woman, despite her customary eloquence.

By two o'clock the members of the legislature had to fight their way to the seats reserved for them. The gallery, the staircase, even the platform, were crowded. Every seat was taken; the aisles and lobby were filled with standees. Men clustered around the windows and doors and many, after waiting patiently for an hour to be admitted, had to leave disappointed.[2] No one, apparently, wanted to miss this unprecedented event. Until this day, no American woman had ever spoken to a legislative body. Women did not vote nor stand for office and had no influence in political affairs. They received inferior elementary schooling and were, with the exception of recently opened Oberlin College, excluded from all institutions of higher learning. No church, except the Quakers, permitted women any voice in church affairs or in the ministry. The belief that a woman's name should properly appear in print only twice in her life, on her wedding day and in her obituary, described accurately the popular dread of female "notoriety." Woman's sphere was the home. There, she was the "grace, the ornament, the bliss of life." With an education which provided her with just enough "skill in household matters and a certain degree of cunning in culinary disposition" she might rule supreme over children and servants and expend what energies she had left after the care of her large family on the care of the community's indigent and poor.[3] This gospel of woman's "proper role" was preached from pulpit and press and enshrined in the law, which classified women with slaves and imbeciles regarding property and voting rights. Married women had no legal rights over their inherited property or their earnings, could not make contracts, could not sue or be sued. While American practice, especially that of premarital contracts, tended to mitigate the generality and severity of these restrictions, the concept of woman's inferior position remained firmly entrenched in the law and in the popular mind. Children were under the sole guardianship of the father; mothers had no rights over them even in cases of legal separation. Few occupations were open to women and in those her wages were often less than half of those of men. As a result unmarried and widowed women were dependent on their nearest male relatives, and spinsterhood was considered a tragic fate. Prescribed in scriptures and fixed by tradition, woman's secondary role in society was taken for granted by most men and women. "A woman is a nobody," declared *The Public Ledger* of Philadelphia as late as 1850 in an article ridiculing the advocates of equal rights for women: "A wife is everything. A pretty girl is equal to 10,000 men and a mother is, next to God, all powerful. The ladies of Philadelphia therefore . . . are resolved to maintain their rights as wives, belles, virgins and mothers and not as women."[4]

One daring woman had attempted to break through this web of restrictions, but she had been a foreigner, a radical and an infidel. In 1828 Frances Wright had lectured to large audiences in several American cities, but had been hooted and jeered as a freak. Her name had become an epithet across the land. It was considered unthinkable that any American woman would follow the example of this "female monster."

Several years later a Negro woman, Mrs. Maria W. Stewart, gave four lectures in Boston, speaking to her own people in favor of abolition and education for girls. But she soon gave up and admitted failure. "I find it is no use for me, as an individual, to try to make myself useful among my color in this city. . . . I have made myself contemptible in the eyes of many." [5]

But the woman who would address the legislators today was not only American-born, white and Southern, but the offspring of wealth, refinement and the highest social standing. Angelina Grimké and her sister Sarah, notorious as the first female antislavery agents, were ladies whose piety and respectability had been their shield against all attacks during their recent precedent-shattering nine months' speaking tour.

Angelina Grimké was well aware that people regarded her as a curiosity and came not so much to listen to her as to stare and scoff. Now, as she approached the hall and noticed the large number of people who could not find room inside, she felt her courage waning.

I never was so near fainting under the tremendous pressure of feeling. My heart almost died within me. The novelty of the scene, the weight of responsibility, the ceaseless exercise of mind thro' which I had passed for more than a week — all together sunk me to the earth. I well nigh despaired.[6]

She knew that a great many in this crowd were at best unsympathetic, at worst openly hostile. They had read derogatory accounts of the Grimké sisters' brazen defiance of public opinion, of their unwomanliness in appearing on public platforms, of their radical and inflammatory speeches against slavery. A Pastoral Letter of the Council of Congregationalist Ministers had warned all the churches of Massachusetts against these dangerous females. Outrageous caricatures of Angelina Grimké and William Lloyd Garrison had daily been hawked in the streets.[7] She was experienced enough in judging audiences to know that a crowd such as this might easily become a mob. Somewhat anxiously, she turned toward the woman walking with her, a beautiful Bostonian of unequalled poise. Maria Weston Chapman was a veteran of the antislavery movement and had an unusually thorough acquaintance with mobs. The intrepid courage of the Boston antislavery women, who had walked through the mob attacking their meeting, their hands folded in white cotton gloves, their eyes fixed sternly on each threatening face had become almost a legend. Now, Mrs. Chapman cast an experienced eye over the waiting crowd and for an instant placed her hand on Angelina Grimké's shoulder. "God strengthen you, my sister," she said quietly and smiled her radiant smile. Angelina relaxed; the faintness left her. She was surrounded by friends, by women who had felt the shame of slavery deep in their hearts as she had. Twenty thousand of them had signed the antislavery petitions she was about to present to the legislators. It was for them she was speaking, for them she must do what no American woman had done before her. If only her sister Sarah could have been beside her to support and sustain her as she had all during their speaking tour. But Sarah, who had been the scheduled speaker today, was suffering from a violent cold and could not leave her room. In a last-minute change of plans, Angelina, who had origi-

nally intended speaking at the next session, had to substitute
for her.

Once inside the hall, Angelina recognized many familiar
faces: Reverend Samuel May with his kindly smile, the Samuel Philbricks, whose houseguests she and Sarah had recently been, Brother Allen from Shrewsbury, nodding encouragement. The delicate features of Lydia Maria Child
expressed her affection and sympathy. The presence of these
friends gave Angelina courage. And, as always, in moments
of tension, her religious faith sustained her. ". . . our Lord
and Master gave me his arm to lean upon and in great
weakness, my limbs trembling under me, I stood up and
spoke. . . ." [8]

In this first moment of hushed attention Angelina Grimké
impressed her audience most of all by her dignity. Slight of
build, often described as frail, she stood before them in her
simple gray Quaker dress, her delicate features framed by a
white neckerchief. Beneath her dark curls deep blue eyes
dominated a thoughtful, serious face.[9] Her earnestness and
concentration transmitted itself to the crowd even before she
began to speak. "For a moment a sense of the immense responsibility resting on her seemed almost to overwhelm her,"
Lydia Maria Child later wrote to a friend. "She trembled
and grew pale. But this passed quickly, and she went on to
speak gloriously, strong in utter forgetfulness of herself." [10]
Angelina was not beautiful in the conventional sense, but
when she spoke in her clear, well-modulated voice her personality and deep convictions captivated her audiences and
transformed her in their eyes. She was often described as
beautiful, powerful, a magnetic, gifted speaker.

Now she reached far back in time for a precedent to her
appearance before the legislature. Like her, Queen Esther of
Persia had pleaded before the King for the life of her people.

Mr. Chairman, it is my privilege to stand before you
on a similar mission of life and love. . . . I stand before
you as a citizen, on behalf of the 20,000 women of Massachusetts whose names are enrolled on petitions which
have been submitted to the Legislature. . . . These petitions relate to the great and solemn subject of slavery.
. . . And because it is a political subject, it has often
tauntingly been said, that women had nothing to do
with it. Are we aliens, because we are women? Are we
bereft of citizenship because we are mothers, wives and
daughters of a mighty people? Have women *no* country
— *no* interests staked in public weal — no liabilities in
common peril — no partnership in a nation's guilt and
shame? [11]

The bold words rang out in the hall. Woman's influence
on the nations, the speaker asserted, had been largely as
courtesans and mistresses through their influence over men.

If so, then may we well hide our faces in the dust, and
cover ourselves with sackcloth and ashes. This dominion of woman must be resigned — the sooner the better;
in the age which is approaching she should be something more — she should be a citizen. . . . I hold, Mr.
Chairman, that American women have to do with this
subject, not only because it is moral and religious, but
because it is *political,* inasmuch as we are citizens of this
republic and as such our honor, happiness and well-
being are bound up in its politics, government and laws.

Here the speaker paused, and a stirring, like a sigh, went
through the audience. Not only the event itself, but the
words here spoken were so daring and novel, it staggered

the imagination. The women in the audience listened in rapt fascination as one of their own sex dared to speak out what many had thought in silence. Some of the ministers present nodded sagely; they were hearing blasphemy, just as they had expected. Not for nothing had this woman been called "Devil-ina" in the daily press.[12] The devil did indeed work through her attractive form, her poised and ladylike manner. But the abolitionists in the audience, even those who had previously expressed their disagreement with the speaker's approach, now were clearly won over. It had seemed to many that it would be best for Angelina Grimké simply to speak about the antislavery petitions and avoid offending the sensibilities of the audience by bringing up the extraneous subject of woman's place in society. But it was obvious that she had the audience spellbound and even those most critical could not help but admire her accomplishment. Angelina felt their sympathetic support, like "a body guard of hearts faithful and true" and drew strength from it.[13] Her voice, previously calm, now took on a passion that gripped her listeners' emotions.

> I stand before you as a southerner, exiled from the land of my birth by the sound of the lash and the piteous cry of the slave. I stand before you as a repentent slave- holder. I stand before you as a moral being and as a moral being I feel that I owe it to the suffering slave and to the deluded master, to my country and to the world to do all that I can to overturn a system of complicated crimes, built upon the broken hearts and prostrate bod- ies of my countrymen in chains and cemented by the blood, sweat and tears of my sisters in bonds.

The audience was deeply moved and eagerly looked for- ward to her next appearance, which was scheduled for Friday, February 23, two days later. The arrangements caused some dissension among the legislators. A Boston representative claimed that the crowds she attracted were so great that the galleries were in danger of collapsing. This caused a witty legislator from Salem to propose that "a committee be appointed to examine the foundations of the State House of Massachusetts to see whether it will bear another lecture from Miss Grimké."[14] This, apparently, ended the discussion.

Angelina described the scene on her arrival for the second session:

> . . . the hall was jambed to such excess that it was with great difficulty we were squeezed in, and then were compelled to walk over the seats in order to reach the place assigned us. As soon as we entered we were received by clapping. . . . After the bustle was over I rose to speak and was greeted by *hisses* from the doorway, tho' profound silence reigned thro' the crowd within. The noise in that direction increased and I was requested by the Chairman to suspend my remarks until at last order could be restored. Three times was I thus interrupted, until at last one of the Committee came to me and requested I would stand near the Speaker's desk. I crossed the Hall and stood on the platform in front of it, but was immediately requested to occupy the Secretaries desk on one side. I had just fixed my papers on two gentlemen's hats when at last I was invited to stand *in* the Speaker's desk. This was in the middle, more elevated and far more convenient in every respect.[15]

It was a bad beginning and might have upset the most seasoned speaker. But Angelina now felt "perfectly calm"; her

"self possession was unmoved." This time, her sister Sarah
had been able to accompany her. In fact, she, whose timid-
ity was proverbial among her friends, had been invited to sit
in the chair of the Speaker of the Massachusetts Assembly.
"We Abolition Women are turning the world upside down,"
thought Angelina.[16]

She was better satisfied with her speech on this occasion
than she had been earlier. She spoke on "The Dangers of
Slavery, the Safety of Emancipation, Gradualism, and Character of the Free people of Color, the cruel treatment they
were subjected to thro' the influence of prejudice — this
prejudice always accompanied *gradual* emancipation." It
was a speech she had frequently given during her New England tour and represented, essentially, her theoretical contributions to antislavery thought. The attention she gave to
prejudice, especially in the North, was characteristic of her
and distinguished her from other antislavery speakers.
Again, the audience was deeply moved. "The Chairman was
in tears almost the whole time that I was speaking," Angelina
reported. "What affected him so much I do not know but I
never saw a greater struggle of feeling than he manifested."[17]
By request of the committee, she was invited to complete
her remarks to them on another occasion, the following
week.

Abolitionists were jubilant and conscious of a triumph.
And the press, as it had done and would continue to do,
sneered:

MISS GRIMKÉ.

She exhibited considerable talent for a female, as an orator; appeared not at all abashed in exhibiting herself in a

position so unsuitable to her sex, totally disregarding the doctrine of St. Paul, who says "Is it not a shame for a woman to speak in public?" She belabored the slave-holders, and beat the air like all possessed. Her address occupied about 2 hours and a half in delivery, when she gave out, stating that she had a sister who was desirous to speak upon the same subject but was prevented by ill health. She, however, intimated, that after taking a breath for a day, she would like to continue the subject and the meeting was accordingly adjourned to Friday afternoon, at 3 o'clock, when she will conclude her speech.[18]

The reporter from *The Olive Branch* concluded an article in which he ridiculed Sarah Grimké's speech, never realizing that it was Angelina Grimké he had heard, with the following cutting remark: "It is rather doubtful whether any of the South Carolina lords of creation will ever seek the heart and hand of their great orator in marriage. . . ."[19]

And from as far west as Pittsburgh came an attack in a similar vein: "Miss Grimké, a North Carolinian [!], we believe, is delivering abolition lectures to the members of the Massachusetts Legislature. Miss Grimké is very likely in search of a *lawful* protector, who will take her for better or worse for life, and she has thus made a bold dash among the Yankee lawmakers."[20]

But there were other voices: "It was a noble day when for the first time in civilized America, a Woman stood up in a Legislative Hall, vindicating the rights of women. . . . This noble woman gave our legislators . . . one of those beautiful appeals for which she alone, as an American female, has been so justly distinguished."[21] And from distant Detroit the reporter of the Detroit *Morning Post* declared, "Miss Grimké, a pretty Quakeress . . . is a woman of splendid eloquence and has made me 19/20 of an abolitionist." [22]

It is obvious that contemporaries had some appreciation of the meaning of this event. The Grimké sisters' pioneering speaking tour, which culminated in Angelina's appearance before the Legislature, took place a full ten years before the Seneca Falls convention. It was at this convention that for the first time in history women organized to demand their rights as citizens. Many of the key figures in the coming struggle for woman's rights, Elizabeth Cady Stanton, Lucy Stone, Susan Anthony, Abby Kelley, were personally inspired by the Grimké sisters. The woman who, in February 1838, stood up and spoke for her sex before a legislative assembly of men, was an emancipated, a "new woman," half a century before the phrase had been coined. In working for the liberation of the slave, Sarah and Angelina Grimké found the key to their own liberation. And the consciousness of the significance of their actions was clearly before them. "We Abolition Women are turning the world upside down."

The Grimké sisters knew they were ushering in a new era.

CHAPTER
TWO

The political power of the cotton kingdom was firmly lodged in the hands of successful businessmen. . . . Laws were made by the owners of plantations; the higher courts were established by their decrees; governors of the states were of their choosing; the members of Congress were selected and maintained in office in accordance with their wishes. . . . They were the ruling members of all the churches. Truly, nothing of importance could happen in the lower South without their consent.

William E. Dodd, The Days
of the Cotton Kingdom; A
Chronicle of the Old South,
1919.

SARAH MOORE GRIMKÉ was born on November 26, 1792, in Charleston, South Carolina, the sixth child and second daughter of John and Mary Grimké.[1]

Her father, Judge John Faucheraud Grimké, was a man of importance and social standing. Planter, slaveholder, lawyer and politician, he was part of the ruling elite in his state. His Huguenot ancestors had settled in Carolina three generations before, living the quietly cultured life of back-country planters and advancing by a succession of good marriages into the best of the old settlers' families.[2] Young Grimké studied law in England and in March 1774 joined his name to that of Ben Franklin, Thomas Pinckney and other patriotic Americans then residing in London in a petition to "His Brittannic Majesty" protesting against the Boston Port Bill. Returning home, he enlisted in the Revolutionary Army as a Captain. At twenty-six he was Deputy-Adjutant General for South Carolina and Georgia under General Robert Howe. Imprisoned at Charleston, later paroled, he rejoined the Revolutionary Army, fought at Eutaw Springs and Yorktown and returned home a Lieutenant-Colonel.[3] In the eight crucial years following the end of the war he served in the State House of Representatives, holding for one year the office of Speaker. He was a delegate to the State convention for the ratification of the Constitution. He became a Judge in 1779 and served his city as Intendant-Mayor.[4]

In 1784 he married prudently and well. Mary Smith's family were direct descendants of the first Landgrave Thomas Smith, which meant a great deal in family-conscious Charleston. Among her ancestors there were two colonial governors, a speaker of the Commons House Assembly and the famed Colonel Rhett, who delivered the city from the pirates. Her father, "Banker Smith of Broad Street," was one of the wealthiest and most respected men in the state.[5]

As was the custom among the Charleston aristocracy, the family lived alternately on one of their plantations and in their town house on Church Street. It was in this handsome house with its elegant stairways leading up to the front door, that Sarah Grimké was christened at the age of four together with her sister Anna.[6]

In keeping with their wealth and position among the leaders of Charleston's exclusive society, the Grimké family's household staff must have been large. Typically, it would have consisted of a housekeeper in charge of the parlormaids and laundresses; "Mauma," in charge of the nursemaids, one for each of the children; the personal servants of master and mistress; the butler and footmen to see after dining room and table service; the cook and kitchen helpers, plus an uncounted host of servants' children. The family coaches and horses would be attended by several coachmen, stable boys and grooms.

From November until the middle of May the Grimkés lived on their Beaufort plantation, with the exception of the carnival season and "race week" in February, which they spent in town. Rice cultivation had turned most of the countryside to swamp land; from May on, the climate was considered unfit for white men. Country fever, dysentery, "the summer sickness," yearly took their toll. Thus the planters' families would twice a year undertake the arduous journey over sandy roads and corduroy causeways to enjoy the combined benefits of city and country living which gave a unique flavor to Charleston society.[7]

In these early years of Sarah's childhood the invention of the cotton gin had effected a transformation in Southern agriculture. Cotton production was becoming more and more profitable and Judge Grimké expanded his cotton lands, litigating successfully for acreage adjoining his own plantations. He had already augmented his inherited holdings by land the government had given him in recognition of his war service. Now, with the prices of slaves rising, his fortune was increasing.[8] He made some profitable investment in navigation companies and served as President of the Board of the Catawba River Company. His professional rise kept pace with the advance of his fortune. Judge Grimké's compilation of law, *South Carolina Justice of the Peace* and *Duty of Executors and Administrators,* received favorable acceptance. His later work and magnum opus, *Public Laws of the State*

of South Carolina was for several decades the most important compilation of laws of the state.[9]

Sarah Grimké grew up healthy, bright and cheerful, not
particularly pretty, but much beloved because of her outgoing, generous disposition. She was different from the other
girls. She preferred her brother Thomas for company and
that in itself was remarkable, for Thomas, six years her senior, was the brightest, most promising of the boys. They
were very close, almost inseparable. The other sisters, Mary,
three years older than Sarah, and Anna, three years younger,
lived in a separate world. Eliza, the baby, was too young to
be considered.

The world of Sarah Grimké's childhood consisted of a well-
ordered system of hierarchies. At its head stood Father, who
was master and judge, unquestioned power, authority and
law, a stern, often forbidding figure. Then came Mother,
awe-inspiring in the beautiful perfection of her laces, silks
and ruffles, final arbiter in all matters of the household, an
unfailing source of information on society and relatives and
family lore. But Mother was busy, surrounded often by
cousins and friends; it was not right to bother her with a
child's concerns. For these, for all matters of daily importance, the child turned to "Mauma," the nurse and comforter,
a black woman of great authority and kindness, who nevertheless, as each child discovered sometime and always with a
remembered shock, was a slave and servant like all the other
black people. Then there were the brothers, ranking in importance according to age: John, Thomas, Frederick, older
than Sarah, Ben, Henry, Charles, the younger ones. All the
brothers were allowed knowledge and activities forbidden
the girls. Girls had to be ladies, boys could do as they
pleased. The house servants, too, were part of the hierarchy

— one knew exactly where each one stood and they, in turn, were jealous of their "place" against the servants of families of less importance. Lowest of all were the servant children, who had to be ready to do anyone's bidding, fetching and carrying, swishing peacock-feather fans behind the chairs at dinner, running for this and that and helping out wherever needed. They were playmates and companions to the white children, when not otherwise needed. One learned, very early, that one might order them around and expect obedience, even if one were a girl who, otherwise, was taught obedience to all.

Later, Sarah acquired "different branches of polite education for ladies" at one of the numerous institutions provided for the daughters of wealthy Charleston. Typically, this would be needlework, white on white, stitchery and cross stitch and if one were good at that, fancywork, beadwork, silk on velvet, colors. Reading, writing, enough arithmetic for managing a home, a little French were the essentials. Drawing was taught from printed patterns and, as the grand accomplishment, came the sketching of a vase with flowers from model. A little singing, sufficient piano to accompany the voice, gave a young lady an acquaintance with music. The most important thing to learn was manners, the proper way for a young lady to comport herself in company. It was a curriculum offering a little of everything and not very much of anything, designed not to tax excessively the gentle female mind.[10]

But Sarah learned more than that, for she studied Thomas' lessons: mathematics, geography, the history of the world, Greek, natural science, botany. When Thomas took up Latin, Sarah asked her father for permission to join in his lessons. But Judge Grimké disapproved; Mrs. Grimké thought the very idea preposterous and even Thomas, Sarah's unfailing friend, ridiculed her presumption. Surely, a girl had no use for Latin. At this desertion, Sarah's resolution collapsed. She might have ventured, with Thomas beside her, to defy her parents and study in secret; alone, opposition was unthinkable.

For all his refusal to let Sarah study Latin, Judge Grimké appreciated her ability. He had recently been appointed Senior Associate Justice, which meant, in addition to the honor, that he had to be frequently absent from home, riding circuit. Still, he took a lively interest in the education of his children and spent much time with them when he was at home. He encouraged his sons to engage in debates and arguments in preparation for their study of the law and, in deference to Sarah's unusual interest, allowed her to take part in these family debates. He is supposed to have remarked that if Sarah had only been a boy, she would have made the greatest jurist in the country.[11]

Once, Sarah was at Beaufort, keeping house for her father in the absence of her mother. She loved playing this role, so different from that which was usually hers. In her eagerness to be useful she went from room to room, cleaning out drawers and closets. In one drawer she found odds and ends of fabric, which she put aside in order to burn them. One day, her father gave her his shirt to mend and told her to look in that drawer for a piece of material for the mending. But the drawer was empty. As it happened the scraps of cloths had not been burned, but distributed to the slaves, "one of whom furnished me the piece," Sarah recalled later, "and mended the garment ten times better than I could have done." [12] She went unpunished, presumably having learned the intended lesson of the value of thrift. But she learned another lesson as well. Any slave could be of greater service to her father than she could. Her work was merely play-acting, make-believe. Judge Grimké, who had perhaps from his Huguenot and German forebears inherited a streak of thriftiness unusual in plantation society, insisted that his children learn useful skills, even if they never needed to use them. In line with this precept, Sarah was taught to spin and weave the coarse cloth used for clothing the slaves. She was made to shell corn and was occasionally even sent to the fields to pick cotton. Typically, it did not occur to Sarah to be grateful for such training, which might be useful to her as future mistress of a plantation. She merely concluded that she never did anything worthwhile during these training sessions. With the clear-eyed realism of a child she perceived that in her world all the "real" work was done by black hands, not by white.

South Carolina plantation society, during the period of Sarah Grimké's childhood, represented a well-functioning social system, as attested by the increasing prosperity of the region, in which her family shared. Why, coming from such an environment, Sarah should become a rebel and a misfit, critical of what others accepted, unable to tolerate what others considered normal, has remained an open question. During Sarah Grimké's lifetime she provided an answer, which became part of the abolitionist rhetoric and myth. It consisted of a series of anecdotes of her childhood designed to show that she had always, instinctively, hated slavery. One incident concerns a very early experience: Sarah was four years old when, accidentally, she witnessed the whipping of a slave woman. She rushed out of the house, sobbing. A half hour later her nurse found her on one of the wharves, trying to convince a captain to take her away to someplace where such things did not happen.[13]

Unfortunately, the anecdote explains little, except to illustrate that Sarah was a sensitive child. Young children of slaveowners often acted that way. As they grew older, they learned to accept the underlying logic of the system. Slaves were like children, who needed chastisement in order to tell right from wrong. Punishment for wrongdoing could be avoided by doing right. Soft-hearted girls like Sarah learned to pray that justice might be tempered with mercy. Whenever Sarah heard that a slave was to be punished she shut herself into her room and prayed that the punishment might be averted. Sometimes her prayers were answered in unexpected ways, but she recalled later in life that she often cried over the chastisement of slaves.

As a child she was, according to custom, given a slave girl to be her constant companion, to wait upon her, to serve her needs. But Sarah simply considered her as a playmate and treated her as an equal. When, a few years later, the girl died after an illness, Sarah was disconsolate. Her attitude puzzled her parents. After all, it was not as if the servant girl were irreplaceable; there were plenty of idle slave children in the Grimké household among whom she might choose. But Sarah refused.

Much later, she described some of her childhood experiences to a friend:

When I was about your age, we spent six months of the year in the back country . . . where we would live for months without seeing a white face outside of the home circle. It was often lonely, but we had many out-door enjoyments, and were very happy. I, however, always had one terrible drawback. Slavery was a millstone about my neck, and marred my comfort from the time I can remember myself. My chief pleasure was riding on

horseback daily. "Hiram" was a gentle, spirited, beautiful creature. He was neither slave nor slave owner, and
I loved and enjoyed him thoroughly.[14]

"It was often lonely" — with nine brothers and sisters and
a household full of slaves? It is a strange comment, even
though it is balanced by Sarah's insistence that they were
"very happy." An explanation for her loneliness might be
found in her description of the horse, Hiram, "neither slave
nor slave owner." If the child actually placed such a condition upon companionship, it is understandable that she was
lonely in Charleston. Yet one must question whether her antislavery feelings occurred really as early as she reported
them, or whether she rather, in retrospect and later memory,
offered them to herself and others as ready-made explanations for a general feeling of discontent. Undoubtedly, discontent was an essential part of Sarah Grimké's childhood.
Yet the important experiences, the deep, decisive events that
shaped her were not so much concerned with slavery as with
her frustration as a girl in a world dominated by men. It
appears likely that this specific feminist discontent merged
only later with her dissatisfaction with the slavery system.

The year Sarah was twelve, Thomas left home to study at
Yale. Like it or not, Sarah had to face the reality of her situation: no matter how she hungered for learning, it was
Thomas who would go on to get an education. She, a mere
girl, would have to continue frittering away her energies at
stitching and lessons in deportment. The schooling Sarah
Grimké received was considered good in her time, but she
would regret for the rest of her days that her education had
been inadequate and superficial and would resent her unful-
filled talents and thwarted dreams. Why had God given

brains to both men and women, if only men were to be allowed to use them? In 1805 there were no answers to such questions. Yet, unanswered, they inevitably led to other questions.

Each Sunday the family, servants included, set out in carriages and on foot to attend Episcopal services at St. Philip's. Religion was a serious matter in the Grimké household. Only sickness could exclude anyone from attendance at the daily morning prayers. All the children attended Sabbath school and, like most children of their day, moved in a small world edged by damnation; only constant prayer, effort and endeavor might avert the inevitable hellfire and doom. Before Sarah was twelve, three of her siblings had died in infancy. Their fate was doubtful; only one of them had been baptized. Only prayer might secure redemption for their infant souls. But what about the slaves and their children? Every Sunday afternoon the Grimké girls taught Bible classes in the colored school. And again it was Sarah who was dissatisfied with the way things were ordered, who asked too many questions and would not accept the answers. It seemed obvious to her that the slave children hungered for the gospel message. Why could she not teach them to read the Bible? Why give them the word of the Saviour secondhand?

It was explained to her that slaves had no use for reading; it would make them restless and rebellious. Their minds were not fitted for such pursuits; it would strain them and make them unfit for the labor they must do. Besides, it was against the law.

How could that be? Sarah refused to believe it. One can well imagine that Judge Grimké, ever approving of an inquiring mind, took that opportunity to instruct his daughter by presenting her with the irrefutable evidence of the printed word. In his own library Sarah might have read the answer in the Statute Book of South Carolina.

AN ACT FOR THE BETTER ORDERING AND GOVERNING OF NEGROES AND SLAVES . . . 1740. SECT. 45. And whereas, the having slaves taught to write, or suffering them to be employed in writing, may be attended with great inconveniences . . . that any person who shall teach any slave to write or to employ any slave as a scribe in writing, shall forfeit 100 pounds.[15]

As for the baptism of slaves, a 1690 statute spoke of it approvingly, "since charity and the Christian religion, which we profess, oblige us to wish well to the souls of all men," but stated specifically that such baptism "notwithstanding such slaves shall not thereby be manumitted or set free." [16]

Printed law or entrenched social custom, Sarah found it impossible to accept either. "My great desire in this matter would not be totally suppressed, and I took an almost malicious satisfaction in teaching my little waiting-maid at night, when she was supposed to be occupied in combing and brushing my long locks. The light was put out, the keyhole screened, and flat on our stomachs, before the fire, with the spelling-book under our eyes, we defied the laws of South Carolina." [17]

It was the one act of open defiance she recorded in all the years of childhood and it ended in discovery. The slave girl barely escaped a whipping and Sarah was summoned before her father, who lectured her sternly on the enormity of her transgression.[18] Perhaps the child was already then sensitive

to the irony that the very books of law cited against her were
the books denied her because she was a girl, denied her maid
because she was a slave. The sense of sisterhood with the
slave, which would be so strong and compelling in Sarah
Grimké, may well have resulted from this incident. Although there was something in Sarah that needed to learn a
lesson repeatedly, she had finally understood. Her attempts
to help the slaves were useless; she was as helpless as they
were. Her father, master and judge, would brook no defiance.

For a time, thereafter, Sarah seemed quite subdued. Her
rebelliousness, her fine spirit, had been broken and turned
inward. It was, in her day, a not unusual pattern in the training of girls; indeed, almost a necessity in preparation for the
reality of their lives. For most of them, a resigned acceptance of their place would, after such an event, become as
natural as breathing.

When, on February 20, 1805, Mrs. Grimké gave birth to
her last child, a daughter, it seemed like a sign to Sarah. Her
mother was tired from the bearing of fourteen children, still
grieving over the infants she had lost, perpetually harassed
by the cares of her large, complex household. Sarah was
going on thirteen; it was high time she took her place in the
household and relieved her mother. She begged to be permitted to become the child's godmother. Although the request was unusual, her parents consented with some reluctance, perhaps hoping the new responsibility might help her
out of her troubled despondency.

The great day came. Sarah stood at the baptismal font,
holding the infant in her arms. Presumably, the minister
spoke the usual ritual formula: "I baptize thee Angelina
Emily Grimké in the name of the Father, the Son and the

Holy Ghost." And Sarah, in giving the ritual response, promised to cherish this child, to protect her and to train her in the ways she should go. But there was nothing usual in Sarah's emotional response. She was deeply in earnest in her pledge and, years later, remembered the profound emotions which caused her to shut herself up in her room after the ceremony and pray to God to make her worthy of the task she had assumed. "Oh, how good I resolved to be, how careful in all my conduct, that my life might be blessed to her!" [19]

At last, it seemed that Sarah Grimké had found a purpose in her life. She would care for this child as though it were her own. But to do so, she would first have to find her own road to self-fulfillment. To show the way to Angelina she herself would have to travel a strange and difficult road. The pledge to this godchild, her sister, became the content, purpose and salvation of Sarah Grimké's life.

CHAPTER
THREE

*While woman's intellect is confined, her morals crushed,
her health ruined, her weaknesses encouraged, and her
strength punished, she is told that her lot is cast in the para-
dise of women: and there is no country in the world where
there is so much boasting of the "chivalrous" treatment she
enjoys. . . . Her husband's hair stands on end at the idea
of her working, and he toils to indulge her with money: she
has liberty to get her brain turned by religious excitements,
that her attention may be diverted from morals, politics
and philosophy; and, especially, her morals are guarded by
the strictest observance of propriety in her presence. In
short, indulgence is given her as a substitute for justice.*

*Her case differs from that of the slave, as to the prin-
ciple, just so far as this; that the indulgence is large and
universal, instead of petty and capricious. In both cases,
justice is denied on no better plea than the right of the
strongest. . . .*

Harriet Martineau:
Society in America, 1837.

THE THREE YEARS of Thomas' absence passed rather
quickly. As she herself grew into young womanhood
Sarah experienced the happiness of mothering an infant and
with it a sort of peace came over her. The baby, her "precious Nina," was a beautiful child, with clear blue eyes and a
profusion of curls; as the youngest in the family she was

loved and petted by all. Sarah delighted in the fact that the baby called her "Mother." [1] When not occupied with her care, Sarah read poetry, painted and waited for the infrequent letters from Thomas. It seemed that everything in her life had improved. Her restlessness and dissatisfaction were stilled; her keen, uncompromising eyes had learned to view the world with delight.

When Thomas returned, a graduate from Yale, he was full of new ideas to which Sarah listened with rapt attention. Under the guidance of the famed Timothy Dwight, President of Yale, with whom he had also been privileged to spend a summer's vacation, Thomas had become alerted to the dangers of Deism and Enlightenment, which threatened to undermine the very foundations of Christian society. He had taken part in the religious revival held at the college and had undergone a conversion. He had come to the conclusion that his true calling was the ministry. The Bible was the foundation of all knowledge; thus educational reform, in which he was greatly interested, must start with making the Bible the cornerstone of all education from primary grades through college.

Education was one of Thomas' favorite subjects. He had had the best classical training offered in this country, possibly as good as that available at Oxford and Cambridge, but he was aware of the shortcomings. What he had learned simply did not measure up to the need. He and his generation, the first to be born and raised in the United States of America, were under an obligation to help create an American educational system adapted to the needs of their own country. There must be general education, universal as a matter of principle. Education was an affair of all the people; it was also the business of every individual. [2]

Sarah was pleased that Thomas meant to include exceptionally gifted girls in his plan for universal education. She was fascinated with his ideas, his conversation, his knowledge. She delighted in little services to him; she made herself useful by copying his notes and writing out the endless drafts of articles he hoped to publish. But she must have noticed, as the weeks went by, that Thomas had intellectually grown beyond her. The painful realization of her own educational backwardness must have weighed greatly upon her and produced a crisis severe enough to overcome her shyness and inhibitions. For Sarah openly revealed the dream she had for so long kept hidden: she wanted to become a lawyer.[3]

Perhaps she first tried the idea out on her brother; perhaps she broached the subject in a general way to her father. She must have known it was a wild and unlikely ambition, but she had reasonable arguments to support her. For one thing, she was not unprepared — she had been secretly studying law for some time. For another, if only her father and her brother would help, she might acquire the finest legal training in Carolina. Perhaps, having mastered the requirements, she might be examined and qualified to the bar, although no other woman before her had been admitted. Sarah felt willing and ready to be a pioneer.

If she first spoke to Thomas it is unlikely that he gave her support, for he himself was unable to stand up for his own ambition. A few months after his return he bowed to the immutable decree of his father, that he should become a lawyer, not a minister. Before long, he would start his legal training with Langdon Cheves, a prominent attorney and a promising connection.[4] Nor is it likely that Judge Grimké, having imposed his will on his most promising son, would encourage such improper and unfeminine ambitions in his daughter. Sarah never, in later life, referred to the scenes and discussions that followed her startling request. But she often referred bitterly to the outcome, her thwarted dream.

"With me learning was a passion," she wrote decades later, describing her reaction to this bitter disappointment. "My nature [was] denied her appropriate nutriment, her course counteracted, her aspirations crushed." [5] The experience was decisive for her development.

Thomas entered law studies and was admitted to the bar in 1809 and Sarah, at the wise and experienced counsel of her mother, entered society at the age of sixteen. And if something was broken inside her, there is nothing in her diary to prove it. And if something was irrevocably altered between Thomas and herself, there is no historical record to document the change. It was a process of growing apart in interests: Thomas was very occupied with developing into the paragon of Charleston respectability, the successful, universally respected lawyer, the speaker before clubs and assemblies, the future church warden and Orphan Asylum President and advocate of various causes of moderate reform. He became increasingly active in the city's cultural circles and took part in the formation of the "Conversation Club" which met weekly to read and discuss learned essays written by its members. It was a process of growing apart — Thomas removing to the circle of Charleston's bright young intellectuals and Sarah, like any daughter of the best families, becoming caught up in the whirl of a fashionable social life.[6]

One arose early and took a heavy breakfast. Morning prayer service was a pleasant duty, followed by some supervisory function in the household, the correction of a servant, perhaps, or a conference with cook over a meal to be prepared. Mornings were taken up with a brief stroll in the garden, a little reading or shopping, the answering of letters. Dinner around two was a slow and extended affair, which required rest afterward.

In the afternoon or early evening one visited friends for tea. This might be preceded by a promenade on the Battery, where in one hour of leisurely strolling one could meet all the fashionable ladies of one's acquaintance while enjoying the sea breeze and a fine view of the harbor and Mount Pleasant. For the younger people there was the more vigorous entertainment of horseback riding in Watson's Garden and on Sullivan's Island. The island offered many fine spots for a picnic and splendid views to those riding along the shore to Fort Moultrie.[7] Sarah must have responded with all the natural joy of vigorous youth to such excursions. Returning to the city, she may have paused at the harbor with its many foreign vessels, bringing cargoes of food and manufactures from New England, slaves from Barbados, rum and sugar from the West Indies. The sailors from many nations and the picturesque small boats of the Charleston fishermen, mostly "f.p.c." (free persons of color), gave the scene an exciting, cosmopolitan aspect. After the boats had tied up, waiting servants and fishermen engaged in the daily ritual of bargaining for fresh fish, which was more entertaining than many a theatrical performance.

Life in the country, from November on, was a busy round of social occasions, visits, balls and parties, teas and picnics and rides. In February one returned to town for the traditional festivities. For the older folks there was the Episcopal Convention, carefully scheduled so as not to conflict with the races which everyone attended. Race week featured Mrs. Mitchell King's ball on Tuesday night, on Wednesday the

Jockey Club dinner and finally — the high point of the social season — the St. Cecilia concert and ball.[8]

Annually, a leading citizen was selected to deliver an oration before the Society of the Cincinnati, another to speak before the "Revolutionary Society" in St. Michael's Church. It was a proud day for the Grimké family when, on the 4th of July 1809, Thomas Smith Grimké rose in St. Philip's Church, by appointment of the State Society of the Cincinnati, and addressed a select audience in a patriotic oration. With fine rhetoric and lofty eloquence he traced the desire of the United States for independence and stressed the need for a permanent strong union of the states. "We are a favored race," he exclaimed with great seriousness. "What matters is the welfare of the whole, not of the part. Let diversity rule; keep the union strong." [9]

Sarah might be forgiven if she did not understand her brother's subtle allusions to the threat of interposition by the New England states over the controversial embargo issue. To men engaged in state politics and ambitious for office such political questions were of vital interest. But Sarah, now leading the conventional life of the Southern belle, was preoccupied with her social life and personal problems. Thomas' oration appeared in print, a fine bound volume which sat next to Judge Grimké's tomes on the library shelf. It presents mute evidence of the separation in the activities of brother and sister. For the manuscript had not been transcribed in Sarah's hand, as had Thomas's previous orations. The printed copy was not dedicated to his sister, but instead, inscribed meaningfully: "Sally D. Drayton from T. S. Grimké." Thomas was moving on.[10]

He married Sally Drayton the very next year. He moved to the city, to the fine old Smith house on South Bay Street which he had inherited from his grandmother, the second Landgrave's fifth daughter, and set up law offices on Broad Street. The family was no longer what it had been. Brother John became a medical doctor and opened up a practice. Brother Fred in turn started on the study of the law. Baby Nina grew old enough to enter Infant Sabbath school and start reading and writing.[11]

Sarah's diary records about this period only her total absorption with "the gaities and vanities" of her social life. She writes that only her brother kept her from rushing into "the whirlpool of an unhallowed marriage" and one notes that once again it was brother, not father or mother or sister, whose advice she sought in a moment of decision.[12]

"An unhallowed marriage." A tantalizing phrase, which makes one wonder what standards of romantic love had formed in the young girl's mind. All around her the young ladies were making sensible, advantageous marriages at an early age. Their husbands were selected from within their own circle of "first families," often uniting cousins or more distant relatives; marriages were a family matter in which landed property, dowry and names were matters of primary concern. Did Sarah object to her parents' choice or did she have reservations about the prevailing order of things?

Undoubtedly, Sarah had formed some impressions of the marriage relationships existing around her. After marriage, the interest of husbands and wives separated. While the husbands moved in a men's world of politics, law, business, hunting and racing, the women were occupied with the frequent bearing of children. Although the care of their offspring was given over to the slave women and they were relieved of all physical labor, the wives of the plantation aristocracy were, for the most part, limited in their interest to children, home and servants. Their education and intellectual growth had ended with marriage; their contact with the world outside their homes was confined to a social life among families of like social standing. Their interests were narrow; their minds confined; only religion offered an escape and outlet. It was not a life likely to appeal to a searching and restless mind like Sarah's.

Another factor which might have deterred her from marriage was what Sarah, in her gentility, referred to as the "moral degradation" of slave society. Harriet Martineau, the British writer and economist, described it more bluntly:

> Every man who resides on his plantation may have his harem, and has every inducement of custom, and of pecuniary gain to tempt him to the common practice. (The law declares that the children of slaves are to follow the fortunes of the mother. Hence the practice of planters selling and bequeathing their own children.) . . . What security for domestic purity and peace there can be where every man has . . . two families, whose existence must not be known to each other; where the conjugal relation begins in treachery and must be carried on with a heavy secret in the husband's breast, no words are needed to explain . . . nor to point out the boundless licentiousness caused by the practice: a practice which wrung from the wife of a planter, in the bitterness of her heart, the declaration that a planter's wife was only "the chief slave of the harem." [13]

Another contemporary of Sarah, daughter of one of South Carolina's best families, mistress of large plantations and many slaves and a staunch Southern patriot, described conditions in her diary as follows:

Under slavery, we live surrounded by prostitutes, yet an abandoned woman is sent out of any decent house. Who thinks any worse of a negro or mulatto woman for being a thing we can't name? God forgive us, but ours is a monstrous system. . . . Like the patriarchs of old, our men live all in one house with their wives and their concubines; and the mulattoes one sees in every family partly resemble the white children. Any lady is ready to tell you who is the father of all the mulatto children in everybody's household but her own. Those, she seems to think, drop from the clouds.[14]

Whether Sarah shared this common notion as to the origin of mulatto children in her family's household is not known. To what extent her refusal to enter an early marriage was influenced by her disillusionment with the marriages she observed is equally a matter of conjecture. But that her sensibilities were as acute as ever, her diary reveals without question: "Often during this period have I returned home, sick of the frivolous beings I had been with, mortified at my own folly, and weary of the ball-room and its gilded toys. Night after night, as I glittered now in this gay scene, now in that, my soul has been disturbed by the query 'Where are the talents committed to thy charge?' "[15]

Although Sarah had learned not to shock her friends with dissenting opinions, her power of observation was not dimmed. The memories of that period to which she returned time and again in later life, reveal that her attention, outwardly turned toward commonplace social pursuits, was actually focused on quite a different aspect of her environment. "As I was traveling in the lower country in South Carolina, a number of years since, my attention was suddenly arrested by an exclamation of horror from the coachman, who called out, 'Look there, Miss Sarah, don't you see. . . .' I saw a human head stuck up high on a pole." It was the head of a slave who had run away from one of the neighboring plantations and whose punishment was to serve as a deterrent to other slaves.

A punishment dreaded more by the slaves than whipping, unless it is unusually severe, is one which was invented by a female acquaintance of mine in Charleston — I heard her say so with much satisfaction. It is standing on one foot and holding the other in the hand. Afterwards it was improved upon, and a strap was contrived to fasten around the ankle and pass around the neck; so that the least weight of the foot resting on the strap would choke the person. The pain occasioned by this unnatural position was great; and when continued, as it sometimes was, for an hour or more, produced intense agony. I heard this same woman say, that she had the ears of her waiting maid slit for some petty theft. This she told me in the presence of the girl. . . .[16]

Such things she noticed, moreover, in "one of the first families of Charleston." Others, making similar observations, found no difficulty in accepting them as necessary. Punishment was an essential ingredient of the master-servant relationship; the need for excessive severity arose from the peculiar characteristics of the Negro which made him lazy, unwilling, deceitful and slovenly. The person to be pitied was the mistress of such disagreeable servants who could not, like the Northern housewife, rid herself of them by hiring more efficient help. To listen to Southern mistresses, it would seem that slavery fell as a severe burden upon them.

How can you [Northern women] understand the position of a Southern mistress — her many cares and anxieties, her responsibilities, her frequent isolation, her daily
self-sacrifice? Would you like to stand all day long with
a pair of heavy shears in your hand, and cut out coarse
negro clothing, till your hand ached with weariness?
. . . Would you like to go into the negro houses and
stand hour after hour by the bed of the sick and dying, cheering and comforting the poor creature? . . .
Would you like to struggle and wrestle with ignorance,
stupidity and the fearful tendency to immorality — alas!
almost inherent in the negro? All around me, throughout the length and breadth of the land, are women who
do this.[17]

Not only did Sarah hear such opinions, but she saw daily
evidence of them in the efforts of her own mother, her
relatives and sisters to make the best of an inevitable pre-
dicament. However, Sarah Grimké never referred to such
thoughts or considerations in later life; if they were presented to her, she discarded them early.

She was just seventeen; sociological arguments had not
reached her, political questions were beyond her ken. She
had no contact whatever with the world outside of Charleston, no contact with anyone in Charleston who could have
given her a glimpse of broader views. What formed her and
shaped her was the experience of her daily life. That was
quite sufficient; plantation society was a stern crucible for
the molding of what was to become an iron conscience.

Sarah frequently visited in the home of a family friend, a
pious member of their church, who was known for her charitable activities. This woman daily assembled her family for

Scripture reading, yet her Christian spirit seemed to desert her when it came to dealing with slaves. One of them, a handsome young mulatto woman, was giving trouble by repeatedly running away. When she was caught, her mistress sent her to the workhouse where she was whipped and made to work the treadmill. But the more severely she was punished, the more she seemed determined to escape. Finally, after a brutal whipping, a heavy iron collar, with three long prongs projecting from it, was placed around this slave's neck and one of her sound front teeth was extracted to serve as a mark to describe her in case of escape. Sarah saw the woman in this condition, which she described as agonizing.

She could lie in no position but on her back, which was sore from scourgings, as I can testify from personal inspection, and her only place of rest was the floor, on a blanket. . . . This slave, who was the seamstress of the family was continually in her mistress' presence, sitting in her chamber to sew, or engaged in other household work, with her lacerated and bleeding back, her mutilated mouth, and heavy iron collar, without, so far as appeared, exciting any feelings of compassion.[18]

To see such things happen without a word or sign of protest, was to become party to the common guilt. And worst of all Sarah could not keep these horrors from attacking Angelina.

Little Nina was now attending a Charleston Seminary, one run expressly for the daughters of the best families by a very genteel couple. One day, Angelina fainted at school. Alarmed, Sarah probed for the reason and finally Angelina blurted out the truth.

A little boy, a slave child of their school mistress, had been
called in during class time to open the window. He was
small, and moved with an uncertain, shuffling gait so awkward that he could barely accomplish the task demanded of
him. When his back was turned toward the class, the reason
for his awkwardness became clear — his back and legs were
scarred by whip-marks, the injuries so recent they were still
encrusted with blood and scabs. At the sight, Angelina had
fainted. Now, in the telling, she wept. Her little world of
friendliness and fairness had collapsed.[19]

It must have been a bitter moment for Sarah. Angelina
asked for moral judgment, a clear-cut condemnation of slavery as an evil — the very same moral judgment Sarah, as a
child, had expected from those she loved. But Sarah could
not help this bewildered child with an answer. If she had
learned nothing else in all these years, she had learned that it
was best to accept what one could not change. Resignation
was the only comfort of the weak. To take any other position
would have meant to assert boldly that the whole world she
knew, the world of the wealthy, successful and wellborn, was
wrong and only Sarah Grimké was right. It was an irrevoca-
ble, an arrogant and frightening position — precisely the
kind she and Angelina would someday take. But the time
was not yet.

CHAPTER
FOUR

My very heart seemed withered at the prospect of going
friendless and alone with my Father to Long Branch.
                                            Sarah Grimké's diary,
                                            Entry dated 1821.

THE NATIONAL BANK, the protective tariff, the outrageous
bill increasing Congressional pay to $1500 annually —
these were the issues agitating her brothers and cousins during Mr. Madison's last year in office, while Sarah passed her
time in a continuous and somewhat hectic whirl of entertainments. The ladies of Charleston, regarding her as an over-
aged social butterfly, watched and waited. Sarah Grimké
obviously had not yet learned the art of turning an eligible
young man's polite interest into a permanent attachment.
Although she was well endowed in regard to family and
wealth, nature had not treated her so favorably. Her rugged
good health was no asset in a society which placed a premium
on female delicacy; the long straight nose and firm jaw
which lent such character to the faces of her male relatives
were distinctly awkward under the bonnet and curls of a
genteel young lady. Her reputation for eccentric opinions
certainly did not improve her chances for marriage. It was
generally understood that Sarah Grimké, at twenty-four, had
need of fairly desperate measures if she wished to avoid
dying an old maid.

There is no indication that Sarah was disturbed by that possibility, although a pathetic floundering, a search for a purpose, is evident in her erratic course over these years. She was deeply stirred by a revival meeting; she decided to give up the gay life; she "back-slid." She was converted again; the process was repeated. She describes in her diary her second, crucial meeting with Rev. Henry Kollock, a Presbyterian minister famed for his eloquence. It occurred while Sarah was vacationing on the island plantation of one of her fashionable friends.

On entering the parlor, I was struck with amazement on seeing the very minister who had so powerfully aroused my feelings. . . . I stood riveted to the spot like a culprit before her judge. . . . I felt . . . totally disqualified for conversation and hardly raised my eyes. . . . During the next day I observed his eyes were often fixed on me in so scrutinizing a manner that I shrunk from his observation.[1]

Sarah chose to regard this fortuitous meeting with somewhat mystical awe as a providential sign. Overcoming her hesitations, she sought out the minister, revealed to him her history of transgressions and was finally converted. Considering that the usual revival conversion was accomplished en masse within one or two meetings, one must credit Sarah with unusual intellectual resistance, for it took the experienced Rev. Mr. Kollock one whole week of daily private conversation to accomplish the saving of Sarah Grimké's soul. Since she had, by her mother's dictum, never indulged in the sinful enjoyment of the theater, her conversion in practice meant giving up novels, dancing and the parties and picnics so favored by her crowd. For these she substituted religious books, attendance at prayer meetings and charitable visits to almshouses and the homes of the poor. That after a few months she returned to her former life must not be laid to the Rev. Mr. Kollock's discredit, for he had labored earnestly and, in the long run, accomplished more than he had bargained for. Rather it is an indication of Sarah's refusal to accept formal gestures for meaningful activity. Her mind hungered for food which tracts could not supply; her energies demanded outlets which poorhouse visits could not fulfill. Her vacillations during this period were actually caused by her steadfastness; she never made changes easily, never let go of an accustomed position until she was more than certain.

Essentially, the Rev. Henry Kollock did his job very well. For he strengthened in Sarah the one feeling which could in the end subdue her: guilt. Remorse over her repeated "backsliding" was raised to excessive intensity when during the year 1818 Judge Grimké fell seriously ill. Sarah regarded the illness as "the merciful interposition of providence" designed expressly to save her from eternal damnation. It was a sign, a message, which she read clearly: her sinfulness had caused her father's illness; her sincere conversion would save him. Total devotion to the sick man, prayer and Christian living would be tokens of the sincerity of her repentance.

This kind of reasoning was what she had been taught since early childhood. Ministers, wrestling with the devil for the soul of their parishioners, made free use of illnesses, death and other disasters to illustrate the workings of providence and convince the sinner to desist from his evil ways. Religious zeal was one of the few emotional outlets permitted society women. Sarah, as usual, seemed to be overdoing it,

although one had to admit that she was relieving her mother
of a strenuous and depressing duty. Thus, when the Charleston doctors advised a consultation with the foremost surgeon
in the country, the famed Dr. Phillip Synge Physick of Philadelphia, it was Sarah, of all the sons and daughters, who was
chosen to accompany her father. No objections were raised
to letting her bear the burden of a strenuous sea voyage with
the sick man nor were, as might have been expected, any of
the servants taken along to make her task easier. Perhaps
under the illusion that a brief consultation with Dr. Physick
would yield results, the journey was undertaken rather casu-
ally, as though it were a pleasure trip.

Two months later, in June 1819, Sarah and her father were
about to leave Philadelphia, but not for home. Judge
Grimké was no closer to a cure than he had been on arrival.
Dr. Physick had been most helpful, kind and reassuring.
Himself a Quaker, he had helped Sarah to find lodging in a
Quaker boardinghouse and had been generous with his time
and interest. But he had made no promises of a cure and, as
the weeks had worn on, his comments had become less and
less specific. "Your father's health is in the Lord's hands,"
was all he finally would say. He recommended a change of
climate to the sick man and spoke with some warmth of the
curative values of sea bathing and the benefits of the sea air.[2]

The trip to the seashore was arduous. From Philadelphia
they started by chaise to Bordentown, where they rested a
few days, then proceeded along the Burlington road to the
famous New Jersey resort, Long Branch. Past Bordentown
the road was little more than an Indian trail, which the Jersey fishermen used to bring their catch to the city market.
Long Branch was a tiny fishing village, some distance from
the sea, with a single dry-goods store and a cluster of farm-

houses on the land side. Rather than lodge in one of these farmhouses, as many people did, Sarah and her father had, at Dr. Physick's suggestion, engaged rooms in the one hostelry on the seashore, Fish Tavern. It was situated on the high bluff above the beach and consisted of several large frame buildings, each equipped to hold about a hundred guests. It was, despite its name, a perfectly respectable establishment, where prayer meetings after supper were habitually held for the benefit of the guests.[3]

Inside, the place was noisy, the rooms drafty and lacking in conveniences. But the sick man was feeling too poorly to care about his surroundings. There was no doctor within a hundred miles. Sarah transformed her father's room into a sickroom, attended to the most necessary practical details and made her patient as comfortable as possible. This proved to be all she could do for him. Within a few days it was quite obvious that Judge Grimké would little profit from the healing effects of sea bathing. He never even left his room; the closest he came to the ocean was to view it from the window, propped up on his pillows, and turning an emaciated cheek to the strong sea breeze. His fierce attacks of pain were with increasing frequency soothed by laudanum. While he lay for hours in drugged, fitful sleep, Sarah sat by his side, watching, praying.[4]

The long sandy bluff stretched before her to the horizon, with nothing to break the line but the thin flag at the top of the stairs which led down to the ocean. At set times the red flag which indicated that gentlemen were permitted on the beach would be exchanged for the white flag, which cleared the scene for the ladies. On these occasions, the giddy laughter of the daring women who, clothed in long shifts and oilskin caps, waded knee-deep in the ocean holding fast to a

stout rope, could be heard in the room.[5] At other times, all
Sarah could hear was the sound of the breakers dashing
against the shoreline. Their rhythmic roaring filled the cor-
ners of the lonely room, as Sarah sat day and night beside the
dying man.

In common with other women of her class, Sarah had a
thorough and intimate acquaintance with death. Young ladies so delicate that they would swoon at the mere mention
of the word "leg," so timid that they would blush and faint at
the slightest provocation — were expected to and in fact did
attend the illnesses and deaths of their male and female relatives, servants, neighbors, and even total strangers. It was an
accepted part of woman's work and Christian duty. Sarah
herself had in the normal course of events assisted at birth-
ings and dyings, dressed wounds and laid out bodies, gaining
in the process a thorough familiarity with every kind of physical pain. Had her father been at home, in Charleston, she
would have taken turns with her mother, sisters and aunts,
always, of course, relieved by servants of the most unpleasant part of these duties. She would have prayed and she
would have wept; she would have felt sorrow and she might
have felt guilt, but it would not have been as this was — a
crucial, cataclysmic experience.

She was alone in a strange land; there was none to counsel,
none to interfere, none to soften the passion with which she
abandoned herself to the situation. There was guilt; there
was responsibility; there was also, above respect and dutiful
affection, a new and intimate bond of love. It seemed to
Sarah that only during these months of illness had she come
to know her father as a person. He had led an active life,
committed to duty as he saw it, rarely idle, always useful.
Now he lay passive, submitting to pain with a fortitude that
amazed her. Their roles now were reversed: he, the strong

respected figure of authority had given himself over totally
to her care, leaning unashamedly upon her strength and
youth and showing, at times, a solicitude and tenderness for
her that deeply moved her. "We lived in the constant sacrifice of selfishness . . . and became friends indeed. I may
say that our attachment became strengthened day by day. I
regard this as the greatest blessing next to my conversion
that I have ever received from God." [6]

This she wrote in her diary, little understanding the complexities that were at work within her. For years Sarah had
been craving an outlet for her affections; for years she had
searched for the satisfaction of being useful. It was an unful-
filled longing, which only the care of Nina had temporarily
filled. But in regard to Nina she had never had full authority
and responsibility. Now, by a series of strange circumstances Sarah found herself in a situation where for the first
time in her life a human being was totally dependent on her.
For the first time in her life she could wholly give of herself
and take full charge of the life of another. That this other
was her father, so long the object of her awe, fear and secret
rebellion, would be of crucial significance in Sarah's future.

In the struggle with death, Sarah forgot meals and sleep,
neglected her dress and her health. Her reliance on prayer
had all the aspects of a child's faith in magic; her intensity
alarmed even the sick man.

In a moment of consciousness he interrupted her incessant
praying and urged her, gently, to go outdoors for a stroll to
refresh her spirits. Sarah would not hear of it.

Judge Grimké, with great effort, tried to convey to her the
reality she dared not acknowledge: "Do not indulge vain
hopes my child. I no longer expect recovery nor do I desire
it." [7] Sarah fought back her tears.

These stately words, which must have cost him considerable effort, indicate that the manner of his dying mattered to Judge Grimké. Having lived decorously and with acceptance of his place in life, he wished to die with the resignation befitting a good Christian. He wished for his daughter the same grace of resigned acceptance, the wisdom of submitting with dignity to the inevitable.

In fact, there was something extraordinary about the manner of Judge Grimké's dying. One can explain the trip North, accompanied only by Sarah, as due to the erroneous advice of the Charleston physician. One can assume that Sarah and the family were lulled by false hopes. It is hard to believe that an old soldier like the Judge would for so many months have held illusions concerning his illness. Why then, after the two unsatisfactory months at Philadelphia and the obviously evasive diagnosis of Dr. Physick, did he not, as reason and propriety would have demanded, return home to Charleston to die? Some years previous a neighbor and fellow Judge of South Carolina, having heard rumors of an intended slave escape, informed Judge Grimké of the danger and expressed himself confident that "Your own prudence will suggest proper measures" to prevent it.[8] One could always be certain that under any and all circumstances Judge Grimké would show prudence and foresight. Why then, after the disastrous trip to Long Branch, did he not make efforts to summon one of his sons from Charleston or, at the very least, write to one of his many business friends at the North asking him to make suitable arrangements in the event of his death? Was it an expression of confidence in Sarah, a belated recognition that of all his children she was the only one whose strength and love he could trust to sustain him through his ordeal?

The sickness wavered; the patient lingered. "This book

used to be the repository of my dear Father's thought and opinions extracted out of different authors. I shall now fill it up with my own reflections and religious experience," Sarah wrote in August of 1819 at the top of her diary, and proceeded to record every detail of her father's last days. On August 6 his condition worsened. For two days and nights he alternately struggled for breath or lay in a coma. Sarah never left him; during the last night she held his hand and spoke to him, although he no longer heard her. He died in his sleep. Sarah recorded in her diary that she left him, when she realized he was dead and spent the rest of the night alone in the adjoining chamber. The following day she returned to his room, prayed beside him and touched his lips, "cold, cold as marble."

Had John Faucheraud Grimké died at home, he would have been buried with the pomp and circumstance befitting his station. Pallbearers, their hats and chests draped with white scarves and streamers would have carried his handsomely ornamented coffin; with wife and daughters heavily veiled in mourning, sons and relatives, grieving neighbors and weeping slaves making up the funeral cortege, he would have been laid to rest in land owned by his family for several generations. The funeral feast would have lasted for days. On the Sunday following the burial a minister, who had known him all his life and could speak with authority of his virtues, would have delivered the funeral oration.[9] But it was otherwise.

He was buried in Long Branch, in alien soil attended by strangers. The man who spoke briefly at the graveside was, presumably, the local minister, for there was no Episcopalian minister in the little fishing village. Judge Grimké was laid to rest in the little churchyard behind the old Methodist church, and of all his family, Sarah alone walked behind the coffin. And the only things familiar were the rough wind of the Atlantic, the sound of waves crashing against the shoreline, the restless cries of seagulls overhead.

In a sense, Judge Grimké had died just in time. The world he had helped to fashion was the world he believed in, whole and sound, standing on eternal foundations. His sons were important men: doctors, lawyers, planters, continuing his tradition of acquisition and public service. His household and fortunes were as secure as were his values. As yet, Denmark Vesey had not struck terror and fear into Charleston society. The Missouri statehood bill, over which debate had raged during the final months of Judge Grimké's life, had not yet passed and awaited discussion and compromise in the winter session of Congress. The aging Jefferson, deeply troubled, predicted with accuracy that the controversy over the slavery question, which this bill had brought to national attention would, like "a firebell in the night," rouse the nation and divide it into hostile camps. Judge Grimké was spared this terrible realization. He died, not knowing that the society he considered perfect was already eaten by a disease more fatal than the one that had taken his own life. Nullification, abolition, secession, these conflicts which would rend the coming generation and set the members of the Grimké family one against the other, were unknown possibilities of a dim and distant future. It was well for Judge Grimké that he died when he did and, in a strange and complex way, it was well for Sarah.

The heritage left by her father was overwhelming. She might free herself, after bitter struggle, of class and caste and wealth; she might abandon all ties that bound her to his world and adopt new friends, new places, new values. But she would never lose the strength of will he had raised in her nor the complex of feelings. Guilt and love inextricably entwined; rebellion and submission all mixed within her and feeding from the same source. No other man would ever share with Sarah the intimacy of these last months together, no other man would ever receive so wholly the love and devotion of which she was capable.

And yet, unwittingly, he had greatly helped her. By bringing her North, by testing her to the limits of her endurance, he had liberated something in Sarah which had long lain dormant. He had made her independent and she had risen to the challenge. From now on, strength and loneliness would never leave her. In death, her father gave Sarah what he had denied her during his lifetime — the dignity of accepting her as his equal. By the manner of his dying, Judge Grimké set his daughter free.

CHAPTER
FIVE

Suppose that our ancestors and we had been exposed to constant servitude, in the more servile and inferior employments of life; that we had been destitute of the help of reading and good company; that amongst ourselves we had few wise and pious instructions; . . . that while others, in ease, have plentifully heaped up the fruit of our labour, we had received barely enough to relieve nature; and being wholly at the command of others, had generally been treated as a contemptible, ignorant, part of mankind; should we, in that case, be less abject than they now are?

John Woolman, Some Considerations
on the Keeping of Negroes,
1762.

FOR SARAH it was a matter now of taking one step at a time. After the funeral she tarried two months in Philadelphia. During this period she was not at all interested in the religion and way of life of the Quaker family with whom she boarded, although there are indications that she was receptive to certain impressions. The calm atmosphere of the Quaker household, the absence of many servants, the simplicity of the furnishings had a soothing effect on her at this time of stress. Similarly, the necessity of facing the pressures of ordinary life alone, the need for making decisions and attending to practical details provided a cushion against the realization of her loneliness. "After a burst of grief I was

able to wear my mourning in solemn tranquility until my return home in the eleventh month of 1819." [1]

On the return trip to Charleston she spent some time on
board ship in the company of a group of Quakers. One of
these was Israel Morris, a successful broker and commission
merchant, husband of a charming wife, father of eight handsome children, member of a highly respected and prosperous Philadelphia family. Their discussions during the voyage must have been of interest to Sarah, for she accepted his
offer of continuing them by correspondence and walked off
the ship carrying a copy of Woolman's works which he had
given her. [2]

Sarah had been gone less than six months, but she was a
changed person and the home she returned to was not the
home she had left. The house was in mourning; the master
was gone. For the family it was a deeply personal loss; for
the slaves it was, above all, a potential disaster. Even in a
case such as this one, where a good master and provider had
carefully drawn up his will so as to insure his widow and
each of his children a fair share of his wealth and a secure
future, the disposition of his estate would inevitably mean
the dispersal and possibly the sale of slaves. Judge Grimké's
will, a painstakingly detailed document which specified for
the use of his widow during her lifetime his "household furniture, plate, plated ware, carriage and two of my carriage
horses, stock of liquors and provisions which shall be on hand
at the time of my death," plus cash and various real estate
specified only that she was to receive "any five of my negroes
whom she shall chuse out of those belonging to me." [3] Presumably the household servants in Charleston were distributed among the Grimké children who had already established
separate households. What became of the several hundred

slaves who were the labor force needed to work plantations of the size Judge Grimké held is not recorded.

Sarah may have known their fate; certainly she was keenly aware of their helplessness.

> From early childhood [I] long believed their bondage inconsistent with justice and humanity . . . after being for many months in Pennsylvania when I went back it seemed as if the sight of their condition was insupportable, it burst on my mind with renewed horror . . . can compare my feeling only with a canker incessantly gnawing — deprived of ability to modify their situation, I was as one in bonds looking on their sufferings I could not soothe or lessen. . . . Events had made this world look like a wilderness. I saw nothing in it but desolation and suffering. . . .[4]

And there was no one to whom she could unburden herself. Thomas, preoccupied with his many good causes and civic endeavors, lived out of town with his family. Frederick was a judge in Ohio; John, for some years a doctor with a good practice, lived his own life. Henry, now studying law, Charles and young Ben were the only brothers left at home; none of them had ever been close to Sarah. Of her sisters she felt drawn only to Anna who had this very summer, after a short year of marriage, lost her husband, the Rev. Thomas Frost. If this loss brought the two sisters closer, it also must have heightened the poignancy of Sarah's loneliness, for Anna's grief was bearable, *she* had a reason for living: her baby daughter Mary Ann, born shortly after Mr. Frost's death.

And Angelina, who for so long had been the focus of

Sarah's existence, Angelina at fourteen had almost become a stranger. Popular Nina felt shy before this somber sister whom she called "Mother" but who, somehow, seemed to expect more affection and closeness than even her real mother did. Sarah was different; Sarah was lonely.

> Tears never moistened my eyes; to prayer I was a stranger. With Job I dared to curse the day of my birth. One day I was tempted to say something of the kind to my mother. She was greatly shocked, and reproved me seriously. I craved a hiding-place in the grave, as a rest from the distress of my feelings, thinking that no estate could be worse than the present. Sometimes, being unable to pray, unable to command one feeling of good, either natural or spiritual, I was tempted to commit some great crime, thinking I could repent and thus restore my lost sensibility.[5]

Even Mrs. Grimké, contrary to her general tendency to let things slide, became alarmed by Sarah's state. Choosing the sensible explanation that the strain of nursing and burying her father had undermined the young woman's health, she sent Sarah to her relatives in North Carolina for a change of climate and a complete rest.

Mrs. Grimké's elder brother Benjamin Smith, who had been an aide to General Washington during the Revolution, had settled in North Carolina, where he had served as Governor. He had encouraged his brother James to leave his Beaufort plantation and bring his family to North Carolina. It was on James Smith's plantation on the Cape Fear River that Sarah spent several months early in 1820.

Aunt Marianna was a lively and intelligent companion and

Sarah should have found some distraction in the large household, especially with her vivacious, fun-loving cousin, Robert
Barnwell. He was an intense, very promising young man, a
few years younger than Sarah. He had recently started reading law under Thomas Grimké's guidance and was now continuing his studies by' correspondence. In later years he
would adopt the name of a distinguished ancestor and as
Robert Barnwell Rhett oppose his former teacher bitterly
over the issue of Nullification, still later winning national attention as the most extreme exponent of secession.[6] Perhaps
during those winter months on the Cape Fear River plantation, the future "father of secession" and the future radical
abolitionist defined their disagreements, for their opinions
must already have been at opposite poles. If so, Sarah remained unimpressed. As yet she saw her problems solely in
religious terms and made it her business to investigate the
different denominations, declaring herself willing to become
"anything but a Quaker or a Catholic." [7] It was in this spirit
that she began to leaf through the book by John Woolman
which Israel Morris had given her. "Having attained the age
of sixteen years, I began to love wanton company . . . at
times . . . I was brought seriously to consider my ways; and
the sight of my backslidings affected me with sorrow. . . . I
had no confidence to lift up my cries to God . . . but in a
deep sense of my folly, I was humbled before him." [8]

It seemed as though the words had been written for her,
the very feelings she had experienced expressed in simple
words by the Quaker tailor, some eighty years ago. His
struggles and spiritual desolation had led to a mystic revelation followed by peace, and the rest of his life was a lumi-
nous record of dedication to a strict and demanding religion.

It gave Sarah hope. She wrote to Israel Morris, asked

questions about Quaker practice and requested more reading
matter. In the mornings when other guests and family members went horseback-riding, she sat under a tree in some se-
cluded spot and read Woolman, over and over again.

John Woolman had been no ordinary Quaker. Even as a
young apprentice he had felt qualms of conscience regarding
slavery. Commanded by his "inner light" to become a "traveling minister of Jesus Christ," he found the bondage of his
fellow creatures deeply troubling to his conscience. "When I
ate, drank and lodged free-cost with people who lived in ease
on the hard labour of their slaves, I felt uneasy." [9]

How closely these words touched Sarah. Daily, hourly,
she was subject to such feelings. Some time ago, on one of her
rambles she had happened upon a Negro cabin in the woods.

A slave, whose head was white with age, was lying in
one corner of the hovel; he had under his head a few
filthy rags, but the boards were his only bed, it was the
depth of winter, and the wind whistled through every
part of the dilapidated building. . . . As he removed
the rags which covered the sore, I found that it extended
half round the body and was shockingly neglected. . . .
[He obtained his food only from slaves who shared their
portion with him.] The master and mistress of this man
. . . were remarkable for their intelligence. . . . The
master had for some time held the highest military office
in North Carolina, and not long previous to the time of
which I speak, was the Governor of the state.[10]

The description of the owner fits exactly her uncle, the
Hon. Benjamin Smith. Such indifference to the suffering of
others shown by relatives she respected and loved, was sheer

torture to Sarah. Now she read how John Woolman had attempted to ease his conscience by offering coins in payment for services rendered by slaves. But this small gesture did not suffice. "Conduct is more convincing than language," he wrote, making his life a living testimony against the evil of slavery.

His words stayed with Sarah, working powerfully on her agitated mind. On her return to Charleston she sought out Thomas, who had access to books, and asked him to supply her with other reading concerning Quakers.

"Thee had better turn Quaker, Sally," Thomas teased her. "Thy long face would suit well their sober dress." [11] But he provided the books. At times he discussed the subject of slavery with Sarah and scoffed at the suggestion that Quakers like Woolman had found a solution to the problem: to stop the buying and selling and holding of slaves.

Thomas, who admitted the evils of the system, put all attempted solutions to the test of "practicability." Like most men of his class, he considered the coexistence of the two races on a basis of equality an impossibility. Belief in the innate inferiority of the Negro was the cornerstone of the Southerner's world-view. Any scheme for the wholesale manumission of slaves or for abolition, which did not provide for the simultaneous removal of the freed slaves was considered "impractical." There was one organization which offered hope to men like Thomas Grimké. The American Colonization Society, founded in 1816 under the leadership of such men as Charles Carroll, James Madison, and Henry Clay, promised to relieve Southerners of their fear of harboring large numbers of an inferior race in their midst. It proposed, with the aid of the states and the federal government, to colonize "(with their consent) the free people of color residing in our country, in Africa." [12] The society hoped that owners would consent to freeing large numbers of their slaves in order to send them out of the country. Thus, gradually, would total emancipation be accomplished and black labor be replaced with white.

While Thomas Grimké worked actively to build the American Colonization Society in South Carolina, Sarah was more attracted to the promises of the Quaker religion. After many months of correspondence with the Quaker Israel Morris, she mustered enough courage to attend their meetings in Charleston. The congregation was small, a mere handful; the meeting-place a simple building. The silent worship, devoid of ritual, affected Sarah deeply; direct, personal communication with God seemed an answer to her spiritual struggles. Yet she hesitated for a long time before coming to a decision. She never was one to give up old loyalties easily; in this case the ridicule, the sneers and disapproval she was subject to merely for attendance at Quaker meetings were powerful warnings of what to expect should she align herself with this despised sect. But Sarah was too far gone in her loneliness to be swayed by such considerations. Her alienation from her environment was all but complete; now she added the final ingredient: personal withdrawal. She had mystical experiences, heard "voices," received commands. The other-worldly messages directing her to become a Quaker could not have been plainer. In the face of family hostility and alarm Sarah used this crutch, and produced at the right moment "an unmistakable call, not to be disregarded" directing her to go North.[13] What Sarah proposed to do was scandalous for a woman of her background. Unmarried daughters lived with their mothers or were tolerated guests in the home of some other relative. Sarah was plan-

ning to leave home, family and church to live alone and un-
protected in a strange city and to become a Quaker. One can
well imagine that her "voices" were the only argument which
might conceivably induce her mother to agree to such a preposterous scheme. Even then Sarah and her mother both
pretended that it was a matter of a temporary separation, a
trip North undertaken for the sake of "health." Mrs. Anna
Frost and her daughter accompanied Sarah, which served, at
least for a time, to allay the worst gossip.

"15th, Fifth month, 1821." She was already then using the
Quaker calendar in her diary. "Expecting to sail this morning for Philadelphia. . . ."

The step was deliberate, taken after years of preparation.
She could not agree to the Southern way of life, yet she had
given up all hope of personally effecting changes. But at
least, by her action, she could bear a witness. "Conduct is
more convincing than language," John Woolman had written.

Although she would return for several brief visits, Sarah
Grimké's break with Charleston was final.

Sarah spent the next seven years in Philadelphia, living at
times at "Greenhill," the country home of Israel Morris and
mostly with his sister Catherine Morris in the city. Through
the Morris family she was introduced in Quaker circles, making friends among their friends and living in a manner designed to win their respect and approval. Although she
began to attend Quaker meetings almost from the time of her
arrival, it was not until a year and a half later that she expressed her intention of becoming a member of the Society
of Friends. When making her application she stated, with
typical honesty, that she did so "under an apprehension of

duty against her natural will and without comfort." Little
wonder that the Quaker committee, which, according to custom, visited with her and questioned her closely in order to
decide her fitness for membership, advised her to wait. Her
formal application was received in February 1823 and on
May 29 of that year she was accepted as a member of the
Fourth and Arch Street Meeting of the Society of Friends.[14]

> On last Fifth Day I changed my dress for the more plain
> one of the Quakers, not because I think making my
> clothes in their peculiar manner makes me any better,
> but because I believe it was laid upon me, seeing that
> my natural will revolted from the idea of assuming this
> garb. I trust I have made this change in a right spirit,
> and with a single eye to my dear Redeemer. It was ac-
> companied by a feeling of much peace.[15]

The spirit of self-denial manifested by these lines is typical
of much of Sarah's thinking during these years. There was
also a practical aspect to her decision, which was taken
shortly before her first visit home. If she had been looking
for a method to insure her relatives' acquiescence to her continued stay North, she could not have found a better one
than to adopt the despised and — to Charleston — ridiculous Quaker habit. One can surmise the Charleston family
breathed a sigh of relief when she removed herself and her
peculiarities from their presence.

Although the income from her inheritance afforded her a
modest living, Sarah frequently expressed her desire to work.
"Oh, had I received the education I desired, had I been bred
to the profession of the law, I might have been a useful member of society, and instead of myself and my property being

taken care of, I might have been a protector of the helpless, a pleader for the poor and unfortunate." [16]

But, except for teaching, there were no professions open to women in the 1820's. It is therefore not surprising that the Quaker ministry as a career appealed to Sarah. The Quakers were the only sect which allowed women to serve as ministers. The gentle and ladylike Lucretia Mott who, in the early 1820's was a member of the same Quaker Meeting as Sarah, was a highly effective and respected minister. Sarah must have been impressed and encouraged by hearing her speak. Catherine Morris, a "spinster" like herself, was living a busy and useful life as a Quaker Elder, constantly traveling about on missions and religious visits and enjoying an independence which seemed most enviable to Sarah. And yet she regarded her "calling" with awe and dread as a terrible burden. "I was not only guilty of actual disobedience when the call was first presented but continued for several years struggling . . . the prevailing feeling of my mind was that it was impossible that I could ever yield myself to this work. . . . My own will was gradually overcome." [17]

By Quaker custom, ministers were made by "recommendation" of their Monthly Meeting. This was a formal recognition that "a gift in the ministry has been committed to this person" and was based largely on the candidate's extemporaneous utterances made during worship.[18] Catherine Morris encouraged Sarah in the belief that she would be recommended in her calling, but Sarah felt no such assurance. She considered herself unworthy; her natural shyness and inability to be at ease in a crowd made her feel out of place in this select group. Speaking in front of others was an ordeal for her, a handicap which she would overcome in later years by careful preparation. Since Quakers placed great stress on spontaneous inspiration for any utterance made in meeting, Sarah's alternately halting and hasty delivery inevitably created a bad impression. Overly sensitive, she was crushed by criticism which she took as personal condemnation. Her diary records only doubts and tribulations during this long period of preparation for the ministry: "I sit down in meeting . . . in a cold and indifferent state which seems as if I hardly care whether a blessing came upon me or not. This is a fearful thing to write but more fearful to experience." An agonizing struggle against the strong demands of her personality absorbed Sarah's energies to the point of exhaustion. The only way she could see for resolving the conflict was to strengthen her religious dedication, to further discipline herself, to break her own will.

But there were other factors at work. In the early 1820's American Quakers were going through a period of change and dissension. The early simplicity of their way of life had been affected by the commercial success and growing political influence of the leading Quakers, especially in Philadelphia. A subtle rift began to divide city and country Quakers, with the former holding almost all the influential positions of leadership, the latter feeling themselves at a disadvantage and highly critical of what they considered the corruption of wealth and position among city Quakers. The leadership began to become more and more orthodox, adopting a Trinitarian creed, while around the person of Elias Hicks a group of dissidents gathered and grew. This dissension convulsed the Quaker church during the years Sarah lived in Philadelphia, finally ending, in 1828, in an open split which engendered much bitterness.[19] The Motts, Lucretia and James, were actively involved in these issues, siding with the Hicksite faction. But Sarah seems to have moved through this conflict as though untouched by the larger issues at stake. One might have expected that her opposition to slavery would draw her toward the Hicksites, who advocated boycotting slave-made products. Sarah was, perhaps, naïve in the ways of organizational struggle; her intellectual and social life was, in these early Philadelphia years, in many ways more restricted than it had been in Charleston. All those who befriended her were trusted members of the orthodox hierarchy. Sarah loyally stood with them, never realizing how profoundly these events affected her situation. As the orthodox leadership felt itself more threatened it became more rigid, more exclusive, more suspicious of anyone but "birthright" Quakers. Sarah blamed herself when her efforts at becoming a minister were discouraged at every turn. Actually, she was an innocent victim of factional struggle.

There was another complication. Israel Morris was forty-two when his wife Mary died in 1820. His children, six boys and two girls, ranged in age from five to twenty years. He was a very handsome man, at the peak of his success, who must have seemed to Sarah a romantic, somewhat tragic figure. For a Quaker, he had the unusual distinction of having served, in 1798, as a member of the Philadelphia Light Horse Brigade. This brief outburst of a warlike spirit had been atoned for by many years of strict observance of Quaker rule and had long been forgiven, as evidenced by the fact that he was now a respected Elder.[20] That he, who had been a friend and support during the period of her mourning, should so shortly after have suffered such a loss himself, would have seemed to Sarah a coincidence fraught with meaning. On the other hand it was quite natural for the widower with his brood of young children to consider the serious young woman, who was so frequently a guest in his house, as a possible successor to the wife he had lost.

Sarah fell in love. At first she acknowledged it only in such diary entries as: "I struggle against feelings and temptations I blush to think of. . . ." But on September 16, 1826, Israel Morris mentioned "the awful subject of marriage." Henceforth Sarah would mark the date each year in her calendar, as though time for her were measured in the distance from this day. "That was a day of solemn heartfelt supplication that nothing might intervene between me and my God . . . to the individual there was sufficient attachment, but my soul shrunk from the fearful responsibility of such a situation." [21]

She refused him outright, but it was an uphill struggle to keep to her resolutions. "I have found it very hard work to give him up, had I never known of his love, I did not covet it, it was bestowed to my astonishment for I am unworthy of it. I have even thought if death had taken him from me I could more easily have yielded him."

They burned their letters to each other; they vowed they would continue as good friends. He renewed his proposal several years later; Sarah rejected him again. But her emotions were deeply stirred; her ambivalent longings are perfectly expressed by a dream which she recorded in her diary.

I thought I was standing on a wharf in Philadelphia looking anxiously at a Ship which was ready to sail for Charleston . . . my sister Anna was on another part of the wharf and like myself was very desirous of getting on board, but between us and the ship there was a place which looked very muddy. . . . I stepped off thinking I could get over the bog . . . my footing gave way and I fell. I rose . . . but my garment was soiled. I went on however but in a short time I again fell. . . . As I was trying to get up the side of the wharf a person came to assist me and after I was up he held out his hand to me and said in a mild manner, I advised thee not to go. As I stood by him I remarked some of the same mud on his coat sleeve of which there was so much of my garment, it looked yellow and shiny and I thought I felt sorry that he had contracted any of it. When I first awoke I remembered who this person was but the recollection vanished, yet since that the impression has revived that it was dear. . . .

As in most other places in her diary, where there is a reference to him, the name of Israel Morris is here cut off. Choked off, suppressed like his beloved name, were her emotions. The reasons she advanced for refusing marriage were somewhat threadbare. Time and again she asserted that she could not accept this "earthly love" because she found herself bound to the ministry. Yet, right before her eyes, Lucretia Mott managed to combine a happy family life with the Quaker ministry and nowhere in the most orthodox interpretation of the rule could there be found strictures against the marriage of ministers. Then again, at times with bitterness, Sarah referred to the opposition of Israel Morris' children, who did not wish to see him contract a second marriage. Considering the frequency with which second and third marriages were entered into during this period, and considering further the patriarchal respect due a man of Israel Morris' position, it would seem most unlikely that this opposition could not have been overcome. Besides, throughout all the years, Sarah was on friendly terms with all of the Morris children. Much more likely Sarah was held back from marriage by a combination of feminism and her obsession with self-renunciation.

The feminism was the outgrowth of the years of repression and thwarting of her talents. Having at last won a limited independence, Sarah was reluctant to give it up. Conventional marriage meant the lifelong subordination of the woman. Perhaps an unusually strong emotional attachment might have overcome her reluctance, as it did that of other early feminists.[22] Why her attachment to Israel Morris was not strong enough, must remain a matter for speculation. Perhaps his conservatism and orthodoxy reinforced Sarah's lingering doubts regarding her choice of him. Perhaps he failed to live up to the masculine ideal represented by her father and brother. Perhaps he was indeed the one great love of her life. But after years of practice, resignation came more easily to Sarah than the acceptance of her feelings. Renunciation was the one mode of living she had long practiced; it was — so she had been taught — the road to lasting happiness. No novice nun ever tried harder to make herself a saint. No slave ever proclaimed more loudly the advantages of the chains that bound her. All to no avail: Sarah Grimké would never find peace as long as she denied her restless mind and her strong personality.

Very few of the women pioneers were able to persist in their course without the support of some one loved person: a father, a brother, a husband, another woman. Sarah Grimké, one by one, shed the ties of affection that bound her. Seen from a long-range viewpoint her eight-year-long struggle to suppress her feelings for Israel Morris was only a brief detour, after all. Essentially, she headed straight for self-fulfillment. Not that it took her so long nor that the struggle was so severe is remarkable. Coming where she came from and fighting the long battle all alone, it is amazing that she made it at all.

CHAPTER
SIX

*Slavery is a system of abject selfishness, and yet I believe
I have seen some of the best of it. In its worst form, tyranny is added to it, and power cruelly treads under foot the
rights of man. . . .*

Angelina Grimké, 1829.

C HILDHOOD was easier for Angelina. Under Sarah's loving
protection she had been allowed to grow up in a gentle
atmosphere of indulgence. The three siblings closest to her
age were boys who, as a matter of course, excluded her from
their male world, so that Angelina, the thirteenth child, actually lived as an only child in a world of adults. The necessity
for finding companionship outside the family developed her
outgoing, strong personality; her popularity strengthened
her self-assurance.

Now, after her father's death, with the older boys married,
the younger ones in school, Sarah and Anna in Philadelphia,
the large family group had become a small, unhappily
matched household of women. That they were women un-
used to independence compounded their problems. Subtly,
the self-willed, eighteen-year-old girl began to dominate the
family circle and assert herself in a manner which led to constant friction. It amounted to Nina's doing as she pleased
and expecting everyone else to do as she pleased.

There was the business with Kitty. In later years members

of the family would bring up this matter as a reproach to Angelina's self-righteousness.[1] Kitty was a troublesome slave, hard to manage and a source of quarrels among the other servants. Increasingly severe measures taken to discipline her failed to produce any results. Exasperated, Angelina offered to take over the management of Kitty provided she could have full control of her. Although she had up to then refused to own any slave, she now took ownership of Kitty "purely from notions of duty." By kind treatment she won the woman's confidence and cooperation, but continuous quarrels with the other slaves threatened to undo her good work. Angelina therefore arranged to have Kitty placed with a friend of hers where she was well treated. Later, when the slave had become converted to Methodism, Angelina transferred the ownership of Kitty back to her mother, because she had scruples about receiving the wages Kitty had earned. In this, as in so many other things, she had her way.[2]

To her family her behavior appeared capricious and irresponsible. But Angelina all her life exhibited a supreme indifference to the standards and values of others. Unlike Sarah, she had a great deal of self-assurance. It never occurred to her that she should abide by the superior judgment of her male relatives or that anyone might consider her inferior, simply for being a girl.

She took an active, confident approach to her religion as well. When religious doubt assailed her, she turned it into action. At the age of thirteen, when the time had come for her confirmation, Angelina dumbfounded the rector of St. Philip's by declaring that after reading the required pledge in her prayer book, she had come to the conclusion that she could not agree with it. And since she could not agree, she could not go through with the ceremony. "If, with my feelings and views as they now are, I should go through that form, it would be acting a lie. I cannot do it," she declared firmly and stuck by her decision.[3]

She passed through the obligatory religious experience without the despondency that had marked Sarah's conversion. Admitting that she was a miserable sinner, Angelina seemed convinced that she would be saved in the end and that all would turn out well. The reasons she offered for her conversion from the Episcopal to the Presbyterian church seem eminently practical. "The Presbyterian, I think, enjoy so many privileges that, on this account, I would wish to be one. They have their monthly prayer-meetings, Bible-classes, weekly prayer-meetings, morning and evening, and many more which spring from different circumstances."[4]

Angelina credited the newly appointed Rev. William McDowell with her conversion and, with her mother's approval, entered his Presbyterian church in April of 1826. Typically, she threw herself into church activity with great zest. Before long she taught a Sabbath school class which ultimately grew to 150 children, took great interest in Bible school education and inter-faith work. Rejecting efforts by her Episcopalian minister to win her back to the fold, she declared:

I could not conscientiously belong to any church which exalted itself above all others and excluded ministers of other denominations from its pulpit — the principle of liberality is what especially endears the Presbyterian Church to me. . . .

I have lately succeeded in establishing a female prayer-meeting among Baptist, Methodists, Congregationalists and Presbyterians — we assemble on the first

Monday of every Month in the afternoon (about twenty attend). It is a sweet meeting to many hearts.[5]

Considering the strict social divisions which existed among Charleston society and found expression in religious affiliation, Angelina's organization of an inter-faith female prayer-meeting must have been quite a shocking unorthodoxy. But, then, the family was becoming conditioned to Angelina's peculiar forms of self-expression.

Angelina enjoyed her church work and made many new friends. But her friendship with the Rev. William McDowell soon transcended the ordinary relationship of a parishioner to her minister. The personable, young minister came from the North and had for nine years been pastor in Morristown, New Jersey, when ill health made it advisable for him to seek a milder climate. He arrived in Charleston in 1823 and stayed for ten years, well beloved by his congregation. However, his own adjustment to Southern life was apparently not the best, nor did he seem able to accept the South's "peculiar institution" with equanimity. In 1831 he would write to his brother in New Jersey:

I hope the state of things in Virginia is different from what it is in South Carolina — but really such is the feeling in this state, such deep rooted hostility to everything northern, such a reckless opposition to the General government, and such is our domestic state in reference to the slaves — that nothing but a hope that I am doing good here — and that I am needed would keep me in South Carolina a single week. . . . Indeed how near we are to a revolution here is known only to him who sees the end from the beginning. . . .[6]

The fact that Rev. Mr. McDowell, as a Northerner, had strong reservations about slavery must have strengthened Angelina's regard for him. He approved of her daily prayer-meetings with the family slaves, a practice she had instituted over her mother's initial opposition. Soon these services were attended by her mother and sisters and by the servants of other masters. Years later, several of these slaves wrote — or dictated — touching letters to Angelina, thanking her for these meetings, the first instruction of any kind they had ever received. There was no reason for her to doubt that she was doing good.

But Angelina was not satisfied. Over and over again she questioned Mr. McDowell as to the morality of a system of chattel bondage by professing Christians over other professing Christians. The Minister agreed that the system was morally wrong, but advised her only to pray and have patience. Angelina did not feel that was enough and urged Mr. McDowell to preach about the subject in his church in the same way as he had spoken to her in private.[7]

It is quite possible that Angelina was totally unaware of the practical realities of Southern life. But Mr. McDowell must have known what had become of ministers who chose to defy or attack the slave power. The Baptist David Barrow had been subjected to violence in Virginia, and to censure and expulsion in Kentucky, for his antislavery views. James Gilliland of South Carolina and George Bourne of Virginia had been charged with heresy and had been silenced by the Presbyterian Synod. More recently, William Dickey, John Rankin and others had been forced to leave the South for their attacks on the system.[8] That William McDowell chose the cautious way of silence is quite obvious from the fact that he remained in his post for a number of years longer as well as from the tone of his later correspondence.[9] But Angelina never accepted the necessity for compromising a moral position and, supremely confident in the rightness of her own convictions, apparently decided to undertake the job of persuasion alone. She appeared at a meeting of the elders of the Presbyterian church, all slaveholders, offering them the fantastic suggestion that they, as a body, should speak out against slavery. Her standing in the church must have been very good, for the elders listened politely, neither threatened nor condemned her, but offered fatherly counsel instead. It was not surprising that at her age she should feel as she did; they trusted that experience and years would show her the wisdom of their position. Naturally, they would not act on her suggestion.

Angelina was disappointed, but did not give up. One by one, she spoke to individual church members. How could they bear to go on living with this system of injustice and cruelty? How could they bear to stand what it was doing to their own character? In private conversation these individuals were quite willing to agree with her. But not one of them would take a public position against slavery.[10]

Sarah, visiting Charleston in the winter of 1827, found Angelina deeply disturbed. When she spoke of Quakerism now, she found a receptive listener in her sister. Under her influence Nina began to see her environment with new eyes. Attracted by Sarah's Quaker simplicity, she began to discard her laces, fancy bonnets and other finery, devoting much attention to these outward signs of protest. After Sarah left for Philadelphia Angelina also curtailed her activity in the Presbyterian church and spent much time thinking and reading.

By the spring, she was certain that she did not belong any

longer with the Presbyterian church. She had joined it largely because of its "principles of liberality"; when she found that these principles extended merely to other Protestant sects and not to people of another race, she felt disillusioned. However, she chose to stand on religious grounds and announced that she felt called to become a Quaker.

> Today is the last time I expect to visit the Presbyterian Church — the last time I expect to teach my interesting class in Sabbath School. . . .
> I saw Mr. McDowell day before yesterday and conversed with him on the subject of leaving his Church. We wept together for this is a painful separation for both — he is totally ignorant of the state of mind and told me that he pitied me sincerely for that I certainly was under the delusions of the arch adversary. . . .[11]

Not satisfied with this dire warning, Mr. McDowell decided to enter combat with the arch adversary and wrote Angelina a long letter, pleading with her to reconsider her decision. She tried to answer it, was interrupted by her sister Eliza, quarreled with her, then showed her the letter. Eliza, who always was close to her younger sister, was sympathetic. The two had a good cry; nevertheless, Angelina answered Mr. McDowell that her decision was firm. She was barely finished with her letter when Dr. McIntire, the Superintendent of the Sabbath school, appeared in person, having heard the rumor, and wanted her to assure him that it was untrue. Quite the contrary, Angelina replied. She was well aware of the impact of her action; she would not reconsider. Dr. McIntire had to leave without her recantation.

Angelina spent all the next day composing a farewell address to Sunday school teachers and students, explaining her

reasons for leaving their church. She was very careful in her
wording, since she expected that her letter would be read
aloud. It was not; it was not even mentioned. Angelina had
a few things to learn about the ways of the world.

Still, on Sunday, while her mother and sisters drove off in
their carriage to worship at fashionable St. Philip's, Angelina, on foot, went to pray at the Quaker meeting house.[12]

But the pressure continued. The next week a committee of
her former Bible scholars came to visit and pleaded with her
to return to the fold. Her family argued, friends made dire
predictions as to her future. Mr. McDowell, gentle but persistent, came visiting. "The whole Christian community are
looking at you with amazement," he informed her. They still
loved her; they pitied her for her delusion.

"They may love me with a feeling of pity," Angelina replied, "but all respect for and confidence in me is destroyed.
Such love is calculated to humble rather than gratify me."

Mr. McDowell wished to point out that it was not too late
to reconsider.

"Our conversation I am afraid was mutually unprofitable
and we parted with less favorable feelings than we met," Angelina commented in her diary.[13]

Her new church proved disappointing. The Charleston
Quaker congregation, small in Sarah's day, had by this time
dwindled to two old men. Sunday after Sunday they met
Angelina at the door, exchanged polite greetings, then
shared quiet worship. It was understandable that they
should be reluctant to talk to her, a newcomer, but why did
they never say a word to each other? Angelina finally asked
one of the men if there was a feud between them. Yes, there
was. Since his Quaker brother was a slaveholder and had,
moreover, cheated him out of a large sum of money, they
were not on speaking terms.

"Christians ought to be gentle and courteous to all men,"
the new Quaker instructed him.

The old man took it badly. He sent her a letter in which
he expressed his conviction that the other Quaker was "a
heathen and a publican" and that she was a "busybody in
other men's matters." In short — would she kindly mind her
own business?[14] It was good advice, but something Angelina
was absolutely unable to do.

Soon she became the target of another kind of attack.
Friends began to visit the Grimké household to inquire so-
licitously about the state of Angelina's mind. It was rumored
that she had become unbalanced. There were not so subtle
hints that she was committing a great sin, shutting herself up
every Sunday in an isolated meeting house with two old men.

Angelina remained unruffled. The windows and doors of
the meeting house were wide open, she informed them
calmly. Anyone was welcome to come and join them.[15]

A summer vacation with Sarah in Philadelphia strengthened her Quaker sentiments and her antislavery views. But
she did not feel convinced by Sarah's experience that she,
too, must leave the South. She was different from her sister.
Criticism and conflict did not frighten her; on the contrary,
she felt that as a Quaker in Charleston she would be able to
exert considerable influence for good. "I feel that I am called
with a high and holy calling, and that I ought to be peculiar,
and cannot be too zealous." [16] This was her comment when
friends remonstrated with her that her Quaker garb merely
served to make her conspicuous. She felt called to leadership; she gloried in opposition with the spirit of the true crusader. Besides, as the old Quaker had discovered, she was a
born meddler.

She set out to reform her family as well.

I am much tried at times at the manner in which I am obliged to live here in so much luxury and ease, and raised so far above the poor, and spending so much on my board. . . . I feel obliged to pay five dollars a week for board, though I disapprove of this extravagance and am actually accessory in maintaining this style of living, when I know it is wrong, and am thereby prevented from giving to the poor as liberally as I would like.[17]

Her paying for room and board was resented by her brothers who thought nothing of staying at their mother's house without paying for it. Angelina was particularly critical of her brother Charles, the family problem, who had never settled into any occupation. In several discussions she berated him for his failings, advised him to live more frugally and eat more sparingly. She was not above pointing out that she, when unable to pay for her board, had taken only water for breakfast. Not surprisingly, Charles took this with ill grace, complained to his mother about Nina's constant fault-finding. Finally he decided to leave home rather than live with her disapproval.[18]

It was not much better with the other family members. Sister Mary reproached Angelina for being unkind to her mother; Angelina reproached Mary with being cruel to the servants. Henry brought his young wife Selina to live in the house; Angelina found her flighty and superficial. Brother John refused to speak to Angelina at all; when she had a skin eruption on her hand he treated her only after Mrs. Grimké insisted — Angelina complained bitterly that his medical care was negligent and ineffective.[19]

Brother John had reason to hold a grudge against Angelina, for when he and his wife came on their weekly visit to their mother, Angelina made it her business to stay in her room. Mrs. Grimké ignored this rudeness, but Angelina insisted on explaining her behavior.

I . . . explained to her that it was not, as she seemed to think, because I did not wish to see brother John and sister Sally that I was tried at their dining here every week, but it was the parade and profusion which was displayed when they came. I spoke also of the drawing-room, and remarked it was as much my feeling about *that* which had prevented my coming into the room. . . .

She said it was very hard that she could not give her children what food she chose, or have a room papered, without being found fault with; that indeed, she was weary of being continually blamed about everything she did, and wished she could be let alone, for she saw no sin in these things.

"I trust," I said, "that I do not speak to thee, mother, in the spirit thou art now speaking to me; nothing but the conviction that I am bound to bear my testimony to the truth could induce me to find fault with thee. . . . I am acting with eternity in view."

Interrupting me, she said if I was so constantly found fault with I would not bear it either; for her part, she was quite discouraged.

"Oh, mother," said I, "there is something in thee so alienated from the love of Christ that thou canst not bear to be found fault with."

"Yes," she said, "you and Sally always say *I* speak in a wrong spirit, but both of you in a right one."

She then went on to say how much I was changed,

about slavery, for instance, for when I was first serious I thought it was right, and never condemned it.

I replied that I acted according to the light I had.

"Well, then," she continued, "you are not to expect everyone to think like Quakers." . . . She . . . said it was because I was a Quaker that I disapproved of a great many things that nobody but Quakers could see any harm in.

I was much aroused by this. . . . Some very painful conversation followed about Kitty. I did not hesitate to say that no one with *Christian* feelings could have treated her as she was treated before I took her; her condition was a disgrace to the name of Christian.

She reminded me that *I* had advised the very method that had been adopted with her.

This stung me to the quick. "Not after I professed Christianity . . . and that I should have done so before, only proved the wretched manner of my education." But mother is perfectly blind as to the miserable manner in which she brought us up.[20]

Waste, display and dissipation were bad, but slavery was unbearable. A child in Angelina's former Bible school class was the daughter of the workhouse master. Since she was frequently obliged to go to the house to mark the child's lessons, Angelina had had occasion to catch glimpses of the activities inside; they filled her with horror. The workhouse was a place where masters, too dainty to perform the office themselves, sent slaves for punishment. Whippings were administered in orderly fashion upon the naked bodies of women as well as men.

The most dreaded punishment was the treadmill, a drum

with broad steps which revolved rapidly. The slaves' arms
were fastened to a handrail above it. Only the strongest and
most agile could move their feet in time with the movement
of the drum, the others were soon helplessly suspended by
their arms, the edge of the steps hitting their legs, knees and
bodies at every turn. Several "drivers" attempted to make
the prisoners move by flogging them with a "cat o'nine tails."
Fifteen minutes on this instrument of torture would cripple
a slave for days afterward.[21]

> These are not things I have heard; no, my own eyes have
> looked upon them and wept over them. . . . No one
> can image my feelings walking down that street. It
> seemed as though I was walking on the very confines of
> hell. This winter being obliged to pass it to pay a visit
> to a friend, I suffered so much that I could not get over
> it for days and wondered how any real Christian could
> live near such a place.[22]

And every day added fuel to her indignation. Returning
from meeting one morning she saw a colored woman in much
distress pleading with two white boys, one about eighteen,
the other fifteen. Angelina suspected that they were leading
her to the workhouse. She wanted nothing more than to
avoid her but could not help hearing the younger boy say: "I
will have you tied up."

Angelina felt ill, her worst fears confirmed. Now the
woman appealed to her: "Missis!" But Angelina could not
utter a sound, it took all her strength to hurry past the pitiful
creature. The woman's cry for help pursued her; that she
had been helpless to answer it made her feel obsessed with
guilt.

"How long, oh Lord, wilt thou suffer the foot of the oppressor to stand on the neck of the slave!" she wrote in her diary.

It seemed to me that all the cruelty and unkindness which I had from infancy seen practiced toward them came back to my mind. . . . Night and day they were before me and yet my hands were bound as with chains of iron. . . . If only I could be the means of exposing the cruelty and injustice . . . of bringing to light the hidden things of darkness, of revealing the secrets of iniquity and abolishing its present regulations. . . .[23]

It became an obsession with her. No occasion passed that she did not insist on bringing up the subject. A group of visitors in her mother's home were speaking, the way they usually did, of the depravity of their servants, their laziness and dishonesty. "What made them so depraved?" asked Angelina, and suggested that it was their degraded situation for which white people were to blame. Was it not a fact that the minds of the slaves were uncultivated? She elaborated on the topic at some length, but the only result was that one of the visiting ladies asked her never to speak on the subject again, for she spoke too seriously. "Truth cuts deep into the heart," was Angelina's reply.[24]

It seemed that not a single day could pass without some painful argument. Angelina objected to the constant commands given the servants. When she went to her mother's room to read to her she did not want to be interrupted by a variety of orders which might easily be avoided. Why could not she shut a window or move a chair for her mother? Why must a slave be summoned?

Mrs. Grimké answered that this was the servants' duty

and she saw no reason to let her daughter do such work. "Mother," said Angelina, "Our Heavenly Father intended that we should be dependent on each other, not on servants." She was convinced that this dependence on servants caused "a real want of natural affection" among many families she knew.[25]

Another futile argument, one of many. Why must slaves be kept waiting outside of doors, standing often for hours in drafty hallways on the chance of being needed? Why must they sleep on the bare floor with only a blanket and be awakened any time their mistress wanted a service performed? Why must they eat their meals at irregular hours?[26] It seemed to Angelina un-Christian to be served by people whose only motivation was fear. "Are not these unfortunate creatures expected to act on principles directly opposite to our natural feelings and daily experience? They are required to do more for others than for themselves, and all without thanks and reward."[27]

Angelina found her own situation daily more difficult. Frequently, she wrote in her diary of her urgent desire to "escape from this land of slavery." Yet she stayed, still hoping that her example and influence might convince others.

Brother Henry had recently punished his slave John within Angelina's hearing. The blows were dreadful to hear, but the angry curses coming from her brother's lips struck her as more dreadful. Yet she did not interfere, even when John told her that he was in pain for a week after the whipping. Now the boy had run away because he had again been threatened with a whipping. Angelina lay awake all night worrying about John, worrying about the cruelty she saw growing in her brother.

The next morning, finding occasion to go to Henry's room, she decided to bring up the matter. She approached her

brother tenderly, placing her arm around his shoulder, and
questioned him about John.

He very openly acknowledged that he meant to give
John such a whipping as would cure him of ever doing
the same thing again, and that he deserved to be whipped
until he could not stand.

I said that would be treating him worse than he would
treat his horse. He now became excited, and replied that
he considered his horse no comparison better than John,
and would *not* treat *it* so.

By this time my heart was full, and I felt so much
overcome as to be compelled to seat myself, or rather to
fall into a chair before him, but I don't think he observed this. . . . I pleaded the cause of humanity. He
grew very angry and said I had no business meddling
with him, that he never did so with me. . . . I had
much better go and live at the North. I told him . . .
that as soon as I felt released from Carolina I would
go. . . . I could not but lift up my voice against his
manner of treating John. . . . To my surprise he readily acknowledged that he felt something within him
which fully met all I asserted, and that I had harrowed
his feelings and made him wretched. Much more passed.
. . . I left the room in tears.

The next night, when John returned, Henry merely told
him to go back to his business. He did not punish him at all.
Angelina was exultant. "My heart sings aloud for joy. Dear
Henry has good, tender feelings naturally," she wrote in her
diary, "but a false education has nearly destroyed them." [29]
If she was harsh in her criticism of others, she was equally
harsh on herself.

It is hard for me to *be* and *do* nothing. My restless, ambitious temper, so different from dear sister's craves high duties and high attainments. . . . For a long time it seemed to me I did everything from a hope of applause. I could not even write in my diary without a feeling that I was doing it in the hope that it would one day meet the eye of the public. . . . I fear I am even proud of my pride.[30]

In an effort at patient persuasion she instituted nightly silent worship, Quaker fashion, in which her mother and sisters joined her. Sitting on a low stool in the silent, dark room, her head in her mother's lap, Angelina prayed that love would conquer over what separated them now.

But humility would not prevail. The nightly meetings did not have the desired effect. Angelina felt clearly that her mother took no interest in them, that the stifling heat, the darkness and silence oppressed her. As the season advanced, the mosquitoes became unbearable and these sessions came to an end, probably to the disappointment of both mother and daughter. Years later, Angelina recalled that each summer the slaves had been tortured by mosquitoes as had their masters, yet they had never been given mosquito nets without which no one in the family would think of sleeping. It is unlikely that Angelina failed to point out this added grievance to her mother, that last summer in Charleston.[31] There was no truce in the battle, no respite.

One day the following letter was delivered to Angelina:

DEAR MADAM:

By order of the Session of the Third Presbyterian Church in this City it is my painful duty as the pastor of said church to cite you to appear before that session . . . to answer to the following charges:

A neglect of the publick worship of God in his house
A neglect of the ordinance of the Lord's supper and
A neglect of the means of grace and the ordinance of
the Gospel generally contrary to your engagement when
you became a member of that Church.

> By order of the Session of the Third
> Presbyterian Church
> WILLIAM A. McDOWELL, PASTOR [82]

Charleston,
May 14th, 1829.

Angelina took pains not to let her mother and sisters find
out about the charge before the Session. Despite her great
anxiety she managed to show a smiling face to the family
until the Monday of her trial. She arranged to take tea at
her friend Rebecca Eaton's house. There Mr. McDowell
called for her, took her arm, smiled, tried to calm her. She
was deeply agitated as she entered the Session room and
stood in awed silence before the seven judges. They came
forward one by one, shook her hand and assured her that
they had nothing but feelings of friendliness and kindness
toward her.

Still, the charges were solemnly read and Angelina was
asked to reply to them.

She defended herself ably, on theological and moral
grounds, maintaining that her change of religion was purely
a matter of conscience.

The Session members, again assuring her of their good
will, explained that personally they would just as soon drop
the matter, but were obliged by their positions as church officials to proceed. Their respectful and delicate attitude toward Angelina somehow took the sting out of the proceedings and left her with friendly feelings toward them. It can

only be explained by the good work she must have done during the two years in their church and by their admiration for her strong moral stand. Still, on the next day she received a letter expelling her from the Presbyterian church.[33]

She had been prepared for it and took it with poise. Much more painful were the letters from Mr. McDowell which now rapidly followed one upon the other. He assured her of his deep affection, he deplored their separation, he complained that she no longer visited his house.

> My beloved friend . . . the change in the whole current of your feelings . . . has appeared to me altogether inexplicable . . . when I see you with so little reflection adopting a system with even the outlines of which you acknowledge yourself unacquainted, when I see you closing your ears against the counsel and warning of your best and most pious friends and when you seem to act on the principle you are altogether infallible and cannot possibly be mistaken I confess, my friend, I feel anxious. . . .
>
> My dear friend I cannot consent to lose your affection. . . . Forget you I cannot. Forget you I do not desire. You must, my dear Angelina, suffer me to see you tomorrow. . . . In the meanwhile rest assured, my beloved friend, you still occupy and will continue to occupy a place in the tenderest affections of your attached Brother.
>
> W. A. McDowell [34]

She replied with an anguished letter in which she defended herself from his accusations. Her conversion was not a sudden one; she had gone through an agonizing six months' struggle. Although she had not read any Quaker books, their principles had been brought to her one by one. She felt that she had been called to be a Friend. She begged him not to see her, since a meeting would only widen the separation between them. "I tho't I had given thee up . . . out of the depth of sorrow my soul still exclaims 'How can I give *thee* up, thou hast been my best earthly friend, my counsellor, my guide, my *all* in this world. . . . Let us drink the cup of anguish to the dregs, let us say *Thy* will be done. . . . Farewell my best beloved Brother. Angelina." [35]

The phrasing of these letters reveals a strong personal attachment, suggestive of love. However, the exalted language commonly used among religious people at that time could frequently be so misinterpreted. Mr. McDowell was a married man and all references to him by contemporaries and biographers stress his high moral character. Moreover, Angelina's later history does not bear out this interpretation of the relationship. Still, there can be no question that the separation from him and loss of his friendship weighed heavily on her.

But the most difficult decision was the separation from her mother. Angelina faced it without the subterfuge of false hope. "If I believed that I contributed to dear mother's happiness surely duty, yes, inclination, would lead me to continue here, but I do not." [36]

For more than a year she had tried to fight against slavery single-handedly, publicly, using every means at her disposal. Now she had concluded that her stand was futile, her struggle useless. One person alone could not act effectively in the South. To continue here would be her living death.

Finally, it was Mrs. Grimké herself who ended a situation which had become distressing for all concerned. "I see very

differently [now]" she conceded, "for when I look back and
remember what I used to do and think nothing of it I shrink
back with horror. . . ." It had been painful to bear the many
hard things Sarah and Nina had said to her but she believed
now that the Lord had raised her daughters up to teach her.
Her fervent prayer was that if they were right and she wrong,
she might see it.[37]

Her mother's blessing and consent to her going North
made the leavetaking a little less painful. Yet Angelina allowed herself no illusions about the future. There was nothing temporary about this separation. "I do not think dear
sister or I will ever see her again until she is willing to give
up slavery," she wrote in her diary.[38]

Sarah had simply fled, in quiet desperation and feeling
deeply guilty and defensive at her flight. Angelina had prepared the way painstakingly, making her inner struggle a
public scandal. When she took the final step there could be
no doubt as to the reasons for her action: her very departure
was a public act of protest against the slavery system.

In November of 1829 Angelina Emily Grimké left Charleston to become, of her own free will and choosing, an exile.

CHAPTER
SEVEN

*God in his inscrutable wisdom has appointed a place and
a duty to females, out of which they can neither accomplish their destiny, nor secure their happiness!*
                                    James Norcom to Mary Harvey,
                                                    May 25, 1848.

IT WAS a relief no longer to be surrounded by slavery, no
longer to feel the obligation of conducting her daily, private warfare against the hated institution. In Philadelphia,
Angelina never tired of appreciating the blessings of a free
labor system: the pride white men and women took in the
work of their hands, the dignity which even the lowliest colored man manifested. Only a displaced Southerner like herself could wax enthusiastic over seeing white men at work as
cobblers, carpenters and glaziers. Only an outsider and newcomer could see anything remarkable in the various colored
peddlers, the charcoal vendor, the hominy man, the peddler
of soft soap and ashes, shouting their wares in the streets and
backyards. To a Southern exile there was a subtle distinction
between these colored peddlers and their Charleston coun-
terparts. These, although sometimes ragged, were free, independent businessmen, while the others were slaves or free
colored persons living under the constant threat of enslave-
ment.

Time and again, in her letters and in her diary, Angelina

compared the peace and calm of her life in the home of
Catherine Morris with the turmoil and friction of her home
in Charleston. Here, many of the values for which Charleston had declared her a rebel and a freak, were commonly
accepted. It was restful and comforting and, for a time, Angelina found it sufficient for happiness. She liked Philadelphia. As Sarah had before her, she easily succumbed to the
charm of the simple brick houses in which her friends lived
on Arch and Cherry streets. She enjoyed the change of seasons, the custom of walking down the streets shaded by rows
of elms and linden trees, a custom considered vulgar and unbecoming by Charleston society. She considered it freedom
to be able to come and go without the services of coachman
and footmen, to shop for her own food in rows of stalls on
Market Street, to mingle with common housewives, farmers
and mechanics when purchasing fish down at the Camden
Ferry slip.[1] Her letters home expressed her enthusiasm and
her conviction that very soon some members of her family
and certainly her mother would be joining her. She extolled
the virtues of the climate, the excellence of the schools, the
cultural attractions. When brother Henry came to visit, she
convinced him of the business advantages of living North.
When Thomas' wife was seriously ill, she urged him to bring
her to Philadelphia for superior medical care. If freedom
meant the absence of slavery, Angelina had found exactly
what she wanted to find in coming North. As for that other,
more personal kind of freedom — a chance to grow in mind
and spirit, a multitude of choices, an unfolding of opportunities, Angelina, at this time in her life, did not even know that
such a concept of freedom was possible. Her aspirations went
no further than becoming a Quaker and being "useful." She
felt well qualified religiously and morally when she applied

for membership in the Society of Friends and expected to be readily accepted.

On the 4th of March 1831, a year and a half after she had arrived, a committee appointed by the Monthly Meeting called on Angelina to determine her fitness for membership.[2]

Most likely she had already met some of the members of the committee: Elizabeth Mason, who sat at the head of the women's gallery in meeting, Elizabeth Cope and John Letchworth.[3] There is no question that she must have known and heard tell of the fourth member of the committee, for Samuel Bettle was no ordinary Quaker. He was an Elder and, next to Jonathan Evans, the most influential member of the orthodox leadership. Samuel Bettle's name appeared on numerous memoranda and "charges," documents in the factional struggle of the 1820's against Elias Hicks. Lately he had been forced to testify in court in law suits regarding valuable Quaker properties now claimed by both Orthodox and Hicksite factions. It was he who, having been Clerk for many years, had at the crucial 1827 Yearly Meeting refused to give up the clerkship to the Hicksite sympathizer John Comly, although Comly had been elected by a majority. Quakers did not, generally, believe in majority decisions, but rather, in the "consent of the meeting" as gathered by the clerk, and Samuel Bettle gathered clearly, that the "weightier members" wished him to continue as clerk. He later stated without a twinge of hesitation, when questioned in court about this decision: "I never considered them [those who disagreed with the orthodox viewpoint] entitled to any weight or influence at all." His action had thrown the Yearly Meeting into a turmoil and had sharpened the already bitter division between orthodox and reformist Quakers, which in 1828 led to complete separation of the factions.[4] Depending on

one's viewpoint, it was said that Samuel Bettle had forced
the separation of the Hicksites from the regular Society or
that he had, by his firmness, salvaged what there was to sal-
vage. But that he was a "weighty man" none would dispute
and his presence on a committee might well overawe any
young woman in Angelina's position. Sarah had frequently
been reduced to despondency when faced with a disapproving glance, a slight or even the hint of criticism on the part of
an Elder, not to speak of an interrogation. Angelina was
painfully aware of the way Sarah had been treated by the
Elders and resented that mixture of condescension, suspicion
and hardness by which her sister's efforts at becoming a
Quaker minister had been dodged. Still, she did not regard
this attitude as typical of the Quaker church as a whole or
she would not have applied for membership. Angelina was
used to dealing with important people: she had not flinched
before the Session of the Presbyterian Church of Charleston;
she would not so easily be intimidated now.

Yet the visit by the committee was important enough to be
entered in her diary, where minor events seldom found a
place. The committee questioned her closely. They expressed doubts whether her action in leaving her home and
her mother was quite in line with the duty of children toward their parents and concluded that, under the circumstances, it might be best for her not to join the Society as yet.

Angelina, undaunted by this unexpected attack, replied in
her usual, spirited way: "I believe the circumstances must be
very peculiar which would render it binding on anyone who
had embraced the principles of Friends to live in a Slave
country — that I could not feel it my duty to subject myself
to the suffering of mind necessarily occasioned by it." Besides, Mother was in excellent health and had other daugh-

ters with her. She had given her blessing to Sarah, Anna and herself and fully consented to their moving North.[5]

Her strong rejoinder must have impressed the committee, for they recommended approval of her application. When Angelina had been tried before the Presbyterian Session in Charleston, she had been left with no feeling of bitterness toward the Elders, although her trial ended in her expulsion. The Monthly Meeting of Friends accepted her for membership, yet the committee's attitude rankled. On May 2, 1831, Angelina attended the Meeting of Women Friends for the first time.[6] But she noted in her diary that she did so in a critical frame of mind, an attitude which ever after seemed to remain with her in regard to Quakers.

Now the circumscribed life of the Society of Friends was her life. Befriended by Catherine Morris, she was accepted by the leading and "weighty" Quakers, while at the Women's Meeting at Arch Street Center she made friends with many of the young women her own age. There was much charitable activity, but little diversion. Quakers considered theater and dancing exceedingly sinful and had little appreciation of music. Sports and entertainments, such as she had known in Charleston, were not permitted by discipline and even such innocent frivolities as a colored ribbon for a bonnet or the bright shade of a shawl would be censured disapprovingly and appear in the Minute Book as reprimands.

A dutiful Quaker lady anxious to be useful, Angelina occupied herself with charity visits and took to holding weekly prayer meetings with the inmates of Arch Street Prison. On occasion she expressed her satisfaction with having held another "solemn meeting" in her diary, yet one cannot help but feel that she left much dissatisfaction unexpressed.[7]

She had come to Philadelphia the year Andrew Jackson

entered the White House. The turbulent years of Jackson's
first administration touched the minds and imagination of ordinary people everywhere, but Angelina and her sister were
as effectively isolated from political events as they had been
in the sheltered society of aristocratic Charleston. The Web-
ster-Hayne debates, the Maysville veto, the Eaton affair all
passed unmentioned and unnoticed. The only issue on
which Quakers showed any political concern was the plight of
the Cherokee nation. Regarding the continued despoliation
of Indian lands by the state of Georgia as a flagrant injustice,
they criticized Jackson's policy and memorialized on behalf
of the Indians. The sisters were interested in this issue and
expressed their sympathy with the Cherokees in a number of
letters to Thomas. It is ironic that it was only through their
brother that they became concerned with the most dramatic
issue of the day, the Nullification crisis.

Ever since the prolonged depression the North had become increasingly committed to protective tariffs and rapid
industrialization, while the South rallied to low tariffs and
Western expansion. Jackson's support of the "tariff of abomi-
nations," though qualified, had brought sectional conflict to a
boiling point. South Carolina, claiming state sovereignty and
minority rights, proposed to nullify the tariff of 1828 and 1832
at a special state convention. Thomas Grimké, a staunch Un-
ionist, was deeply involved in the controversy. The Nullifi-
ers, under the leadership of Vice-President Calhoun and the
Grimkés' cousin, Robert Barnwell Rhett, took a belligerent,
even secessionist stand. At the height of the crisis, Thomas
Grimké issued a courageous letter addressed to Calhoun,
pleading with him to uphold the Constitution and set aside
sectional considerations. For this he had to face an angry
mob of his constituents,[8] who dispersed without carrying out

their threats of violence when he met them calmly, unarmed, on the porch of his house and declared himself ready to be mobbed for the cause of the Union.[9] By 1832 the tariff issue had become for the South only one aspect of the larger states' rights question. President Jackson coupled his efforts at working out a compromise tariff with his strong *Proclamation to the People of South Carolina,* in which he asserted the supremacy and indivisibility of the Federal Union and termed secession an "impractical absurdity." Passage of the Force Bill, authorizing use of the military to enforce federal revenue laws, left no doubt as to the intentions of President and Congress and led to a compromise which ended the Nullification episode. Secession was averted, for the time being, but the crisis marked a turning point in North-South relations. It had become clear that slavery was at the core of the sectional conflict. And for the first time in the North as well as the South, intransigent radicalism began to raise its voice.

In January of 1831 a Boston printer published the first issue of his paper, *The Liberator.* Pledging himself to the cause of immediate abolition he announced his earnest determination to be heard. "The apathy of the people is enough to make every statue leap from its pedestal, and to hasten the resurrection of the dead," he declared.[10] Angelina, unaware of William Lloyd Garrison's stirring rhetoric, seemed to be part of the general apathy. She was well insulated from all possibility of deeper knowledge and involvement. The only source of current information she and Sarah read was *The Friend,* the weekly newspaper of the Society of Friends. This worthy "religious and literary journal" printed in fine point and close columns a variety of edifying matter: long and detailed theological and organizational diatribes against the Hicksite Quakers, scientific lead articles such as

"Herschel's Discourse on the Study of Natural Philosophy," J. J. Gurney's "Biblical Notes," essays on such varied topics as "The American Locust," "On Sacred Poetry," "Anatomical Structure of the Hand and Arms," "The Jews," and "Cuba." With much space devoted to news of interest only to Quakers, there was room for an article condemning tea parties as a waste of time and similarly uplifting pieces.

Of more interest to the sisters may have been a discussion on the subject "Woman." The opponents squared off with these contrasting views: "It is no derogation from the dignity or utility of woman to declare that she is inferior to man in moral as well as physical strength. She has a different part to act . . . from the being who has been pronounced her superior by the Almighty himself. . . ." And: "There does not appear any reason why the education of women should differ in its essentials from that of men. . . . [Women] are part, and they ought to be in a much greater degree than they are, a part of the effective contributors to the welfare and intelligence of the human family. . . ." [11] That the latter view was not shared by most Quakers, including the editors of The Friend, was shown by the paper's reaction to a young Englishwoman who asserted woman's equality at about this time, the first woman ever to do so publicly in America.

Frances Wright had, in 1828–1829, scandalized the nation by her public lectures on a variety of topics, chief among them free thought, a system of public education for all children, equal rights for women and a ten-hour day for the workingman. Her political activities on behalf of workingmen and mechanics were as shocking as her unorthodox behavior in going about unescorted and speaking in public. The Friend repeatedly referred to her as "the notorious Frances Wright" and found it convenient to accuse any

Hicksite Quaker it wished to destroy of association with her. "It has often been declared that there is but one step from Hicksism to infidelity: and that sooner or later, the disciples of the former would be found among the advocates of the latter." [12]

Sarah and Angelina, had they read the writings of Frances Wright or heard her speeches, might have been spared many years of agonized intellectual struggle, for the ideas the young Englishwoman projected so boldly and prematurely were those they themselves would later advocate to a similar chorus of defamation. But as yet their religion kept them from the very possibility of free intellectual inquiry. All they knew about Frances Wright was material such as this, reprinted in *The Friend* from the *Allegheny Democrat:*

> Pittsburgh, Dec. 8. Frances Wright. This celebrated female commenced a course of lectures . . . in this city. Her fame and misapplied talents attracted crowded audiences. . . . The dogmas inculcated by this fallen and degraded fair one, if acted upon by the community would produce the destruction of religion, morals, law and equity, and result in savage anarchy and confusion. [13]

Better by far to read "Rambles of a Naturalist" or "Hicksite Views Examined."

For both sisters, personal concerns were during this period predominant. They had, over the years, developed a respectful friendship with Jane Bettle, the wife of Samuel. Like her husband, Jane Bettle was a leading figure in Philadelphia Quaker circles, very active in the Women's Meeting, several times nominated for overseer and frequently occupied with religious visits to other Meetings. Like Catherine Morris, she had taken a motherly interest in the two unattached young women. Nothing could be more natural than that her younger son, Edward, should begin to visit his mother's protégées. "In the latter end of the 5th month," Angelina wrote in her diary,

> E. B. began to visit me in such a way as induced me to believe he designed to win my affection if he could; this was no surprise to me for I had long believed from his conduct that as soon as I became a member of Friends Society such would be the course he would pursue. I had always respected him and soon became attracted toward him, having in earnest prayer first inquired after the Master's will and believing He had put his seal on it.[14]

Apparently, the young man's visits met with tolerant approval by the ever-watchful matrons. Quakers regarded a young man's "calling" on a young lady more seriously than Angelina realized. The young lady, if she encouraged such calls at all, would soon find herself engaged, which engagement would in due course lead to an entry in Quaker Minutes to the effect that so and so had with approval of his parents proposed marriage to Miss so and so and requested the consent of the meeting. Such consent, when forthcoming, would be duly entered in the Minute Book and announced at the meeting and marriage would soon follow.

Such an orderly and compliant courtship was as foreign to Angelina's temperament as it must have been natural to Edward's. While she admitted being attracted to Edward, she still retained other interests. She had realized for some time that charitable visits would not satisfy her need for useful

work. Her widowed sister Anna Frost, who had come to
Philadelphia at the same time as Sarah, was faced with the
necessity of supplementing her inheritance by earnings in
order to support her daughter, and took the only way open to
a gentlewoman by starting a school. Since her school was
never listed in the Philadelphia directory in her name as an
independent venture, one must assume that she took care of
her fourteen scholars in the manner of the usual "Dame
school," herself and possibly one assistant offering what instruction they could in all subjects. Angelina tried to help
Anna but was dissatisfied with an arrangement whereby the
teachers kept just one step ahead of the students. If she were
to be a teacher, she decided she wanted to be trained and
qualified. She had for some time been considering the possibility of attending Catherine Beecher's Female Seminary at
Hartford, Connecticut. Although she must have been aware
of the subtle disapproval of her Philadelphia friends, Angelina reported in the summer of 1831 that:

> My feelings did not however deter me from going with
> Susan Warner to visit the Hartford Seminary. . . .
> Whilst there I became very much interested in Educa-
> tion and thinking I might be more useful as a teacher
> than in any other way I gave my mind up to the subject
> and tho't that I would sacrifice my private feelings, re-
> turn to Hartford in the winter and prepare myself to
> teach a School.[15]

The institution Angelina Grimké wished to attend was
outstanding of its kind and bore the strong imprint of its remarkable founder. Catherine Beecher, the eldest daughter
of the celebrated Lyman Beecher had, after raising her eight

orphaned brothers and sisters, turned her grief over the death of her fiancé into a fierce determination to serve society. Equipped with an extraordinary mind and a strong will, she had built her school in the short span of eight years from the usual ladies' academy staffed by two teachers into one of the foremost institutions for the education of women in the United States. In 1827, by subscription of Hartford residents, she had raised the $5000 necessary to erect a model school building with accommodations for 150 pupils, library, lecture rooms and all the latest equipment. Her teachers specialized in two or three subjects, which was in marked contrast to the usual practice of teachers attempting to cover as many as twenty different "branches of education." Her students had to pass entrance examinations and were awarded diplomas only after passing stringent tests. Later, she would pioneer by setting up teacher training institutions in the East and West, and by writing textbooks and articles on education. While she regarded housework and home-making as woman's primary profession — a subject on which she would later publicly clash with Angelina — Catherine Beecher equally strongly believed that women, in extension of their role as mothers, must raise educational standards. Similarly, she believed that the work of the housewife and mother must be upgraded by scientific instruction in the various domestic subjects, a need she supplied by a home economics book which became a national best-seller.[16]

At the time of their meeting Catherine Beecher must have appeared an awe-inspiring figure of female accomplishment to Angelina, who suffered from an exaggerated sense of her own ignorance and lack of formal training. She was closer to Catherine's youngest sister Harriet, a graduate of the Female Academy who had just begun teaching there.

The two young women chatted and walked on the lawns of the Hartford Female Academy. Harriet, shy and moody, but blessed with a keen sense of humor, may have smiled inwardly at this graceful Southern lady in her unbecoming Quaker bonnet who worked so zealously at self-improvement and admired the accomplishment of any schoolgirl who could rattle off a few memorized facts. Angelina, happily aware of Edward Bettle's intention, may have silently pitied this insignificant petite woman, so obviously living in her sister's shadow and destined for spinsterhood. If, in the manner of young women getting acquainted, they made plans for the future, they could not have reached any further than the next year when they might be working together at Hartford nor aimed much higher than at becoming good teachers and influencing a small number of girls in the direction of self-improvement. That their fame would at any time eclipse that of the formidable and accomplished Catherine Beecher was not likely. That Angelina, within only a few years, would in a public exchange of letters demolish Catherine's colonization views of slavery was not a possibility they could have then foreseen. But that between the two of them they were destined to furnish much of the intellectual ammunition which equipped a generation of Northerners to accept the necessity for civil war, would have seemed a preposterous thought to them both. *American Slavery as It Is* and *Uncle Tom's Cabin* lay years ahead. Harriet Beecher, as yet quite unconcerned about slavery, questioned the one woman from whom she might have drawn authoritative information on the subject, about the odd habits and customs of Quakers, something that interested her very much. And Angelina, liking Catherine's younger sister, thought her rather unimpressive but sweet. They chatted pleasantly, and that was all.

At the end of her stay Angelina took the entrance examination and was gratified to learn that she had passed it easily. Catherine Beecher thought that after six months of proper training, she would be qualified to teach. Angelina, weighing "another prospect" in her mind, felt she needed time for reflection. But she was tempted.[17]

When, on her return to Philadelphia, she told her friends how much she had liked Hartford and that she wanted to return in the fall for study, the effect was quite unexpected. Jane Bettle tried to discourage her from going by the earnest suggestion that "it might be dangerous for her there among so many Presbyterians." Other Quakers expressed opposition to her leaving her sisters and abandoning her charities. And Edward Bettle stopped calling on her altogether.

Angelina was bewildered. It was impossible for her, without permission of her Meeting, to move to another town or even to travel and, obviously, such permission would be denied her for going to Hartford. And worst of all was Edward's absence: "It seems they were all tried at my going away instead of staying at home to receive his visits — they cannot understand it and I believe he felt discouraged and tried and I have no doubt had no idea of my affection being engaged." [18]

For a short while she floundered. Then her feelings won out. "I very soon saw that tho' it had been right in me to go to Hartford, it was wrong for me to have yielded my mind up to going back, for that this was not required and that every *unrequired offering* is an *unhallowed one*. Obedience is better than sacrifice." [19] With her usual aptness for finding the appropriate Bible sanction to suit her decision, Angelina thus rationalized in her diary and hastened to inform Jane Bettle of her changed plans. Edward, however, "finding that [her] mind had been unsettled" still did not resume his visits.

While Angelina was thus preoccupied, an event occurred in Virginia which had far-reaching impact both North and South. Nat Turner, known among his fellow slaves as The Prophet, led an armed uprising in Southampton County, in which fifty-seven white persons, mostly women and children, were killed in the first twenty-four hours, while in the days following hundreds of Negroes, including all the conspirators, were killed in an orgy of vengeance. The Nat Turner rebellion struck fear in the South and made the subject of slavery of particular urgency in the North. One would expect a dedicated enemy of slavery to be very much concerned with such an event. But Angelina seemed not to have noticed. She was still trying to find herself.

Catherine Morris, noticing Angelina's disappointment about not going to Hartford, made a constructive proposal. In her capacity as a member of the school committee she supervised a number of the Quaker schools. One of them, the new Infant School, was in need of an assistant teacher — perhaps Angelina could find a useful function there?

Dutifully, Angelina spent weeks in observation at the Infant School and finally began teaching. But it was work she did not enjoy and to which she felt ill-suited. She went about her duties mechanically. She rose before seven in her unheated room, read the Bible for an hour, then went down to breakfast with Catherine. She attended the health and temperance lectures of Sylvester Graham. She spent much time with Anna, trying to be helpful to her. Every hour of the day was given over to some useful occupation, but all of it was meaningless. Angelina was in love, and had, by her own inept actions, driven Edward away from her.

In December she wrote to Sarah, who was in Charleston on a four-month visit: "Lydia Reeve . . . was willing to take the part of keeping the children in order, which was

most wanted and which I was unwilling to undertake and
incapable of. I went constantly for two weeks, but have believed this was designed to convince me that school keeping
was not my business. . . . I was truly glad of a release." [20]
Nevertheless, she continued studying. Two nights a week,
she and Anna read history, chemistry, anatomy and arithmetic and enlisted the aid of a Quaker friend to study geometry.
They found the work absorbing, but difficult.

During this time occurred an event which would, in later
years, be of great interest to Angelina, but which passed unmentioned in her correspondence then. In December of
1831 the Virginia House Assembly had begun its momentous
debate on slavery. Slaveholders and non-slaveholders alike
stood united in condemning the evils of the system, but
differed sharply as to the remedy. In three months of hard
arguments, many possible solutions were discussed, mostly
centering on various schemes for gradual emancipation with
colonization outside the state. The one solution never discussed was the emancipation of slaves without resettlement,
there being unanimity that it was impossible for whites and
blacks to live in the same community as equals. After long
debate, agreement was reached that while slavery was "evil,"
no legislative action should be taken on it at this time. However, in panicky response to the Nat Turner rebellion, the
Assembly acted to tighten oppressive laws against free Negroes. While the debate aired much that had hitherto been
swept under the rug, the outcome was a victory for slavery
and became even more so when Thomas R. Dew, in his essay
on the debate, furnished the South with the apologetic ideology for slavery which was to dominate the next several decades.[21] After this debate, the issue was joined. The South,
having forced the opponents of slavery into exile individu-

ally, would henceforth restrict freedom of speech within its borders. After 1832, with a few notable exceptions, slavery was no longer a debatable issue in the South.

During Sarah's absence in January, Edward Bettle suddenly resumed his visits. From then on, all of Angelina's diary entries concern only him. They seemed to have reached some kind of understanding, although he never "spoke." Angelina hinted that lack of privacy might have been what prevented him from proposing, for every time he visited her he had to displace Catherine Morris from her parlor. Accordingly, in March, Angelina abruptly decided that her sister Anna needed her help and financial support and that it would be best for her to board with Anna. Undoubtedly, her sister's need played a part in her decision. But the decisive factor Angelina admitted only to her diary: she believed Edward was more likely to call on her at Anna's, where there was more privacy.

It was as natural for Angelina to take such an action as it was for her to find a good rationalization for it. Obviously, her decision would be a cruel blow to Sarah, who in her state of unhappiness and dissatisfaction very much needed the support and love of her younger sister. Angelina was quite aware of that and worried considerably over how to break the news to Sarah, as well as to Catherine Morris. In February, in a letter to Sarah who was then visiting Charleston, she urged her warmly to return to Philadelphia in time for Yearly Meeting.

Precious . . . I have much desired that we might at the time be permitted to mingle in tender and holy feeling, in sympathy and love — truly we have known . . . the agony of separation. Those months of thy deep and

lonely suffering I count the most unhappy of *my* life and
often this winter in my own trials have I been made
truly thankful that I was only suffering for myself.
. . . To see thee suffer is to me a far greater affliction
than to suffer myself. . . .[22]

In the same letter she mentioned that she had visited Sam
and Jane Bettle and consulted them about her proposed
move to Anna. They approved, a factor which weighed
heavily with her. "Their opinion seems to have quite decided me." She had even sought and gained her mother's approval — now all that remained was Sarah's. "It seems to me
thou canst not disapprove of it . . ." she wrote with some urgency.

Angelina obviously did not understand Sarah's capacity
for martyring herself to please those she loved. Clearly, if
Angelina wanted to move away so badly, Sarah would put no
obstacle in her way. She would simply suffer in silence. On
her return, in March, the sisters talked the matter over. Sarah declared herself "willing to give Angelina up." That
phrasing is revealing of Sarah's actual feelings — Angelina's
leaving was not just a casual matter to her, but meant a total
"giving up." But Angelina replied, with staggering lack of
sensitivity, that she did not think Sarah was losing anything.
She, Angelina, could be nothing to anyone, being much too
absorbed in her own affairs.[23]

So she moved to Anna Frost's house and Edward called a
little more frequently than he had, but not enough to make
any real difference. Two weeks later Angelina suddenly decided to take Elizabeth Walton, a young Quaker woman dying of a lingering illness, into Anna's house in order to nurse
her. This charitable gesture would have done her more credit,

if not for the fact that Elizabeth Walton was Edward Bettle's cousin.

In May she noted in her diary that Edward had not come to visit her, but had come several times to pick up Elizabeth for a ride. She thought of him constantly, but did not let him know her feelings.

This state of affairs continued throughout the summer, with Edward visiting his cousin, and occasionally exchanging a few words with Angelina. The cousin turned out to be a difficult and ungrateful patient and the summer dragged on.

In July 1832 the first case of cholera occurred in Philadelphia. For several months cholera had been raging in Europe, then in England, finally in Quebec. An American medical commission had gone to Canada to study the disease. On the very day the first victim died in Philadelphia the medical commission issued its report to the public. It declared that the disease was "atmospheric" in origin, recommended "prudence in living, tranquility of mind and body and the wearing of flannel next to the skin." It advised the public to eliminate all fresh fruit except blackberries and most vegetables from the diet, with special cautions against cucumbers and watermelons, which were considered deadly food. Despite these warnings, a number of cases occurred in different sections of the city. By the last week of July it was an epidemic. The Board of Health ordered the evacuation of crowded tenements. An asylum was set up for children whose parents were sick or had died. Daily at noon, large numbers of people assembled on Fifth Street before the Board of Health office, listened in deep silence to the announcements, separated immediately afterward and carried the news to every part of the city.[24]

The Friend covered the epidemic extensively. Quaker

physicians were heroically active; many of the Quaker ladies helped at the children's asylum or did other charitable services for the victims. Angelina must have been aware of the horror that occurred in Arch Street Prison late in August when the disease struck savagely in the crowded quarters. Healthy prisoners forced into close contact with the sick and dying pleaded pitifully to be released in someone's custody, while even the guards dreaded their duty and tried to find means of escape. Although in the end the prison authorities took the desperate step of freeing the remaining healthy prisoners, the decision was made too late. Out of 131 prisoners, 70 had died of the cholera within a few weeks. No doubt Angelina, who had spent so many hours with these prisoners, must have felt for them but her diary entries and the few letters available from that period are silent on the subject. Sarah commented on the experience in one line. "The Pestilence has come and is now within our city." [25] The epidemic came to an end early in October; by that time 935 people had died of cholera in Philadelphia.[26]

During this time of horror and suffering Edward Bettle continued his visits, making his feelings so plain that Angelina felt they did not need to be put into words. On September 21, he visited her again, but did not come two days later, when he fell sick. Angelina was not worried, since his sickness was not serious. On the 24th of September she attended a wedding at Arch Street Meeting House and wrote in her diary: "I saw myself in imagination passing through the solemn scene."

The next morning Sarah came to tell her that Edward was gravely ill. A few days of prayer and anxious waiting passed, during which Sarah stayed very close to Angelina, brought her news, consoled her and sometimes simply let her weep in her arms. Suffering restored the two sisters to the close intimacy they had temporarily lost.

Edward Bettle died after a short illness. Angelina's dream was irretrievably lost. Grief-stricken, she expected to find some consolation through Edward's parents. Approaching them as a bereaved daughter she was shattered when she was coldly informed that her presence was not desired either during the mourning or at his funeral.[27] Obviously, the parents blamed her for having ruined their son's last year of life with her behavior, which appeared to their conservative minds as merely capricious.

And now there was nothing for Angelina but to join the army of disappointed spinsters, cut off from love and clutching at religion, trying to bury their unhappiness in uplifting work. The first bitter lesson to be learned was resignation and it came harder to Angelina than to most. But, supported by Sarah, she succeeded in turning her bitterness toward the elder Bettles into a feeling of guilt. It was, she decided, her own sinfulness which had brought this grief and suffering upon Edward's parents.

This kind of wrenching of feeling and emotions into unnatural channels was quite what was expected from women of her day. Sarah had long since become expert at it. None who saw her calm face and gentle manner would have guessed at the storm still raging within her. Her intense suffering is revealed in this pathetic outcry:

This alienation of heart, mind and soul from him who has been the dearest object of earthly regard, this sad estrangement from good towards those who are near him, this vain endeavor to withdraw from among them, oh, I thought I had gained a victory over these foes of

my own house . . . but it seems not. . . . The presence of Israel fills me with dismay, but I must endure
it. . . . I must be kindly, affectionate, tender-hearted,
forgiving, while my sad heart is a stranger to good.[28]

But it was only a commonplace of her time, after all. Like
other young women doomed to resignation, Sarah and Angelina turned toward their brother for support, comfort and
contact with the real world.

Thomas Grimké had recently become vitally interested in
the peace reform, a subject on which he spoke and wrote
eloquently and which had colored his stand in the Nullification crisis. "No controversy between the nation and the
states, or between the states themselves shall ever be settled
by the sword. . . . Peace is the unchangeable, universal
law of my land," he had written to the fire-eaters.[29] Sarah
and Angelina responded strongly to his pacifism which was
so close to their Quaker beliefs. Thomas, having joined the
American Peace Society, went further than many of its members in opposing not only capital punishment, the present
penal code, aggression and aggressive war, but also defensive
war and even the American Revolution. He pointed out that
since each side considers the war it is waging defensive,
nothing but opposition to *all* wars would stop war.[30] Sarah
was particularly interested in his views on peace and was
helpful in placing his articles with the printer, editing and
proofreading them. Angelina, in her correspondence with
Thomas, was more concerned with fine points of theology,
such as the exact date of the second coming of the "adorable
Redeemer." Both sisters, under Thomas' influence, adopted
his spelling reform, a scheme designed to simplify spelling in
order to enable more people to become literate.

That was their life, their substitute for a life in 1833, while the bank crisis, labor problems and questions of Indian policy were agitating their countrymen. The sisters undoubtedly were thrilled by the abolition of slavery in the British colonies in 1833. Their hopes that America might soon follow the British example may have been raised by the formation of the American Anti-Slavery Society in Philadelphia the same year. But as yet, their interest was purely theoretical.

In September of 1834, when their brother Thomas visited with them, they criticized his colonization views and challenged him to examine the subject of immediate abolition. Thomas replied that he had for a long time planned to study the subject of slavery, but professional pressures had seemed to make it impossible. Now he would delay no longer. He asked them to get for him all the books on abolition, both American and English, which in their judgment, were worthy of consideration. When he returned from his six-week trip to the West, he would take them with him and study the question thoroughly. The sisters were very pleased; they would have liked nothing better than the reassurance of Thomas' approval for their ideas.[31]

Thomas went to Cincinnati, where he delivered an oration before the College of Teachers. On October 10 he left for Columbia by stage to visit his brother Frederick, but was taken ill and had to be left behind at a stage stop. He died on October 12, "a beautiful Sabbath morning," of Asiatic cholera.[32]

The news reached Philadelphia on November 2. Sarah's diary entry for that day notes that she was able to feel at peace and accept her brother's death as a blessing. One wonders at such correct feelings untinged by emotion. Was

Sarah finally no longer able to admit pain even to herself?
The same day's entry in her diary continues: "Sister Anna
and her daughter sailed for Charleston on the 27th — and my
dear Angelina is once more my companion." [33]

Actually, both sisters, but especially Sarah, had been
deeply affected by Thomas' death. He was their last close
friend, their last meaningful link with the family and the
world they had left in Charleston. For a while they occupied
themselves in issuing a memorial to Thomas, "A Sketch of
T.G.'s life written by his sisters in Philadelphia and sent to
his friends in Charleston for their approbation." In it Sarah
attempted to evaluate his many contributions, showing her
good judgment in assessing Thomas' talents as "rather solid
than brilliant." They continued to live through Thomas in
editing another book of his writings, to which they affixed a
touching foreword signed "His Afflicted Sisters." [34]

Angelina's diary stopped with Edward Bettle's death.
Sarah's stopped shortly after the death of Thomas. Sarah
had personally burned all her letters of that period and had
requested her family to destroy all her correspondence to
them. While the two sisters were once again living together,
there is little on record of their feelings and reactions.

But there is much one can surmise and reconstruct from
later accounts. Their personal experience with Quakers had
not been happy. Both were somewhat disillusioned, both
had been unhappy in love. Through Thomas' death their last
contact with the wider social concerns seemed cut off. Their
religion sustained them in resignation and grief, but it
seemed now that their search for a purpose had ended in failure. They had come North and found freedom from slavery,
but no freedom for themselves. Their feelings were dead,
their intellects stifled. It was a familiar story and it should

have ended here. They had reached the limit of freedom their age permitted to women. They were spinsters, aged forty-three and thirty, alone, without training and occupation and purpose — by the standard of their day, their lives were over.

Instead, it was like the long incubation of the butterfly in the cocoon — all that had come before was merely preparation. Their real life, their role as pioneers of a future freedom, was only just beginning.

CHAPTER
EIGHT

I sometimes feel frightened to think of how long I was
standing idle in the marketplace. . . .
                                        Angelina Grimké, Aug. 1836.

T HE SISTERS had only each other now and their need for
"usefulness" became desperately urgent, because there
was nothing else left in their lives that mattered.

It was especially hard on Sarah, because of the long years
lost in suffering and waiting. Only Thomas' death helped
Sarah finally to free herself from her hopeless passion. In the
hour of her bereavement she had expected at least a sign of
friendship from Israel Morris. But there had been none. Bitterly disappointed, she expressed what she felt in a poem she
sent him. He responded with a stiff, embarrassed note, sug-
gesting that she stop presuming on their relationship. For
once, Sarah understood. The long, hopeless struggle was
over.[1]

At this very time, even her religion failed Sarah. In February 1835 she reviewed in her diary her nine years of struggle
within the Society of Friends, the false accusations made
against her, the animosity of the orthodox Elders, her self-
doubts and uncertainties. For the first time she admitted to
herself a change of attitude: "Now everything looks and feels
different . . . the servitude I have been in for years is no
longer felt." [2] This new intellectual independence found no

reflection in her activities as yet. She continued her close friendship with Catherine Morris, performed religious and social duties the same as ever. And when her sister became more openly concerned with abolition, Sarah for a long time resisted any commitment to the cause.

The formation of the American Anti-Slavery Society in Philadelphia on December 4, 1833, marked a turning point in the antislavery movement. Uniting the three main strands of radical abolitionism, Garrison's Massachusetts Anti-Slavery Society, the New York Anti-Slavery Society and the Western antislavery movement, the new organization marked the final break with Colonization ideas. Immediate emancipation, improvement of the lot of the Negro by education, and an end to race prejudice were the main demands which defined the new organization against the older antislavery groups. The several groups coming together at Philadelphia had their differences, but they were united in their rejection of Colonization, which they exposed before the public in terms which had been previously formulated by the free Negroes of Philadelphia. Colonization was based on prejudice, directed against free Negroes and offered no practical solution to the slavery question. Their most radical demand for "immediate emancipation gradually accomplished" was not as novel an idea as Southern attacks contended. It had first been formulated by the British Quaker Elizabeth Heyrich in her 1824 pamphlet, *Immediate, not Gradual Abolition*.[3]

In America "immediatism" had been variously defined. The position taken in 1833 by an association of Southern gentlemen, the Kentucky Society for the Gradual Relief of the State from Slavery, represented the most conservative definition. The Society's stated aim was "immediate preparation for future emancipation based on the recognition that

slavery is an evil the continuance of which cannot be justi-
fied." By this was meant, first, "a decision that slavery shall
cease to exist — absolutely, unconditionally and irrevocably." Second, preparation, immediately begun, for future
emancipation, such as the liberation of all slave children,
born after a certain date, at age twenty-five.[4]

Garrison's position, as stated in the Minutes of the Massachusetts Anti-Slavery Society, was more forceful: "immediate
and unqualified emancipation without compensation to the
owner." But in elaborating on the meaning of this slogan,
Garrison offered extensive qualifications:

> Immediate abolition does not mean that the slaves shall
> immediately exercise the right of suffrage, or be eligible
> to any office, or be emancipated from law, or be free
> from the benevolent restraints of guardianship. We
> contend for the immediate personal freedom of the
> slaves, for their exemption from punishment except
> where law has been violated, for their employment and
> reward as free laborers, for their exclusive rights to their
> own bodies and those of their own children, for their
> instruction and subsequent admission to all the trusts,
> offices, honors and emoluments of intelligent freemen.[5]

The position taken by the American Anti-Slavery Society,
derived from both the British and the Garrison formulation,
was not essentially different. It was understood by all who
subscribed to it to mean an immediate declaration of emancipation to be followed by a series of gradual, unspecified
steps to prepare the slave for full citizenship. With differing
emphasis abolitionists were now united in demanding that
slavery should at once be recognized as a sin, emancipation

should be declared at once as a principle, but they left unspecified the steps to be taken after such a declaration.

Perhaps more important than the theoretical slogan was the image created in the public mind by the American Anti-Slavery Society's insistence on bringing the Negro into the antislavery movement as an equal. The organization was interracial from its inception and looked upon slavery not only from the white man's point of view, but from that of the Negro. With supreme disregard for the fears and prejudices of their contemporaries, the abolitionists coupled their attack on slavery with an attack upon race prejudice and asserted boldly that the Negro, free or slave, was a human being and a citizen and was to be considered as such in the antislavery debate. This viewpoint which seemed novel and unsettling to the North, incendiary and highly dangerous to the South, was familiar and easily acceptable to the Grimké sisters. Unlike Northern abolitionists, to whom Negroes were mostly an abstraction, they had known Negroes all their lives. They would never forget that the slaves were human beings, with rights and needs, with good qualities and failings. Given their background, it was natural that Garrisonism should appeal to them.

Yet, for several years, their circumscribed life kept them from further involvement. It was in these years that they clarified their own thinking on Colonization in their debates with brother Thomas. In this they were somewhat ahead of most antislavery people, to whom the issue became clear only after the Lane Seminary debates of 1834. The foundation of Lane Theological Seminary was an indirect outgrowth of the work of the dynamic revivalist Charles Grandison Finney. Finney's interpretation of salvation as a turn from selfishness toward benevolence expressed in good works

released a dynamic force for reform in his converts. One of
the most important of these converts was Theodore Weld,
whose highly successful stint as a member of Finney's Holy
Band was merely a preparation for a lifetime of leadership in
reform. From revival preaching Weld had turned his oratorical talents to temperance and the promotion of manual labor
schools, which would enable poor students to finance their
college education by doing all the manual work necessary for
the running of the institution. Arthur and Lewis Tappen of
New York, who were enthusiastic followers of Finney, hired
Theodore Weld in 1831 as general agent of the Society for
Promoting Manual Labor in Literary Institutions. In this capacity Weld traveled 4575 miles in a year and made 236 public speeches. He helped to select the site for Lane Seminary,
an institution largely financed by the Tappans, helped to set
up the school and recruited students for it. He was pleased
with the selection of the Rev. Lyman Beecher as president
of Lane.[6]

Weld had been an antislavery man for years. During his
travels he had begun to read *The Liberator* and had debated
"immediatism" with the president of Western Reserve College, Charles Storrs, and two faculty members, Elizur Wright
and Beriah Green. His recent travels through the South had
made Weld ripe for conversion to immediatism. On his return to New York he resigned his manual labor agency in
order to finish his theological studies at Lane and make abolition his life's work.

Elizur Wright, who had left his teaching to head the New
York Anti-Slavery Committee, kept Weld informed of all
developments of the young movement. He made several
efforts to get Weld to give up his studies and become an
agent for the new society. But Weld considered the West

more important for antislavery development and saw his chance to do fruitful work where he was. He declined all offers for agencies and instead turned his attention to the situation at Lane Seminary and the town of Cincinnati.

President Beecher, an antislavery man of strongly Colonizationist views, did not object when Theodore Weld, in the spring of 1834, arranged a series of debates on slavery and abolition. Beecher had the greatest respect for Weld and considered him the leader of the student body.

But the debates turned out differently from what Lyman Beecher had expected. He himself was at Boston during the crucial time of conflict, but his daughter Catherine attended in his place. Also present at Lane during this period and the ensuing months were the other Beecher children, among them Harriet, and one of the Lane professors, the widower Calvin Stowe, who would later marry Harriet Beecher. The debates lasted for eighteen nights and resulted in the conversion of the majority of the students and some of their professors from Colonization ideas to immediatism. Trouble began when the students, many of whom were Southerners, insisted on carrying their newly won principles into practice. Despite opposition from faculty and town, they organized schools, Bible classes, an employment agency and social services among the Negroes of Cincinnati in order to prove that free Negroes could, with proper help, make a valuable contribution to the community. But the trustees of the school disapproved and outlawed their antislavery society and all the activities which had flowed from it. President Beecher felt compelled to support the trustees. Weld and another student leader were threatened with expulsion, whereupon all but a handful resigned from the school.

Their action initiated a free-speech struggle in many col-

leges on the slavery issue and demonstrated a new militancy
in the attack on race prejudice. It dramatically called attention to the plight of the free Negro and demonstrated the
effectiveness of a "direct action" approach to the vexing race
problem. Indirectly, it led to the founding of Oberlin College. Since most of the Lane rebels decided to dedicate their
lives to the cause, they became a crucial force in antislavery
organization. Theodore Weld, who had given up all thought
of the ministry, emerged as the leader of the Western anti-
slavery forces.

Sarah and Angelina learned of these events sometime during the winter of 1834. They had already noticed that slavery was a subject seldom mentioned among Philadelphia
Quakers. Angelina once questioned an elderly Friend about
it and was told that all such matters were properly handled
by a committee, the Meeting of Suffering. Individuals ought
not to concern themselves with such things. Angelina considered this explanation unsatisfactory and began to read
some of the antislavery papers. Exposure to *The Emancipator* and *The Liberator* soon convinced her that the abolitionists had been grossly slandered. "She found to her surprise,"
as Sarah later told it, "that their principles were her principles, and that they were men and women with whom she
could work for the slave." [7]

Sarah still had hopes of reforming the Quakers. After the
death of Thomas she began a correspondence with William
Ladd, of the American Peace Society, who had been a close
personal friend of her brother's. Ladd tried to enlist her to
his cause and Sarah made a feeble attempt to form a Peace
Society among Friends. She was told that Friends must not
join any group led by other sects, and gave up the effort. [8]

Always more independent, Angelina had begun to attend

antislavery meetings, much to Sarah's consternation. On February 12, 1835, she attended a lecture by Andrew Gordon, sponsored by the Philadelphia Female Anti-Slavery Society and one month later she heard George Thompson speak.[9] The British abolitionist had, since his arrival in America in October 1834, lectured in Maine, New Hampshire and Massachusetts, attracting large audiences and apparently converting many to abolitionism, for local agents report the formation of quite a number of antislavery societies after his lectures. He had already been subject to mobs, intimidation and sharp attacks from press and pulpit. The charges against him were that he was a "foreign incendiary" and "intermeddler" who had no right to interfere in the affairs of another country. Perhaps Angelina Grimké had heard the rumor that Thompson had been sent to the United States by "a bevy of old maids at Glasgow who pay his board, wages and travelling expenses." This charge, designed to render Thompson ludicrous, was more likely to attract her to the lecture than not. It was varied by the accusation that Thompson had been sent at the expense of the British government and was a foreign agent. All the careful denials and explanations offered by Garrison and other abolitionists did not satisfy the attackers. Thompson's appearances had, so far, been frequent occasions for riots. It took a certain amount of courage, under these circumstances, to attend his lecture on the evening of March 3, 1835, at the Reformed Presbyterian Church on Cherry Street.[10]

Although no public announcement of the meeting had been made, over a thousand persons turned up to hear Thompson. The speech he made that night has not been preserved, but one may assume that it followed the pattern of his other American speeches. If so, Angelina was subject to

as thorough and well-rounded an exposition of the argument
for immediate abolition as she was likely to hear. Thompson,
after recounting a few incidents illustrating the brutality of
the slavery system, compared Biblical and American slavery
to the latter's detriment and concluded that the Bible did not
sanction slavery. He then spoke of gradual emancipation as
being impractical and dangerous and illustrated the benefits
of immediate emancipation from the British experience. Yet
he urged specifically that children and old slaves be freed
first, slave marriages legalized, the internal slave trade outlawed, a system of apprenticeships set up and a time limit set
for total abolition — all of which seemed to imply a period of
gradual transition from slavery to total emancipation. He
welcomed questions and opposition from the floor, answered
arguments of opponents, and urged all sympathizers to join
the antislavery organizations.[11]

In later years Sarah and Angelina usually dated their involvement in the antislavery struggle from this meeting.
Since Sarah did not attend it, this most likely was more a
symbolic dating than an accurate statement. The exact date
at which either of them joined an antislavery society is not
known. Angelina's name appears for the first time in the
Minutes of the Philadelphia Female Anti-Slavery Society of
May 14, 1835, as a member of the committee for the improvement of the people of color. The Society held monthly
meetings, and since one can assume that she was a member
for a little while before serving on a committee, she must
have joined between February 12 (the date of the Gordon
meeting) and April 1835.[12]

George Thompson, undaunted by the ridicule heaped
upon his Glasgow "philanthropistisses" in America, always
stressed the need for the participation of women in the anti-

slavery movement. At the time of his tour there were several female antislavery societies in existence. Of these the Philadelphia Female Anti-Slavery Society was one of the oldest and most active. Up to 1833 American women had traditionally limited their organizational activities to charitable and religious societies, with here and there a group interested in schooling. It is significant that the first women ever to participate in an organizational convention were Quakers, long used to free speech for women in mixed assemblies. Even so, Lucretia Mott, Lydia White and Esther Moore spoke at the Philadelphia convention of the American Anti-Slavery Society only at the special invitation of the chairman. Although several of the suggestions offered by Lucretia Mott on this occasion were adopted as resolutions, none of the women present presumed to vote on them. Since custom and prevailing ideas of "propriety" made participation in an organization with men impossible, twenty women under Mrs. Mott's leadership met a few days after the convention, and formed the Philadelphia Female Anti-Slavery Society.[13]

Despite the excitement of new ideas and new activities, these were troubled months for Angelina. It was a time not unlike the one she had passed through nine years before, when she had known that she must leave the South, though lacking as yet the courage to face the consequences of her decision. Once again, she was faced with a serious decision — alone. For Sarah left no doubt that she considered the road Angelina was taking a temptation of the devil.

An invitation from a friend, Mrs. Margaret Parker, to spend the summer at her seashore home in Shrewsbury, New Jersey, came as a welcome diversion. Angelina hoped, in the quiet of sun and sea, to find some rest from challenging decisions.[14]

Instead, she found herself in Shrewsbury, oblivious to the enjoyments of the resort and anxiously scanning the Quaker paper and *The Pennsylvanian* for antislavery news. The young abolition movement was embattled everywhere. That the South had reacted violently to the spreading of abolitionist literature was, certainly to Angelina, not surprising. But she, who had fixed her hopes on the free spirit of the North, was appalled by the opposition the antislavery message encountered there. In 1834 there had been violent riots in New York and Philadelphia, directed at first only against abolitionists, then focusing their fury on helpless Negroes. It had taken state troops to end the mob action in New York; the Philadelphia riots left forty-five Negro homes destroyed, many persons wounded, one killed. In May, the poet John Greenleaf Whittier and the Unitarian minister Samuel May were stoned in Concord, Massachusetts. Antislavery organizers in the West and Northeast were regularly heckled, attacked, stoned and beaten. One might well wonder whether abolition was not a lost cause. And, like a personal warning to Angelina that even the most respectable lady was not immune to attack when allied with the despised cause, was the eighteen-month harassment of the Quaker schoolteacher Prudence Crandall, who had dared to run a school for colored girls in Canterbury, Connecticut. Miss Crandall had been mobbed, reviled and jailed; she had lost her school, her house, her reputation.[15]

Angelina became obsessed with the news. In July there was yet another anti-Negro riot in Philadelphia. August brought a report of an attack on the mail in Charleston, South Carolina, by persons who were determined to destroy a shipment of antislavery literature which had reportedly arrived. The crowd forced the Post Office windows open, rifled the mail and confiscated the sacks containing all "incendiary" literature. "The pamphlets . . . were burned at 8 P.M. the next evening, opposite the main guard house, 3000 persons being present. The effigies of Arthur Tappan, Dr. Cox and W. L. Garrison, were at the same time suspended. At 9 o'clock the balloon was let off, and the effigies were consumed by the neck, with the offensive documents at their feet." [16]

Angelina could fairly see it — the familiar buildings, the square, the masts of the ships in the harbor in the background. How many in the crowd were members of her family or old friends? It was as though a hand had reached out to her from the distant land of childhood. Had she thought to escape the guilt and horror? The mob was the same in Charleston and in Philadelphia — there was no escape in running away. The only answer was a firm commitment to those being mobbed.

A few weeks later, Garrison, in *The Liberator*, appealed to the citizens of Boston to repudiate mob violence and give George Thompson a fair hearing. Angelina, deeply moved, wrote Garrison a personal letter. Although she did not know him, she spoke freely and forthrightly of her fears and concern: "I can hardly express to thee the deep and solemn interest with which I have viewed the violent proceedings of the last few weeks. Although I expected opposition, I was not prepared for it so soon — and I greatly feared abolitionists would be driven back in the first outset, and thrown into confusion. . . ." But Garrison had shown her that her fears were groundless — he stood ready to die rather than yield an inch. For this she was grateful. "The ground upon which you stand is holy ground: never — never surrender it," she urged. "If you surrender it, the hope of the slave is extinguished." As for mobs, they had always persecuted reform-

ers. "If persecution is the means which God has ordained for
the accomplishment of this great end, EMANCIPATION;
then . . . I feel as if I could say, LET IT COME; for it is
my deep, solemn deliberate conviction, that this is a cause
worth dying for. . . ." [17]

Angelina had hesitated before writing the letter, now she
delayed sending it. She laid it aside and prayed "to be preserved from sending it if it was wrong to do so." After a few
days, she suddenly felt that she must send it and after bringing it to the post office she felt "as if I had nothing more to do
with it." [18]

Without asking her permission, Garrison published her
letter in *The Liberator* with a lengthy foreword in which he
introduced her as the sister of Thomas Grimké, explained
that she had not authorized publication, but that he felt he
could not, dared not suppress it. He felt certain that one
who had given utterance to such sublime words would not
shrink from having her private letter published, if in the
"opinion of her friends it will essentially aid the cause of
mercy and righteousness." Garrison shrewdly predicted that
the letter would be read widely and admired by posterity.[19]

"I had some idea it might be published," Angelina confessed to her diary, "but did not feel at liberty to say it must
not be, for I had no idea that, if it was, my name would be
attached to it." [20] Three weeks passed, and she heard no
more. Then a Quaker friend came one afternoon and told
her, outraged, that a letter of hers had been published in *The
Liberator*. He was very angry with her for having written it.
He expressed an opinion she was to hear many times in
the following days: that Garrison's words of introduction to
her letter were the "ravings of a fanatic" and his mention-
ing her own and her brother's name was a disgrace. He urged

her strongly to write Garrison and ask him to withdraw her letter. This Angelina absolutely refused to do. Others of her Quaker friends put pressure on her to retract the letter or at least alter it. Sarah wrote her disapprovingly and expressed her grief at the suffering Angelina had brought upon herself.

Angelina had not expected such general condemnation. "I was indeed brought to the brink of despair," she wrote in her diary. She believed her reputation was ruined among her dearest friends. "To have the name of Grimké associated with that of the despised Garrison seemed like bringing disgrace upon my *family*, not myself alone. . . . I cannot describe the anguish of my soul. Nevertheless I could not blame the publication of the letter, nor would I have recalled it if I could." [21]

She could no more recall it than she could deny the essence of her past life. It was a symbolic act, a public gesture of commitment from one world to another. All the years of floundering and searching had finally brought her to this single moment. Judge John Faucheraud Grimké's daughter from Charleston, South Carolina, had burned the bridges behind her.

CHAPTER
NINE

*I appeal to you, my friends, as mothers: are you willing
to enslave your children? You start back with horror and
indignation at such a question. But why, if slavery is not
wrong to those upon whom it is imposed?*

Angelina Grimké, 1836.

WITH HER letter to Garrison, Angelina had become committed to the cause of radical abolitionism. Now, step by step, she was drawn more deeply into the struggle. Her letter was reprinted in the New York *Evangelist* and various other religious and reform papers. Theodore Weld read it and was deeply affected, amazed at this young woman who with one gesture had tossed her past away to ally herself with the most unpopular cause of her day.[1] In October *The Liberator* reprinted enthusiastic reader reaction to the letter. "Its ultimate effect will be superior to a thousand speeches like that of Peleg Sprague and Harrison Gray Otis," wrote one reader, referring to the pro-slavery speakers at a recent rally held at Faneuil Hall. The same issue of *The Liberator* carried a detailed account of the mob of respectable citizens who, looking for George Thompson, had broken up a meeting of the Boston Female Anti-Slavery Society, then caught Garrison and dragged him through the streets of Boston by a rope. The Mayor had personally rescued him from the angry mob and lodged him one night in

the jail for safekeeping.[2] At the insistence of the Mayor and
of his own friends, Garrison left town for a time. In his absence, his brother-in-law, George Benson, ordered 1000 copies of a pamphlet printed, which consisted of Angelina
Grimké's letter, Garrison's *Appeal to the Citizens of Boston*
and Whittier's poem, *Stanzas for the Time*.[3] In November
The Liberator advertised a pamphlet "Angelina Emily
Grimké's Letter to William Lloyd Garrison just after the
Boston mob." This was actually a one-page reproduction of
Angelina's letter, correctly dated August 30, 1835, and supplied with a headline SLAVERY AND THE BOSTON RIOT and the
introductory remark that "the letter was written, shortly
after [*sic*] the Pro-Slavery Riot in Boston."[4] Thus, her letter
was linked in the public mind with the Boston riot, although
she had written it earlier. Without any direct action on her
part, she was placed before the public as an active abolitionist.

If it had taken courage to write the letter to Garrison, it
took infinitely more courage not to back out of the consequences. In the fall of 1835 opposition to abolitionism took
on violent form in the North. On the day of the Boston
mob, a violent crowd sought to prevent the formation of the
New York Anti-Slavery Society in Utica, New York. It succeeded only in forcing the convention to adjourn to a private
home, the large estate of the wealthy Colonizationist, Gerrit
Smith, who became a convert to immediatism during the
conference.[5] The mobbing and beating of antislavery speakers became commonplace. Charles Stuart was attacked in
western New York; Amos Phelps was almost killed by a
brickbat while he gave an abolitionist lecture in Farmington,
Connecticut.[6] The brunt of these attacks was borne by Theodore Weld, Henry B. Stanton, James A. Thome and several

others of the Lane rebels, who were determined to spread
the antislavery message in the West. Every effort was made
to deny them a hearing, frighten their audiences away and
keep free Negroes from attending their meetings. Usually
the press prepared the ground for violence with a barrage of
distorted interpretations of abolitionist views or outright lies.
At their meetings hecklers abounded, sometimes drummers
or other kinds of noisemakers invaded the hall and kept up a
steady racket. Frequently the speakers were pelted with rot-
ten eggs and vegetables; at times they were hit with bricks,
sticks or other handy weapons. Occasionally they were
tarred, feathered, and ridden out of town on a rail.[7] But
Weld and his little band, deeply convinced that they were
doing God's work, were not alarmed by personal danger. In
time they came to consider a riot a part of their introduction
to a community. Pacifists by conviction, they developed
"non-violent resistance" into a working technique. On the
first night in a new community their main task was to stand
up to the mob without fear. Weld discovered that by folding
his arms across his chest and calmly staring down a mob, he
usually could impress the crowd enough to escape serious
injury. The next night (or perhaps the third, if resistance
was particularly virulent), he would have found enough
men curious to see what was the source of his courage to
guarantee him a hearing. Often a few of these would form
an escort and handle the disturbances. Once the audience
was willing to listen, he would speak without further reference to the violence, using all his persuasiveness and oratorical skill. He would usually end up by making enough converts to form a committee to carry on the work after his
departure. In town after town, village after village in Ohio,
Pennsylvania, upstate New York and Rhode Island the foun-

dation for abolition organization was laid in this painful manner.[8]

Angelina followed these events in the press with a mounting sense of frustration. It seemed intolerable to be merely an observer at a time like this. What can I do? Angelina kept asking herself. What can I, a mere woman, do to help the slave? Her Quaker friends made no secret of their disapproval. Sarah cautioned patience and asked her to stay away from antislavery meetings for a while, so that she might see her way more clearly. But through the Philadelphia Female Anti-Slavery Society Angelina could keep in touch with reform movements in other parts of the country; here she worked with and met an interesting group of women, very different from those she had previously known. Lucretia Mott, a gentle lady and mother of six, whose demure appearance hid a brilliant intellect, patient wisdom and iron convictions, was beloved and respected among advocates of every humanitarian cause. Two other Quaker members, Lydia White and Sydney Ann Lewis, ran Free Produce stores.[9] Mrs. Lewis also sold antislavery literature in her store, which made it doubly obnoxious to her neighbors. Once, when the Mayor called on her and asked her to remove her offensive sign, Mrs. Lewis replied quietly: "I thank thee for thy friendly advice, but I do not feel disposed to follow thy suggestion. . . ." The antislavery sign remained and the store stayed in business for many years.[10] Other members of the Female Anti-Slavery Society were Abba Alcott, wife of the transcendentalist educator Bronson Alcott, the Forten girls, Charlotte, Marguerite and Sarah, daughters of the wealthy Negro shipbuilder James Forten, and Harriet Purvis, wife of Robert Purvis, an outstanding leader of the free Negro community. Here, Sarah and Angelina met Sarah

Douglass and her mother Grace, two Negro women with whom they formed a lifelong friendship.[11]

In September 1835, David Lee Child of Boston was the speaker at the Society's monthly meeting.[12] His wife, a well-known and popular fiction writer, had in 1833 published a forceful abolitionist essay, *An Appeal in Favor of That Class of Americans Called Africans*.[13] Overnight her literary popularity had vanished, her earnings had dropped. Pretty Lydia Maria Child was the sort of woman Angelina could love and admire. Mrs. Child in turn was so impressed by Angelina's self-assurance and dignity that she wrote about their first meeting to her friends in Boston. The evening the Childs first met Angelina Grimké, slavery was the topic of discussion. A lady present chided Angelina for being too absorbed with the subject. In her opinion the right time for action had not yet come. Quietly, Angelina replied: "If thou wert a slave, toiling in the fields of Carolina, I apprehend thou wouldst think the time had *fully* come." This total identification with the slave as a human being seemed apparently remarkable even to abolitionists, since the Boston Society saw fit to reprint this anecdote in its annual report.[14]

There were other indications that Angelina's antislavery reputation was growing. Already, she was the object of celebrity hunters. A Miss Susan Cabot from Boston, when planning a trip to Philadelphia, requested an introduction to Miss Grimké from Garrison.[15] A Ladies' Society from Concord, Massachusetts, corresponded with her.[16] The Olive Branch Circle of Essex County, Massachusetts, a literary and philanthropic organization concerned with peace, honored her. Angelina, in her reply, took notice that the Olive Branch Circle was a woman's organization and praised the ladies for carrying out their "responsibility as intellectual, moral and spiritual beings" in helping men in "that great work of regenerating the world." [17] This comment is an indication that already Angelina's feminist convictions were beginning to take shape.

Although Sarah Grimké at this time still shied away from greater involvement, there was one antislavery activity that even she felt she could support, the Free Produce movement. The idea that slavery could be weakened by a boycott on slave-made products had originated with the Quaker John Woolman and the Presbyterian Benjamin Rush. Another Quaker, Elias Hicks, who had advocated the idea for some fifteen years, finally carried it into practice in 1827. The formation of the Free Product Society of Pennsylvania was one of the factors contributing to the split in the Society of Friends between Hicksite and orthodox Quakers. The leading figures in the Free Produce movement, James Mott, Isaac Hopper, Thomas Shipley, were all Hicksite Quakers.[18] Angelina and Sarah enthusiastically took to the Free Produce idea, which Angelina preached to all who would hear. Whether it was practical or feasible on a large scale, they never considered. That the South at no time showed the slightest sign of alarm at this boycott movement was of little concern to them. The important thing was that it was a way in which one could manifest one's abhorrence of slavery, a way in which one could purge oneself of the sin of it. If this meant a personal sacrifice, so much the better. It did in fact mean such a sacrifice, for the Free Produce movement had difficulty organizing adequate supplies; its cotton goods were of poorer quality than the English or New England-woven product of slave-grown cotton, and repeated attempts to raise beet-sugar crops profitably were unsuccessful. Free Produce was expensive and scarce. Still, the Grimké sisters maintained their personal boycott until the Civil War, although many other good abolitionists gradually fell away from this form of protest.

Although neither of the sisters had personally owned a slave since their girlhood, their slaveholding past seemed to weigh more heavily on them at this time. They increased their pleas to their mother to give up her slaves. Angelina also renewed her inquiries about Kitty, the slave girl she had once undertaken to educate. Kitty, the property of Thomas Grimké's widow, was now the mother of several children. Angelina and her sister Anna Frost offered to buy the woman and her children from their sister-in-law, but their repeated requests and letters were ignored. Later, Angelina would follow the purist position of other abolitionists and refuse to buy a slave in order to free him, since the very act of buying him meant acceptance of the hated slave system. But Kitty always weighed on her conscience.[19]

As a result of their close personal friendship with Negro women the sisters became more and more sensitive to race prejudice. They began to notice and protest instances of discrimination against Negroes in Quaker Meeting. They noticed with dismay that in Arch Street Meeting-House the colored members sat on a separate "colored bench," all except Grace Douglass, who because of her age and respectability was permitted to sit on a bench against the wall. But none of the white Friends sat near her. When the sisters questioned Catherine Morris about this practice, they found that she approved of it. This further alienated them from her. A year later, on their return from New York, they would take their seat demonstratively on the "colored bench" and encourage their abolitionist friend Mira Orum to do likewise.[20] They also noted bitterly that this was no isolated instance of segregation in Quaker Meeting, but that there were other, similar cases in meetinghouses in Philadelphia and New York.

The experiences Sarah Douglass and her mother shared with them undoubtedly made them more acutely aware of the subtle but deep-seated pattern of segregation which existed among Philadelphia Quakers. There was the time Grace Douglass, who had for years been attending North Meeting, appeared at the home of a deceased minister of the Meeting to attend her funeral. The family spoke to her politely enough in a separate room, away from the other guests, but when it came to forming the funeral procession, Mrs. Douglass was left to walk behind it together with the two colored family servants. All the other women had been seated in carriages. The fact that Grace Douglass was never admitted to membership in the Meeting, although she attended services and wore Quaker dress, also greatly distressed the sisters.

Similar acts of discrimination by Quakers in New Jersey and New York came to their attention. Sarah Douglass told them of an incident that took place while she was visiting New York City. At a Quaker Meeting she attended no one spoke to her except one young woman, who addressed her with this question: "Doest thee go out a house-cleaning?" When Mrs. Douglass answered that she was a school teacher, the white lady expressed her astonishment and lost interest. Mrs. Douglass, however, said that she wept through the entire meeting.[21]

Such stories, even if only secondhand, were enough to arouse the sisters to indignation and to make them feel uncomfortable and frustrated in the Quaker environment. Yet, in February 1836, when they attended Yearly Meeting in

Providence, they were pleasantly surprised to find among the
Rhode Island Quakers many convinced and active abolitionists. They commented on the freer, more liberal atmosphere
they found in Providence. Sarah referred to it as a "door of
escape for me out of that city of bonds and afflictions." In
Providence Angelina made the acquaintance of two New
England cotton manufacturers, both Quakers, father and
son. Effingham Capron later became a good friend, although
he must have been startled at their first meeting to find this
very impassioned young lady lecturing him on the need for
boycotting slave-made products. Angelina felt so secure and
liberated outside of Philadelphia that she spoke her mind
freely to various people. Apparently she made a great impression on several, for she received an invitation to come to
New England to do antislavery missionary work among
Friends. Angelina spoke to a woman from New York, possibly Mrs. Abby Cox, and asked her to try to interest Gerrit
Smith in promoting a free cotton factory, a project for which
she offered to advance $100. While there was no immediate
response to this offer, Angelina had impressed the New York-
ers so greatly that they began to discuss ways of using her in
the antislavery cause.[22]

The trip to Rhode Island fortified both sisters in the feeling that they could no longer accept Catherine Morris's hospitality. As they began to move away from Quaker influence, they felt it impossible to stay within that circle, yet
they had no friends outside it. Where to live became a serious problem. As unattached females they could not, respect-
ably, live alone. Angelina had tried living with her sister
Anna, but it had not worked out satisfactorily and neither of
the sisters ever considered this a practical possibility. For a
short time Sarah stayed with Jane Smith in Philadelphia.

This young Quaker woman, who lived with her widowed mother on Cherry Street, was one of the few friends with whom the sisters felt at ease at this time. She offered Sarah permanent hospitality but did not have the necessary space to make this a practical solution. Jane Smith, who remained a lifelong close friend, later became an abolitionist herself and joined the Philadelphia Female Anti-Slavery Society.[23]

For the summer of 1836 the sisters found a temporary solution to their housing problem. Sarah was the guest of orthodox Quaker friends, Peter and Abigail Barker in Burlington, while Angelina, as she had done the previous summer, visited the Parkers at Shrewsbury, New Jersey.

Once again, Angelina made every effort to have a real vacation. She went bathing, riding and visiting. As though to force herself to stay away from the dangerous subject of slavery she occupied herself with various writing projects. But she was restless, and kept flitting from one thing to another. First she began to work on a project which had interested her since the death of Thomas: a history of the United States based on "peace principles." Feeling unequal to the task, she gave that up and began to write a "little book on the Beauty and Duty of Forgiveness, as illustrated by the Story of Joseph." This too was quickly abandoned. For several weeks she read and studied theological works and compiled quotations in order to write a "Sacred History of the Bible." Together with Margaret Parker she read various theological debates of British Quakers. From her comments on these it becomes clear that she was, perhaps unconsciously, building up theological arguments against the views of the Quaker Orthodoxy. Repeatedly, in her letters to Sarah she quoted "proof" that sound faith had to be based on no other testimony than that of the Bible. She found quotations in Fox and Penn to prove the "unsoundness of submission to the Church." It was just like Angelina to construct a careful rationalization to precede what would come to her almost as mystical revelation. She had done this in Charleston, during that long winter before she felt ready to leave. The difference between her and Sarah was that Sarah would simply obey the "voices" or "commands" she suddenly perceived, while Angelina, long before allowing such inner commands to be heard, had worked up what amounted to a lawyer's brief to fortify and justify her position.[24] During this summer of 1836 she certainly made every effort to convert Sarah to her viewpoint. One reason the letters from Shrewsbury to Burlington were so full of theological argument may have been Angelina's awareness that these were the kind of arguments best designed to win a response from Sarah. As for herself, theological problems could not long absorb her interest. She grew increasingly restless. Each evening she spent reading the newspapers; but this year it was the antislavery *Emancipator* and *Liberator* she read. No doubt, the news disturbed and upset her. More so since there came various offers, forcing her to make decisions regarding her future.

Catherine Morris and another Friend proposed to her, once again, that she open a school in Philadelphia. This Angelina rejected out of hand. "I cannot think of acceding to it [the proposal] because I have seen so clearly that my pen, at least, must be employed in the great reformations of the day, and if I engaged in a school, my time would not be my own. No money that could be given could induce me to bind my body and mind and soul so completely to Philadelphia."[25] Philadelphia, in Angelina's mind, had become a symbol of Quaker Orthodoxy. Her reply shows how far she had come in rejecting what it stood for. Sarah remonstrated with her for this decision, and Angelina expressed herself more strongly: "I feel no openness among Friends. My spirit is oppressed and heavy laden, and shut up in prison. What am I to do? The only relief I experience is in writing letters and pieces for the peace and anti-slavery causes. . . . My mind is fully made up not to spend next winter in Philadelphia, if I can help it. . . . I know not what is to become of me. I am perfectly blind as to the future." [26]

A few weeks later Angelina received another offer, which she found much more difficult to reject. It came from Elizur Wright, secretary of the American Anti-Slavery Society, who invited her in the name of the Executive Committee to come to New York and speak to women in sewing circles and private parlors on the subject of slavery, as she had done so effectively in Rhode Island. But it was one thing to speak to friends and acquaintances when her heart was full, quite another to make advance arrangements and speak at the invitation of the American Anti-Slavery Society. Angelina hesitated, then wrote to Sarah about it, obviously hoping to be strongly discouraged by her. But Sarah, always submissive, refused to stand in her way. Once again she declared herself willing to "give up her precious child." [27] Angelina, reassured and relieved by her sister's understanding, now confided her own doubts to her: "The bare idea that such a thing may be required of me is truly alarming, and that thy mind should be at all resigned to it increases the fear that possibly I may have to do it. It does not appear by the letter that it is expected I should extend my work *outside* of our Society. One thing, however, I do see clearly, that I am not to do it *now*. . . ." [28]

For meanwhile, Angelina had experienced her revelation. Her hostess, who for some time had been alarmed by Angelina's state of perplexity, had urged her to confide in her. Angelina did not need much persuasion and for days the two women did nothing but speak about slavery and the various possibilities open to Angelina. Although Mrs. Parker in no way agreed with Angelina's extremism, she could not help but be affected by the desperate sincerity with which the young woman repeated the question: What can I do? How can I help? One morning, after a sleepless night and much weeping, she appeared radiant and informed Margaret Parker that God had shown her the way. She would write an appeal to the women of the South. Southerners who had closed their minds to the words of Northern abolitionists would not be able to resist an appeal by one of their own. An address to men would not reach women, but an address to women would reach the whole community, if it could be reached at all.[29]

She began at once and in two weeks wrote her *Appeal to the Christian Women of the Southern States,* a work unique in abolitionist literature.

In simple, direct language, as though addressing them in person, Angelina Grimké appealed to former friends to listen to her for the sake of old bonds. Those who did not know her, she asked to listen because she addressed them in *love.* Slavery was contrary to human law, contrary to the teachings of Jesus, contrary to the Declaration of Independence. The core of her argument was her belief in the manhood and equality of the slave and in his *natural* right to freedom.

Man, who was created in the image of his Maker, never can properly be termed a *thing,* though the laws of the Slave States do call him a "chattel personal"; Man, I assert, never was put under the feet of men by the first charter of human rights which was given by God.[30]

She refuted the Bible argument for slavery in detail, review-
ing the many biblical laws which made Hebrew servitude
more favorable than Southern slavery. Unlike Hebrew servitude, with its provisions for the periodic freeing of all slaves
and its careful safeguarding of the rights of slaves, the legal
structure of the Southern states robbed the slave of all his
rights as a man.

It has been justly remarked that *"God never made a
slave,"* he made man upright, his back was *not* made to
carry burdens, nor his neck to wear a yoke, and the man
must be crushed within him, before *his* back can be
fitted to the burden of perpetual slavery; and that his
back is *not* fitted to it, is manifest by the insurrections
that so often disturb the peace and security of slaveholding countries.[31]

But why appeal to women on this subject since they did
not make laws?

I know you do not make the laws, but I also know that
you are the wives and mothers, the sisters and daughters
of those who do; and if you really suppose you can do
nothing to overthrow slavery, you are greatly mistaken.
. . . 1st. You can read on this subject. 2d. You can
pray over this subject. 3d. You can speak on this subject. 4th. You can act on this subject. . . .
    Speak to your relatives, friends, acquaintances, be not
afraid . . . to let your sentiments be known. . . . Try
to persuade your husband, father, brothers and sons that
slavery is a crime *against God and man*.[32]

More important than words was action. She urged women, if
they owned slaves, to set them free and pay them wages. At

the very least, they must educate their slaves. If the law for-
bade it, "such wicked laws ought to be no barrier in the way
of your duty. . . . If a law commands me to sin I will break
it: if it calls me to suffer, I will let it take its course unresist-
ingly." True, such action might bring great suffering to
Southern women. But martyrs, reformers and prophets had
always been willing to suffer for the truth and among them,
from biblical times to the present, had been a long line of
heroic women. Besides, such suffering might prevent the
much greater suffering of a servile uprising.

> It is manifest to every reflecting mind, that slavery must
> be abolished. . . . Now there are only two ways in
> which it can be effected, by moral power or physical
> force, and it is for *you* to choose which of these you pre-
> fer. Slavery always has, and always will produce insur-
> rections wherever it exists, because it is a violation of
> the natural order of things, and no human power can
> much longer perpetuate it.[33]

She urged women to appeal to the legislatures with petitions.

> If you could obtain but six signatures to such a petition
> in only one state, I would say, send up that petition, and
> be not in the least discouraged by the scoffs and jeers of
> the heartless or the resolution of the house to lay it on
> the table. It will be a great thing if the subject can be
> introduced into your legislatures in any way, even by
> *women*.[34]

Taking up the various charges against abolitionists, she attempted to disprove them one by one and ended with a glow-

ing account of the effectiveness of immediate emancipation as carried out in Santo Domingo, Haiti and the British West Indies. "I have done — I have sowed the seeds of truth . . . but God only can give the increase." [35]

There was nothing novel in the antislavery Bible argument or the defense of abolitionism Angelina Grimké offered. Yet her *Appeal* is unique in abolitionist literature because it is the only appeal by a Southern abolitionist woman to Southern women. It is remarkable also for its simple and direct tone, the absence of fashionable rhetoric and its bold logic which in the name of righteousness advises even lawbreaking with Garrisonian unconcern. It seems strange that Angelina, who in Charleston had personally tried all the advice she was giving women and had experienced nothing but failure, should still have faith in the efficacy of her program. Perhaps she expected much from greater numbers. More likely she was already beyond practical considerations. Had not God shown her the way? If she did as He bade her, He might show the way to others.

Angelina often thought of her role in such terms. As soon as she had finished the *Appeal* she sent it off "to the publishing committee of the American Anti-Slavery Society of New York, for revision, to be published by them with my name attached, for I well know my name is worth more than myself and will add weight to it." And a few days later she wrote to her sister: "I feel as if He directed and helped me to write it." [36]

It was almost at the same time that Sarah experienced a personal revelation. All during the summer she had struggled increasingly with her rebellious feelings toward the Quaker leadership. She was in such a state of distress that she prayed for sickness in order to be relieved of the duty of attending Yearly Meeting. But her physical health was unimpaired, despite all her mental torture. On the third of August, 1836, she went to Orange Street Meeting and after silent prayer felt moved to speak. But soon she was sharply interrupted by the presiding Elder, Jonathan Edwards, with the suggestion that she stop speaking. This unprecedented act on the part of the most powerful man in the Philadelphia Orthodoxy was obviously intended as a personal rebuke, since there was no sanction in Discipline for cutting short the utterance of any member in meeting. For Sarah, it was the last straw. "The incident has proved the means of releasing me from those bonds which almost destroyed my mind," she wrote. At last, she felt herself released from the ministry.[37]

Sarah poured out her heart to her sister in a long letter and indicated she, too, was now ready to leave Philadelphia for good. Angelina responded to Sarah's story with great sympathy, consoled her with the Scriptural quotation, "I will break your bonds and set you free," and invited her to come to visit in Shrewsbury so that they could, together, make plans for the future. The way things had turned out seemed to Angelina only another sign of the mysterious working of Providence.[38]

Meanwhile, Elizur Wright had sent an enthusiastic response to Angelina's letter. "I have just finished reading your Appeal and not with a dry eye. . . . Oh that it could be rained down into every parlor in our land."[39] The American Anti-Slavery Society had it printed as a pamphlet and advertised it in the antislavery press. It was widely distributed. An English edition with a foreword by George Thompson appeared a few months later and aroused much interest there.[40] Elizur Wright renewed his request that she come to New York as a speaker. Angelina still felt that she owed her first loyalty to the Society of Friends. She wrote to Effingham Capron, the Massachusetts Quaker she had met in Rhode Island, and inquired whether she might be useful as an antislavery missionary in New England. He replied that she would find most doors closed to her if she wished to do antislavery work among Quakers.[41] Angelina then communicated her plan to Catherine Morris and asked her opinion. The answer was that she could not leave Philadelphia without a certificate from her Quaker Meeting and a companion. Catherine Morris and Angelina both knew that such permission would never be granted her for the purpose she had stated. No doubt because she knew this, Angelina objected heatedly to the whole idea. "Didst thou ever hear anything so absurd as what Catherine says about the certificate and the companion?" she demanded of Jane Smith. "I cannot feel bound by such unreasonable restrictions if my Heavenly Father opens a door for me, and I do not mean to submit to them. . . . I do not expect ever again to suffer myself to be trammelled as I have been. It is sinful in any human being to resign his or her conscience and free agency to any society or individual." [42]

As Angelina had expected, there was consternation among the Philadelphia Quakers about her *Appeal*. Catherine Morris came to Shrewsbury in person to try to argue Angelina out of her dangerous ideas. She hinted that Angelina would most likely be disowned by the Society if she traveled without their permission and indicated that this would mean the end of their friendship. Angelina did not take this lightly, but felt that if Friends did not want her services as an antislavery missionary, she must work where she could do some good. "It really seems as if Friends were determined we should not be useful among them," she declared to Sarah.[43]

Early in September Sarah came to Shrewsbury. The sisters had a long and thorough discussion. Sarah tried her best to dissuade Angelina from public work for an antislavery organization. She pointed out all the criticism and difficulties Angelina would face, the notoriety, the lack of privacy. She begged her sister to wait with a decision. But Angelina had already decided to accept the offer of the New York Committee.[44] She hoped her sister would go with her, but if she did not, her friend Jane Smith had declared her readiness to join her. Sarah, still hesitant, offered to go with her for a short visit to New York, so that they might speak to the Anti-Slavery Committee members in person and see what was expected of them.

The sisters made the visit, met Elizur Wright and stayed for a day with Abby Ann Cox, whom they had earlier met in Providence. Mrs. Cox, who was very interested in the organization of antislavery women, tried to persuade the sisters to stay on and work as agents for a national female antislavery organization which the Philadelphia, Boston and New York women hoped to organize shortly. Angelina was willing to work for either one organization or the other.[45]

There the matter rested when the sisters returned to Philadelphia. Sarah, who had become convinced of her sister's sincere determination, was still uncertain as to her own future. Then a letter from her mother decided her. Although Mrs. Grimké was opposed to abolitionism, "her maternal feelings were aroused at the prospect of Angelina's going on such a mission alone, and she entreated me to accompany her. It was like a voice from the Lord," wrote Sarah, "and I instantly resolved to do so." Her decision once made, Sarah was able to meet the disapproval and threats of disownment by a committee of Quaker Elders with a certain degree of equanimity. "Friends were aware they would be in an awkward position for disowning us for an activity in which they themselves had been engaged and which was interwoven with their principles." [46] Angelina hastened to inform Elizur Wright that she and her sister would come to New York to work as the antislavery committee had proposed. They would not accept any pay for their efforts and would bear their own expenses. Perhaps, in thus assuming financial responsibility, Angelina felt she could retain a degree of independence from the Society. It was the only trace of hesitation or caution she showed as she and Sarah launched on a strange and unprecedented career.

The sisters from South Carolina had become the first female abolitionist agents in the United States.

CHAPTER
TEN

Why are all the old hens abolitionists? Because not being able to obtain husbands they think they may stand some chance for a negro, if they can only make amalgamation fashionable.

Reprint from New Hampshire Patriot
in the Boston Morning Post
August 15, 1837.

ALL DURING the month of October *The Liberator* ran advertisements and excerpts of Angelina Grimké's *Appeal.* Reader comment was enthusiastic. "We have just finished reading this eloquent and powerful product," wrote one. "It needs no puffing. . . . It speaks in a tone of high moral courage, of noble daring. . . . It is recommended to every woman's attention." [1] Under the heading "What the Ladies of Massachusetts think," a Miss Ellen Ladd told this anecdote:

Mrs. A. and Mrs. B. were no abolitionists. Miss Grimké's Appeal fell into their hands about the same time. . . . "I must go," said Mrs. B. "and see Mrs. A. and get her to read Miss Grimké's Appeal, and she will become as strong an abolitionist as I am."

"You are a 'day after the fair,' " we replied. "Mrs. A. was converted yesterday." [2]

It must have been about this time that copies of the *Appeal* reached Charleston. Like other abolitionist literature, it was publicly burned by the postmaster. The Charleston police warned Mrs. Grimké that they had been instructed to prevent her daughter from ever visiting the city again. If she should attempt to come and elude the police, she would be arrested and imprisoned until she could be placed on a boat and sent North. Feelings against her were running so high that even in her mother's home she would not be safe from mob violence. Angelina, who had, in fact, been entertaining the idea of a long visit home, was informed of this threat. She replied that she realized her visit would probably compromise and endanger her family. She had no right or intention to do that. Otherwise, threats of violence and penalties would not keep her from exercising her right as an American citizen to visit her home town.[3]

These were brave words, and most likely Angelina meant them sincerely. She would very soon prove that threats of violence or mobs could not stop her from doing what she considered her duty. She would not have shied away from the hostility of her former neighbors and friends, but the estrangement from her family, the inevitable conflict with mother, brothers and sisters was probably more than she could face. In any event, neither she nor Sarah saw Charleston again.

The sisters came to New York in October 1836 and stayed at the home of Dr. Abraham S. Cox, whose wife, Abby, they had met in Rhode Island. In consultation with Elizur Wright at the office of the Anti-Slavery Society they worked out their future activities. A Female Anti-Slavery Society was to be formed in November and they were to speak under the auspices of this organization to groups of women in private homes. In order to prepare them better for their future duties, they were to attend the Agents' Convention of the American Anti-Slavery Society.[4] The "agents' convention" had been called for the purpose of training "the seventy" newly recruited agents to spread the abolition message throughout the Northern states.[5] It marked a new level of antislavery organization, a refinement of method and theory and a temporary unification of leadership. Sarah and Angelina were the only women among the forty abolitionists who met daily between November 8 and 27 in an intensive training course under the leadership of Theodore Weld. The men the sisters met during these two weeks were experienced agitators, writers and organizers; they represented the different approaches and currents within the abolitionist movement.

Theodore Dwight Weld, the "master spirit and chief organizer" of the Convention, had been chosen by the Executive Committee of the American Anti-Slavery Society to enlist and train the agents, because of his great success and experience in the dynamic Western abolitionist movement. Weld had demonstrated the effectiveness of well-trained field workers, when in one year of spectacular work he and six others of the Lane rebels had "abolitionized" Ohio. Henry Stanton, an orator second only to Weld, had been highly successful with similar tactics in Rhode Island and upstate New York. Augustus Wattles and Marius Robinson were doing very effective work among free Negroes in Ohio. The twenty Lane-Oberlin men, a dedicated fraternity who looked up to Weld as their mentor and spiritual father, were the experienced core of the agents' convention.[6]

The New England abolitionists were represented by William Lloyd Garrison and Arnold Buffum. The sisters, who like so many others had been moved to new levels of participation in the cause by Garrison's stirring writing, were amazed to find him a soft-spoken, mild-mannered man of great personal sweetness. The man who had become the symbol of radicalism in the South and whose intemperate rhetoric and rigidity made him the focus of controversy among abolitionists, was personally likable, modest and gentle. Sarah was delighted to find him a "peace man." Uninitiated and unsophisticated as they were in organizational matters, the sisters did not regard Garrison so much as the representative of the New England Anti-Slavery Society — an organization he had founded in 1831 and which he was to dominate throughout its existence — but as the voice of the abolition movement. This first impression was quite accurate historically, for Garrison, despite his contrary claim, represented not so much organizational strength as the strength of an idea.

Through the Quaker Arnold Buffum, who himself was the first full-time antislavery agent ever appointed by the Society, the sisters came in contact with a group of Quakers quite different from those they had known. Some Hicksites invited them to tea and freely discussed antislavery. At another time Orthodox Quakers encouraged them in their work and invited them to their home. "A great contrast to Philadelphia," Angelina noted.[7]

New York antislavery was represented by the Tappan brothers, whose leadership was very much in evidence during the convention. Lewis and Arthur Tappan ran a flourishing business in New York City, which owed its success largely to their one-price policy, an innovation at the time. Strict in their religion to the point of fanaticism, they considered reforming their sinning fellowmen a sacred duty, which they carried out to perfection in supervising the mor-

als of their clerks. They had generously supported many phi-
lanthropies, but abolition was their greatest concern and
they were the financial mainstay of the movement. In 1830
they paid the fine for Garrison when he was jailed for "libel-
ing" a slave-trader, contributed to *The Liberator* and were
converted to immediatism by Garrison's pamphlet, *Thoughts
on African Colonization. . . .* They were close friends and
supporters of Weld. In 1833, following emancipation in the
British Colonies, they were instrumental in calling together
the founding meeting of the New York Anti-Slavery Society.
A few months later, they helped organize the American Anti-
Slavery Society, of which Arthur Tappan was president.
Their position was more conservative than Garrison's; their
organizational emphasis was on winning over the clergy and
community leaders. They were much influenced by and kept
closely in touch with the British abolition movement. That
movement, which had been such a stimulus and inspiration to
American reformers, was represented in the person of Charles
Stuart, a colorful, somewhat romantic figure. He had retired
from the British East India Company's forces with the rank
of Captain, a pension, a land grant in Ontario and a reputation for tenderheartedness toward the natives. After a brief
career as schoolmaster, he had devoted himself to antislavery
and temperance work, both in Britain and the United States.
At the same time as Weld he had come under the influence
of the evangelist Finney and had joined his band of revival
preachers. He had a great fondness for Weld, upon whom
he, a bachelor, looked almost as a son. It was he who had
first interested Weld in abolitionism, and who had paid for
his education. Recently Stuart had worked as an agent in
upstate New York, Ohio and Pennsylvania. In his perpetual
frock of Scotch plaid with a huge cape he cut an eccentric
figure whom casual acquaintances considered somewhat

crazy. But those who knew him thought of Stuart as a "true man of God." [8]

The sisters, in letters to their friends in Philadelphia, reported meeting all these men and more, but their attention was focused on the "lion of the tribe of Abolition," Theodore Weld. "At first sight there was nothing remarkable to me in his appearance," Angelina confided to Jane Smith, "and I wondered whether he was really as great as I had heard. But as soon as his countenance became animated by speaking, I found it was one which portrayed the noblest qualities of the heart and head beaming with intelligence, benevolence, and frankness." [9]

Angelina described the meetings as "increasingly interesting" and considered a two-hour speech by Weld a "moral and intellectual feast." "I never heard so grand and beautiful an exposition of the dignity and nobility of man in my life," she wrote.

After this meeting Garrison introduced the sisters to Weld. He greeted them with the appellation "my dear sisters" and Angelina at once felt "as though he was a brother indeed . . . a man raised up by God and wonderfully qualified to plead the cause of the oppressed." [10]

Although Weld, in the years of strenuous outdoor speaking, had seriously damaged his voice, he did not spare himself during the agents' convention. He spoke for two hours on the question "What is slavery?" For four straight days he developed "The Bible Argument against Slavery." "His labors were intense — I have heard him speak 8 or 10 hours in a day at three sessions of the Convention, notwithstanding he had a severe cold," Angelina reported. "Human nature could not endure it . . . for besides his speaking he would be up night after night until 2 & 3 o'clock." [11]

The future agents were hardly allowed time to eat. Every

objection raised by the public to their cause was presented, discussed and refuted. Weld saw to it that they benefited from the experience of those agents who had been in the field for some time. Henry Stanton, Charles Stuart and Beriah Green shared their experiences in the handling of audiences with these novices. One night a large meeting brought together the abolitionists and the leaders of the free Negro community. The Negro minister, Theodore S. Wright, lectured and "our hearts were one and love reigned over all," as one enthusiastic participant described it.[12] Another time, Amos Dresser told of his ordeal in Nashville, Tennessee. An itinerant Bible agent, he had been suspected of abolitionist leanings. His trunk was broken open and when a few anti-slavery pamphlets were found in it, Dresser was sentenced to receive twenty lashes on the bare back. The sentence was carried out publicly in the town square in the presence of the mayor and the elders of the Presbyterian church from whose hands Dresser had, the Sunday before, received Holy Communion. "His countenance betrayeth that he had been with Jesus," Angelina commented, deeply impressed.[13]

"It is so good to be here that I don't know how to look forward to the end of such feast," Sarah wrote with new-found enthusiasm. "We sit from 9 to 1, 3 to 5, and 7 to 9, and never weary at all. It is better, *far* better than any Yearly Meeting I ever attended." [14] The agents' convention was for both sisters an exciting and stimulating experience, especially since they had been invited, by unanimous vote of those present, to participate in the discussion equally. Even Sarah felt bold enough to make use of this unusual privilege and spoke freely of her firsthand knowledge of slaves and slavery.[15] When the meeting adjourned on November 27 and the agents scattered to their various assignments, Sarah and

Angelina, for the first time in their lives, felt themselves no longer in opposition, but part of a group of like-minded people.

Their own work began a few weeks later with a series of "parlor talks" under the auspices of the newly formed Female Anti-Slavery Society. But it was soon obvious that there were so many ladies eager to attend that no parlor would be large enough to hold them. A Rev. Mr. Dunbar offered them the session room of his Baptist church. The announcement of their first meeting there caused consternation. The idea of women *lecturing* in a church was outright shocking. "I speak of our talks as lectures," Angelina Grimké wrote a friend. "Well, that is the name that *others* have given our poor effort and I don't know what to call such novel proceedings." [16] Several of the leading New York abolitionists had second thoughts. Gerritt Smith, whose name and opinion carried much weight, advised them to cancel the proposed meeting. He feared it would be considered a "Fanny Wright affair" and would do more harm than good to the cause. The sisters, appalled, were ready to reconsider their decision. [17] But Weld encouraged them to go on. In several conversations with them, he deplored the state of society which bound up the energies of women instead of allowing them to work for the good of their fellowmen. "His visit was really a strength to us," Angelina reported. "I felt no more fear. We went to the meeting at three o'clock and found about three hundred women there. It was opened with prayer by Henry Ludlow; we were warmly welcomed by brother Dunbar, and then these two left us. After a moment, I arose and spoke about forty minutes, feeling, I think, entirely unembarrassed. Then dear sister did her part better than I did." [18] Thus Angelina described their first meeting.

The audience demanded another, and Rev. Henry G. Ludlow offered them the session room of his church.

After the meeting they went to tea at the Tappans' home, where Weld was waiting for them, anxious to hear about the meeting. Julia Tappan told him how successful it had been and mentioned, laughingly, that a man had tried to get into the meeting and had to be put out by Rev. Mr. Ludlow. "How ridiculous," exclaimed Weld, "to think of a man being shouldered out of a meeting for fear he should hear a woman speak." His sympathetic words affected Angelina deeply. For the rest of the evening, she sat and listened to him talk. How had he first become interested in abolition? she queried. Weld told her that as a boy of six or seven in Hampton, Connecticut, he had seen his schoolmates and teacher mistreat and ridicule the only colored boy in class. He had felt so badly about it that he had asked for permission to sit next to the boy, which had stopped the persecution. Weld had regarded himself as an abolitionist ever since. "A fair specimen of the nobility of his character," Angelina commented.[19]

The lectures ran all through January and February. The audiences were soon so large that the session room of the church was inadequate and they had to move to the church itself. "We ascended the sacred pulpit and there held forth," Angelina wrote her friend Jane Smith. It was at this meeting that another man slipped into the back of the room, but refused to leave on request. This seemed so odd an action to Angelina that she suspected him of being a "Southern spy," who might "publish them" in some Southern paper.

At first Angelina approached each meeting full of self-doubt and fears. "I can truly say that the day I have to speak is always a day of suffering, and I now understand what friends mean when they say, they speak for the *relief of their mind.* I feel like a totally different being after the meeting is over. . . ." [20]

But a few weeks later she could dismiss the criticism some of her Quaker friends made of her manner of speaking with a good deal of self-assurance. She was told she was using too many gestures; it was much more dignified for a woman to stand motionless while speaking. "I am so absorbed in my subject I forget myself," Angelina explained. "To stand motionless when the feeling is deeply excited is perfectly unnatural and I cannot admire or approve it." [21]

Apparently her audiences agreed, for she continued to speak to good crowds. As she gained experience, she began to develop her ideas more fully. Trying to answer the objection against women speaking on a "political subject," which she had repeatedly encountered, she took the position that women were citizens and had duties to perform for their country as well as men. She backed up this daring and novel contention by showing how the women of the Bible had participated in civic and religious affairs.

Sarah, too, spoke at these meetings, although Angelina remained the main attraction. Sarah usually dealt with moral and theological questions, while Angelina developed the political and organizational arguments. Sarah was obviously happy in her new field of work. "I would not give up my abolition feelings for anything I know," she wrote to Jane Smith. "They have given a new spring to my existence." [22] Sarah also had begun to write. Her *Epistle to the Clergy of the Southern States* had been published late in 1836 as an antislavery pamphlet. She appealed to the Southern clergy to take moral leadership in opposing slavery and developed a logical and compelling argument to show the irreconcilable contradiction between the laws and tenets of Christianity and the practice of slavery. She used quotations from the slave codes of the Southern states and from the debate in the Virginia House of Delegates with great effectiveness. Although her style was not as fluid and lucid as Angelina's and she showed no originality of style, her arguments were well-reasoned. Her boldness in directly challenging the church, to which she had felt hopelessly subject for so many years, was a sign of her intellectual and personal growth.

She also felt bold enough to suggest to Weld that she would be willing to undertake the editing of the speeches made in the great debate on slavery in the Virginia House of Delegates and that she would write a preface for it. Apparently nothing ever came of this project.[23]

During this winter, while they stayed at Rev. Henry Ludlow's house and gave their course of lectures, the sisters did a great deal of reading. They deepened their understanding of the antislavery cause and underwent a rigorous period of guidance and education under the direction of Weld. The days when their reading had been limited to theology and Quaker pamphlets were gone. They followed political events and antislavery news with equal interest. In March they were ready to develop a full legal and political argument to prove the involvement of the North with the slavery question. A writer, over the signature of Clarkson, had addressed a letter to them in the New Haven *Religious Intelligencer* in which he asked them to stop preaching to the people of the North against slavery. "Ladies, what would you have us do?" He challenged them to present practical proposals by which Northerners could put an end to slavery in the South.[24]

The sisters, in their letter to Clarkson, cited the existence of the slave trade in the District of Columbia and of slavery in the territories, the admission of seven slave states to the Union, the participation of Northern states in delivering fugitive slaves to the South as evidence of Northern involvement in slavery. They pointed to the silence of Northern churches and ministers on the subject, to the participation of Northerners in the economic exploitation of slaves by their commerce and banking ties with slaveholders and by their purchase of slave-made products. Lastly, they sharply castigated the North for color prejudice. "Northern prejudice against color is grinding the colored man to the dust in our free states, and this is strengthening the hands of the oppressor continually." [25]

The practical program they advocated called for an end to each of these practices. They made an especially strong plea for the North to end racial prejudice. This statement, stylistically and in its content, bears all the earmarks of the most mature writings of the Grimké sisters. Already, one of their special contributions to antislavery thought was beginning to take shape — the hard-hitting and specific attack on race prejudice as a support of slavery.

The sisters' Southern life experience had brought them in close personal contact with Negroes; their sensitivity to the manifestations of race prejudice was unusually keen. In this, their close contact with Weld was also beneficial, for he was outstanding among abolitionist leaders in his intellectual understanding of the damaging role of race prejudice and in his alertness and constant vigilance against all evidences of it. Weld had, in Cincinnati, pioneered in fusing abolitionist work with a practical program of self-help for free Negroes. In those days he had lived and worked among Negroes to a degree most unusual for a white man. "If I ate in the City," he wrote later, "it was at their tables. If I slept in the City it

was in their homes. If I attended parties, it was *theirs* —
weddings — *theirs* — *funerals* — *theirs*. *Religious meetings*
— *theirs* — *Sabbath Schools* — Bible classes — *theirs*. . . . I
was with the colored people in their meetings by day and by
night." [26]

During these months in New York Weld encouraged the
sisters to teach colored Sunday school and visit in the homes
of their pupils. He sometimes accompanied them on these
visits and Angelina noticed Weld's attitude of perfect ease
and friendliness with these disadvantaged people. "I have
seen him shine in the Convention and in refined circles," she
noted. "But never did I admire him so much. His perfect
ease at this fireside of poverty showed me that he was accustomed to be the friend and companion of the poor of this
world." There was, she began to realize in these visits, an
essential difference between the charitable inclinations of
the rich and the genuine humanitarianism of the reformer.
"To visit them as our inferiors, the recipients of our bounty,
is quite a different thing from going among them as our
equals." [27]

In line with this new awareness Angelina took a special
interest in securing the active participation of Negro women
in the forthcoming Convention of Anti-Slavery Women. She
criticized the Ladies' Anti-Slavery Society of New York: "On
account of their strong aristocratical feelings . . . they were
most exceedingly inefficient. . . . We have had serious
thought of forming an Anti-Slavery Society among our colored sisters and getting them to invite their white friends to
join them, in this way we think we could get the most efficient white females in the city to join them." [28] She also took
the initiative in inviting colored women to the forthcoming
convention, trying to secure the work of the pupils of the

colored schools for exhibition and seeing that the convention be presented with an address to the free colored people. She urged Lucretia Mott to prepare such an address, believing her particularly qualified to undertake such a work because she had "put away prejudice, that monster of iniquity." [29] Lucretia Mott did not agree, and the task finally fell to Sarah Grimké.

After their New York lectures ended, the sisters spoke at similar meetings in various communities in New Jersey. In Poughkeepsie, New York, they spoke to their first "mixed audience," a group of men and women in a Negro church.

"My feelings were so overcome at this meeting," Sarah wrote to Sarah Douglass, "that I sat down and wept. I feel as if I had taken my stand by the side of the colored American willing to share with him the odium of a darker skin. . . ." [30]

After a short rest at Gerritt Smith's spacious country home in Peterboro, New York, the sisters returned to New York. They could be well satisfied with their work of the winter. The meetings they had held had been singularly successful. Undoubtedly, through the women who had attended them, many men had heard of these remarkable Southern women. Despite dire predictions, they had spoken to hundreds of women without damaging in any way the abolitionist cause. True, some of the Southern newspapers had written about them. The Richmond *Whig* had published several editorials about the "fanatical women," but the reaction had been no worse than after the publication of Angelina's *Appeal*.[31] To judge from the several offers that were made to the sisters at this time, the abolitionists were aware that they had found a pair of singularly effective agents.

From Boston came a broad hint that, should they decide to visit there, they would find a "field for Herculean labor." [32]

From Asa Mahan, President of Oberlin College, came an inquiry to Weld regarding the possibility of employment for Miss Angelina Grimké as an assistant teacher in the college's Female Department. If this should not be possible, would Weld at least persuade Miss Grimké to write to the Oberlin Young Ladies Anti-Slavery Society or Literary Society? It would give a new impulse to them.[33] There is no record of Angelina's response to this request. Meanwhile, the sisters had joined a newly formed Temperance Society and signed the pledge. After their intensive work during the winter they looked forward to devoting their time to "reading borrowed books."[34]

They made a brief visit to Philadelphia during the spring, which marked their final alienation from the Quaker environment. This was the time they demonstrated their feelings by sitting with the Douglasses on the "colored bench" in Meeting. The committee of Overseers, which visited them, took the occasion to reprimand them for their conduct and bring up various other charges against them, such as their attendance at Presbyterian services in New York. The sisters defended themselves with considerable spirit. The committee then urged them to resign their membership in order to save the Meeting the embarrassment of having to disown them. The sisters replied that they still believed in the great principles of the Quaker faith. "Upon Friends, not upon us must rest the responsibility of depriving us of the right of membership," they asserted.[35] With this politically sophisticated challenge they left Philadelphia and the realm of Quaker Orthodoxy. They were not surprised that the Elders failed to act on their threat. The Philadelphia Meeting would disown them in time, but over a technicality, not a controversial issue.

During May the sisters attended the Anti-Slavery Convention of American Women in New York City. Thus, convention leaders Lucretia Mott from Philadelphia; Lydia Maria Child, Maria Weston Chapman and her sister Ann Warren Weston from Boston; Julia and Susan Tappan from New York were joined by two "delegates from South Carolina." The sisters actively participated in the preparation and the proceedings of the convention. Since this was the first major organizational effort of American women, some of the male reformers apparently thought the women very much in need of advice and counsel. Far from needing such help, the seventy-one delegates from eight states ran an efficient convention, issued publications and resolutions, and set up executive committees in Boston, New York and Philadelphia to launch their campaign for one million signatures on antislavery petitions.[36] Angelina seemed to take particular pleasure in giving Weld a message from one of the convention secretaries: "Tell Mr. Weld . . . that when the women got together, they found they had *minds* of their own, and could transact their business *without* his direction." To which she added her own comment: "The Boston and Philadelphia women were so well versed in business that they were quite mortified to have Mr. Weld quoted as authority for doing or not doing so and so." [37]

The particular contribution of the Grimké sisters to this convention was their insistence that race prejudice must be fought in the North as well as in the South. In an article Angelina had prepared for the convention she stressed the bond of women of all races: "They [the female slaves] are our countrywomen — *they are our sisters;* and to us as women, they have a right to look for sympathy with their sorrows, and effort and prayer for their rescue. . . ." She stressed the particular burden slavery placed on women and charged Northern women with prejudice.

> Our people have erected a false standard by which to judge man's character. Because in the slave-holding States colored men are plundered and kept in abject ignorance, are treated with disdain and scorn, so here, too in profound deference to the South, we refuse to eat, or ride, or walk, or associate, or open our institutions of learning, or even our zoological institutions to people of color, unless they visit them in the capacity of *servants*, of menials in humble attendance upon the Anglo-American. Who ever heard of a more wicked absurdity in a Republican country?
>
> Women ought to feel a peculiar sympathy in the colored man's wrong, for, like him, she has been accused of mental inferiority, and denied the privileges of a liberal education.

To the frequent objection she had encountered, that women should not concern themselves with a political subject like slavery, she answered: "The denial of our duty to act in this case is a denial of our right to act; and if we have no right to act, then may *we* well be termed 'the white slaves of the North,' for like our brethren in bonds, we must seal our lips in silence and despair." [38]

This was indeed new and bold reasoning. That it reflected thoughts held in private by some of the most advanced women abolitionists, was shown by the warm reponse of women such as Mary T. Parker, Anna Weston and Lydia Maria Child. Angelina Grimké's *Appeal to the Women of the Nominally Free States* was published by the convention, as was Sarah Grimké's *Address to Free Colored Americans*.

Invitations to speak came from many different places in the North and West and in New England.[39]

In consultation with the executive committee of the American Anti-Slavery Society it was decided that, two weeks after the convention, the sisters were to go to Boston and speak there and in the neighboring towns to groups of women, as they had done in New York. A touching letter of recommendation from the Ladies' New York City Anti-Slavery Society to "Our Sisters in the Anti-Slavery Cause" expressed its "every confidence in the necessity, the propriety and the ultimate, if not immediate success of their mission." [40] The concern of the abolitionist ladies of New York over the fate of their venture was understandable. As the first women abolitionist agents in the country, the Grimké sisters would undoubtedly face more than the usual hostility and censure directed against antislavery agents. That they were Southern ladies, the only white Southern ladies ever to have embraced the abolitionist cause publicly, would make their position even more difficult. But the time for their unique undertaking seemed propitious. At this moment the abolitionist movement seemed united in purpose and strength as never before. The different factions and regions had submerged their separate interests to the common goal of spreading the abolition gospel. The agents were the means; tens of thousands of antislavery petitions were the end of their joint effort. More than anyone else, the two new female agents symbolized in their person the newly won unity of the various factions and trends in the cause. Members of the Philadelphia Female Anti-Slavery Society, they had been discovered by Garrison, trained by Weld, launched by the American Anti-Slavery Society. There was every reason to believe that their agency would be a unifying force.

Instead, their New England tour placed these two young

women for a brief time in the front lines of the antislavery struggle and made them the focal point for sharp controversy. Their presence caused a furor; their actions heightened conflict over leadership and brought ideological disagreements into open controversy. Refusing to be merely instruments of the policies of others, they became shapers of events and leaders of a new cause. The controversy they created has, to this day, obscured the remarkable accomplishments of their mission. To some, Angelina and Sarah Grimké would become the women who started the split in the abolition movement. To others, they would be the abolitionists who added the cause of woman's rights to the cause of abolition, to mutual benefit.

The sisters, however, as they set out on their way to Boston on May 28, 1837, had no intention of accomplishing anything so controversial. They simply wanted to lecture to the women of New England on the subject of abolition.

CHAPTER ELEVEN

*But I suffer not a woman to teach, nor to usurp authority
over the man, but to be in silence.*
                                        St. Paul. I. Timothy, ii, 12.

A T FIRST, in Boston, it was no different from what it had
been in New York. There were reform meetings to attend, parlor meetings in the homes of leading abolitionists at
which they spoke, and the huge public meeting of the Boston Female Anti-Slavery Society in Washington Hall, where
Angelina addressed over 400 women.[1] There were the familiar faces of the reformers they had met in New York, Garrison and Stanton, William Goodell, and the man who had
helped defend Prudence Crandall, Charles Burleigh. The
Childs and Mary Parker were old friends from Philadelphia
days. There were others of the Garrison crowd whom they
met for the first time: Francis Jackson, the lawyer; Henry
Chapman, the wealthy merchant whose wife, Maria Weston
Chapman, was a leader of the Female Society; and Samuel
Philbrick, at whose beautiful country home the sisters addressed the first antislavery meeting ever held in Brookline.[2]

Yet the sisters became conscious of a different spirit in Boston from what they had known in Philadelphia and New
York. "There is some elasticity in this atmosphere," Sarah
commented. "I feel as if I was helped, strengthened, invigo-
rated."[3] "In New York we were allowed to do nothing," An-

gelina observed, "here invitations . . . press in from all sides." [4] In New York they had been discouraged and criticized for speaking in public, but here, where for more than four years the Female Anti-Slavery Society had accustomed reformers to seeing women participating in public meetings, their pioneering met with friendly interest and approval. "At Friend Chapman's, where we spent a social evening, I had a long talk with the brethren on the rights of women," Angelina reported, and found a very general sentiment prevailing that it is time our fetters were broken. L. M. Child and Maria Chapman strongly supported this view." [5] In this atmosphere, the sisters felt free to express some of their ideas on the subject, which they had up to then confided only to each other and to a few friends. At a meeting they presented their "new approach" to some 300 women. The reform must begin in women themselves, they told the audience. Women must cast off their embarrassment and restraint in the company of men and begin to look on themselves as responsible moral beings. "After we had finished many women came up and expressed their pleasure and satisfaction at this part particularly . . . they were their own feelings, but they had never heard them expressed before." [6]

Even on a purely social visit the subject of woman's role was on Angelina's mind. On June 6 the sisters accompanied Garrison on a visit to John Quincy Adams at Quincy. The aging ex-President, now a representative from Massachusetts, had recently been beset by a succession of visiting abolitionists, who urged upon him a greater public commitment to their cause. This Adams circumspectly avoided. He refused to attend any public antislavery meetings, believing that he could best serve the cause "by such services as I could render to it in the discharge of my duty in Congress." [7]

There, he had since early in 1836 led a vigorous fight for the right to present antislavery petitions over Southern opposition. Through this campaign which, with passage of the "gag-rule," broadened into a free-speech fight and which Adams conducted with great resourcefulness and a stubborn dedication to principles, he greatly aided the antislavery cause. As for the organized abolition movement, Adams noted in his diary: "Upon this subject of antislavery my principles and my personality make it necessary for me to be more circumspect in my conduct than belongs to my nature." [8]

This attitude was as incomprehensible to Garrison as the latter's disdain of practical politics must have been to Adams. Already under Garrison's influence, Angelina Grimké echoed his appraisal of Adams in commenting on the visit. "He [Adams] has no idea of the power of moral right, the supremacy of the laws of God over those of men." [9] Sarah reported that they "came away sick at heart of political morality." [10] That the man who so resolutely defended the right of women to send antislavery petitions to Congress would at the same time oppose abolition in the District of Columbia because he did not consider it practical, could be understood by Sarah only as a surrender of moral principle to "political expediency." [11]

But Angelina was interested in testing her new ideas. Typically, she put the matter with bluntness. "I asked him whether women could do anything in the abolition of slavery." Adams, always the perfect gentleman, answered smilingly: "If it is abolished, *they* must do it." [12]

It was an answer that must have given the sisters great satisfaction. Undoubtedly, in Adams' case, it was more than a courteous phrase offered a visiting lady. John Quincy

Adams, of all men, had already had ample occasion to weigh the contribution of women to the antislavery petition campaign.[13] The intriguing aspect of the conversation is that Adams could not know that the very ladies with whom he was here discoursing would soon reach more women than anyone had before them with the abolition message. The rush of female activity they would set in motion was to find its expression in the ever-increasing flood of antislavery petitions. These Adams would dutifully present to a Southern-dominated Congress in the face of the "gag rule" although he continued to disagree with some of the petitioners' objectives.[14] The female effort he now politely encouraged was to reveal a dynamic political potential.

With characteristic singlemindedness the sisters concentrated on their work. The letters never mention any of their impressions of the city of Boston and the beautiful countryside surrounding it. Angelina's comments on the people she met are curiously devoid of characterization and personal impressions. But her long and detailed reports to Jane Smith, and through her to the Philadelphia Female Anti-Slavery Society, are filled with names and dates and attendance figures and reveal her growing awareness of her pioneering role. Although all their meetings had been arranged for women, the sisters found, within two weeks of the start of their tour, that there were more and more men in their audiences. At Roxbury Angelina spoke to 250 women and 30 men.[15] Several days and several meetings later, she addressed 550 women and 50 men in the Methodist Church on Boston's Church Street. It was, Angelina reported, "very easy to speak, because there was great openness to hear." [16]

At Lynn, where there was an active group of Quaker abolitionists, the antislavery society which had made the arrangements announced the meeting open to all. On the evening of June 21, the sisters addressed their "first, large mixed audience. Over one thousand present, great openness to hear, and ease in speaking." [17] After this, all their meetings were open to men and women.

That the audiences did not object is obvious from the success of the Lynn meeting. The meetinghouse was "crowded to excess. About 600 seated, many went away, about 100 stood around the door . . . on each window on the outside stood three men with their heads above the lowered sash." The meeting was too crowded to attend to the usual practice of signing up new members and taking a collection. The sisters had to return the next day, and again the next week.[18]

After several weeks, Angelina commented:

It is wonderful how the way has been opened for us to address mixed audiences, for most sects here are greatly opposed to public speaking for women, but curiosity and real interest in the antislavery cause . . . induce the attendance at our meetings. . . . Our compass of voice has astonished us, for we can fill a house containing 1000 present with ease. We feel that the Lord is with us.[19]

It was needful that they feel the living presence of the Lord to sustain them. For by now the novelty and excitement of their position had worn off; their trip was no longer quite the thrilling, liberating experience it had been at first. They had, of necessity, settled down into the wearing routine of the itinerant lecturer, traveling from town to town in all kinds of weather, in uncomfortable conveyances and at inconvenient schedules. They would lodge at the home of a local

abolitionist in a town or village where there was an established antislavery society and lecture there, if possible, several times and in different churches. Escorted by a local
minister or leading abolitionist, they would then meet speaking engagements in most of the surrounding villages and
towns, frequently in places where abolitionist organization
had not previously reached. This crowded schedule did not
permit them sufficient rest between engagements. Frequently there was no time for regular meals, while the endless
teas and receptions given in their honor added to the demands made upon them. They were almost continuously in
the public eye. And now they were beginning to meet with
hostility. After they had successfully lectured in Lynn and
the neighboring villages of Danvers, Salem and New Mills, it
was in South Danvers that they first ran into difficulties. Unable to secure a church in which to lecture, they had to hire a
hall. Owing to the active opposition of Rev. Mr. Park, the
Congregational minister, they had difficulty even in giving
notice of their meeting.[20]

This proved to be only the first incident of many. As they
more and more frequently experienced opposition on the
part of individual ministers, it became clear to Sarah and Angelina that this was due to their twofold role as women and as
abolitionists. All churches, except for the Quakers, were opposed to women speaking in public, but since the issue had
never been put to the test before, many individual ministers
and congregations were open-minded. It was as abolitionists
that they ran into severe opposition.

The New England churches had been strong supporters of
the old Colonization Society. Garrisonians expected, by the
sheer persuasiveness of their argument, to transfer this
church support to their own brand of antislavery doctrine.

They considered Christian ministers their natural allies and expected a strong attack on slavery to be made by the Northern clergy. In this expectation they were bitterly disappointed.

In 1834 a meeting of Congregationalist ministers in Boston had voted by a large majority to refuse to read notices of abolitionist meetings from the pulpit.[21] Two years later the Congregational General Association of Connecticut, under the leadership of Rev. Leonard Bacon and Rev. Lyman Beecher, passed a resolution against "itinerant agents" speaking in churches without the advice and consent of pastors and regular ecclesiastical bodies.[22] A few days later, the General Association of Massachusetts, again under Beecher's influence, unanimously passed a resolution to the same effect. The proscription of itinerant agents was merely a device for closing the churches to abolitionist argument which church leaders considered divisive and therefore dangerous.

As a result the abolitionists of Boston found it impossible, early in 1837, to secure a single church or meeting hall, and had to hold their convention in a converted stable.[23]

Clerical opposition to the abolitionists focused its attack on the vituperative language of *The Liberator* and the extremist demand of its editor that the churches exclude slaveholding members and deny them communion. The Garrisonians, in turn, believed that the denial of meetinghouses to abolitionist speakers was added proof of the "sinful" silence of the churches in regard to slavery and felt driven to the use of ever stronger language in condemning the churches.

The Grimké sisters' tour served to bring the issue more sharply to the attention of local congregations and to point up dramatically that denial of free speech to abolitionists was possible only by reversing the century-old tradition of the

Congregational church serving as a community forum. In other denominations as well, their appearance precipitated controversy over the free speech issue.

An incident of this kind occurred only two days after their meeting in South Danvers. The Yearly Meeting of Friends, which had met only a few weeks earlier in Newport, Rhode Island, had — at the suggestion of the Philadelphia delegates — passed a resolution ordering all Quaker meetinghouses closed to antislavery lecturers.[24] This measure was designed to keep the abolition controversy from creating dissension in Quaker ranks. News of this policy reached Salem, Massachusetts, only after permission to speak at the Quaker meetinghouse had already been granted to the Grimkés; consequently Sarah was able to address 600 people there on "The Heathenism of India compared with Southern Slavery."[25] Angelina followed her and took the occasion to express her disillusionment with the Quakers' current indifference to slavery. The principles which had moved a Benezet and Woolman had by now become mere formulae. Abolitionists, she told her audience of Quakers, had expected too much in assuming Friends would be antislavery leaders. Friends thought they knew all about antislavery principles, yet they must be converted to them just like members of other churches.[26]

Angelina and Sarah were of great help to each other. Angelina, who was more gifted as a speaker, never failed to encourage her elder sister and often wrote her friends about Sarah's successful lectures. Sarah, in her usual motherly way, worried about her younger sister's health. Long used to self-denial and an attitude of resignation, Sarah saw her role strictly as that of a helper and support to Angelina. "I only pick up the chips for her," she wrote to Gerrit Smith.[27] When the Salem Female Anti-Slavery Society voted a life membership to Sarah Grimké as a token of their admiration, Sarah endorsed the letter with "I take it for granted I am honored and praised for the sake of my A.E.G." [28]

Although for a long time she carried her full share of lecturing and most likely the larger share of research and preparation, Sarah continued to disparage her own contributions. "The work in which we are engaged is in a peculiar manner dear Angelina's. . . . My precious sister has a gift in lecturing, in reasoning and elucidating, so far superior to mine, that I know the cause is better pleaded if left entirely in her hands," she confided to her good friend Sarah Douglass, adding that it had not been easy for her to resign herself to "thus being laid aside." [29]

This comment, offered in September 1837, is curious and seems rather a last welling up of the old self-pity and desire for martyrdom than an accurate statement of her situation, for this was the very period in her life when Sarah was finally coming into her own as an individual. It was Sarah who had noticed the plight of the women and children working in the factories and mills of Lynn and Danvers at wages far lower than those of men. This interest would find expression in the continued stress in her writings on the discrimination against working women, an issue on which she was far ahead of most reformers of her day. It was Sarah who began to be more and more concerned with the "woman question" as a separate issue. While both sisters made it a point to avoid all issues other than slavery and abolition in their lectures, Sarah was gradually developing a theory of woman's right to equality before the law and a concern with the abuses to which women, as a group, were subjected.[30]

Intellectually, Sarah Grimké was growing by leaps and bounds. Her development was often erratic and would, occasionally, lead her into byways, but she was no longer the

same person who had for so many years been fettered by a
rigid theology. "I feel sometimes as if my soul was just emerging from the darkness of ignorance," Sarah wrote to Weld.
"For many years I have been inquiring the way to Zion and
now I know not but I shall have to surrender all, or many of
my long cherished parts of religion and come back to the one
simple point: 'Follow after holiness without which no man
shall see the Lord.'" [31] Indeed, the more radically a theory
questioned every point of faith she had previously held, the
more it appealed to Sarah at this time. That was why the
perfectionist theories of John Humphrey Noyes attracted her
strongly.

Noyes, a former divinity student at Andover and Yale, had
become convinced that the millennium was close at hand and
that by his own insight he could reach a state of perfection.
Such a condition was attainable by others as well. Noyes
preached this new theology in the columns of his paper, *The
Perfectionist.* He rejected civil government, public worship,
observance of the Sabbath, and the paid clergy. He had recently converted Garrison to some of his ideas, to the extent
that the editor had allowed Noyes' definition of the United
States Government to be printed in his paper.

> I picture to myself a bloated, swaggering libertine,
> trampling on the Bible — its own Constitution — its
> treaties with the Indians — the petitions of its citizens:
> with one hand whipping a negro tied to a liberty-pole,
> and with the other dashing an emaciated Indian to the
> ground. . . . Every person who is . . . a citizen of the
> United States, i.e. a voter, politician etc., is at once a
> slave and a slaveholder — in other words a subject and a
> ruler in a slaveholding government.

. . . Is it not high time for abolitionists to abandon a government whose President has declared war on them? I cannot but think that many of them hear the same great voice out of heaven which has waked me, saying, "*Come out* of here, my people, that ye be not partakers of her sins and of her plagues." [32]

This "come-outer" doctrine, which enraged Garrison's clerical opponents, held a strong fascination for Sarah Grimké. To an extent it was an outgrowth of ideas she herself had previously adopted. The Quaker doctrine of the "inner light" bore a certain resemblance to Noyes' perfection by inner revelation. Sarah, who had long suffered from the tyranny of an orthodox ministry, was sympathetically inclined toward Noyes' generalizations. A few months earlier, she had taken the drastic step of writing an "address," exposing the errors of the Quakers and attacking the stifling rule of their Orthodoxy. This pamphlet she had offered to Theodore Weld for publication, fully aware that such a step would expose her to disownment by the Quakers. But Weld, considering the pamphlet too controversial, refused to publish it, and Sarah apparently took no further step to publicize her views.[33] From opposition to the "paid clergy" and the Orthodoxy, it was only a step to rejection of all the clergy. Having witnessed in several churches the acceptance and even the defense of slavery by professing Christians, Sarah was ready to reject all churches. From this position it was only a logical step to the rejection of all government. Sarah was well prepared for religious anarchism by her own experiences and development. Now, she began to test these ideas in her letters to Weld and Gerrit Smith.

She belabored Gerrit Smith in letter after letter with her

"ultra peace principles," revealing the typical reformer's certainty that whatever revelation she had just experienced must be immediately shared with friends to save their souls from otherwise certain perdition. She urged on Smith the necessity of one's "acknowledging no government but God's," in order to be free of "all dominion of man both civil and ecclesiastical." Viewing slavery as only an "offspring of war," she was now convinced that "peace principles" offered the only solution to the slavery question.[34] In this she was not only showing the impact of Noyes' and Garrison's ideas, but was falling back on the pacifist preoccupations of her brother Thomas. Gerrit Smith, an idealistic but highly unstable man who was attracted to fads as easily as to worthwhile ideas, discussed these questions with great seriousness. Weld, for the moment, ignored this aspect of Sarah's correspondence. He was greatly concerned with the obviously increasing influence upon the sisters of Garrison and Henry C. Wright, but as yet refrained from commenting upon it.

Henry C. Wright, an agent assigned by the New York Committee to do "children's work" in Massachusetts, had become the self-appointed escort and sponsor of the sisters. Early in July, they made his home in Newburyport, Massachusetts, their headquarters. Wright, a former hatmaker, had studied theology at Andover and served as a Congregational minister in West Newbury until 1833. While working as an agent of the American Sunday School Society he attended a session of the New Hampshire House of Representatives. Wright found the inattentiveness and indifference of the representatives shocking. "I do not believe that one in ten of all the members in this House have any knowledge of the contents of those bills or care more for them than do brute beasts. . . . This is the God-ordained institution of human government! It is a costly farce. . . . The people will not always be spellbound by this cheat." Disillusioned by what he had witnessed, Henry C. Wright moved toward the "no-human government" doctrine of Noyes. "The God in whom I believe . . . never made man to be an appendage to institutions," he concluded.[35] Wright joined the abolitionists in 1835 and became a worshipful admirer of Garrison and an extreme radical. A happily married man, he had a particular interest in children and pedagogy and would, in later years, write extensively on educational questions. His belief in the absolute equality of the sexes and in the dignity and rights of children would lead him to develop strikingly modern ideas of marriage and education, which he published and dispensed by direct consultation in an informal marriage counseling service. His religious convictions underwent drastic change. He now confessed himself an "infidel to a war-making, slave-holding and man-oppressing religion . . . an atheist to a God with whose nature slavery or war ever was or ever can be reconciled." [36]

Wright made himself very useful to the sisters, planning their itinerary, making advance arrangements and acting as their escort. He must have been a pleasant companion whose original, often brilliant conversation was stimulating, more so because in so many particulars they found their own unorthodox new ideas expressed and accepted by him. For years the sisters had charted their own intellectual course, deprived of the support and sustenance of like-minded people. They had come into the abolition movement humbly, as novices, worshiping at the feet of such great men as Garrison and Weld, and ever conscious of their own deficiencies of education and "mental training." During the months of work as "female agents" they had been alternately idolized

and treated as freaks by their audiences, while male reformers were ever conscious of the need to patronize and protect them. It was taken for granted that they needed advice
and would willingly accept it. In all the correspondence between them and other reformers there is no evidence that
anyone had ever sought their advice, nor that they themselves saw fit to offer it. But in Henry C. Wright they found a
man willing to accept them not only as fellow workers in the
cause of reform, but as intellectual equals. The effect of this
attitude on them was overwhelming — for a time, it seemed,
Henry Wright could say or do no wrong.

At Amesbury there was an unpleasant interruption at one
of their lectures. Two young men challenged Angelina's statements from the floor. They had recently spent several years
in the South and had found the conditions of the slaves not
bad at all; they thought the slaves were "no worse off than
the yeomen and manufacturers of the North." [37] Amesbury
was a shoe manufacturing town and there were a good many
factory workers in the audience with whom this remark did
not sit well. By public request Angelina agreed to a full debate with the two young men at a subsequent meeting.[38]

The next few days were crowded with lectures in Ipswich,
Essex and Byfield. On Monday, July 17, they returned to
Amesbury. There was such an overflow crowd at the Monday meeting that a second one had to be scheduled for
Wednesday. A moderator presided over the debate, which
opened with Mr. John Page giving the traditional Bible argument in favor of slavery. This point of attack was an unfortunate choice for him, for Angelina was an expert at the
abolitionist Bible argument, which she herself had helped to
develop in her *Appeal*. She ended the debate in high spirits,
as can be seen from her request to Mr. Page to refrain from

addressing her as his "fair opponent." Bristling with feminism, she heartily disclaimed all such "un-Christian flattery." Angelina was aware of the historic significance of this first debate held in public between a male and female platform speaker and, characteristically, she wished to be judged on her intellect rather than on her looks.[39]

On the return engagement Angelina had much the better of the argument. She concentrated on castigating the un-Christian aspects of slavery: the separation of families, the destruction of marriages, the denial of the right to property and the denial of education. After citing examples for each of these indictments, she asked dramatically whether the farmers, mechanics and workers of Amesbury were in a similar condition? Employing a well-tested oratorical technique, she ended her speech by reading a testimonial from a factory girl, who described her elevated status compared with that of a slave. "This was very effective" Wright reported, in demolishing her opponent's "main" argument. A somewhat biased eyewitness reported that Angelina

had compassion on the poor little soul and was far more inclined to help him out of the difficulty into which he had indiscreetly fallen, than to hold him up to ridicule and contempt. . . . She was calm, modest, and dignified in her manner; and with the utmost ease brushed away the cobwebs, which her puny antagonist had thrown in her way. Her whole deportment was a model of propriety. Her conduct throughout was admirable and her triumph complete.[41]

On the other hand, this debate so scandalized the editor of the Amesbury *Morning Courier* that he found it "too indeli-

cate" for publication. In her speech Angelina had attacked
the abuses of power of the white planter over the female
slave. This remark served as the excuse for censorship of the
entire speech. "The character of the white ladies of the
South, as well as of the ladies of color, seems to have been
discussed, and the editor of the Courier was of the opinion
that the reputation of his paper, and the morals of its readers,
might be injuriously affected by publishing the debate." [42]

The Amesbury debates had enhanced the sisters' reputation as speakers, so that more and more people came to hear
them in the surrounding towns and villages. At the same time
they began to meet more serious opposition. The spectacle
of "two Massachusetts men defending slavery against the accusations of two Southern women" and emerging somewhat
the worse, made these women look pretty dangerous to those
opposed to their ideas. The publicity provided for them by
Henry C. Wright was not designed to quiet the apprehen-
sions of their opponents.

For weeks Wright had kept the readers of *The Liberator*
informed of the daily progression of the sisters in a column
headed, "The Labours of the Misses Grimké." "What a
blunder and that of a most ridiculous kind he has fallen
into," James Birney exclaimed, "the 'LABORS' ? of the Miss
Grimkés!! . . . Can he not be stopped?" [43] But there was
worse to come.

Early in July the readers of *The Liberator* were treated to
the following from Wright's pen: "A DOMESTIC SCENE.
It was Sabbath Eve. The table was spread, the lamp lighted.
. . . The family circle drew around the table, each one
with a Bible. In this domestic circle of peace and love were
those devoted sisters, S. and A.G." Then followed a description of a lengthy philosophical debate on (1) Had God given
man domination over man? and (2) Had God authorized

man to control man by violence? The debaters settled the
question by deciding God alone had the right to rule man.
Man had no right to rule over his fellowmen, nor had he the
right to rule over women. "Thus did we conclude that no
institution designed or necessarily tending, like human government or slavery, to subject man to the domination of man,
can be approved of God." [44]

Thus, with one stroke of his pen, had Henry C. Wright
managed to saddle the Grimké sisters with his "no-human
government" and "peace" principles and to convey the idea
that all three of them, agents of the American Anti-Slavery
Society, were advocating a new cause — woman's rights. To
what extent this was an accurate representation of their beliefs is difficult to determine. But it did create a furor among
abolitionists and was, if nothing else, considered to be in
very bad taste. James Birney wrote to Lewis Tappan in
alarm and asked that Wright be disavowed. [45]

Weld was particularly outraged by the "Domestic Scene."
Still, Wright continued his weekly column until, several
weeks later, he was transferred to Philadelphia by order of
the New York Executive Committee. The sisters considered
this move a personal affront to them and accused Weld of
treating Wright unfairly. In a bitter exchange of letters
charges and countercharges were made, with Weld hotly denying any personal animosity toward Wright and then proceeding to accuse him of vanity and poor judgment. In view
of later developments it is doubtful whether Weld ever held
the lofty neutral feelings he claimed to hold. He had every
reason to be annoyed with Wright; moreover, the conflict between the Executive Committee and Wright involved basic
questions of policy. Essentially, Wright expressed in extreme form everything in the Garrisonian position that the
more conservative and practical-minded abolitionists found

objectionable. At this early date they could not strike directly at Garrison, but they could and did dispose of Henry C. Wright. When, somewhat later, Wright's term as an agent expired, it was not renewed.[46]

At the beginning of August, after more than eight weeks of speaking, the sisters were very tired. Sarah had for some time been suffering from colds and a bad cough, and Angelina had had to do most of the speaking. Now, at the Philbrick's farm near Boston, where they spent a week, they had a chance to rest and to review their situation.

The initial phase of the speaking tour was over. Everything they had been most afraid of had worked out much better than they had expected. Their ability to attract and hold crowds was no longer in question. Their audiences had been large, mostly peaceful and generally sympathetic. They had proven to themselves and others that they could speak before any crowd without self-consciousness. They had been challenged by new ideas, complex problems, for which they were not adequately prepared. Unsure of themselves, they had looked for intellectual leadership to Garrison, Noyes and Wright. Now they found themselves being criticized for the new theories they had embraced — criticized not only by their opponents, but by friends and co-workers. This was a new and unsettling experience.

But there was worse to come. They would be attacked not so much as abolitionists, but as *women*. And in this situation, there would be no past experience, no theory to guide them. All at once they would stand alone, with friends advising them to retreat from their isolated position.

But they would not choose to retreat or stand pat. They would move forward — on an uncharted road in defense of women.

CHAPTER
TWELVE

*We have given great offense on account of our woman-
hood, which seems to be as objectionable as our abolitionism. The whole land seems aroused to discussion on the
province of woman, and I am glad of it. We are willing to
bear the brunt of the storm, if we can only be the means
of making a break in that wall of public opinion which lies
right in the way of woman's rights, true dignity, honor and
usefulness.*

Angelina E. Grimké,
July 25, 1837.

THIS WAS the way Angelina saw their situation. It was
quite true that from their first speech before "mixed audiences" they had been attacked as women and as abolitionists. Such attacks should not have been unexpected. As it
happened, all during their tour they published serialized articles in the reform press, agitating their two favorite causes
in such a way that it was impossible to ignore their connection. Angelina, in her *Letters to Catherine Beecher*, was making herself one of the foremost spokesmen for abolition,
while Sarah, in her *Letters on the Equality of the Sexes*, was
bringing the woman's rights question squarely before the
public. Whether by accident or design, the Grimké sisters
had come to represent in the public mind the fusion of abolition and woman's rights. It was this that precipitated an ideological crisis among reformers.

Early in 1837, Catherine Beecher, eldest daughter of Rev. Lyman Beecher, had published *An Essay on Slavery and Abolitionism with reference to the Duty of American Females,* which she had addressed to Angelina Grimké.[1] In a foreword, the director of the Hartford Female Seminary, whose learning Angelina had once so greatly admired, explained that Angelina's *Appeal* had come to her notice while she was preparing an essay against abolition societies, and had struck her as deserving an answer. In her essay, Catherine Beecher defended the Colonization Society and gradualism as against the radicalism of the abolitionists. In particular, she declared herself against any effort to organize women in abolition societies, since the subordination of women to men was "a beneficent and immutable Divine law." And this pioneer of woman's education, who in her own life exemplified the ability of women to achieve independence through a career, declared that women's influence must be confined to the "domestic and social circle." Lecturing Angelina Grimké as though she were, indeed, the scholar at her academy she had once wished to be, Catherine Beecher declared herself strongly against women petitioning Congress: "Men are the proper persons to make appeals to the rulers whom they appoint, and if their female friends, by arguments and persuasions, can induce them to petition, all the good that can be done by such measures will be secured. But if females cannot influence their nearest friends, to urge forward a public measure in this way, they surely are out of their place in attempting to do it themselves." [2]

Angelina had decided, early in May, to answer this essay, a decision in which Weld strongly encouraged her.[3] She wrote a series of letters during the longer stops on her tour and sent them off, one by one, to be published in *The Eman-*

cipator and *The Liberator*. The finished series was later revised and reprinted in book form.

In her *Letters to Catherine Beecher* she offered a forceful defense of abolitionist tactics and theory and demolished every argument offered by Colonizationists. In this she followed the arguments developed by Theodore Weld during the Lane Seminary debates and gave respectful attention to the opinion of leaders of the free Negro community of Philadelphia, men such as James Forten and Robert Purvis who had attacked the Colonization Society as an instrument for depriving free Negroes of their rights.[4] She wrote:

That the Colonization Society is a *benevolent* institution we deny. . . . And it is a perfect mystery to me how men and women can *conscientiously* persevere in upholding an association, which the very objects of its professed benevolence have repeatedly, solemnly, constantly and universally condemned. . . . Yes, the free colored people are to be exiled, because public opinion is crushing them into the dust; instead of their friends protesting against that corrupt and unreasonable prejudice, and living it down by a practical acknowledgement of their right to *every* privilege, social, civil and religious which is enjoyed by the white man.

Surely you never want to "get rid" of people whom you *love*. . . . It is because I love the colored Americans, that I want them to stay in this country; and in order to make it a happy home to them, I am trying to talk down, and write down, and live down this horrible prejudice. Sending a few to Africa cannot destroy it. No — we must dig up the weed by the roots out of each of our hearts. . . .[5]

This strong and uncompromising attack on race prejudice as the chief buttress of slavery was central to Angelina Grimké's thought and led her directly to an acceptance of immediate emancipation. She suggested that gradualism stemmed essentially from race prejudice. Defining what she understood by emancipation she listed a series of concrete steps: freedom for the slave, payment of wages for his labor, his right to marriage and to guardianship over his children, legal rights, education and the protection of equitable laws. Then she asked: Now, why should not all this be done immediately? Which of these things is to be done next year, and which the year after? . . . I have seen too much of slavery to be a gradualist.[6]

She discussed immediatism, the connection between North and South, the lesson to be drawn from the British Emancipation Movement. Quoting from an interesting collection of letters and anecdotes, she endeavored to show the effectiveness of abolitionist doctrine in converting individual slaveholders and discussed in detail every point of attack made by Miss Beecher on abolitionist methods. This clear-cut and strong defense of abolitionism occupied ten separate letters. Only in two letters did she answer Miss Beecher's strictures on "women's sphere" and develop her defense of woman's rights as a citizen into a full-fledged feminist argument.

The right of petition is the only political right that women have: why not let them exercise it whenever they are aggrieved?

The fact that women are denied the right of voting for members of Congress, is but a poor reason why they should also be deprived of the right to petition. If their

numbers are counted to swell the number of Representatives in our State and National Legislatures, the *very
least* that can be done is to give them the right of petition in all cases whatsoever; and without any abridge-
ment. If not, they are mere slaves, known only through
their masters. . . .

Now, I believe it is woman's right to have a voice in
all the laws and regulations by which she is to be governed, whether in Church or State: and that the present
arrangements of society, on these points, are a *violation
of human rights, a rank usurpation of power,* a violent
seizure and confiscation of what is sacredly and inalien-
ably hers. . . . If Ecclesiastical and Civil governments
are ordained of God, *then* I contend that woman has just
as much right to sit in solemn counsel in Conventions,
Conferences, Associations and General assemblies, as
man — just as much right to sit upon the throne of England, or in the Presidential Chair of the United States.[7]

And, boldly linking the causes of slaves and women, Angelina Grimké charted the path of common struggle for greater
democracy: "The discussion of the rights of the slave has
opened the way for the discussion of other rights, and the
ultimate result will most certainly be the breaking of *every*
yoke, the letting the oppressed of every grade and description go free, — an emancipation far more glorious than any
the world has ever yet seen. . . ."[8]

Meanwhile, starting in July, Sarah's *Letters on the Equality of the Sexes* appeared in the New England *Spectator* and
were reprinted in *The Liberator.* These letters were addressed to Mary Parker, the President of the Boston Female
Anti-Slavery Society, at whose suggestion the topic had been

chosen as "The Province of Woman." It was she who had suggested to the editor of *The Spectator* that the Grimké sisters write such a series of articles — a suggestion the sisters considered "providential." [9] Since Angelina was already occupied with her rebuttal to Miss Beecher, Sarah undertook to write the series for *The Spectator*.[10]

The growing irritation of the New England churches with the abolitionists had been further aggravated by several articles in *The Liberator* which smacked of theological subversion. Garrison had not only reprinted J. H. Noyes' heretical doctrines, but had expressed his approval of Noyes' and H. C. Wright's "no-human-government" principles.[11] These eccentricities of Garrison, which happened to appear in print just about the time the two female abolitionist agents were lecturing to approving crowds in many New England communities, seemed to conservative churchmen dangerous threats to the established order of things.

Oliver Johnson, a friend and close co-worker of Garrison, describes the prevailing mood:

> The women at that day, as in the present, were the strongest allies of the clergy, and in many things their main reliance. The ladies from South Carolina were making a very deep impression upon their sex wherever they went, and proslavery ministers felt that some strong measures must be taken to counteract their influence. . . . I believe they were more afraid of those two women than they would have been of a dozen lecturers of the other sex.[12]

The 1836 resolution of the Congregational General Association against antislavery speakers had not been as effective outside of Boston as its proponents had hoped it would be. Now the Grimké sisters' tour provided the necessary impetus for another attack. Rev. Nehemiah Adams, whose friendliness to the Southern viewpoint would later earn him the sobriquet "Southside Adams," took the lead in drafting a statement which was approved and issued on July 28, 1837, as a "Pastoral Letter of the General Association of Massachusetts to the Congregational Churches under their care."

Without naming names, the Pastoral Letter berated Garrison and the Grimké sisters. In a slap at Garrison it declared: "The perplexed and agitating subjects which are now common amongst us should not be forced upon any churches as matters for debate, at the hazard of alienation and division." Stressing the importance of deference to the pastoral office, it enjoined the churches not to permit "strangers to preach on subjects the ministers do not agree with." It went on to warn all churches against "the dangers which at present seem to threaten the female character with widespread and permanent injury." Denouncing the behavior of females "who so far forget themselves as to itinerate in the character of public lecturers and teachers," it exhorted women to abide by their "appropriate duties and influence . . . as clearly stated in the New Testament." Woman's strength derived from her dependence and weakness. "But when she assumes the place and tone of man as a public reformer, our care and protection of her seem unnecessary . . . and her character becomes unnatural. If the vine, whose strength and beauty it is to lean upon the trelliswork, and half conceal its clusters, thinks to assume the independence and the overshadowing nature of the elm, it will not only cease to bear fruit, but fall in shame and dishonor into the dust." [13]

The first effect of this Pastoral Letter, which was read

from the pulpits and widely published, was to split the more conservative clerical abolitionists from Garrison and thus sharpen the leadership struggle within the abolition movement. It was followed by two "Clerical Appeals," denouncing Garrison for his intemperate and indiscriminate attack on the clergy. The first, signed by five ministers who claimed to be sincere abolitionists, was more damaging to the movement than the Pastoral Letter.[14] In reply, Garrison rushed into print with a long and heated editorial, which only aggravated the division in abolition ranks.[15] The New York Committee, and particularly the Tappans, Weld and Elizur Wright, although they were highly critical of Garrison, tried to avoid further damage by playing down the controversy.

The second Clerical Appeal emanated from Andover Theological Seminary. It directly involved the Grimkés and continued, in the vein of the Pastoral Letter, to link the attack on Garrisonism and on women lecturers.

As it happened, the sisters had lectured at Andover two days before the appearance of the Pastoral Letter, speaking there to 200 women and a few men in the Methodist Church at the invitation of the Andover Female Anti-Slavery Society. A few days later, thirty-nine students and faculty members of the Seminary published a signed statement in which they expressed their opposition to slavery, but insisted that only "moral" means must be used to bring it to an end. The means they approved were: "conversation, education and prayer." They went on to condemn "certain abolitionists" for surrounding the cause of abolition with "so many foreign and repulsive associations" and concluded, "the public lectures of females we have discountenanced and condemned as improper and unwise." [16]

The Andover Female Anti-Slavery Society replied to this statement: "We wish to have it known that the lectures . . .

were designed for the Ladies, and that those Gentlemen
who were present must sustain the responsibility of a mixed
meeting." They also declared they saw no reason to regret
their invitation to the Grimké sisters and recommended them
to other women's organizations.

Some abolitionists responded to the Pastoral Letter with a
chivalrous defense of the ladies as abolitionists and Quakers.
Whittier's poem, "The Pastoral Letter," set the tone.

> So this is all — the utmost reach
> Of priestly power the mind to fetter!
> When laymen think — when women preach —
> A war of words — a "Pastoral Letter!"

He recalled to New England the shameful history of the persecution of heretics and witches and asked these modern-day
bigots to learn from the past. He urged them to honor "Carolina's high-souled daughters" and predicted that "the pure
and good shall throng to hear/ and tried and manly hearts
surround them." [17]

Maria Chapman's amusing poem, "The Times That Try
Men's Souls," sought to reduce the impact of the Pastoral
Letter by ridicule:

> Confusion has seized us, and all things go wrong,
>   The women have leaped from "their spheres,"
> And, instead of fixed stars, shoot as comets along,
>   And are setting the world by the ears!
> In courses erratic they're wheeling through space,
> In brainless confusion and meaningless chase. . . .
>
> They've taken a notion to speak for themselves,
>   And are wielding the tongue and the pen;

They've mounted the rostrum; the termagant elves!
And — oh horrid! — are talking to men!
With faces unbalanced in our presence, they come
To harangue us, they say, in behalf of the dumb. . . .[18]

Women rallied to the support of the sisters. Anna Weston
joined them in Groton and accompanied them to some of
their lectures. Mary Parker sent word that the Boston
women would stand by them "if everyone else forsook
them." [19] Most encouraging of all were the women in their
audiences, who responded warmly to every allusion to the
rights of women. That many of them walked six and eight
miles to hear the sisters was better proof than words could
give that they were expressing the hopes and aspirations of
many.

It was Sarah Grimké with her *Letters on the Equality of
the Sexes* who "preached up woman's rights most nobly and
fearlessly." [20] Attacking the Bible argument, which was the
strongest point of those who claimed woman's inferiority was
God-given, she held that the Scriptures had necessarily reflected the patriarchal society which had produced them.
She claimed that women had been created by God as man's
companion, in all respects his equal. "I ask no favors for my
sex. . . . All I ask our brethren is, that they will take their
feet from off our necks, and permit us to stand upright on
that ground which God designed us to occupy." [21]

She characterized the Pastoral Letter as of a piece with
Cotton Mather's pronouncements on witchcraft. As for its
injunction that women must be instructed by their ministers
before listening to speakers of their choice, she dismissed it
harshly. "This I utterly defy. I have suffered too keenly
from the teaching of man to lead anyone to him for instruction." [22]

After a historical and worldwide survey of the condition of women, she devoted one chapter to their situation in the United States. She decried the inferior, marriage-centered education given women, and cited Thomas Grimké in support of her demand for equal educational opportunities for women. In a survey of laws which worked to the detriment of women and deprived them of their rights as citizens Sarah Grimké anticipated by a dozen years the main arguments of the feminist movement. She even demanded equal pay for equal work and wrote at length and with bitterness about the low wages paid to women workers. She drew parallels between the status of the slave and that of women, and attacked with particular sharpness the degradation of slave women.

Addressing herself directly to women, she urged them to abandon all frivolity, love of fashion and the false protection of chivalry. Instead, they must become conscious of their own dignity and worth. "Woman must feel that she is the equal, and is designed to be the fellow laborer of her brother." [23] While she charged men with most of the responsibility for holding women in subjection, she pointed to specific examples of women acquiescing in their own degradation. The practice of having ministers open a meeting of a woman's organization she considered "ludicrous." Women were perfectly capable of taking charge of their own meetings. Women, who in sewing circles earned money to supply ministerial students, would do better to work for the advancement of their own sex.[24] She urged full and active participation of women in all the moral and social reform movements of the day. ". . . whatsoever it is morally right for a man to do, it is morally right for a woman to do." [25] Men and women have the same rights and duties.

She ended her appeal with a strong bid to men. Equality

of the sexes would be to their benefit: they would find woman as their equal "unspeakably more valuable than woman as their inferior."

In their abolition speeches and writings the Grimké sisters had often given a new and different emphasis from that of other abolitionists. But they had not originated theoretical or legal arguments; their strength lay in their approach and their incisive presentation of tried and tested material. But their feminist argument was original. Its strongly religious derivation made it particularly adapted to the American scene. Considering that it appeared ten years before the Seneca Falls Convention and seven years before Margaret Fuller's *Woman in the Nineteenth Century*, the outraged reaction with which so many of even the most radical reformers greeted it, is quite understandable.

If those who had issued the Pastoral Letter had expected it to force the sisters to stop speaking, they must have been greatly disappointed. One of the most successful meetings of the tour took place a few days after the appearance of the Letter. One thousand five hundred people crowded into Lowell City Hall and several hundred had to be turned away.[26] It is even possible that the Pastoral Letter increased their audiences by attracting curiosity seekers, many of whom came to sneer at the preaching women and stayed because they became interested in the subject. As the sisters continued speaking at Groton, Brookline, Charlestown and Cambridgeport their popularity was undiminished.

Still, the Pastoral Letter made their task infinitely more difficult. They felt its effect in Pepperell, Massachusetts, where they found every church closed to them and had to hold their meeting in a barn. At another town the minister, after reluctantly consenting to open their meeting with a prayer, left as soon as he was finished, declaring he would sooner rob a hen-roost than hear a woman speaking in public.[27]

At Bolton they were shut out of the churches and notices of their meeting were torn down. Still, they lectured in the town hall to 300 people.[28] At Leicester, they had arranged with the substitute minister to speak at the large Congregational church, but the regular minister, who returned just before the meeting, declared he would never speak in his pulpit again if they did. The sisters did not wish to be responsible for so drastic a step and chose to speak at the Town Hall. In neighboring Worcester they lectured in a church to more than 1000 people, while hundreds stood outside, some on ladders, some on wagons.[29]

And so it went — town by town, their arrival posing a problem of conscience and free speech for the community and the ministers. Audiences flocked to them. Through August, September and October they continued at the grueling pace of five to six meetings a week, each in a different town. They traveled by stage and carriage, on horseback and on wagons. Sometimes they spoke after a ten-mile ride without a chance for a meal or rest, at other times they left a meeting, hurried to a waiting stage and moved right on to the next place. The halls in which they spoke were overcrowded, ill-ventilated, drafty. Often crying babies disrupted the meeting. At Woonsocket Falls, where Sarah lectured, the beams holding up the gallery began to crack. Two carpenters were called, who pronounced the building dangerously overcrowded and asked that at least one third of those present leave. Not enough volunteers could be found and the sisters had to close the meeting for reasons of safety.[30]

The physical and mental tensions of the tour were hard to

bear, especially since the sisters had become "notorious." Conservatives had begun to see them in stereotypes, as "infamous" fallen women. James Birney, with expressions of considerable outrage, recorded an incident which illustrated this attitude. Traveling on a boat to New Haven, Birney met the Rev. Leonard Bacon, pastor of the First Congregational Church of New Haven, and took the occasion to question him about a remark attributed to him regarding Sarah Grimké.

"And what was that?" asked Rev. Bacon.

"I have been told," said Birney, "that in speaking of fanaticism, at one time in New England, you said a Quaker woman had been known publicly to walk through the streets of Salem, *naked as she was born* — But that Miss Grimké had not been known to make such an exhibition of herself *yet*. Did you say this?"

"I did," Bacon readily admitted and added after a pause: "And should I have said that she *did?*"

Birney was so incensed about these remarks, that he refused to exchange any further civilities with Rev. Bacon.[31]

No doubt, there were many respectable men and women who thought of the sisters as did the Rev. Mr. Bacon. But Sarah and Angelina were not deterred by attacks of this nature, although they must have felt them painfully. What was much harder to bear was the necessity of opposing their own friends.

Many abolitionists were greatly disturbed by the intrusion of the woman's rights issue upon their cause. Rev. Amos Phelps, a staunch abolitionist, wrote the sisters a long, kind letter, asking them to confine their lectures to women. The sisters rejected this advice, and pointed out that he was aligning himself with the author of the Pastoral Letter in offering it.[32]

Rev. Samuel May, a loyal supporter of Garrison, was at first "not a little disturbed in my sense of propriety" by the female agents. But he looked the facts fully in the face and decided that his attitude was "nothing but miserable prejudice." Always a man to act on his convictions, the Rev. Mr. May invited the sisters to his home and parish at South Scituate. They spent a week there in October 1837, a week which Mr. May considered one of "highest, purest enjoyment to me and my precious wife and most profitable to the community."

Angelina spoke from his pulpit and lectured in various churches in Scituate, Duxbury and Hanover. The Rev. Mr. May reported: "I have never heard from other lips, male or female, such eloquence as that of her closing appeal. The experience of that week dispelled my Pauline prejudice. I could not believe, that God gave them such talents as they evinced to be buried in a napkin." [33]

Much more upsetting to the sisters than the objections of a few ministers were the letters from the New York Executive Committee and especially from Theodore Weld.

Early in July, when they had first begun to speak before "mixed audiences," the sisters had asked Weld for clarification of their status. Were they officially "agents"? Were they subject to the control of the Executive Committee in regard to their meeting arrangements? Weld, after consulting with other members of the Committee, informed them that their status was "a sort of *cooperative* relation," not one of "*authority* on the one hand and a *representative* agency on the other." The Executive Committee no more sanctioned their speaking to "promiscuous assemblies" than it did their Quaker clothing. Thus, if anyone objected to their public speaking, it was an objection directed not against the antislavery movement but against Quaker practice. Weld went on to express his own views. Personally, he was strongly in favor of antislavery women preaching and considered it "downright slaveholding" to keep men away from their meetings. Why, people talked about women's preaching as though it were highway robbery. "Pity, women were not born with a split stick in their tongues!" He considered all ideas of this kind "ghostly dictum, proxy-thinking, expediency, tomfooleries." [34]

But Angelina, already in the thick of the controversy, feared this "hands-off" policy of the Executive Committee would not be maintained. "I am waiting in some anxiety to see what the Executive Committee mean to do in these troublous times, whether to renounce us or not," she wrote to Weld two weeks after the Pastoral Letter. While she was aware that this issue might divert attention from the abolition question, she pointed out that it had been raised by a "concatenation of circumstances over which we had no control." Angelina rejected Weld's position, that their being Quakers could serve as the excuse for their public speaking. "We do not stand on this ground at all; we ask *no* favors for ourselves, but claim rights for our *sex*." Here, for the first time, Angelina clearly stated to Weld the feminist position the sisters had evolved. "What we claim for ourselves, we claim for *every* woman whom God has called and qualified with gifts and graces," Angelina reiterated and demanded, perhaps with slight anxiety, "Can't *thou* stand *just here* side by side with us?" [35]

It appeared that Weld could not. A supremely capable organizer, he was not concerned with abstract theoretical questions, but with policy. His task was the promotion of antislavery organization in the Northern states, with the tangible objective of collecting a maximum number of signatures for the petitions to Congress. All matters not directly leading to this goal had to be excluded from consideration. Thus to Weld, as to most of the leadership of the American Anti-Slavery Society, the woman's rights issue threatened the concentration of reformers on the antislavery cause. Weld regarded the subject in the same light as he might the "peace" issue or the Graham diet — as a side issue which the enemies of abolition might seize on, in order to distract reformers from their main goal. Undoubtedly, the growing personal irritation between Garrison and his New England followers and the New York leadership fed into this attitude. Weld might have reacted much differently to the Grimké sisters' raising of the issue had they not, at the time it happened, been so closely associated with Garrison. The coincidence was unfortunate, for there was a basic difference between the extraneous issues of Garrison and the issue of woman's rights.

When Angelina demanded of Weld: "Can you not see that women could do and would do a hundred times more for the slave, if she were not fettered?" she had caught hold of a fundamental organizational principle, which even so experienced an organizer as Weld had overlooked.[36] To mobilize activists in an embattled cause, they must be mobilized as equal participants, not as tolerantly suffered inferiors. In regard to Negroes, abolitionists had perceived this principle quite clearly; Weld himself was one of those who demanded that colored abolitionists be treated as equals, if one ex-

pected their full support. But women, too, were kept away
from the cause by their own repressed status. Few women
could brave the disapproval of their friends and neighbors in
order to take a public stand and actively participate in community affairs. Weld looked on the woman's rights question
entirely as something affecting a few outstanding women in
leadership positions, but the Grimkés saw the need of mobi-
lizing the vast, untapped reservoir of antislavery sentiment in
women and harnessing it to the cause.

As if in support of his "Quaker" argument, Weld enlisted
the aid of the Quaker Whittier, a man the sisters greatly respected. Whittier's letter to them linked the issues of war,
human government, church and family government as matters that ought to be held "far aloof from the cause of abolition." He attacked Wright and Garrison for tying these
causes to abolition. As for the rights of women, the sisters
were asserting these rights by their current lectures. "Why
then, let me ask, it is necessary for you to enter the lists as
controversial writers in this question? . . . Is it not forget-
ting the great and dreadful wrongs of the slave in a selfish
crusade against some paltry grievances of our own?" [37]

Weld's next letter was written after he had read the first
several of the *Letters on the Equality of the Sexes*. "Woman,
in every *particular* shares equally with man rights and responsibilities," Weld stated, describing his views on women
as "ultra." He believed that qualified women could and
should make laws, administer justice, govern — even propose marriage! Yet he deeply regretted that the sisters had
started their articles. Writing of this sort was something any
woman could do. But in their function as female antislavery
speakers they were unique. He asked them to let others do
the lesser work, let *them* do the work they were best qualified to do.[38]

"Brethren beloved in the Lord," Angelina began her reply, addressed jointly to Whittier and Weld, saying that she was writing for both herself and Sarah. She explained how they came to write the articles and insisted that they could see no harm in publishing their views on women in a paper which was not an abolition paper.[39] It was not these articles which aroused the public on the subject of woman's rights, it was the Pastoral Letter that did the damage. Angelina saw it as an attack on free speech. *"This invasion of our rights* was just such an attack upon *us,* as that made upon Abolitionists generally when they were told a few years ago that they *had no right* to discuss the subject of Slavery." At that time abolitionists did not ignore the attack. "The time to assert a right is *the time* when *that* right is denied. *"We must establish this right* for if we do not, it will be impossible for *us* to *go on with the work* of Emancipation." Could they not see that the clergy, in attacking their right to lecture, were trying to prevent people from hearing what they had to say? "If we surrender the right to *speak* to the public this year, we must surrender the right to petition the next year and the right to *write* the year after and so on. What *then* can *woman* do for the slave when she is herself under the feet of man and shamed into *silence?"* As for the Quaker argument, Angelina pointed out that *their* feminism was as different from the Quaker view on women as *their* abolitionism was from the Quaker variety. Quakers regarded woman "as equal to men on the ground of *spiritual gifts,* not on the broad ground of *humanity.* Women may *preach:* this is a *gift;* but woman must *not* make the discipline by which *she herself* is to be governed." This insight reflected years of practical experience in "Women's Meeting." Neither of the sisters had forgotten the Quaker practice whereby Women's Meeting recommended acceptance of membership or other disciplinary matters, which were then acted upon at the Meeting of male members. But these were trifles compared to the basic issue. This was the participation of women in abolition as active workers. "We are actuated by the full conviction that if we are to do any good in the Anti Slavery cause, our *right* to labor in it *must* be firmly established." [40]

Weld answered each argument, point by point. He agreed that opposition to speaking in public was a "stereotyped notion," held by men who regarded women as inferior. He had run into this before, when he had worked with the revivalist Finney. He himself had, over a good deal of opposition, first urged women to pray in public during these revivals. He agreed with their aims; it was their methods he disagreed with.

> Now, if instead of blowing a blast through the newspapers, sounding the onset, and summoning the ministers and churches to surrender, you had without any introductory flourish just gone right among them and lectured, *when* and *where* and *as* you could find opportunity, and paid no attention to criticism, but pushed right on, without making any ado about "attacks" and "invasions" and "opposition" . . . within one year you might have practically brought over five hundred thousand persons, of the very moral *elite* of New England. You may rely upon it.

No moral enterprise had ever failed, if its advocates had pushed the "main principle." And what could be plainer than that the main principle for which they were struggling was human rights, from which the rights of woman were purely derivative? [41]

The sisters answered, Sarah sweetly and patiently, Angelina with some heat. The only new argument added to the debate was their insistence that they were not lecturing on woman's rights and had not in any way lessened their anti-slavery effort. Weld replied that he understood Angelina proposed to hold a course of lectures on woman's rights in Boston. Angelina, who had, indeed, been considering such a course at the urging of the Boston women, gave up the idea.[42]

The practical result of this correspondence was a compromise. The Grimké sisters were restrained by Weld from putting any further public emphasis on the woman's rights question. On the other hand, they did not discontinue Sarah's article series. *Letters on the Equality of the Sexes* actually benefited by Weld's lucid and sharp criticism, which forced the sisters to sharpen their own thinking.

It is dubious whether the effectiveness of the sisters on their tour would have been increased had they followed Weld's advice. The woman who became the first female abolition agent would have aroused controversy no matter how she behaved or how she reacted to the attacks upon her. The attendance figures at the Grimkés' lectures and the fact that their speaking dates were as frequent at the end of their tour as they had been at the beginning, seem to indicate that their effectiveness as agents was in no way impaired by their stand on woman's rights. On the contrary, the attacks made upon them increased their audiences.

All during September and October 1837, while this debate by correspondence was carried on, the sisters continued their lectures at the same pace as before. Owing to Sarah's bronchitis Angelina had to do all the speaking for several weeks. More and more frequently, she, too, complained of extreme fatigue and suffered from colds and pains in the chest. The week they stayed at Rev. Samuel May's house was particularly strenuous for her, with five lectures in five different places and many social engagements in between. Sarah was still unable to hold up her end and by Sunday Angelina felt quite ill. Although she had a fever, she fulfilled her speaking date in Hingham. But she was near collapse. Alarmed, Sarah took her to Brookline, where they accepted the hospitality of Samuel Philbrick. For weeks, Angelina hovered between life and death, gravely ill with typhoid fever.[43]

For all practical purposes, the speaking tour was ended.

CHAPTER
THIRTEEN

The Misses Grimké have made speeches, wrote pamphlets, exhibited themselves in public, etc. for a long time, but have not found husbands yet. We suspect that they would prefer white children to black under certain circumstances, after all.

The Boston *Morning Post*,
August 25, 1837.

THEODORE WELD was a tall, thin man of striking appearance. Careless in his dress to the point of slovenliness, he walked with a slouching gait, let his shoes run down and his coat go unbrushed, neglected to comb his hair and frequently forgot to cut his beard.[1] Yet the impression he made on others was overpowering and intimidating. His face arrested attention with its heavy lines, irregular eyebrows, thin nose and sensitive mouth. Before strangers his expression was one of forbidding sternness. One of his friends commented on the "deep, wild gloom" of his appearance. His stern, silent fierceness reminded another of the Inquisitor-General. An artist, to whom he went to have his miniature painted, commented that it would be easy "to hit the outlines" of his face, but very difficult to catch the expression. "Its SEVERITY is like a streak of lightning." A woman who was in the audience at one of his lectures later recalled her first impression of him as he stood waiting to speak: "Mercy," she thought, "I hope that young man never gets married. I should pity his wife. He'll break her heart." [2] But as soon as Weld began to speak, the expression of his face changed and his kindliness and warmth shone through. His full, rich voice, his deep sincerity, his persuasive charm and keen intelligence made him irresistible alike to huge audiences and intimate circles of friends. Theodore Weld was known as a spellbinder on the platform, one of the most formidable orators of his generation. His ideas were original and profound and he knew how to reduce the most complex concepts to simple statements. One of his admiring co-workers stated that the "rapidity of his mind is equalled only by its strength" and went on to marvel at Weld's brilliant imagination.[3]

His great physical energy, which in childhood had found expression in reckless stunts leading to innumerable injuries, enabled him, at the age of fourteen, to take full charge of his father's 100-acre farm in Pompey, New York. With the proceeds of two years' labor he was able to pay for his schooling at Phillips Academy in Andover. In his eagerness to make up for lost time, he overworked and neglected his health. His eyesight began to fail. Reluctantly, he abandoned his studies and became an itinerant lecturer on the "science of mnemonics." The subject attracted him because he himself suffered from strange lapses of memory and all his life was extraordinarily absentminded, to the point of being unable to remember the day of the week or the month of the year.[4] He traveled extensively and returned after three years with little money but increased self-confidence, and with his eyesight greatly improved. Weld now entered Hamilton College at Clinton, New York, determined to prepare for his father's profession, the ministry. The course of his life was altered by his contact with Charles Grandison Finney, the great revivalist, who, despite Weld's long and stubborn resistance, converted him spectacularly. Finney's novel methods of persuasion, based on focusing community censure on the individual sinner until he staggered forward to the "anxious seat," ready to give up, were extraordinarily effective. His methods and techniques became not only the prototype for revivalism, but also exerted considerable influence on the abolitionist movement. Young Weld developed his oratorical and organizational talents while traveling with Finney's "Holy band" and, characteristically, worked with unremitting zeal until his health began to fail. A stint of several months as a sailor on a whaling vessel brought him back strong and fit, eager to resume his education. While working with Finney, Weld had met Charles Stuart, the retired British officer and reformer, who was to become his closest friend.

Stuart helped to finance Weld's education and directed him toward Oneida Institute, a manual labor school, where Weld resumed his theological studies. There, his physical energy found ample outlet in the endless round of farm chores the students had to perform, while keeping up a rigorous schedule of study and religious activities. During these years Weld also made a reputation as a temperance speaker and, through the Tappan brothers, became connected with various other reforms. Finally, in 1831, he traveled West to draw up a plan and select a site for a model manual labor institution — Lane Seminary.

It was on this trip that Weld was almost drowned in an accident in flood-swollen Alum Creek in Ohio. Thrown into the water when his coach overturned, he was dragged under several times by the struggling horses, carried downstream in the freezing cold February night, knocked against rocks and, finally, exhausted, caught in a protruding tree along the deeply forested shore. That his feeble cries for help were heard by some men living in a log cabin on the opposite shore — the only inhabitants along the stream for miles — seemed to Weld providential. His miraculous deliverance confirmed him in the decision to consecrate his life to God's purposes.[5] To a disciple of Finney this meant practical good works. During a cholera epidemic at Lane Seminary Weld selflessly risked his life to nurse the sick students. But it was only after the Lane debates that he found his true vocation: Theodore Weld's ministry was to be abolition.

This was the man Angelina met for the first time during the agents' convention of 1837. She had read a letter of his in *The Liberator* some years before and had been deeply impressed by his ideas and spirit. Now, meeting him in person and hearing from all sides stories and anecdotes of his life, she could not help become his devoted disciple. Weld, whose legendary accomplishments in organizing Ohio, Pennsylvania and upstate New York for abolition had earned him the title, "the most-mobbed man in the United States," had once again recklessly sacrificed his health in the service of the cause. His fine voice was now barely a whisper; it was most unlikely that he would ever again speak from a lecture platform. But for a reformer like Weld there could be no retirement. Inability to work in the field meant simply transferring his labor to headquarters.

Work at the New York office of the American Anti-Slavery Society was not to Weld's liking. He was suspicious of big cities and did not consider them to be the place where reform effort should be concentrated. "Let the great cities *alone*," was his advice to antislavery agents, "they must be burned down by *back fires*. The springs to touch in order to move them *lie in the country.*" [6] Weld disliked the wealthy and socially prominent among the reformers, who made their benevolent activities an occasion for ostentation. The "artificial and factitious life" which existed among the wealthy he found so abhorrent that it was "almost martyrdom" for him to meet such people.[7] Weld's shyness in social gatherings, his modesty and his refusal to accept the amenities of polite society were well known among reformers. His dislike of ostentation carried over into organizational matters; Weld refused to take part in the innumerable anniversaries, which were the spice of the reformer's hard life. He equally steadfastly refused to accept committee appointments and chairmanships, no matter how often and how urgently these were pressed upon him.

"The stateliness and Pomp and Circumstance of an anniversary I loathe in my inmost soul," he wrote to Lewis Tappan. "It seems so like ostentatious display, a mere make believe and mouthing, a sham and show off. It is an element I was never made to move in. . . . I am a Backwoodsman — can grub up stumps and roll logs and burn brush heaps and break green sward. Let me keep about my *own* business and stay in my *own* place." [8] The habit of antislavery agents of "gadding, attending anniversaries . . . clustering together, six, eight or ten of them in a place at a big meeting, staying a few days and then streaming away some hundred miles to another and another" seemed to him a trend dangerous to the cause. "The great desideratum in our Cause is *work, work,* boneing down to it." [9] Perhaps it was to impart this conviction to others that he overcame his dislike of meetings and accepted the responsibility for the training of antislavery agents. Weld's personal leadership at the convention sessions, the long hours he made himself available to the partic-

ipants despite his obvious physical disabilities — all these set
the tone for the work of the agents. To Angelina, and no
doubt to many of the other aspiring agents, Weld represented an ideal of perfection after which to mold themselves
— the reformer incarnate.

After the convention the sisters saw a good deal of Weld.
They met a number of times at the home of Lewis Tappan
and the sisters accompanied Weld on some of his charitable
visits. Weld lived in the home of a colored man, where he
slept in a tiny attic room. Every morning he rose at dawn,
took a long walk before breakfast, chopped and carried up
his own wood and was at his desk at the office of the Anti-
Slavery Society before eight. He took his meals with a Negro
family downtown, close to his office. After working all day,
he would visit sick and poor people and return to his lodg-
ings late at night. Out of conviction and long habit, he attended church in a colored congregation.[10]

The more she saw of him, the more she saw of his life and
work, the more Angelina was attracted to Weld. For a brief
time, she entertained hopes that this idol of perfection might
regard her with more than just brotherly love. But it was
well known in abolitionist circles that Weld had pledged not
to marry until slavery was abolished. This pledge, in which
he had been joined by John Greenleaf Whittier, seemed
quite in keeping with his total dedication to the cause and
discouraged Angelina. She prayed for strength to conquer
her own feelings, especially since there seemed to her to be
many indications that Weld in no way reciprocated them.
On the contrary, he appeared to go out of his way to show
his indifference to her. One night, when Weld escorted her
and Sarah to church, he did not offer her his arm and walked
in total silence all the way. After the meeting he kept back
until someone else offered to walk her home. When the time

came for the sisters' departure for Philadelphia, Weld dutifully escorted them to the steam boat landing, but his farewell was so impersonal and cold that Angelina's hopes crum-
bled. It was the last time she saw him before her speaking
tour. Angelina was deeply hurt, but she had to conclude that
all his attentiveness toward her and Sarah had been impersonal and due entirely to their role in the movement.

Still, there was friendship; and for many weeks and
months a lively correspondence flowed between New York
and New England. An increasing intimacy is evident in
these letters. Angelina teased Weld about his impossible
handwriting and refused to correspond unless he improved
his "scratchifications." She scolded him for his tardiness in
answering their many requests. Sarah did her share by
motherly questions concerning his health and a warm concern for his well-being. Weld seemed perfectly willing to
tolerate these female intrusions. Always incapable of humor,
he responded with earnest and lengthy explanations and
offered much helpful guidance and advice on organizational
and practical questions. Angelina had every reason to believe that she was winning his respect and friendship.

When the furor broke out over the "woman question,"
nothing was more natural than that Angelina should look for
support and encouragement to Weld, who had always been
in favor of her public speaking. When Weld joined the others in opposing the sisters' course and attacked Angelina as
sharply as he would have any male abolitionist, she felt hurt
and disappointed. Under the circumstances, she fought back
with much spirit. The debate between Weld and Angelina
on the theory and tactics of reform was sharp and vigorous
and, for a while, strictly objective. But emotions could not
be forever restrained.

Perhaps Weld bore an unreasonable animosity toward

Henry C. Wright. At least, to Angelina it appeared that he
did. But then, she over-reacted in rushing to Wright's defense. Weld was highly irritated by her accusation that the
New York Executive Committee had acted dishonestly toward Wright, and struck back angrily. "Why dear child!
What is the matter with you? Patience! Rally yourself.
Recollect your womanhood, my sister, and put on charity.
. . ." He refused to even discuss her charges and expressed
his grief and disappointment that she should suspect such
men as Tappan, Leavitt and Dr. Follen.[11] "This reiterated
accusation, based on trifles light as air, argues a state of mind
in you that makes me mourn and weep with an aching
heart," he wrote. "You talk like one in a trance." In the Finney tradition of frank, harsh criticism designed to perfect the
friend and co-worker, which he had practiced throughout
the years with his young disciples from Lane and Oberlin,
Weld proceeded to analyze Angelina's habits of reasoning,
her motivations, her faults and inadequacies. "Go to God,"
he advised. "His searchings will bring to light . . . even the
subtlest form of pride. . . . To KNOW and to RULE ones
own spirit is the rarest and most difficult of human attainments." It took two separate letters to say all he had to say.
Finally, having covered page after page in his nearly illegible scrawl with the scathing words of a teacher upbraiding a
disappointing pupil, he allowed himself a personal word.
"Long and desperate conflicts with my own tempest
wrought and [illegible] spirit have taught me that the souls
grand conquest is *self* conquest." [12]
Angelina was so stunned and hurt by the last letter that
she read it once and never again. If she had reread it in a
more quiet frame of mind, perhaps the meaning of Weld's
self-confessed torment might have become clearer. As it

happened, this letter, written in the middle of October, must have reached her during the final weeks of her speaking tour, when she was already deeply exhausted and ill. A few weeks later Sarah reported to Weld in a hasty note that Angelina was sick "owing to over exertion" and that they planned to spend the winter in Boston.

A Massachusetts abolitionist, visiting in New York, gave Weld the information that Angelina's lungs were seriously affected. The news upset Weld greatly. He pleaded with the sisters to give up public speaking and return to Philadelphia for the winter. Other abolitionists had ruined their health, even lost their lives by neglect and overwork. "I entreat you as a brother," he wrote, obviously highly agitated and worried, "to save yourselves for the slave, for human rights, for womans rights, for the coming and kingdom of Christ Jesus our Lord." [13]

Sarah replied with a calming account of Angelina's gradual recovery, assured him there was no involvement of the lungs and asked him a number of factual questions to which she needed answers for her writings and speech preparation. Weld supplied all the information posthaste and continued his worried admonitions over the state of Angelina's health.

In November, Elijah Lovejoy, abolitionist editor in Alton, Illinois, whose press and home had been repeatedly attacked by proslavery mobs, took the desperate decision to meet violence with violence. Attacked once again by an armed mob, Lovejoy had fallen, gun in hand — the first victim slain in the antislavery struggle. His murder won thousands to the antislavery cause, because it symbolized the connection between free speech and abolition. But abolitionists debated hotly whether Lovejoy's armed defense of his home and press was compatible with antislavery principles. Believers

in non-resistance seemed more concerned with Lovejoy's violation of their principles than with his martyrdom. True to
form, Sarah Grimké stood with the non-resistants. "My heart
sinks within me when I remember the fearful scenes at Alton.
Will God continue to bless an enterprize which is baptised
in blood?" she queried of Weld. She felt strongly enough
about the issue to write a long letter to *The Liberator*, in
which she attacked Lovejoy's position.[14]

For once Weld let an occasion for edification and theoretical debate pass unnoticed. In his correspondence with the
sisters the Lovejoy incident served only as warning illustra-
tion. If the sisters were serious in expressing their horror at
Lovejoy's taking of human life and considered it "murder,"
then they must realize that any violation of the sixth com-
mandment was as bad as "killing outright." The gradual destruction of "the cord of life" through the neglect of one's
health must be considered a form of suicide. No matter how
worthy the cause in which the sisters labored, to neglect
their health for the cause was a violation of God's law. He
admitted that he himself had sinned in this respect, but he
now repented.[15] To which Angelina, with her usual practical approach, replied gently: "How is it my brother that
H. B. Stanton tells us *thou are now* working far harder than
is good for thee?" [16]

Now that Angelina was recuperating, the sisters asked
Weld's opinion regarding the possibility of republishing Angelina's *Appeal to the Women of the Nominally free States*.
They would be happy to bear the expense of printing 5000
copies and would Weld think it improper if Angelina's name
were attached to it? [17]

Weld thought reissuing the book an excellent idea and had
no question but that Angelina's name should be put on it.

"Anything coming from a southerner even if it be no better nor even equal to what a northerner might say, will secure ten times as many readers," he said with his usual brutal honesty. But he advised cutting and editing. "Just put on the condenser and press the thought so close together as to produce spontaneous combustion then their explosion upon mind will work wide execution." [18] Weld had had a great deal of experience in editing; he was currently cutting James A. Thome's *Emancipation in the West Indies* from seven hundred pages to about three hundred fifty and had recently finished a similar editing job on the third edition of his Bible argument against slavery.[19] As for the cost of printing the *Appeal*, the American Anti-Slavery Society would bear the expense, but would welcome a contribution toward it.

Weld assisted Angelina in editing and preparing for publication both her *Appeal* and the reprint in book form of her *Letters to Catherine Beecher*. His suggestions were accepted by Angelina without debate or controversy. Increasingly, a tone of friendly intimacy pervaded the correspondence. Angelina consulted Weld about a variety of matters and went so far as to ask him to pray for her mother's soul, that she might be preserved from dying as a slaveholder. Sarah wanted to know minute details about Weld's daily life. How much did he spend for his clothing? Did he have congenial friends? Did he think, as she now did, that all churches were places of "spiritual famine"? And what were his views on the "peace question"?

Weld answered all these inquiries patiently. In a carefully worded letter to both sisters he explained that he had always been a firm believer in personal non-resistance. But the "no-government" doctrine made him shudder. He was certain that both of them were sincere and believed themselves logical in proceeding from "peace" principles to an opposition to all government. He had read what they had both written on the subject and had failed to be convinced. "That your habits of *investigation* are all wrong, and that you are exceedingly liable to arrive at conclusions without either stating your premises at all or from false ones, I believe; and knowing the vast influence that you are exerting on an immense mass of mind, I conjure you by love of Christ to *prove*, PROVE all things." [20]

"Let me tell you how often I have thanked God for such a friend as you have proved to me," Angelina replied, "one who *will* tell me my faults. . . . I know I find it very hard to bear, but this only proves the dire necessity which exists that you should probe deep. . . . And yet, Brother, I think in some things you wronged me in *that letter never to be forgotten.*" She explained that she had asked him to take a position on the "peace" question because she feared he might, under similar circumstances, do as Elijah Lovejoy had done. "For you ever to die as he did I could not endure to think of," she confessed.[21]

The next mail brought a letter from Weld to Sarah in which he recommended to the sisters that they attend the lectures of Sylvester Graham, the health reformer, who would give them more knowledge of the laws of life than any books could. There was another letter, addressed to Angelina, marked PRIVATE. Angelina opened it with a heavy heart, expecting another lengthy review of her failings.

"A paragraph in your last letter, Angelina, went *to my soul*," she read. "You feel that I have wronged you and think what I said 'was not written in the spirit of love.' . . . I have not a word to utter either in justification or in palliation." And with this, remorse-stricken, horrified at the effect of his harshness, which had caused her abiding pain, Weld cried out his confession: "I know it will surprise and even amaze you, Angelina, when I say to you as I now do, that for a long time *you have had my whole heart.* . . . Your letter to Wm. Lloyd Garrison formed an era in my feelings and a crisis in my history that drew my spirit toward yours by irrepressible affinities. I read it over and over. . . ." But he had heard that she was so strict a Quaker, that she would consider any-one not of her denomination a heathen. "Notwithstanding this my heart turned toward you. . . . I strove long against it. . . . From the time that I met you in New York to this moment in which I write, this same state of mind has contin-ued unvarying, except that it has gathered strength with every day. . . . I have no expectation and almost no hope that my feelings are in *any degree* RECIPROCATED BY YOU." And he urged her, if this were the case, to tell him so frankly, the whole truth. He would bear it, conquer his feel-ings and consider the outcome God's will.[22]

"Your letter was indeed a great surprise, my Brother, and yet it was no surprise at all," Angelina replied. "It was a sur-prise because you have so mastered your feelings as never to betray them; it was no surprise because in the depths of my own heart there was found a response." His disclosure, "so full of strength and power," had made her content. Her heart trusted him wholly.

And in calm, almost serene words, with the sudden self-assurance of a woman who finds herself loved, Angelina re-vealed the long history of her own secret love, her struggles against her feelings which had suddenly, in the last few weeks, returned in full force. As for her religion, she had as long as five years ago disapproved of the Quaker restrictions against marriage outside of Quaker ranks. Marriage, in her

view, was too sacred and private a compact to be interfered
with by ecclesiastical rules. But why, why had he so long
struggled against his love? How could he have no hope that
his feelings were shared by her? "I feel my Theodore, that
we are the two halves of one whole, a twain one, two bodies
animated by one soul and that the Lord has given us to each
other."

In that unique fusion of private and public concerns which
their entire relationship had manifested, Angelina in this
rapturous love letter proceeds to discuss without further
transition an organizational responsibility she had undertaken. Some time ago Henry Stanton had, half in jest, proposed that Angelina speak before the legislative committee
of the Massachusetts State Legislature on behalf of the anti-
slavery petitions presented by women. To his astonishment,
Angelina had agreed to do it. New England abolitionists,
even Stanton, who had been all in favor of woman's rights in
the abstract, now drew back; no woman in the United States
had ever spoken before any legislature. Only Francis Jackson and the Boston ladies supported Angelina. But the
chairman of the legislative committee was favorably inclined
to the idea. Would the New York Anti-Slavery Committee
approve? "If not, I feel that I must bear my own burden
entirely and speak on my *own* responsibility alone, for woe is
unto me if I speak not." The hearings would be sometime
the following week, and she asked for Weld's prayers.[23]

Sarah added a few lines, giving her blessings to their relationship. "Since our first meeting I have felt as if you were
kindred spirits. . . . You have my prayers, my love my sympathy. Dear as A. is, the dearest earthly friend, I can resign
her to one who loves God supremely. . . ." It was as final as
that for Sarah. One after another she had given up the peo-

ple she loved and blessed the Lord for the sacrifice. Now, once again, she was "resigning" Angelina. But surely none had ever sacrificed with better grace than Sarah Grimké.

Weld's reply was an emotional outburst:

> My heart is full! THAT LETTER found me four days ago! I tried to answer it immediately but could not, and again the next day but could not write a word! . . . I dared not trust myself to write to you. . . . The truth is, Angelina . . . I have so long wrestled with myself like a blind giant stifling by violence all the intensities of my nature that when at last they found vent and your voice of love proclaimed a deliverance . . . all the pent-up tides of my being . . . broke forth at once and spurned controul. [!] [24]

Weld was thirty-five, a strong, passionate man, dynamic and vital, who had dedicated his mind, body and soul to the cause of Christ and abolition. To him, as to many of the other reformers, there was no distinction between the two — their battle against slavery was their battle for Christ. Their love of the Savior was as tangible and concrete as that of any religious and found expression in their zeal for reform. But what of human affection? Weld had found fellowship and warm friendship with Charles Stuart, he had given affection and sympathy to his brothers in the movement, but he had never loved a woman. Now the dam had broken — the newness, the violence, the totality of the experience overwhelmed him. For days he struggled for his former self-control and tried intellectually to comprehend what was happening to him. Although Angelina asked him to come at once to see her, he waited almost six weeks. Despite her

pleas, that he confide his happiness to one of his friends and
unburden himself, as she had so often unburdened herself to
Sarah, Weld took a perverse pride in his ability to hide his
feelings. He dared not, he could not, he would not speak to a
soul. . . . He worked ceaselessly at the office, where he
served as editor of special publications. With James Birney,
the newly appointed executive secretary, Stanton, the financial secretary, Joshua Leavitt, Elizur Wright and John
Greenleaf Whittier he directed the work of the American
Anti-Slavery Society — and made certain that his work in no
way suffered because of the alarming state of his feelings.
He kept up the spartan discipline of his daily routine, slight-
ing not a single one of his duties. True, he passed a number
of sleepless nights, he lost weight and began to observe himself as though he were a stranger. And he poured out his
observations, his sensations and thoughts and reactions in
more than usually illegible letters to his beloved.

"I thought I had the mastery of my spirit and power to
quell its wildest insurrection . . . but your letter has taught
me that I am a novice in the one department of self restraint.
In truth . . . I am as ignorant and artless and simple as a
child. . . . I have no experience to draw upon, no habits
formed, nor accurate knowledge, nor elements analysed, nor
principles fixed, nor any materials out of which to draw principles." He worried endlessly that he would be unworthy of
her. She had seen him through a "magnifying medium," had
judged him through the affection of his friends. He insisted
on her knowing every one of his failings, so that she might reconsider, if she wished. "I fear I shall always be startling
you with alarm or breaking your heart by the wild rockings
and tossings of my stormy spirit." [25] He was "a quivering
mass of intensities kept in subjection only by the *rod of iron*

in the strong hand of conscience and reason and never laid aside for a moment with safety." [26] He went on to catalogue his weaknesses. His pride: "I am too proud to be *ambitious*, too proud to seek applause . . . too proud to *betray* emotions, too proud ever for an instant to loose my self possession . . . there is no end to my pride." This astonishing revelation from a man, who was known to his contemporaries and almost forgotten by posterity because of his inordinate modesty, provides an unusually perceptive insight into the psychology of the reformer. Few men have ever seen themselves so harshly, fewer yet have revealed their insights with such merciless clarity. The catalogue continued: he had a bad temper and was given to impatience. He was, at times, extremely intolerant. His severity stemmed often only from fear that he would betray emotion or affection. His excessively severe criticism of Angelina had been a case in point. For fear of betraying his love, he had forced himself "with such unyielding purpose up to duty that it gave everything I said or wrote . . . an artificial and unnatural *severity*." And Weld, whose spartan devotion to unceasing work was a source of constant concern to his fellow workers, revealed that at heart he was downright lazy.

The lesser sins were listed unsparingly: his notorious absentmindedness, his indifference to clothing and appearance, his taciturnity, his aversion to social amenities. Besides, he was extremely deficient in education. Although, given a chance for education, he had taken hold of study "as he had of the plow" with all his might, poor eyesight and the demands of the various good causes he had given his time to had left their mark. He had not looked at an arithmetic book since the age of eleven; in algebra, geometry, botany, geology, even geography he had never had a single lesson; except for natural philosophy, he was totally ignorant of all the liberal sciences. Eighteen months' instruction in Latin and Greek, a few weeks in Hebrew and a smattering of theology, sacred history and philosophy were "the sum total" of his "acquisitions — about equal to that of the learned pig!" [27]

"I read your letter every day, sometimes twice a day until I get another," Angelina reported. "I slept tolerably, rejoice that you could sleep one whole *night;* I cant yet." [28] At this moment, Angelina could not allow herself the luxury of indulging her private feelings. Ten days after Weld's declaration of love she appeared in public session before the Legislature of Massachusetts. Sarah, who had been scheduled to make the first day's speech, had been laid up with a severe cold and could not even be present at the first session. But many good friends stood by her and gave their encouragement: the Childs, the Chapmans, the Philbricks, abolitionists from many of the New England towns. Among the crowd of the hostile and the merely curious, their good kind faces had given her comfort. And the Lord has sustained her, Angelina wrote Weld, despite her fear and trembling.

Her second session before the Legislature passed. Angelina's effective speech elicited great praise among the public and the legislators. Astonishing as it seemed, it was indeed possible for a woman to present cogent argument and deliver it with dignity and grace. Abolitionists were delighted and rallied round in greater numbers for the third session at which both sisters spoke to the legislators. Angelina felt more satisfied with her own performance than she had previously, yet she had to struggle to keep her mind on her public speaking. "It seems all like a dream. I can hardly realize what I have been doing only three hours ago," she confessed. And for once she could afford to pass over the sneers and smears of the press. "It is rather doubtful whether any of the South Carolina lords of creation will ever seek the heart and hand of their great orator in marriage," a witty journalist speculated.[29] Angelina could well afford to smile tolerantly at such malice.

Her worries were of a different nature. Was she sinning and idolatrous in her love, that the love of the Saviour was not enough to satisfy her? "I am a mystery to myself. . . . Why must I have *human love?*" she anxiously asked her beloved. "Why do I feel in my inmost soul that you, *only you,* can fill up the deep void there is?" Why could not those of her own sex, a sister, a friend, satisfy her emotional needs? "Why do I so anxiously desire to hear from you, to see you?"[30]

This was indeed a deep topic, Weld replied earnestly. He, too, had been considering it and would be glad to accept a crumb of "true teaching" on the subject. He felt ill-prepared to deal with the "philosophy" of sex. But he could answer some questions of fact. He believed that sex must be mingled with the higher "affinities" of chaste love. He believed it was a necessity of human nature, which combined mind and body in one, that it also mingled affinities of different kinds. "I suppose that persons of the *same* sex cannot so intensely be drawn toward each other by a love that baffles all expressions. . . . For being of the *same* sex their love is *not* aided by the combinations and strengthened by the contributions and stimulated and borne outward by the united and simultaneous affinities of *all* the susceptibilities of the compound nature acting together. . . . In a word, my dearest," he concluded several pages of speculation, "I suppose you and I feel for each other more absorbing affinities than tho we were of the *same* sex; and we feel them . . . from the

fact that we are — from the law of our nature sublimely assigned by God as the reason for creating a difference of
sex." [31] All of which left the topic as much in the dark as
ever, but seemed to satisfy Angelina that she was not the
worst of sinners.

In fact, she seemed a good deal more composed and self-
assured than Weld in this novel situation and replied calmly
to his catalogue of sins, that, no doubt, she could send him
"just as revolting a picture of herself." She confessed to
pride, selfishness, impatience and irritability. But why go
on, since he had proven already that he knew her "altogether" and had studied her character profoundly. She was
delighted to find his views on courtship agreeing with her
own. The true end of marriage was spiritual communion
"the union of heart and mind and soul." And yet, on second
thought, she begged him to reconsider his commitment to
her, for she feared only that she could not make him happy.

"Talk not to me of giving you up," Weld replied and
brushed aside all the objections she had raised, her fears of
inadequacy, her worries that domestic cares might hamper
his antislavery work. "God sparing me, come what will," he
declared passionately, "I'll marry you in spite of earth or
hell." And demonstrating that he had, after all, greatly matured in the past weeks of emotional turmoil, he summed up
his views on marriage:

> We marry, Angelina, not *merely* nor *mainly* nor *at all
> comparatively* TO ENJOY, but together to do and dare,
> together to toil and testify and suffer . . . to keep our-
> selves and each other unspotted from the world, to live a
> life of faith . . . rejoicing always to bear one anothers
> burden, looking not each on his own things but each on

the things of the other, in honor preferring one another and happy beyond expression.[32]

And with this definition, satisfactory at last, of a reformer's marriage, he announced that he was ready and determined to come and see her. He would arrive for a visit that very week.

CHAPTER
FOURTEEN

*No man who remembers 1837 and its lowering clouds
will deny that there was hardly any contribution to the
anti-slavery movement greater or more impressive than the
crusade of these Grimké sisters through the New England
States.*

*Wendell Phillips,
Funeral Oration for
Angelina Grimké Weld,
October 28, 1879.*

THE SISTERS' APPEARANCE before the Massachusetts Legislature was a fitting climax to their New England tour.
Depending on the viewpoint of their contemporaries, they
had been hailed as heroines or condemned as troublemakers.
Most frequently the judgment of press and public did not go
beyond a disapproving awareness of their "notoriety" and
sniggering speculations as to their motivation in abandoning
respectability and its comforts. They were described as old
maids anxious to attract men, abnormal creatures lusting for
the degenerate pleasures of "amalgamation," embittered
spinsters venting their frustrated emotions by public attacks
on the sacred and time-honored institutions of society or,
simply and most frequently, as cranks. Historians of a later
time have, generally, not gone beyond that contemporary
judgment. The sisters themselves, chafing under the barrage
of hostile criticism, considered their speaking tour a duty

which had turned out to be far more onerous than they had anticipated. Neither they nor Weld were in a position at that time to evaluate the results and the significance of the tour objectively.

The sisters had been in New England twenty-three weeks, during which time they had spoken before at least eighty-eight meetings in sixty-seven towns. They had reached, face to face, a minimum of 40,500 people in meetings.[1] To have reached even half that number would still have been an impressive accomplishment.[2]

In quite a number of communities they stimulated the formation of abolition societies. In West Amesbury, Holliston, Andover, West Newbury and Brookline, societies were formed within six months of their visit. To what extent their lectures contributed to such organizations one can only surmise. In at least one instance, in Worcester, they were specifically invited in order to help in the formation of an abolition society.[3]

In the first two weeks of their tour the sisters kept a record of the new members who joined abolition societies at their meetings. Unfortunately, they later abandoned the keeping of such records. At six meetings in the Boston area a total of 154 new members were enlisted at their lectures. If anywhere near this level was sustained during the rest of the tour, Wendell Phillips was right in regarding their tour not only as a propagandistic, but as an organizing success.

There can be no question that the tour served to raise the free speech question in many churches and towns. Like all other abolitionist speakers, they created controversy by their appearance and in so doing, focused attention on their cause. Because of their unique role as Southerners and women, the Grimkés did this more effectively than most. They were in many cases able to break through prejudice and church-imposed restrictions. More importantly, because they were ladies, they could reach their audiences without stirring up mobs and riots. Their presence forced many communities and community leaders to think through their attitude toward women. The impact of this is hard to measure. But at the very least, as Weld had pointed out, they won the right for respectable, religious women to speak in public in many communities.

An indication of the interest they had aroused in the subject was a public debate held at the Boston Lyceum in January 1838 on the question, "Would the condition of woman and of society be improved by placing the two sexes on an equality in respect to civil rights and duties?" The two pro-feminist speakers stressed the intellectual accomplishments of women and their contribution to reform causes and predicted that the granting of full civil rights to women was an inevitable development and would greatly benefit society. The two "antis" granted woman's intellectual accomplishments, but declared that woman's sphere had been ordained by divine Providence as different from that of man. They anticipated the humorous approach of latter-day anti-feminists by describing the dire consequences of having a frigate "womaned" for a cruise. The debaters were all men and the decision was, predictably, against equal rights for women.[4] "Never was a completer farce enacted," Angelina reported indignantly to Weld. "There our Lords and Masters undertook to discuss *our* rights and settle what was most to *our* benefit, but we were not permitted to plead our own cause nor were *we* called upon to give our votes. As well might the Slaveholders of the South hold a meeting to discuss whether the condition of Society and the slave would be improved by emancipation, whilst they sat gagged before them and the question decided by acclamation of the masters without the voice of the slaves." [5] Angelina notwithstanding, the very fact of such a debate being held in 1838 was progress.

A few months later the sisters themselves were the featured speakers in Boston's largest meetinghall, the Odeon, for a course of weekly lectures under the sponsorship of the Boston Female Anti-Slavery Society. Angelina reminded Weld that she would not be able to see him after March 22, when the lectures were to start, since his presence would be too upsetting to her. This had the desired effect: Weld finally set the date for his visit for the weekend of March 17. Now it was Angelina's turn to falter and, once again, to express her fears that their marriage might impair Weld's usefulness to the cause. And, as though to subject his love to a final test, she confessed her past attachment to Edward Bettle.

Weld brushed aside her hesitations and responded to her disclosure with a somewhat naïve and typically Victorian gush of sentiment: "My hearts desire, you have knitted me to you still closer if possible by the free disclosure of your deep and tender affection for that loved one who was snatched from you by death. I love you the more Angelina that you *loved* and *love him still* . . . instead of *consenting* that you should forget him or love him less than you do — Oh *no no.* Let me help you love him more. To do so will be to me a sweet privilege and a dear delight." [6]

Meanwhile, however, he complicated arrangements for his visit no end by his abnormal concern with secrecy. "I expect no poor slave ever passed through our land under more suffering from fear of exposure," Angelina teased him. "You did not tell me that *vanity* was among your defects, but I find to my surprise that you are so vain as to suppose that you cannot possibly even pass thro' Providence or Boston without the blast of wonder and rejoicing being blown on the arrival of so great a personage. Why Theodore, I tho't when you came, you were to come as a man." And she assured him that all arrangements had been made to give them privacy and that the Philbricks could be trusted to keep their secret.[7] All the same, Weld did not come by the common route, but traveled by way of Hartford and Worcester to Brighton, where Sam Philbrick met him with a carriage.

At last, these shy and reluctant lovers were united for a few days of private happiness. Weld later confessed that all during his visit he kept himself "tied up with a tetherline" so as not to be carried away with emotion. Nothing in his life had prepared him for the problems of awakening sexual desire and he struggled bravely to "keep an extinguisher" on his spirits. Often, when embracing his beloved, he suddenly would rush out of the room for fear of losing control of his feelings. Angelina took the situation more calmly and found that a settled contentment began to replace the turmoil of feeling under which she had been living these past months. The happiness she experienced made even the parting bearable. And Weld matured enough during these few days to face the world with his emotions without embarrassment. On his return trip he told his brother and sister in Hartford of his forthcoming marriage and received their and his parents' blessings.[8]

The first of the Odeon lectures took place while Weld was still in Boston. According to plan, the sisters were to share the responsibility by alternating each week as speakers. Sarah led off at the first meeting. She was very apprehensive, especially since there had been rumors of a planned disturbance. The meeting started off with some hissing and noise in the galleries, which abolitionists countered by clapping. Sarah had difficulty making herself heard. Still, she delivered her prepared lecture, which included an attack on the Governor of Massachusetts for having expressed his willingness to send troops to the South in the event of a slave insurrection. Garrison, who attended the lecture, was concerned that this daring personal attack would provoke further trouble, but Sarah had apparently captured the audience of 2800 persons. Unfortunately, she lost track of the time and spoke for over two hours, yet, "with a few exceptions," the people stayed quietly.[9]

Although Weld had not attended Sarah's lecture, he heard it discussed on the stagecoach ride from Worcester on his way home. What he heard alarmed him and caused him to write a letter to Sarah, which he knew would pain her.

It seemed that both abolitionists and pro-slavery people on the coach had agreed "that Angelina's lectures before the legislature had done more for the abolition cause in Massachusetts than any or *all other measures together* for the whole season." However, abolitionists were distressed about the first Odeon meeting. They had come to hear Angelina and only waited patiently through Sarah's speech in expectation of hearing Angelina. They felt that the future lectures would be failures, if Angelina did not deliver them all. Conversely, anti-abolitionists had expressed their hope that Sarah would continue to lecture, to the damage of the abolition cause. All agreed that it was Sarah's delivery which was at fault; her lectures were dull, her manner of speaking "monotonous and heavy." Weld appealed to her to step back voluntarily. He hoped that she would appreciate that his suggestion was offered for the good of the cause and in "all

abounding love." Despite this protestation, Weld was not
unaware of the effect his letter would have, for he begged
Sarah not to show it to Angelina for fear of distressing her.
His curious request only compounded this demonstration of
personal ruthlessness where the good of the cause was concerned, especially since Weld's judgment of Sarah's performance was based on nothing but hearsay evidence. At the
very least, the Boston abolitionists and especially the
women, who had sponsored the meetings, might have been
consulted and their opinions considered. In fact, they did
not agree with Weld at all. But he knew that to get the desired result it was simpler and much more efficient to discourage Sarah directly.

Sarah disregarded Weld's desire to shield Angelina. The
younger sister was "mortified," but quickly recovered, trust-
ing in Sarah's well-tested "sweet humility." Sarah told Weld
frankly that his letter had crushed her. "It seemed as if God
mocked me." For a time she considered never again opening
her lips for the antislavery cause. But after a calm review of
her Odeon lecture she did not regret having given it. She
had been officially invited to speak by the Boston Female
Anti-Slavery Society, and those who had invited her were
well satisfied with her performance.[10] Still, she complied and
offered to let Angelina give the third lecture, which had been
originally planned for her. She volunteered, instead, to give
an afternoon lecture in Dorchester.

"That day was one of deep suffering," Angelina wrote to
Weld. "Dear Sister . . . could not rise above thy letter. I
saw it and was troubled for her. I don't know what kind of
meeting she had except that they wish her to hold another
there."[11]

"I have had a fearful struggle to know the path of duty,"

Sarah confessed to Weld a few days later. "My sisters in Boston after hearing why I declined partly were earnest to have me deliver one more of the Odeon lectures. I was willing to do it. . . ." [12] But it was Angelina who delivered the last two lectures and ended in triumph on April 19, "full of solemn pathos and deep feeling." John Tappan, who was in the audience, thought she had kindled a fire which would never go out.[13]

"I shall never forget the wonderful manifestation of this power [Angelina Grimké's eloquence] during six successive evenings in what was then called the Odeon," Robert F. Wallcutt recollected years later: "The four galleries rising above the auditorium all crowded with a silent audience, carried away with the calm, simple eloquence which narrated what she and her sister had seen from the earliest days." [14]

Wendell Phillips, himself acclaimed as the greatest of all the reform orators, recalled listening to the Odeon lectures, "to eloquence such as never then had been heard from a woman. Her own hard experience, the long, lonely, intellectual and moral struggle from which she came out conqueror, had ripened her power and her wondrous faculty for laying bare her own heart to reach the heart of others shone forth, till she carried us all captive." [15]

As for Angelina, she was only grateful that this last and most exacting of her public obligations was over. Now preparations for her marriage could take first place. During Weld's visit they had set a tentative date for the wedding for the last week in April, depending on the convenience of Weld's family and their antislavery friends. The wedding was to take place in Philadelphia at the home of Angelina's sister, Mrs. Anna Frost. They had also agreed that Sarah was

to live with them for the rest of their lives. Since Weld and
Sarah loved and respected each other and Angelina's only
reservation about her marriage had been the fear of a possible separation from Sarah, this arrangement was "mutually
pleasant" to all concerned.[16] Besides, it was in no way
unusual in nineteenth-century America, when unmarried
women frequently joined the household of a parent, brother
or sister.

While Weld, in New York, was occupied with househunting, the sisters set to work sewing Angelina's trousseau. Everything, including the mattress, would be fashioned out of
"free cotton." [17] Since Angelina was very conscious of Weld's
poverty "in worldly goods," simplicity was the watchword.
She expected to get no new clothing at all and to furnish her
household with only the barest essentials. Weld would continue to work for the American Anti-Slavery Society and expected to meet the needs of his family by part-time farming.
The simplest of household arrangements would enable the
sisters to spend a minimum of time housekeeping and to give
them a chance to write for the antislavery cause and occasionally to lecture. But never again would they work "so un-
remittingly" as they had during the New England tour.[18]

This question of Angelina's future career as a lecturer was
one that would crop up time and again in the next few
weeks. The first to bring it up was her mother. In a warm
and generous letter Mrs. Grimké gave her blessings to her
daughter's marriage and assured her of her motherly love
"notwithstanding our difference of opinion." She was greatly
relieved by Angelina's now having a protector, who, she felt
certain, was suitable to her daughter in all respects. She had
always believed Angelina was acting from conscientious motives; now she hoped that marriage would bring retirement
from the "busy scenes of publicity." [19]

Few of Angelina's friends could react to the news of the impending marriage without concern over her public role. Maria Chapman, who had guessed at the turn of events, was overjoyed with Angelina's happiness and let it go at that.[20] Not so Anna Weston, who was "perfectly delighted," but could not keep from commenting that Weld had risen 50 percent in her estimation. No other man would marry a woman who had so far stepped out of the "ordinary lot of women." Angelina's engagement was, in her opinion, "a complete triumph over the ministers who had threatened that women such as she would never find husbands."[21] Angelina was somewhat taken aback by this comment, but soon realized that she would encounter it frequently. Her Philadelphia friends were "almost offended" by the idea of her marriage, considering both her and Weld "public property." Some feared that from now on Angelina would be "good for nothing . . . to the cause." It was generally assumed that Weld was opposed to her speaking in public in the future. "If they think so, they are very excusable for grumbling about it," Angelina commented with equanimity.[22]

Most of Weld's friends reacted to the news of his engagement with sincere pleasure. But Lewis Tappan unintentionally hurt Weld's feelings, when he commended him for his moral courage in marrying a woman like Angelina.[23] Another abolitionist, who did not know that Weld was the man in question, commented that he thought it impossible for a "man of high feeling" ever to marry Angelina Grimké. "He thought that *nature* recoiled at it," Weld informed his bride without, at all, seeing the humor in the situation. It seemed to Weld that at this moment there was probably no other female in the country so well known and talked about as she was. Typically, he could see this only as an added challenge. Angelina would be the first known advocate of woman's rights to be tested in marriage. "I feel also most solemnly that a peculiar responsibility rests on ME too, on this very account. . . . Married life will be the touchstone to test me and to show how I reduce to practice what I have long and perhaps pertinaceously contended for in *theory*." Besides, since both of them were strong-willed people, to whom others had usually deferred, there was a danger that in close daily contact they would "more or less try each other." To prevent this, Weld suggested that they exercise a spirit of "mutual concession" in their marriage. In all non-essentials, each should decide in advance to yield; in all other matters everything should be done by mutual consultation.[24]

So fortified with good resolutions, Weld was better able to bear the teasing of his good friend Whittier, who professed to be greatly aggrieved by Weld's having abandoned him in their celibacy pact. He wrote a humorous poem of congratulations, in which he complained that Weld's betrayal was worse than Benedict Arnold's and berated him for "scoffing at Love and then sub-rosa wooing."[25] In later years he commented that Weld "did the best thing a man could do, and married A.G. — a woman of great beauty of mind and person, and an eloquent pleader for the slave."[26]

There was only one man whose reaction irritated Weld — the unfortunate H. C. Wright. "Brother Wright *says* he is rejoiced and he really thinks so doubtless, but dear me! he *looks* as tho' his heart was broke when he speaks of it."[27] Weld, usually so tolerant of all foibles of abolitionists, could not conquer his jealous dislike of Wright. He even refused to sign the wedding invitation to him. "The thought that *you* should marry *me* is to him like *poison*," he insisted, but assured Angelina he had nevertheless issued a kindly oral invitation to Wright.

As soon as Weld had begun househunting, he had encountered the usual difficulties. Large houses were too expensive; houses with seven or eight rooms and an acre of ground were hard to find. He had decided definitely against sharing a house with another family. The two of them and Sarah were, after all, "a strange trio, different from all the world in their mode of life, their tastes and habits." Close proximity with others, no matter how congenial, would lead to friction. Weld was also concerned over the difficulty in finding plain furniture. "Everything is so tricked out and covered with carved work and bedizzened and *gew gawed* and gilded and tipt off with variegated colors that the mark of the beast is omnipresent." [28]

He decided at last on a house in Fort Lee, New Jersey, a little way up the Hudson from New York and accessible by steamboat from Brooklyn. The rooms were large and were to be newly plastered and painted before occupancy. Now the host of domestic decisions really crowded in on him. Did they prefer cane or flag bottom chairs? Were the bureaus to have two small drawers at the top or only large ones? What shape were the knobs of the drawers to be? And what style parlor table did the sisters prefer? [29]

The couple's insistence on making their wedding an interracial affair complicated arrangements. Angelina was not certain that her sister Anna would approve and asked Weld to secure an alternate place, in case Anna objected. Weld assured her that both Lewis Tappan and James Birney would be delighted to have the wedding take place in their homes. But sister Anna finally agreed, although Angelina discerned that she consented "from a principle of *duty*, but has no pleasure in it. Her aristocratic feelings I can plainly see are galled at the very anticipation of such a motley assembly of white and black, high and low, as we expect to have there." [30]

Wedding invitations for May 14, 1838, went out to over eighty friends and acquaintances in many states. Preparations included arrangements to have a colored confectioner, who would use only "free sugar" in the baking, supply the wedding cake.

Another aspect of the wedding plans proved more difficult of solution. Angelina could not have a Quaker ceremony, since she was marrying out of the faith. Sarah made inquiries and found out that under Pennsylvania law a marriage was regarded as merely a civil contract, legal if made in the presence of a competent number of witnesses, one of whom was to be a justice of the peace.[31] Weld pointed out that the presence of a justice of the peace was necessary only to give validity to the marriage in such matters as property settlements. Since their marriage would be such an extraordinary and public event, it was most unlikely it would ever be challenged. As for property, he would be delighted to have no record proving his legal right as husband to his wife's property. "I am quite thankful for this unexpected opportunity to give a little testimony against a vandal law which prostrates a woman at the feet of her husband the moment after marriage, suing for the *favor* of a pittance of the property just plundered from her by the law, and put at his *sole disposal*." [32] Angelina concurred and it was decided that the couple would be married in a ceremony of their own devising, but would sign a legal marriage contract witnessed by their friends.

The sisters left Boston on April 23, stayed two days in Providence, where they gave several lectures, then went to New York for a brief reunion with Weld. They spent an afternoon visiting their future home in Fort Lee, then Weld

saw them off at the boat for Philadelphia. He had to stay on
in New York to attend the annual convention of the American Anti-Slavery Society. But it was a wasted effort; his mind
was not on business. Although there was heated controversy
on the convention floor concerning the "constitutional question," namely whether the United States Constitution, properly interpreted, was to be considered a document prohibit-
ing slavery — a proposition which finally lost by a few votes
— Weld absented himself for long periods of time in order to
run down to the post office and see if there was mail for him
from Philadelphia.[33]

The last week before her wedding was a busy one for Angelina. She visited old friends and found time to attend a
meeting of the Female Anti-Slavery Society and to meet the
visiting British Quaker Joseph Gurney. Both she and Sarah
accepted organizational responsibilities for the day immediately following the wedding. They would represent the Female Society at the Free Produce Convention, in addition to
attending the four-day Anti-Slavery Convention of American
Women. About this time, Garrison and Henry C. Wright arrived in Philadelphia. While making a social call on the
Grimké sisters, Garrison took the opportunity of having
"considerable conversation about the approaching marriage"
with them. He told Angelina frankly of his fears that Weld's
"sectarianism" would enslave her, unless she could succeed
in "emancipating him." He was worried about Weld's "sab-
batical notions, church-going worship etc." When Angelina
admitted that she would join Weld in family worship, Garrison despaired of her ideological purity and thought if she
went that far she was likely to go further. To all of which
Angelina answered mildly, that she expected the "experiment" of her marriage to be "mutually serviceable." [34]

On Monday, May 14, 1838, busy abolitionists and reform-

ers from many parts of the country gathered in the morning
to attend the opening ceremonies of newly built Pennsylvania Hall and ended their triumphant day of celebration at
the wedding of the most-mobbed man and the most notorious woman in America.

The little house at 3 Belmont Row, Spruce Street, over-
flowed with its thirty to forty guests. Judge Grimké's youngest daughter was getting married in a manner calculated to
shock and dismay the pillars of Charleston society, among
whom she had been raised. "I would only ask if something is
not due to Sister Anna's feelings and opinions," sister Eliza
had fretted in her letter of congratulations. "What a motley
crew did you assemble to witness the solemn scene," Mrs.
Grimké had commented in turn.[35]

One cannot help but feel a certain amount of admiration
for the fortitude of Anna Frost, who suppressed her prejudices and notions of propriety to provide her sister with a
family wedding. She herself had had a difficult time as a
young widow with a child to raise alone, and it cannot be
said that Angelina had ever exerted herself very much on
Anna's behalf. But Anna seems to have had large shares of
that capacity for tolerance which was so unevenly spread
among members of the Grimké family. Perhaps she found
some comfort in the presence of such obviously dignified and
respectable persons of wealth as the Chapmans, Westons,
Tappans and Gerrit Smiths. But what of W. L. Garrison,
"the worst of men," according to Mrs. Grimké. If Anna Frost
had hoped that his irritating skin condition, for which he had
only a short while ago sought hospital treatment, or his expressed disapproval of the marriage would keep him away,
her hopes were disappointed. There he was, slight and tidy
with his rimless spectacles and bald head, mild-mannered,
precise and appearing more like a country schoolteacher

than the fiery agitator of abolition. He acted in every way as though the whole affair, from beginning to end, were of his doing. Had he not introduced the bride and groom? And if it were not for him, would there have been a "Letter to Garrison" which served to bring the lovers to one another's attention? Surrounded by his admiring Bostonians, the Chapmans, Fullers and Philbricks, Garrison was in his element, a kindly godfather to the young couple. Seeing him thus, even Mrs. Grimké might have approved.

Mrs. Frost had, no doubt, been briefed in advance on the eccentricities of some of her guests. Charles Callistus Burleigh could be forgiven his bushy black beard and shoulder-length curls, if one knew of his gift of oratory. The Lane rebels, Amos Dresser, Hiram Wilson, George Avery and Henry Stanton looked rather respectable and inoffensive, so that it was hard to imagine them facing down roaring mobs and braving lynch parties. But what could one make of a handsome, almost elegant man like Henry C. Wright? His romantic good looks made it utterly impossible to connect him with the fanatical heresies against church and government he had uttered.

As for the mixing of colors, Mrs. Frost must have been more embarrassed about it in principle than in practice. What the neighbors would think must have been a matter of concern to her, for, unlike her sisters, she would continue to live on Spruce Street. As for the colored people present, Mrs. Frost was familiar with most of them. The Philadelphians, Sarah Douglass and her mother, were respectable, well-educated Quakers with whom Angelina and Sarah had been intimate for many years. And the presence of former house slaves of their father, Betsy Dawson and her daughter, whom Mrs. Frost herself had freed, must have seemed as natural to her as it did to them. So that personally, the presence of these Negroes offered no difficulty and yet it was this very presence which made the event so unique and shocking. And there was no denying that it was a deliberate demonstration on the part of the hosts. "They were our invited guests," Sarah explained on behalf of herself and the Welds, "and we thus had an opportunity to bear our testimony against the horrible prejudice which prevails against colored persons, and equally awful prejudice against the poor." [36]

Having thus arranged their wedding as a testimonial and a demonstration, bride and groom looked radiant in their matching wedding outfits. Angelina wore a simple brown dress; Weld, in his matching coat, white vest and beige pantaloons, stood tall and handsome beside her, as they addressed each other "in such words as the Lord gave them at the moment." Weld took the occasion to denounce the unrightful power of laws, which gave the husband control over the property of his wife. He acknowledged "only that authority which love would give to them over each other as moral and immortal beings." Angelina responded by promising to honor him, prefer him above herself and love him with a pure heart. All present knelt, while bride and groom each led a prayer. Then a colored minister prayed, followed by a white minister. After them, Sarah felt moved to a prayer of thanksgiving. Garrison read the marriage certificate aloud and passed it around to be signed by each guest.

With this simple ceremony Angelina Grimké and Theodore Weld were married. Surrounded by friends and those they loved, they had fashioned of their most private feelings a moving, public testimonial to their basic faith in the equality of men and women of all races before God. This belief had brought them together; this belief would be the motive of their union.

CHAPTER
FIFTEEN

The old falsehood, that the slave is kindly treated, shallow and stupid as it is, has lullabied to sleep four-fifths of the free north and west; but with God's blessing this sleep shall not be unto death. Give facts a voice, and cries of blood shall ring till deaf ears tingle.

Theodore D. Weld
November 28, 1838.

Angelina and Weld allowed themselves only one day of privacy before stepping once again into their public roles. It was important to them both to demonstrate that marriage would in no way lessen Angelina's involvement in reform activities. It was with this in view that they had planned to participate, "as though nothing had occurred," in the conventions scheduled to be held all week in newly dedicated Pennsylvania Hall.[1]

Pennsylvania Hall, the biggest building of its kind, stood as a monument to the perseverance and dogged courage of the reformers. It was their answer to the harassment, intimidation and mob violence which had restricted free speech for advocates of unpopular causes all over the country. Renting a hall for a meeting had become an almost insurmountable problem. Reformers in Philadelphia had decided to meet this difficulty by building their own hall. It was a handsome building with stores and committee rooms on the first floor, a huge hall with a gallery on the second and third floors. Its construction cost $40,000 and was financed by the sale of twenty-dollar shares to 2000 associates, among whom there were a large number of women. It was to be a symbol of free speech, open to all opinions "not of an immoral character." The dedication ceremonies on Monday, May 14, 1838, featured warm messages of greeting from John Quincy Adams, Thaddeus Stevens, Gerrit Smith, Judge John Jay and Theodore Weld.[2] For the rest of the week reform meetings and conventions had been programmed daily. But it was soon apparent that the citizens of Philadelphia did not intend to let this occasion pass unnoticed. On Tuesday following the opening of the hall, placards were posted in many parts of the city: "A convention to effect the immediate emancipation of the slaves throughout the country is in session in the city, and it is the duty of citizens who entertain a proper respect for the Constitution of the Union and the right of property to interfere." It was suggested that people assemble at Pennsylvania Hall the next day and demand the immediate dispersal of the convention.[3]

Abolitionists later claimed that these posters and the campaign to promote mob violence had been instigated by the many Southerners, especially a large group of medical students, resident in the city. This was never proven. At all events, ugly rumors were circulated all over town, based on the flimsiest of evidence. The fact that people "of all races" had been seen entering and leaving Pennsylvania Hall became certain proof that the real purpose of the abolitionists was to practice "amalgamation." Soon it was rumored that whites and blacks had been seen "parading" arm in arm on Chestnut Street; some accounts had it that there were 500 such "amalgamated" couples, others that there were just a few, who had actually been hired by abolitionists in the hope of provoking a riot. Elsewhere it was stated for a fact that at the wedding of Theodore Weld six whites and six blacks had acted as groomsmen and bridesmaids.[4]

Yet Wednesday morning came peacefully enough. The Welds and Sarah attended the opening session of the Anti-Slavery Convention of American Women in Pennsylvania Hall, which was taken up with discussing the progress and future of the petition campaign. The women vowed that for each petition rejected by Congress they would send five in the coming months.

But in the evening the results of the incitement were plainly in evidence. A hostile, noisy crowd surrounded the hall, as over three thousand reformers arrived for the evening meeting which featured as a special attraction male and female speakers on the same platform. William Lloyd Garrison gave the opening address, at the end of which there was a commotion, and a shouting mob broke into the hall. The audience rose; there was momentary confusion, but the women on the platform remained seated and Maria Chapman began to speak, as planned. This quieted the audience; the intruders retreated into the street. But they were not done — throughout Mrs. Chapman's brief speech the shouting, groaning and stamping of feet could be heard outside. Soon missiles began to hit the walls.[5] It was a dramatic moment when Angelina Grimké Weld, bride of two days, was introduced to the audience, while bricks crashed through the windows and glass fell to the floor. The audience showed some uneasiness, but the calm presence of mind of the slender woman before them held them in check. It was her finest, most accomplished performance as an orator, unforgettable to all who witnessed it. She spoke as a Southerner who felt it her duty to stand up and bear testimony against slavery.

I have seen it! I have seen it! I know it has horrors that can never be described. I was brought up under its wing. I witnessed for many years its demoralizing influences and its destructiveness to human happiness. I have never seen a happy slave. I have seen him dance in his chains, it is true, but he was not happy. There is a wide difference between happiness and mirth. Man can not enjoy happiness while his manhood is destroyed. Slaves, however, may be and sometimes are mirthful. When hope is extinguished, they say, "Let us eat and drink, for tomorrow we die."

At this point in her speech, another shower of stones hit the windows. The audience stirred apprehensively, but Angelina continued, only briefly remarking on the disturbance. "What is a mob? What would the breaking of every window be? Any evidence that *we are* wrong, or that slavery is a good and wholesome institution? What if that mob should now burst in upon us, break up our meeting and commit violence on our persons — would this be anything compared with what the slaves endure?" [6]

The din outside was unabated while Angelina lectured for over an hour. She was followed by a young woman who had never before spoken in public. Abby Kelley, a Quaker abolitionist, had been inspired by hearing the sisters speak in Lynn on their tour. Her speech that night was brief, but forceful. It so impressed Theodore Weld that after the meeting he spoke to her at once about becoming an antislavery lecturer. "Abby, if you don't," he said in his vehement and direct way, "God will smite you!" [7] Abby Kelley later became one of the most effective lecturers in the antislavery movement.

The strong-arm mob outside Pennsylvania Hall failed twice that night, despite its size and clamor: it failed to stop the pioneer of female orators from making what turned out to be her last public speech for many years. And it failed more importantly, to arrest the growth of the movement she had inspired. Young Abby Kelley was taking up where Angelina and Sarah were leaving off.

The next morning, although a hostile crowd again surrounded the hall, Lucretia Mott opened the second session of the convention of antislavery women, who proceeded to a spirited discussion of their work in educational institutions and churches. Meanwhile, the trustees of the hall had become alarmed and appealed to the Mayor, the Sheriff and the police for protection. The Mayor answered by requesting the women to keep colored people from attending the evening session, since their presence was particularly infuriating to the citizens of Philadelphia and endangered the safety of all. This request was read to the assembly by Mrs. Mott and was, at her suggestion, rejected. The women were determined not to give in to intimidation. When they left the hall they walked arm in arm, a white woman with a colored woman. It was a tactic they had used during the Boston riot, three years ago — then their display of solidarity and non-violent resistance had overawed the mob and brought them all out safely. Now it worked again, although this time they were met not only with shouting and curses, but with stones which injured one woman.[8]

Fearing further violence, the managers decided to close the hall for the evening and give the Mayor the key. Mayor John Swift thereupon informed the crowd that they had succeeded in stopping the meeting. He saw no point in calling out the police, since he could trust his fellow citizens to keep

order. Bidding them all a good night, he departed amid
cheers. But as night fell the streets around Pennsylvania
Hall were still densely packed. Suddenly, the public lamps
in the neighborhood were extinguished. The mob surged
forward, breaking down the doors. When the Mayor and the
police came back on the scene, the assault was well on the
way. Fires had been kindled on the ground floor of the hall;
venetian blinds, furnishings and chairs were fed into the
flames. When the chief of police attempted to restore order,
he and his force were attacked by the mob. Someone ripped
down the gas pipes, letting the gas stream into the roaring
fire. The policemen withdrew, while another group of activists ransacked the antislavery office on the first floor, throw-
ing pamphlets, books and records into the flames.[9]

For several hours, a crowd of many thousands stood in silence, watching the destruction. Some of the abolitionists
stood by helplessly, but John Greenleaf Whittier, seeing his
editorial office threatened, grew bold and inventive in his
desperation. He rushed to the nearby house of a friend, put
on a coat and a wig and so disguised mingled with the mob
that entered the office. By this ruse he managed to save a
few of his precious records from destruction. But all of Benjamin Lundy's papers, which had been kept there, were
burned.[10]

The firemen came late on the scene, and lifted not a finger
to save the building. Instead, they set to work very efficiently to protect the neighboring buildings and roofs from
the fire. At ten, the roof of Pennsylvania Hall fell in; another
hour and the interior was gone. With a tremendous crash
the entire front collapsed, as the crowd cheered wildly. The
symbol of free speech was a charred and gutted ruin.

Many of the antislavery women had gathered at the

nearby home of Lucretia and James Mott during this riotous night. After the hall was destroyed, some of the mob decided to attack the homes of abolitionists. The Motts and their guests were saved only by the presence of mind of an abolitionist who, pretending to show the way to the Motts, diverted them from their goal. Meanwhile, members of a vigilance committee, headed by Robert Purvis, spirited Garrison out of town to safety.[11]

In the following days nationwide attention was focused on the arson and riot in Philadelphia. Condemnation of the mob action was universal, although it was generally coupled with attacks on the reformers. The press was outspoken in its contempt for the Mayor's silent encouragement of mob violence. But it was also noted with approval that no lives had been lost. Significantly, the next night, when a smaller mob attacked and set fire to the Shelter for Colored Orphans, run by the Society of Friends, firemen and police swiftly managed to save the building. This show of civic energy most likely served to prevent a race riot of the kind that had convulsed the city in 1834 and 1835.

The city council of Philadelphia later appointed an investigating committee, which called many witnesses. One of them was Robert Purvis, the wealthy sailmaker, who offered to explain the incident which had inspired the most lurid "amalgamation" stories. Any number of people had reported seeing a white woman being let out of a carriage and escorted into the hall by a Negro. Robert Purvis freely confessed that he had been the guilty party — the lady was his wife, a light-skinned colored person like himself. Still, the committee concluded the victims were to blame for the mob action, because they had tried to promulgate "doctrines repulsive to the moral sense of a large majority" of the community. This widely accepted doctrine, blaming the victims for the crime, sanctioned mob violence in the name of majority opinion.[12]

The morning after the fire, while the ashes of the building were still hot, Philadelphians were treated to another display of that fanatical persistence which so alarmed the ordinary citizens. The antislavery women, as though nothing had happened, returned to the business of holding their convention. Naturally, they had trouble securing a hall and finally had to accept the hospitality of Sarah Pugh, one of their members, who offered her schoolroom. But riot or not, they met bright and early Friday morning.

Both sisters had been elected vice-presidents of the Convention and played an active role throughout. In this session Sarah offered several resolutions. In one, which was passed unanimously, she linked the mob action of the previous night with the "spirit of slavery" of the South and with the spirit of the "reform convention who have recommended that the people of Pennsylvania should wrest from the free people of color the right of suffrage."[13]

This represented an astute political analysis on her part. The sudden outbreak of mob violence in Philadelphia was not unconnected with the efforts to disenfranchise the free colored population of the state. The amendment to the state constitution, limiting the vote to white freemen, had been passed in January 1838 and, at the time of the riot, awaited ratification. It was a sharp departure from the past, when Negroes had been voting as freemen, and was bitterly protested by the well-organized free Negro community. The mob actions against Pennsylvania Hall and the Negro orphan asylum were object lessons in terror directed as much against the Negro community as against their white sympathizers.

The amendment was, in fact, ratified in the October elections and was part of a pattern by which expanded voting rights in the North were coupled with suffrage restrictions on free Negroes. No Negro voted in Pennsylvania between 1838 and the Civil War.[14]

The second resolution presented by Sarah Grimké was one of the few not adopted unanimously at the convention. It resolved that prejudice against color was the very spirit of slavery and that it was "the duty of abolitionists to identify themselves with these oppressed Americans, by sitting with them in places of worship, by appearing with them in our streets, by giving them our countenance in steamboats and stages, by visiting them at their homes and encouraging them to visit us, receiving them as we do our white fellow citizens." [15]

The antislavery women showed generally greater awareness of race prejudice and all its implications than did their contemporaries. Their meetings were integrated and their Negro members were given a chance to take leadership positions. Still, this call for a conscious policy of demonstrations against segregation in public places was considered controversial even by abolitionists. In advocating it year after year, and personally carrying it into practice, Sarah and Angelina made one of their most significant contributions to the ideology of the antislavery cause. It was an issue on which they consistently were in advance of most white abolitionists.

The excitement and activities of the conventions were over and the Welds and Sarah looked forward to their "sweet retirement." Their home was small, but comfortable, beautifully situated with a sweeping view of the Hudson. The sisters enjoyed their daily walks to the river and along the heights of the Palisades, their work in the orchard and vegetable garden and the unaccustomed and challenging chores of housekeeping.

Sarah was forty-six years old and Nina thirty-three; neither of them had ever kept house or lived in a home of her own. It was a long time since Sarah had been taught how to weave Negro cloth and pick cotton and neither of these plantation skills was any help when it came to keeping house on an isolated little farm in New Jersey. "Pray, have you got no servants?" Mrs. Grimké wrote in considerable dismay, when informed of the household arrangements. "This, my daughter, is like some of your other strange notions." [16]

But Sarah and Nina were delighted to do without household help. Nina was ashamed to let anyone see how ignorant she was of domestic skills and was determined to learn the rudiments before undertaking to direct others. All the more, since she was not simply an inexperienced bride — she and Sarah were public lecturers. It was "absolutely necessary" that they should show that they were not "ruined as domestic characters" — in that way they could do as much for the cause of women as they had done by public speaking.[17] They wanted to prove that women like themselves, who had taken a public role, could be efficient housewives and that "well regulated minds" could "with equal ease occupy high and low stations and find true happiness in both." [18]

So, cheerfully taking on herself the burden of the feminine cause, Angelina burnt her stewed apples, learned how to boil potatoes, swept and dusted and shook out her matting and claimed to be far prouder of her accomplishment in baking "very nice bread" than she had ever been of her lectures.[19]

In this, as in other matters, the sisters were sustained by their theories and reform principles. They were converts and fervent advocates of the Graham diet. Both sisters had taken a course of lectures with Sylvester Graham while in Boston and had become fully convinced that his simple, largely vegetarian diet was the "most conducive to health and besides . . . such an emancipation of woman from the toils of the kitchen." They cooked hot food only once a week and ate cold meals the rest of the time, which saved "much precious time for purposes of more importance than eating and drinking." They would make a meal of rice and molasses, another of bread and milk, breakfast on raw apples and cold water, lunch on stewed beans and dine on pears.[20] They never used sugar, tea, coffee or spices because of their boycott of slave-grown products and eschewed butter, fish and meat from Grahamite principles. They thought nothing of offering their guests pie without shortening, potatoes, mush and cornbread with fresh fruit from their garden. Fortunately, they were all three "of one heart and mind" as to the physical and spiritual benefits of this Spartan diet and most of their reformer friends were similarly inclined or at least mildly tolerant of this particular fad. No doubt, in an age of heavy over-eating and over-drinking, when the better part of woman's life was apt to be spent in baking, cooking and serving huge meals, the Graham diet simplified housekeeping and was a nutritional improvement. "Graham bread" remains to this day the monument to Sylvester Graham's energetic educational campaign for better nutrition. Also, the Graham diet had another, not inconsiderable advantage for reformers: it was cheap.

"As to our poverty," Angelina had assured her friend Jane, "neither of us can feel any uneasiness on that score. I suppose if IEL never does pay what he owed me, TDW will rather rejoice for he says he wishes it was all sunk in the ocean — this is the only thing that troubles him in marrying

me." [21] The money here referred to constituted Nina's pater-
nal inheritance and was, of course, for Weld, money tainted
by the exploitation of slaves. On the day of their wedding,
Weld and Angelina had received a statement from the
Quaker Isaac Lloyd, who had held and invested Angelina's
money, to the effect that she would remain the sole owner of
the sum of $5328, "regardless of any marriage or other cove-
nants." Having thus carried out the protest against the auto-
matic transfer of a wife's property to her husband, Angelina
later signed a separate document, in which she transferred to
her "beloved husband all right and title to the sum of $5000
. . . and also of the $328 in trust for the American Anti-
Slavery Society." [22]

Sarah's money, which had also been invested with Isaac
Lloyd, always remained her independent property. She contributed a fixed sum arranged by mutual agreement to the
household. With Weld's earnings of $1000 a year from the
American Anti-Slavery Society they could expect to live adequately, though simply. They did not reckon with the depression and the vagaries of investment. As it happened,
their major problem concerning the tainted money would be
how to collect it from the almost bankrupt Mr. Lloyd. In the
happiness of her early married life Nina could smile at the
recklessness of her "Thoda," who never laid up anything for
the future and "danced over the empty purse," even as her
mother wrote touching letters to her unknown son-in-law,
pleading with him to think prudently of the future and every
year lay aside something toward sickness.[23] The young couple were cheerfully prepared to make a virtue of a life of
simplicity and small creature comforts; but for most of their
married life they were to face actual poverty and a hard
struggle for their daily living.

But cares and worries were far from their minds that lovely summer and fall of the first year of their marriage. Weld was patient and tolerant of his bride's inexperience in domestic matters and worked out with Sarah a fond and mutually respectful relationship, in which she gradually adopted the role of an older sister or aunt. The young couple worked together in the garden and field, took long rambles and spent many hours reading. Several days a week Weld went to the Anti-Slavery office. In the evening, the sisters would stand in front of their house and watch for the steamboat *Echo,* on which Weld would be returning. Then Angelina would go down to the landing and meet him. The sisters helped him with the editing and correction of the third edition of his *Bible against Slavery* and of the yearly *Anti-Slavery Almanacs.* They made a few friends in the neighborhood, spent Sundays visiting the poor, kept up an extensive correspondence and fended off all requests for speaking engagements which kept coming in. Weld refused them because he needed to give his throat a complete rest; Angelina, because she felt her contribution at the moment was to prove the capacity of female reformers in the "domestic sphere"; Sarah because she did not as yet feel called upon by the Lord to leave her retirement.[24]

Their idyll was barely disturbed by the announcement of the sisters' disownment by the Society of Friends — Angelina for marrying out of the faith, Sarah for attending her wedding. These acts having been deliberately performed in full awareness of the consequences, the committee appointed by the Monthly Meeting of Friends could only regret that they had not more highly prized their membership. The sisters replied promptly that they did not feel they had committed any offense against Christ and wished the "discipline of the Society of Friends to have free course" with them. Their only regret was that the Society should have adopted a discipline without foundation in the Bible or reason and they remained "in that love which knows no distinction in color, clime or creed" respectfully etc.[25] Thus easily was the affiliation dissolved, which they had long since outgrown spiritually and intellectually.

Early in 1839 the British Quaker Elizabeth Pease asked the sisters to furnish any facts they might have concerning discrimination within the Society of Friends, so that British Friends might bring pressure to end such practices in America. The request came just at the right moment and gave Sarah a chance to set down her accumulated grievances in writing and for publication. She solicited statements from Sarah Douglass and asked her to include details of her own and her mother's personal experiences with prejudice among Quakers. She incorporated Sarah Douglass' reply in her forty-page statement, in which she recounted in detail her own and Angelina's experiences with Philadelphia Quakers. Throughout, she freely named names, but these were omitted in the parts of her letter which were quoted in the British pamphlet, *Society of Friends: Their Views of the Anti-Slavery Question, and Treatment of the People of Colour.* Later, when the Quaker William Bassett was preparing his defense in proceedings which ended in his disownment because of his abolitionist activities, Sarah induced the Douglasses to provide him with a statement similar to the one they had furnished her. She took an active interest in Bassett's case and identified herself with his position. Her blind loyalty to the Quakers had turned into bitter disappointment.[26]

One might wonder why the sisters never considered joining the Hicksite Quakers, especially in view of their frequent contact with Hicksites both in Pennsylvania and in New England. It is quite possible that they intended taking such a step on their return from their speaking tour, but as they became exposed to the different state and local antislavery organizations and became enmeshed in the personal feuds and sectarian squabbles of the leadership, their faith in all organizations weakened. At the time of their disownment, when they might logically have moved into a more liberal Quaker sect, they were already far gone toward a radical "come-outerism" and a distaste for all organized churches. From this it was not far to a vague Pantheism of their own devising. A decade later, they would give up even the observance of the Sabbath and engage in a long and serious flirtation with spiritualism. All that remained was to live their humanitarian convictions according to their own, very personal interpretation of the Bible. The religious reformer ended up in making a religion of reform.

Angelina's marriage had led to an increasing warmth in the relationship with her mother. Mrs. Grimké now wrote frequently and at length, giving motherly advice, family gossip and local news. She sent homemade pickles and three pairs of stockings for Weld, with the rather touching comment that he should return them, if he had any scruples about wearing something made of slave-grown cotton. Mrs. Grimké was generous in showing her love and affection for her daughters, yet she had her own dignity and refused to be badgered. She admonished Sarah to stop trying to convert her. "I must ask you to consider that I have as much proof that I am acting from principle as you have . . . the only way to carry on our correspondence with satisfaction and affection is to agree to disagree and not to expect from me more than I expect from you." [27]

The sisters found it difficult to abide this tolerant position. They felt an increasing urgency to convert their mother from the sin of slavery and asked her outright to free her slaves and send them North. Mrs. Grimké refused to do so, but told them they could have the slaves as their portion of the inheritance after her death. The rest of the family obviously did not share her attitude toward the abolitionist sisters. Brother John, the doctor, who had suffered a paralytic stroke, did not write to them at all, while sister Eliza wrote stiffly and frequently disapprovingly.

Sarah and Angelina did nothing by halves; once their interest in the family slaves had been revived they were generous with advice and financial help. This was especially so in the complex case of Stephen. He was a former house servant of Mrs. Grimké, who had been hired out to work on the docks. This kind of arrangement was not infrequent and enabled the owner to realize a cash income from the labor of a slave. Stephen claimed that stevedore work was too hard for him and that he had had several bad falls while at work. He then began to have "fits," which may have been epileptic or due to mental illness, as his owner believed. He was married; his wife Juda was owned by a different owner, a Mrs. Bizan. An arrangement had been made by the owners to permit Stephen to live with his wife, but when he became "deranged" Mrs. Bizan feared for the safety of her children and turned him out. He was sent to the poorhouse, since there was no hospital for sick slaves. When Sarah and Angelina heard this story, they begged their mother to take charge of Stephen, promised to pay all the necessary expenses and asked that he be sent to them, if he wanted to come.

Several weeks later Mrs. Grimké found Stephen in the

poorhouse "in good health and perfectly in his right mind and so rejoiced to see me that I was afraid the excitement would occasion a return of his malady." She spoke to the doctor who had attended him and who was of the opinion that Stephen was an intelligent, conscientious servant, whose health had so greatly improved since his commitment that he could now return to work. Stephen himself was very anxious to work; "he knew he was a great expense" to the sisters and wanted to compensate them for what he had cost them. Mrs. Grimké arranged with his wife's owner to take him back and hired him out to a Dr. Frost at the Medical College. Apparently, the arrangement lasted only a few months, for Stephen became violent again and was returned to the poorhouse. Mrs. Grimké was obliged to pay his keep out of the wages he had earned, which she considered quite an imposition.[28]

The sisters continued to send money for Stephen's expenses and were kept informed of his erratic progress. Released from the poorhouse, he was back at work, but far from well. He would gladly have come North, especially since Mrs. Grimké was now willing to let him go, but he did not want to leave his wife behind. The sisters wrote to Mrs. Bizan and offered to purchase Juda, so that she and Stephen could both be freed, but the old lady refused, since she depended entirely on Juda's services. She would allow her to be freed after her own death, but not before. When Stephen had another relapse, Mrs. Bizan told him never to set foot on her property again. Mrs. Grimké had to keep him at her place, which caused her considerable annoyance. He was barely able to earn enough for his room, not to speak of his board. Mrs. Grimké made very clear that she felt under no obligation to him; she had done what she could, and if he had any more fits he would have to go to the poorhouse for good. In desperation, Stephen decided to leave without his wife, since he was forbidden to see her and she was "of no service to him."

But before he could carry out his plan to go North, Juda found a way of making her mistress retract. She told Mrs. Bizan plainly, "that she could never be of the same service to her that she ever had been, if she was the cause of separating her from her husband." Juda must have reinforced this statement with some effective malingering, for her mistress changed her mind and permitted Stephen to visit his wife during the day, but not at night. This accomplished, Stephen improved and things went on as before.[29]

The correspondence concerning Stephen offers an unusual insight into the complexities of personal relationships under the slavery system. It shows that there was considerable room for maneuvering and personal initiative on the part of a resourceful slave. It also illustrates the slaveholders' dilemma.

The sisters, in their public speaking, had frequently encountered the argument that the slaveholder's economic interest in the welfare of the slave was guarantee of the latter's decent treatment. Here was proof that even a humane and responsible owner, when faced with a steady expense for the upkeep of a sick slave, could quickly conclude that the slave was a liability to whom no further consideration was due. Even so kind a lady as Mrs. Grimké saw nothing strange in her willingness to give his freedom to a sick slave, while absolutely refusing to part with the healthy ones. All of which was perfectly familiar to the sisters and astonished them not at all, especially since just at that time they were daily exposed to the worst side of the system. Compared with that, the fate of Stephen was an exercise in benevolence.

Weld had undertaken to issue a series of pamphlets for

the American Anti-Slavery Society, which were to refute the major arguments against abolitionism. The first of these was to be a factual study, based on Southern sources and the testimony of reliable eyewitnesses. Thome and Kimball's *Emancipation in the West Indies,* which Weld had recently edited, had proven the propaganda value of a factual, documentary approach. Now Weld wanted to present to the American public a study of slavery as an institution and of the actual position of the slaves within the system. Moreover, he wanted to "establish all these facts by the testimony of *slaveholders* in all parts of the slave states, by slaveholding members of Congress and of state legislatures, by ambassadors to foreign courts, by judges, by doctors of divinity, and clergymen of all denominations, by merchants, mechanics, lawyers and physicians, by presidents and professors in college and professional seminaries, by planters, overseers and drivers." [30]

This was a novel and ingenious approach and although Weld's abolitionist viewpoint permeated the questions asked and the selections made, he took great pains to arrive at unimpeachable and honest conclusions. He addressed a circular to abolitionists of Southern origin in various parts of the country, asking them to state all facts known to them in writing. In case they included the testimony of others, he wanted assurance of the witness' reliability, his name, address, calling, religious affiliation. Weld urged all respondents to "great care and accuracy." [31] All testimony was checked by the members of the executive committee — Birney, Tappan, Stanton, and Weld — and every effort was made to verify facts. In addition, and perhaps more importantly, Weld included quotations from judicial decisions and law codes, from the speeches of Southern members of Congress and from statements made by prominent slaveholders.

But his most important sources were Southern newspapers. Weld bought the discarded files of the New York
Commercial Reading Room from 1837 to 1839, including
daily newspapers from New Orleans, Charleston, Vicksburg,
Memphis, Montgomery, Raleigh and Mobile. He brought
these papers home to Fort Lee and for months Sarah and
Nina read, clipped and filed news items, trial records, advertisements for runaway slaves, speeches, anything that might
provide facts adverse to slavery. "Angelina and myself had
been engaged all winter in looking through files of Southern
papers which God, in his providence, placed in our possession, and have collected an abundance of testimony which
Theodore has arranged. . . . I think . . . this work will
wake up the nation to renewed and more effectual efforts," [32]
Sarah wrote to a friend.

Providence, by way of the New York Commercial Reading
Room, provided Weld with an enormous mass of corrobora-
tive evidence of the cruelties inflicted upon slaves as part of
the normal workings of the system. Numerous advertisements for runaway slaves described their physical characteristics, including scars, whipmarks, brandings, iron collars,
cropped ears, etc. Trial decisions, accounts of the punishment of slaves convicted of crimes, law codes detailing the
harsh penal code imposed on blacks and the total lack of
legal rights for their protection — all these provided a horri-
fying picture of one-sided justice and cruelty practiced
widely and consistently.

Weld and the sisters spared no effort to prove their case.
"The fact is," Weld recorded,

those dear souls spent six months, averaging more than
six hours a day, in searching through thousands upon

thousands of Southern newspapers. . . . Thus was gathered the raw material for the manufacture of "Slavery As It Is." After the work was finished we were curious to know how many newspapers had been examined. So we went up to our attic and took an inventory of bundles. . . . When our count had reached *twenty thousand* newspapers, we said: "There, let that suffice." Though the book had in it many thousand facts thus authenticated by the slave-holders themselves, yet it contained but a tiny fraction of the nameless atrocities gathered from the papers examined.[33]

Weld investigated the housing and feeding of slaves, compared their diet to that of the armed forces of the United States, of European countries and of the prison populations of the United States and Great Britain. He added up facts and figures concerning the clothing, medical care and work loads imposed on slaves, collected facts on slave breeding, internal slave trading and the number of slaves illegally smuggled into the country.

The result was a devastating indictment of the slavery system, an exposé of horrors and barbarities, which became a model for documentary "black books" of various kinds. Setting fact upon fact, it presented overwhelming evidence that the slaves were undernourished, overworked, poorly clad, badly housed, neglected in sickness and old age, deprived of education, human and civil rights and elementary safeguards of justice, subject to barbarous punishments and a widespread system of terror and oppression. Weld had set out to answer, once and for all, the myth that the slaves were well cared for and happy. He demonstrated with innumerable examples that the concept of the slave as a "chattel personal" inevitably led to the need for destroying what humanity was left in the slave by terror. "The greatest provocation to human nature is *opposition* to its will. . . . The idea of property having a will, and that too in opposition to the will of its *owner*, and counteracting it, is a stimulant of terrible power to the most relentless human passions, and from the nature of slavery and the constitution of the human mind, this stimulant must, with various degrees of strength, act upon the slaveholders almost without ceasing." [34]

Angelina and Sarah, in addition to their research work and editorial collaboration, each provided a lengthy statement of her own experiences in the South. Sarah's statement revived every personal memory of brutality she herself had witnessed in Charleston. When one considers her sheltered life and her limited circle of activity, the number of the incidents she witnessed is in itself an indication that such things were commonplace, rather than excesses.

Angelina pointed out that all her own experiences were based only on the treatment of house servants, who were generally treated much better than field labor. "In a multitude of instances," she wrote, "even the master can know very little of the actual condition of his own field-slaves, and his wife and daughters far less." She herself had never visited the fields on her father's plantation, where the slaves were at work. But she had first-hand impressions of the effects arbitrary uses of power produced on both master and slave.

"I remember very well that when I was a child our next door neighbor whipped a young woman so brutally, that in order to escape his blows she rushed through the drawing room window in the second story, and fell upon the pavement below and broke her hip. This circumstance produced no excitement or inquiry." At a friend's house, she once saw the mistress with a cowhide in her hand, upbraiding her manservant.

> She was a cruel mistress, and [I] had heard her daughters disputing whether their mother did right or wrong, to send slave children (whom she sent out to sweep chimneys) to the work house to be whipped, if they did not bring in their wages regularly. This woman moved in the most fashionable circles in Charleston. The income of this family was derived mostly from the hire of their slaves, about 100 in number. . . .
>
> Everything cruel and revolting is carefully concealed from strangers, especially those from the north. . . . I have known the master and mistress of a family send to their friends to *borrow* servants to wait on company, because their own slaves had been so cruelly flogged in the work house, they could not walk without limping at every step, and their putrefied flesh emitted such an intolerable smell that they were not fit to be in the presence of company. . . .
>
> I repeat it, no one who has not been an *integral* part of a slaveholding community, can have any idea of its abominations.[35]

A unique aspect of Angelina's testimony was her attention to the "utter disregard of the comfort of the slaves in little things." Slaves, to her knowledge, were given no bed, bedding or firewood, allowed no mosquito nets in a tropical climate, were fed only twice a day and never at table, not allowed to leave the house without permission, separated from their families, humiliated needlessly and constantly watched. She explained that she entered into a description of the "minutiae of slavery" because this part of the subject was often overlooked. "Slaveholders think nothing of them, because they regard their slaves as property, the mere instruments of their convenience and pleasure. One who is a slaveholder at heart never recognises a human being in a slave." [36]

Weld had been scrupulously careful to document all his evidence, but his evidence was entirely one-sided. It never occurred to him that a truly documentary approach might have included evidence on the other side. He would, to such an objection, have replied that the whole nation was flooded with information in defense of slavery, and further, that any system capable of such atrocities in such numbers could not be defended on any grounds. Besides, to Weld and the sisters such objections would have seemed immoral; they were not interested in writing with scientific objectivity — they were forging a powerful antislavery weapon.

And that it was — the most powerful pamphlet in the antislavery literature until the advent of *Uncle Tom's Cabin,* which is partially based on the content and wholly influenced by the spirit of *American Slavery As It Is.* It was printed in 1839 and soon sold more copies than any antislavery pamphlet ever written. Over 100,000 copies were sold in the first year; it was also widely distributed and read in Great Britain. [37]

The sisters found the months of work on this project both physically and emotionally exhausting. Angelina, in particular, was very wrought up by this intense exposure to Southern documents and the memories they recalled. The more so, since the finished pamphlet evoked a violently hostile response, when she sent it to members of her family. This is hardly surprising, but it is interesting that none of the family members ever disputed a single incident mentioned in the sisters' testimony. A few months after the publication, Mrs. Grimké, who had been ill for some time, died in Charleston. Anna Frost, who had attended her mother during her illness, informed Sarah and Angelina of her death with the comment that their mother had been spared "a bitter cup" in not having to read their "last infamous publication." [38]

"What we have written we have written from a deep and solemn sense of duty," Angelina replied. "It cost us more agony of soul to write these testimonies than any thing we ever did. . . . We wrote them to show the awful havock which arbitrary power makes in human hearts and to incite a holy indignation against an institution which degrades the *oppressor* as well as the oppressed." To Anna's suggestion that she had hidden cruelties which she herself had committed against slaves while still in Charleston, Angelina replied that she did not remember the incidents Anna hinted at, but would be glad to publish them, if Anna could remember them. "I have no wish to cover up my own sins, but will make use of it as an additional evidence of the horrible effects of the system." [39]

Sister Anna did not come up with any specific evidence and continued, as did the other sisters, a respectful and fairly friendly correspondence with Sarah and Angelina. They corresponded about the disposal of their mother's home and furnishings and carried out the sisters' instructions with regard to their inheritance and the slaves. Mrs. Grimké had, as promised, left her two slaves and their young children to Sarah and Angelina, who promptly arranged to free them. They continued to pay for the care of Stephen and offered to take him in, should he ever decide to come North. It must have been a special consolation to them to know that their mother, whom Sarah had told of the project they were working on, nevertheless treated them in her will exactly as she did her other children. Of all the Charleston family, their mother had proven to be the most understanding and tolerant of her radical renegade daughters.

CHAPTER
SIXTEEN

*If you could obtain but six signatures to such a petition
in only one state, I would say, send up that petition, and be
not in the least discouraged.*

Angelina E. Grimké,
Appeal to the Christian Women
of the South, *1836.*

THE AGENTS sent out by the American Anti-Slavery Society had done their work well. The number of abolition societies had more than doubled since 1835 and in 1837,
the peak year, reached 1006, with a membership of more
than 100,000.[1] Success and growth brought innovations in
method, a change of emphasis, decentralization and, eventu-
ally, a most serious organizational crisis.

Local societies spread the antislavery message through
three principal means: meetings with guest speakers, furnished by state and national leadership, the sale of tracts and
pamphlets provided by the national society, and the circulation of petitions. There was also a proliferation of state and
county antislavery papers, which eked out a precarious existence. The effect of meetings was, of course, purely local.
The antislavery press suffered from small circulation, which
was generally restricted to those already converted. It
reached a wider public only because the general press frequently reprinted abolitionist articles, even in distorted
form, in order to attack and refute them.

Tracts and pamphlets had proved disappointing as a method of reaching a wide audience. With a very few exceptions, of which *American Slavery As It Is* was the outstanding example, they were haphazardly used and there was no telling how effective they were. Even when efforts at systematic mailings were made, such as to members of Congress or selected groups of lawyers, there was no follow-up. They were an irritant in the South and became an excuse for censoring the mails and excluding all controversial literature from the Southern states.

It was otherwise with petitions. Here was a most effective way of reaching community and neighborhood with a simple, brief message and garnering immediate results in the form of signatures. It enabled the local societies to measure their appeal in a tangible, way, utilize antislavery literature as a direct means of influencing sympathizers and win new adherents. It also made it possible to overcome sectarianism and isolation. Through the use of similar petitions, the various local groups could combine their strength and call attention to their existence on a state and national level. Petitions were, of course, nothing new on the American scene. Individual slaves and voluntary societies had petitioned since colonial days. But these early antislavery memorials and petitions amounted to little more than random personal letters to which at times a number of people affixed their signatures.[2] The reform movements of the later 1820's discovered the potential power of petitions applied in a concerted way as an expression of the "popular will." By 1830 petitions reached the House in large numbers on such varied issues as the tariff, currency, the Bank, abolition of Sunday mail, support of the Cherokee Indians and the ten-hour day. Petitions served to give the ordinary person a sense of participation in the democratic process and provided a means for those outside the political power structure to make their weight felt. The innovation made by the antislavery societies in the 1830's was the use of petitions in a systematic way as a means of agitation and a basis for organization.

The American Anti-Slavery Society had recommended their use from its inception, but it was not until 1837 that petitioning became the major form of antislavery activity. This was largely owing to the influx of women into the movement. Women took to petitioning with enthusiasm and perseverance, probably because it was the only means of political expression open to them at the time. They had been shown the way by British abolitionist women, who had swamped Parliament with petitions by the tens of thousands and were largely credited with providing the final thrust of militancy which led to the passage of the British Emancipation Act in 1833. British women appealed directly to their American sisters to emulate their example. As early as 1830 the Philadelphia Female Anti-Slavery Society circulated petitions on a sporadic basis. In 1834 this became a regular activity and in 1837 the work was organized in a businesslike way.[3]

Angelina Grimké had, no doubt, already been involved in this activity when she wrote her *Appeal* in 1836 and urged Southern women to petition their legislatures. She pointed out that petitions were a particularly appropriate means of expression for women, even if progress were slow and results disappointing. "If you could obtain but six signatures to such a petition in only one state, I would say, send up that petition, and be not in the least discouraged."[4]

In 1837, the Anti-Slavery Convention of American Women appointed a central board in charge of petitions in Boston,

Philadelphia and New York. Its aim was to obtain one million signatures before the opening of the next Congress. Instructions and sample petitions were sent to all affiliated societies. Following a procedure similar to that of the American Anti-Slavery Society in its simultaneous national petition campaign, the local female societies appointed a petition chairman for each county, set goals and standards and followed up on results. The convention issued an appeal to women, stressing petitions as the "first and foremost object." It evoked the British example and shrewdly anticipated the organizational effect of this activity. A signature on a petition answered "a three-fold purpose. You not only gain the person's name, but you excite inquiry in her mind and she will excite it in others; thus the little circle imperceptibly widens until it may embrace a whole town." [5]

That this was a realistic appraisal can be seen from the experience of a young woman in Worcester, Massachusetts, which may be considered fairly typical. She had, in 1836, received some antislavery petitions from Maria Chapman in Boston and had gone from door to door with them in her hometown. From among the signers she won enough supporters to have more than a dozen women circulating petitions the following year. With this group and some new converts, a Female Anti-Slavery Society was formed in 1838.[6]

Petitioning taught women, who were inexperienced in political work, to be methodical, reliable and persevering. It was a practical lesson in committee work and did not always proceed smoothly. "Although we took good care to appoint what we considered a competent committee to circulate the petitions, yet it appears that some did not adhere to the injunction so often laid on them, to make each petitioner, if possible, write her own name," complained Abby Kelley from Lynn.[7]

It was tedious and often discouraging work. "My husband and I are busy in that most odious of all tasks, that of getting signatures to petitions. We are resolved that the business shall be done in this town more thoroughly than it has been heretofore. But, 'Oh Lord, sir!'" Lydia Maria Child complained with her usual good humor.[8]

Wealthy Juliana Tappan of New York spent many hours knocking on doors in her district and discovered, as did many of the other volunteers, that her own sex was ill-informed, apathetic toward larger social issues and ignorant of simple political facts. "Ladies sitting on splendid sofas looked at us as if they had never heard the word Texas and I presume some of them would be unable to say whether it was north or west or south of Louisiana, or whether or not it belonged to the United States." She reported finding a better and more intelligent reception in the homes of some colored people in her district.[9]

Angelina and Sarah had, as lecturers, done much to promote the petition campaign. Now, as housewives, they took an active part in the work. Early in 1839 Sarah told Jane Smith of her experiences collecting signatures in Fort Lee. She complained of the selfishness, unfeelingness and ignorance she met "almost everywhere. . . . One woman told me she had rather see the slaves all shot than liberated, another said she would sooner sign a petition to have them all hung, than set free; she complained bitterly that she was not paid enough for her work, but thought it all right that black people should work for nothing." But not all her neighbors were so hostile; many signed readily.[10]

This was true wherever petitions were circulated. Over half the memorials sent to Congress were signed by women and it is fair to assume more than half were circulated by them. "There would be but few abolition petitions if the

ladies . . . would let us alone," Congressman Walker from
Mississippi complained in the 24th Congress.[11]

The internal effect of the petition campaigns on the anti-
slavery movement was to develop leadership and efficiency
on a local level, thus strengthening the decentralizing tendencies already in existence. By involving large numbers of
volunteers in practical political work on a grass roots level, it
aroused their interest in political action. The next step was
to question political candidates on their views regarding
slavery, an innovation which soon became a standard
method of exerting pressure on candidates and office holders.
The development of political abolitionism and a third party
logically followed.

But the external effect of the petition campaign was even
more important. It was the effort of Southern Congressmen
to dam the flood of petitions which broadened the abolition
agitation into a free speech campaign. Each denial of free
speech to abolitionists by mobs, violence and repression had
increased the number of antislavery activists, but the fight
against the "gag rules" made the connection between slavery
and the denial of free speech persuasively clear to large
numbers of citizens who had been previously indifferent to
antislavery. This, more than anything else, widened the base
of the antislavery movement.

The rule establishing the practice of tabling without further action all petitions on the subject of slavery or the abolition of slavery, known as the Pinckney "gag," had passed the
House in May 1836. It was followed by yearly gag resolutions until, in 1840, the refusal to accept antislavery petitions
became a standing rule of the House. John Quincy Adams'
firm opposition to the first gag rule, despite his objection to
the content of the antislavery petitions, encouraged the

flooding of the House with these petitions. No longer were they signed only by abolitionists, but by all who wished to protest the denial of the right of petition. In fact, it was the Southerners' nervous reaction to the relatively few antislavery petitions before 1836 which unleashed the flood of petitions and the mass campaign against the gag-rule in 1837.[12]

The exact number of petitions is impossible to estimate. James Birney, in 1838, estimated that the total number of signatures on petitions to the third session of the 25th Congress had been one-half million. There were petitions on eight different topics, of which by far the most signatures were against the annexation of Texas and in favor of abolition of slavery in the District of Columbia. Birney's estimate covers only the period between January 1837 and March 1838 and lists only those petitions sent to Congressmen through the office of the American Anti-Slavery Society. A large number, possibly one fourth of the total, were sent by signers directly to their representatives.[13]

The number of signatures on the individual petitions increased year by year, an indication of the growing favorable popular response. In 1836–1837 there had been an average of 32 signatures on each petition, by 1839–1840 the number was 107. In April of 1838 the bundles of abolition petitions presented and tabled at that session filled a room $20 \times 30 \times 14$ feet, closely packed to the ceiling. By 1840 antislavery petitions were no longer received by the House and no record of their number is available. But John Quincy Adams noted during that session "a greater number of petitions than at any former session." [14]

For Angelina and Sarah the public events of 1839 were only of peripheral concern. After the exhausting months spent in the preparation of *American Slavery As It Is,* rest and diversion would have seemed indicated, at least for Angelina, who was expecting a baby. Instead, the summer of 1839 was taken up with an endless succession of houseguests and visitors.

Jane Smith and Sarah Douglass were among the earliest visitors, the former staying for a week, the latter, at her own suggestion, staying only one day. Afterward, Sarah Douglass thanked them for their hospitality and their "Christian conduct." But the sisters were not pleased with this polite gesture. "It seemed to me thy proposal 'to spend a day' with us," wrote Sarah, "was made under a little feeling something like this: 'Well, after all, I am not quite certain I shall be an acceptable visitor.'" She could well understand that her friend might feel that kind of apprehension, but hoped she could "rise above thy suspicions." Angelina put the matter more bluntly. She and Theodore had been disappointed that Sarah Douglass had come for only one day; they had hoped for a visit of at least a week. Sarah's gratitude for their "Christian conduct" had caused them pain. "In what did it consist? In receiving and treating thee as an equal. . . . Oh, how humbling to receive such thanks!" They understood that it was only the bitter experience of prejudice which could have made their friend react this way and they hoped that the time might soon come when she could "no longer write *such* a letter!" And she warmly suggested that next summer Sarah and her mother be their houseguests for a week.[15] This frank discussion of the difficulties inherent in their interracial friendship only deepened the relationship. Sarah Douglass was a frequent visitor thereafter and the sisters reciprocated when they came to Philadelphia.

Abby Kelley was their next visitor; she came not solely for social reasons. Already in 1838, at the New England Anti-

Slavery Convention in Boston, she had become the storm center of another struggle over "woman's rights." The meeting had, under Garrison's leadership, voted to accept women to membership and proceeded to elect Abby Kelley to one of the committees. This had unleashed a storm of protest on the part of the clerical members. Anti-Garrisonians seized upon the incident to bolster their charges that Garrison was dividing the movement by saddling it with irrelevant side issues. Garrison promptly added fuel to the flames by his active leadership in the organization of the Non-Resistance Society. This peace society, based on "ultra" perfectionist principles, declared itself opposed to any human government. Its members were pledged to abstain from voting, office holding and politics. Garrison not only organized the founding convention at Boston's Marlboro Chapel and drafted the Declaration of Sentiments, but he gave ample space to the proceedings and to Non-Resistance ideas in *The Liberator*. In his imperious manner, he acted as though henceforth Non-Resistance were to be a basic principle of abolitionism. The Welds and Sarah were greatly interested in these developments. They could and did approve completely of the equal participation of women in the antislavery societies, and defended Abby Kelley against all rumors that she had been domineering and overbearing in her behavior. They were, however, very cautious and reserved in regard to Non-Resistance, especially since they feared that this issue would only aggravate the deep personal and organizational rift developing in the movement. Maria Chapman and her circle in the Boston Female Society had followed Garrison loyally and had, for some time, unsuccessfully tried to commit the sisters to public support of their position. Now rumors had begun to circulate that the sisters were back-sliding, weakening in their dedication to the cause and leaving the field of battle. Abbe Kelley's visit was designed, at least in part, to clarify the truth of these rumors.

She reported to Mrs. Chapman that the sisters claimed not to have had time to study the subject of Non-Resistance and did not want to commit themselves. Weld, however, had strong opinions in opposition to Non-Resistance principles, and declared flatly that abolitionists who actively endorsed them were losing their usefulness to the antislavery cause. Regarding the charge that the sisters were leaving the field of battle, Abby Kelley was fair enough to admit that it was untrue. She delicately hinted at Angelina's condition and sadly described the state of "prostration" in which she had found her. She blamed it on the lasting exhaustion produced by the speaking tour, Angelina's illness and the shock produced by her research in Southern newspapers. Sarah found it impossible to leave her sister under the circumstances. Abby Kelley also reported that Angelina exerted herself "far too much in order to keep up *appearances* when in company." [16]

There was much company: Anna Frost, her daughter and son-in-law, Llewellyn Haskell, during the winter, Gerrit Smith and his wife early in the summer. In May 1839 the sisters went to Philadelphia for the Female Anti-Slavery Convention, but could not attend because of Angelina's ill health. They stayed for several weeks at Jane Smith's, taking a good rest. In July, all three made a visit to Weld's family in Manlius, stopping at Peterboro for a few days with the Gerrit Smiths.[17] In August, C. Stewart Renshaw, a former Lane student and antislavery agent, who expected to go to the West Indies as a missionary, lived at Fort Lee. A few weeks later, John Scoble, secretary of the British and Foreign Anti-

Slavery Society, came for a brief visit.[18] In the fall, Betsy Dawson, the former family slave who had been freed by Mrs. Frost, joined the household. She was in attendance, together with a midwife, when Angelina, on December 14, 1839, gave birth to a healthy nine-pound boy. Theodore and Sarah were also present; the birth was simple; all went to bed at nine and slept well.[19]

Unfortunately, the report "mother and child doing fine" was somewhat premature. The baby, whom they named Charles Stuart, was doing well, but Angelina was quite ill with mastitis, a "gathered breast," and for weeks was unable to nurse her baby. This upset her greatly, although the baby enjoyed his bottle feedings.

Angelina had never had any experience with small children, and found her baby a delight and a marvel. In line with her dietary ideas, she tried to follow too literally Graham's advice on not over-feeding babies and for several weeks kept the infant on an insufficient diet. In her inexperience she had no way of knowing that his listlessness and fretting were caused by her rigid feeding schedule. Then, during Angelina's first absence of a few days, Sarah decided to experiment and fed the baby as many bottles as he would take on self-demand. The result was a remarkably placid, cheerful baby. The young mother learned her first lesson in child raising and abandoned rigid principles for practical flexibility.[20]

Shortly after the baby's birth and most likely too soon for the health and comfort of the mother, the family made a move. Weld had for some time wanted a real farm, so as to reduce their living expenses and increase their income. Also, with their enlarged family and with all the visitors, they found their little house inadequate. In March 1840 Weld and the sisters bought a fifty-acre farm in Belleville, New Jersey, for $5750. The property was located along the Passaic River, slightly elevated from the road and surrounded by a stone wall. Two gigantic weeping willows flanked the entrance gate; the yard was filled with lilacs, pines and roses. In the garden grew grapes, berry bushes and fruit trees. There was a meadow and a woodlot, a run-down barn and corn crib and a fine Colonial stone house with a wooden addition at the rear. The fifteen-room house was well preserved and comfortable.[21]

Although the Welds and Sarah thought the new home a great improvement, the purchase had drawbacks. For one, it took all their ready cash; for another, the farm needed constant repair and improvements. Also, now that they had ample space, they could indulge their reckless hospitality to a point of physical and financial exhaustion. It was as though in a few short months the sisters and Weld wanted to make up for all the years in which they had not been able to enjoy the normal give-and-take of family and social life. They had a vast circle of friends and had, during the time of their "agency," depended on the hospitality of others. Not unnaturally, they now felt it a pleasure to reciprocate and every letter they wrote contained an urgent invitation to the recipient to spend a week with them on their farm. There is no doubt that they overdid it to the detriment of their own health and comfort, but selflessness was not only a habit with them, it was part of their way of life. Many abolitionists were equally generous — the hospitality of the Motts in Philadelphia, of Gerrit Smith in Peterboro and the Philbricks in Brookline was proverbial; the only difference was that these families could well afford their generosity.

The Welds could not, for Weld had recently taken a cut in

salary. The American Anti-Slavery Society was in serious financial difficulties, owing both to the depression and to the organizational crisis. Decentralizing tendencies had first manifested themselves in the refusal of local societies to make good their financial obligations toward the state organization. The states, in turn, defaulted on their promised pledges to the national office. "Better one dollar spent at Utica than three dollars spent at New York," said Alvan Stewart, the agent for Western New York, expressing the general sentiment. The hard-pressed New York office responded by sending its own agents into the states to collect the necessary — and previously promised — funds. This was a source of serious friction between the Massachusetts Anti-Slavery Society and Stanton and Gould, the fund-collection agents sent into the state on behalf of the New York executive committee. By 1838, the national office was in serious straits, its situation aggravated by the drying up of the usual source of emergency funds, the personal contributions of wealthy philanthropists. Many of these were, like the Tappan brothers, close to bankruptcy themselves because of the depression, and were unable to contribute with their usual largesse.

A year later, the twenty agents still in the field had to be dismissed for lack of funds, and Weld voluntarily cut his salary from $1000 a year to $700. But even this sum was partially owed him at the time he purchased the farm. Isaac Lloyd, who had promised to pay back the money he held for the sisters, kept stalling and delaying and in the end partially defaulted. Weld needed to get his fields manured and plowed, his fences repaired and his chickens housed. He appealed to Lewis Tappan for payment of the money due him, otherwise "I don't see but we must *stop eating* — at least we shall be pretty sure to stop SLEEPING." [22] Lewis Tappan lent him the necessary money and Weld worked hard all spring and summer to get his first crop into the ground. He was still holding down his job as editor of the Antislavery Almanac and continued to collect facts regarding the connection of the North with slavery.[23]

Angelina, who had been sick so much of the previous year and seriously ill after the birth of the baby, was expecting again. Still, her obligations as a housewife and hostess continued. Jane Smith came for a month; Weld's parents and sister Cornelia visited and looked around for a farm to buy in the neighborhood. Weld's brother Lewis came with his family and the oldest son stayed for the summer. Elizabeth Bascom, Angelina's childhood friend from Charleston, and her daughter, who were in debt and unable to support themselves, made their home with the Welds for a year. James Thome, who was working on antislavery research with Weld, brought his wife on a brief visit, which extended to several weeks, during which the wife had to be nursed through an illness. And so it went, not to mention the visitors who came for a day or two. Angelina barely found time to sew baby clothes and quilts for the new arrival and diapers for Charlie. Small wonder she gave vent to some exasperation. "Oh how I long to have our little family alone to sit down without any stranger at our meals. . . ." But that was too much to expect, and she added dutifully: "At present we have a young man from Oberlin who will remain until he finds a passage to Jamaica where he is going to teach the emancipated slaves." [24]

While the sisters were occupied with domestic concerns the antislavery movement passed through its greatest crisis. The petition campaign and the very success of the earlier

organizing drives, with their proliferation of abolition societies, had brought with them the seeds of dissension. In
1838, the "woman question" had driven the conservatives
and anti-feminists under Rev. Amos Phelps' leadership out of
the Massachusetts Anti-Slavery Society. A year later, at the
1839 state convention, Garrison was faced with organized
opposition, inspired by New York and directed by Stanton.
Garrison met this "plot" to undercut his leadership with a
spirited defense, in which the "woman question" emerged as
a handy club to use on his opponents. With the support of
the Negro and women abolitionists Garrison carried the day,
but a rival Massachusetts Abolition Society was formed and
a rival paper, *The Massachusetts Abolitionist*, with Elizur
Wright as editor, was set up. A similar division between radicals and conservatives soon split the state's female abolition
society into two rival factions.

As the "woman question" served Garrison to separate the
contending parties, so "political action" served the anti-
Garrisonians. At the 1839 national meeting the two groups
clashed again; this time the advocates of political action had
their way, beating down Garrison's resolution that abolitionist participation in electoral activity would imperil the integ-
rity of the movement.[25]

After this confrontation the factions polarized. There
emerged, essentially, two large groups: a radical-utopian
group under Garrison's leadership and a more orthodox-
practical one under Tappan, Stanton, and Birney. Their
differences were quite basic, not on long-range goals but on
tactics. The radical-utopian wing was concerned with conducting a moral crusade and bearing witness to arouse the
conscience of the nation. It was quite uninterested in numbers of adherents, but deeply concerned with keeping its pu-

rity of purpose. It refused to compromise, taking abstract principles to their most extreme consequences. It saw its chief aim as being an effective irritant of complacent and indifferent minds. In this it often succeeded, precisely when it used the most shocking tactics.

The orthodox-practical wing was as firmly committed to immediate emancipation as were the Garrisonians. Where they differed was in method and outlook. While the Garrisonians had given up all hope of forming viable alliances and put their trust in utopian and millennial conversions, they became more and more convinced that their hope lay in coalition. They were careful not to alienate the clergy and respectable community leadership; they welcomed the broadening support to be derived from the free-speech issue, and experimented with various forms of political activity which would later culminate in a third-party movement. Their tactic was to win allies; they were interested in numbers and votes and in tangible pressure on the power structure. They represented the forward-moving current in the antislavery movement, the current moving toward an antislavery coalition with ever vaguer and more pragmatically diffuse principles.

That the split occurred between these two factions was necessary in order to break out of sectarian isolation. Typically, in the American setting, factionalism is the symptom of a weak minority movement trying to find new organizational forms. The most radical leadership, unable to admit that its methods are no longer valid, turns utopian and retreats into isolation in order to maintain its purity of purpose, while the majority compromises its program in order to win alliances. The abolitionist factions, debating woman's rights, financial arrangements, intemperate language and political action, were actually talking past each other, no longer using the same vocabulary. An open split was not only inevitable, but both sides knew it would come at the 1840 national convention.

In April 1840 a national Abolitionist Nominating Convention in Albany, New York, decided to form the Liberty Party and nominate James Birney for President and Thomas Early of Pennsylvania for Vice-President. Birney, Stanton, the Tappans, Gerrit Smith, Leavitt, Alvan Stewart and Myron Holley now stood firmly and publicly committed to political action. Garrison regarded their position as a betrayal of principle, accused them of acting from motives of personal ambition, and determined to stop them from turning the national society into a political party. He aroused all his followers to the expected crisis and urged their attendance at the anniversary. Concerned with providing maximum attendance of Garrison's adherents at the anniversary meeting in New York, John Collins chartered a steamer, which waived discrimination rules so that Negro and white abolitionists could travel together. This boatload of New England men and women, nearly 450 of them, provided a handy voting bloc for Garrison among the more than 100 delegates at the meeting.

The political abolitionists had been as vituperative and abusive of their former co-workers as the Garrisonians. Lewis Tappan was particularly embittered at the turn of events and decided that unless the middle-of-the-road political action group's views could prevail, there was no sense in maintaining the national organization any longer. "Our organization is a stench in the nostrils of the nation, and the approaching meeting will increase it," he complained to Weld.[26] Fearful that the other faction would capture the so-

ciety, the executive committee of the American Anti-Slavery
Society transferred *The Emancipator* to the New York state
society and the books and debts of the national to Lewis
Tappan and S. W. Benedict, ostensibly for the purpose of
liquidating the debts. This in fact dissolved the American
Anti-Slavery Society before the anniversary, and was an action bitterly denounced by the Garrisonians. The political
abolitionists in turn made every effort to pack the meeting
and control the outcome.

The crisis came quickly when the acting chairman, Francis Jackson of Boston, appointed a business committee of ten
men, including Lewis Tappan, and one woman, Abby Kelley.
Objections to the nomination of women were raised from
the floor; a lively debate followed. The vote went 560 to 450
in favor of Miss Kelley, giving a clear indication that the
Garrisonians could control the meeting. Thereupon Lewis
Tappan, Amos Phelps and Charles Denison refused to serve
on the committee and Tappan invited all who had voted with
him to withdraw from the meeting and form a new society.
All but one of the members of the old executive committee
and most of the ministers joined the walkout and proceeded
to form the American and Foreign Anti-Slavery Society, its
membership specifically limited to male abolitionists and
with *The Emancipator* as its newspaper. The Garrisonians
took over what was left of the old American Anti-Slavery
Society, set up the *National Anti-Slavery Standard* with Nathaniel P. Rogers as editor, and elected women to the permanent executive committee.

Thus the schism was formalized and final. Both splinter
groups were seriously weakened, neither of them was ever
again able to exert effective national leadership. The anti-
slavery focus had shifted to the state organizations and political abolitionism was the coming trend.

To Weld and the sisters these developments were distressing and painful. Weld had the closest ties to the New York executive committee, to the Tappans, Stanton, Wright and Gerrit Smith, all of whom were intimate personal friends. He had early taken a vigorous stand against perfectionism and "Non-Resistance" and continued to do his best to influence others against these doctrines. He had always tended to stress local leadership as against central authority and was particularly hostile to the kind of personal leadership exerted by Garrison. The strife, contention and personality feuds he saw among abolitionists revolted him and only strengthened his determination to stay away from organizational meetings, conventions, anniversaries and all they entailed. He had no faith or enthusiasm for political action and especially not for third party movements, but he could very clearly perceive the potential power of such activity. By temperament, background and training he was committed to the Tappan-Stanton-Birney group, but he could not accept their political action program and their stand against the participation of women.

The sisters had closer personal ties to the Garrison-Chapman-Wright group and were, by experience and background, more inclined to accept the ultra-radical utopian stance of that group. In addition, their friends in the Philadelphia society were in the Garrison camp, although their methods and attitudes were much more flexible than those of the New Englanders. But the sisters' commitment to petitions, their interest in the influencing of political candidates, the educational work they had done, which was designed to convert men in places of power — all this reinforced the tradition of legal thinking and confidence in the Constitution in which they had been raised. Of the two, Sarah was perhaps more utopian, unrealistic and anarchistic, while Angelina had a much more rational and practical approach to political questions. But it was obvious, to both the Welds and Sarah, that they could not make a clear-cut decision between those who favored woman's rights and rejected political action and those who enthusiastically endorsed political action and excluded women from participation in it. To them, the split was a personal disaster. All they could do was temporarily withdraw from activity, rather than engage in a bitter and hopeless "family feud."

On January 3, 1841, Angelina gave birth to another son. They named him Theodore. This time they had hired a nurse for the baby, an English girl who was a great help to Angelina. Reassured by her presence and with adequate rest and care, Angelina was able to nurse her baby. She had abundant milk and was soon able to take care of the infant by herself. "I cannot tell thee what a comfort it is to me to nurse him," she wrote to a friend. She had feared that she would love the new baby more than she loved Charlie, but it was not so. "I love Charles the better of the two still, for towards him my soul was drawn out in sympathy and sorrow and suffering. I do not believe I can ever love a child as I love him." [27]

Her guilt feelings regarding Charlie were not unnatural in an age in which breast feeding was taken for granted as a normal part of motherhood. But they must have been greatly aggravated by the attacks to which she had been subjected for her stand on woman's rights. One can well imagine that this young mother, who had married relatively late in life amid a chorus of dire predictions, regarded her inability to nurse her first child as a divine judgement against her and that she must have awaited with fear and dread the birth of her next child. The happy denouement of the second birth undoubtedly wiped out some of these bad memories and anxieties, but their effect remained profound. It must have greatly increased in later years when this very baby, Theodore, was afflicted by an incurable and mysterious ailment which became the burden and grief of his family for many years. There is no doubt that both physically and psychologically the first three years of her marriage were a turning point in Angelina's life.

Her husband, describing the years of her "invalidism" which date from this period, explained that she had always been in good health except for having little muscular strength. Occasional fainting spells were preceded by periods of "nervous prostration" and "anxiety from which later years were never exempt. With these exceptions and the chronic effects of certain bodily injuries, her health was uniformly good." So much so that she had only one serious illness in her life, the typhoid fever attack at the end of the speaking tour from which, according to her husband, "she never wholly recovered." The bodily injuries Weld explained discreetly as follows: "Early in her married life, she was twice severely injured. These injuries, though wholly unlike, were in their effect a unit, one causing, the other intensifying a life-long weakness. Together they shattered incurably her nervous system. The one was wholly internal; the other caused a deep wound which never healed." This vague and unscientific explanation was accepted by Catherine Birney, the Grimké sisters' biographer and personal friend, as accounting for Angelina's ensuing poor health. It has never been re-evaluated. The search for an alternate explanation is intriguing and frustrating. There is no reference of any kind to an accident during this early period. It seems most unlikely that, had there been an accident involving a

well-known reformer like Angelina, the ample correspondence available from these years, when the farm was constantly crowded with visitors, would not have revealed a
single item of corroborating evidence.[28]

A more plausible explanation is offered by several references made by Sarah years later, which indicate that "accident" is a euphemism for a "female condition," which may
have occurred between the first and second pregnancies and
which, apparently, was greatly aggravated by succeeding
pregnancies following quickly one upon the other. In correspondence with her friend Harriot Hunt, the first female
medical practitioner in the United States, Sarah referred to
this condition as a prolapsed uterus, so severe that at times
it protruded externally, causing great pain. This condition,
which with modern medical knowledge is easily corrected,
was incurable during Angelina's lifetime. The second "injury" referred to by Weld may have been a miscarriage between the second and the third baby; or, possibly, Weld was
referring to a hernia condition which developed later.[29] This
too, readily repairable with modern surgical techniques, was
incurable in the mid-nineteenth century and, remaining un-
treated, was at times a source of excruciating pain and for
the rest of Angelina's life a source of discomfort. She shared
the fate of countless nineteenth-century women who were
doomed by medical ignorance, inadequate obstetrical care
and too frequent pregnancies to suffer chronic disabilities
and pain with patient resignation as God-given — the normal
"trials" of a woman's life.

But Angelina Grimké was no ordinary woman; she was an
exception, the "new" woman. To see her worn out by the
daily struggle with household chores, child care, ill health
and financial worries, was to admit that "women's rights"

was as yet little more than a dream. Weld and Sarah, in circulating the story of Angelina's "accidents," were being not only Victorian, but also somewhat defensive. For neither of them could have borne the thought that Angelina's gifts had been stifled by anything as prosaic as childbearing and domesticity. Accidents of an unmentionable nature were much more "providential." Weld had no intention of cutting short his wife's public career nor did he believe that this was an inevitable consequence of marriage. He would have been aggrieved at such a charge and would have angrily denied it. Actually, Angelina and Sarah continued to be active in both the abolition and woman's rights movements. But the nature and intensity of their activity was changed; they were never again in the front lines nor in the active leadership. For this an explanation had to be offered, both to their contemporaries and to themselves. The story of the accidents served well and removed both the question of guilt and the necessity for digging more deeply into the problems opened up by the campaign for woman's rights. There was, of course, no conscious deception here; both Sarah and Weld believed firmly in Angelina's weakness, debility and infirmity which she bore with the patience of a saint. Angelina lived, in fact, to the age of seventy-two, through typhoid and influenza epidemics, and on a diet which would be considered seriously inadequate by modern health standards. Except for her deliveries, she never consulted a doctor. She was constantly active, both physically and mentally, except for the very last years of her life. It is therefore difficult to give credence to Weld's story that she was "hardly able to lift an empty teakettle." [30]

There is no doubt, however, that married life made a decisive difference. "How many changes have come over the spirit of the dream," Abby Kelley wrote with a touch of compassion, after seeing Angelina tired and ill in the spring of 1839.[31] But Angelina had not given up her "dream"; she could not and never would give up her struggle for fuller social participation. The fact is that neither she nor Sarah ever "retreated" from public life. They simply entered a different phase of activity.

Before Angelina's marriage they had functioned as spinsters, independent, wealthy and free from personal responsibilities. In the early years of the marriage they had continued their writing and petitioning and were active in the organization of antislavery women. Sarah gave a speech in Philadelphia and both were certain that they would soon return to active participation in the conventions.

Then about 1840, when the split developed in the antislavery movement, they and Weld refrained from activity for a period. This was a deliberate political decision on their part. It was only in 1841 that domestic problems began to stand in the way of activity for both sisters. At that time Weld had returned to active involvement in the antislavery movement, which left the domestic burdens entirely in the hands of the two women.

It was during this period that ill health, poverty and domestic problems became the kind of personal obstacles they have always been in the way of active social participation of women. It was one thing to advance the slogan of woman's equality and her equal rights in society, it was quite another to live that equality and make it come true. Angelina and Sarah, for the first time in their lives, began to understand what the "woman question" was all about. They were no longer sheltered by wealth, privilege or spinsterhood from the basic problem that was to haunt the average woman for the next century: how to have enough energy left over after a day of cooking, housework and childcare to concern herself with issues outside of the home or to do anything about them, even if she cared. The theoretical debate over "woman's sphere" had not yet reached the point where this basic problem could even be debated. Nor had the social structure of society reached the point where it might be amenable to a solution. But the Grimké sisters, at long last, were no longer debating it — they were living the full and common lives of ordinary women.

CHAPTER
SEVENTEEN

Where is Theodore D. Weld and his wife, and Sarah M.
Grimké? All "in the quiet," and far removed from all strife!
. . . Once the land was shaken by their free spirits, but
now they are neither seen nor felt.

Wm. L. Garrison,
The Liberator, Aug. 12, 1842.

EARLY IN 1840 Henry Stanton brought his young bride to
visit the Welds. The announcement of Stanton's impending marriage to Elizabeth Cady had been greeted with
less than enthusiasm by his abolitionist friends, who feared
that the pampered, wealthy girl would hamper Stanton's
antislavery work. Sarah and Angelina had already heard
about Judge Cady's daughter from Gerrit Smith, whose
cousin she was. What they had heard had been enough to
arouse their curiosity. Young Elizabeth had spent many
months at the Smith home in Peterboro. She had had ample
opportunity to contrast the stiff, formal respectability of her
father's conservative home with the unorthodox spirit and
the enthusiasm of the reformers and radicals who were always welcome guests at the Smiths. It was here she had met
Henry Stanton. She had married him after a brief romance,
despite her father's strong objections. Judge Cady had little
use for his son-in-law's heretical opinions and feared, with
some justice, that he would be a poor provider. But Elizabeth had heretical ideas of her own. For years she had sat in

her father's law office, observing with increasing frustration the many women who brought their complaints to Judge Cady hoping for redress, only to be told that the law in almost every respect discriminated against women. These offending laws seemed thoroughly "bad" to Elizabeth and she once had childishly attempted to cut them out of her father's law books, so that he might be able to help his female clients.[1] She had learned since that it took more than scissors to change bad laws; her sympathies were with the reformers, but her enthusiasm was as yet vague and unfocused. Sarah Grimké, who could look back to similar experiences in her own childhood, appeared to Elizabeth Stanton an admirable heroine. She awaited meeting the sisters with eager anticipation.

The Stantons, accompanied by Charles Stuart, Weld's old friend, arrived in Belleville after a long, tiring drive and were greeted warmly by their hosts. Still, the young bride was somewhat disappointed. "There was nothing attractive at first sight in those plain, frail women, except their rich voices, fluent language, and Angelina's fine dark eyes. The house . . . was severely destitute of all tasteful, womanly touches, and though neat and orderly, had a cheerless atmosphere." The peculiar table arrangements under the influence of "the Graham dispensation" only increased the young visitor's disappointment, for instead of the hot beefsteak and steaming tea she had anticipated, they were greeted by cold dishes, served in utter simplicity with only the "memories of tea and coffee for stimulus."[2] Under the impact of three days of earnest and wide-ranging conversation to which the young bride listened with "pleasure and benefit," these first impressions soon wore off. The atmosphere of that home seemed transformed, the simplicity admirable, the hospitality unsurpassed, the "sacrifice of wealth and fame and ease" positively heroic. Those talks, young Elizabeth later remembered, were of lasting benefit to her. The sisters also revised their preconceived notions of Henry Stanton's bride and warmed to her keen intelligence, high spirits and quick enthusiasm. Their first contact ripened into a lasting friendship.

In the following months Elizabeth, through her informative, well-written letters, kept them in touch with one of the momentous events in reform history. The sisters had themselves been invited as delegates to attend the World's Anti-slavery Convention, meeting in London in June 1840, but had had to refuse because of ill health and family obligations. Henry Stanton, however, was one of the delegates, and brought along his bride on this somewhat unconventional honeymoon trip.

The London convention had been called by the executive committee of the British and Foreign Anti-Slavery Society, who invited "friends of the slave of every nation and clime." Forewarned that the Massachusetts society might send female delegates, the sponsors subsequently qualified this invitation by a second one, which specified that "gentlemen only" were expected to attend. Actually, it was a "world" convention in name only, all arrangements being under the firm domination of a self-appointed committee of the British society. As had been expected, the Massachusetts Anti-Slavery Society sent Ann Phillipps and Emily Winslow among its accredited delegates, with Abby Southwick representing the Boston Female Society. From Philadelphia came Lucretia Mott, Abbie Kimber, Elizabeth Neall and Mary Grew, with Sarah Pugh as the official delegate of the Female Society. The question of seating these delegates became the subject of heated controversy, which occupied the entire first day's session.³ The American speakers divided clearly along organizational lines. The Garrison group, under Wendell Phillips' leadership, defended the right of women to attend on the grounds that they were duly elected representatives of their organizations. The New Organization position was taken by James Birney, who pointed to the recent split in the American movement and the exclusion of women from one section of it. To Elizabeth Stanton's dismay, Charles Stuart took the antifeminist view. The vote finally went overwhelmingly against the seating of the women delegates. It is noteworthy that Henry Stanton, although a representative of the New Organization, voted for the seating of women.

The decision made, the women were escorted to the gallery, there to sit behind a curtain during the remaining sessions. Mrs. Stanton, out of a sense of solidarity, joined them. Lucretia Mott's fellow delegates from the Old Organization — Garrison, Nathaniel Rogers and Charles Remond — arrived only after the credentials controversy had been settled. In a dramatic gesture of protest, all three took their seats with the rejected delegates and refused to participate in the convention proceedings.

Underlying this procedural squabble were, of course, more complex issues. British abolitionists were gravely concerned with the rift in the American movement. The Garrisonians, who understood very well that what was at stake at the convention was the moral and financial support of British abolitionists for one faction or the other, naturally sought to demonstrate their militant leadership. Cognizant of the important role women had played in the British movement, they expected to carry the day with their advocacy of woman's rights. But they had overestimated the militancy of

British reformers on this subject and failed to take into consideration the undercurrent of religious factionalism which complicated the picture. Lucretia Mott and several of the Philadelphia female delegates were Hicksite Quakers, while the leadership of the British abolition society was firmly in Orthodox Quaker hands. The suspicion that religious, as well as anti-feminist prejudices were at work, were advanced at the time of the convention by several delegates in the know.[4] They maintained that, had Mrs. Mott been an Orthodox Quaker, the women would have been seated or, conversely, that any group of Hicksite Quakers, regardless of sex, would have met with similar difficulties. This analysis seems somewhat weakened by the fact that Lucretia's husband was seated without difficulty, although he and his wife were ostracized outside the convention by Orthodox Quakers. The fact remains that the London convention only aggravated the rift among American antislavery people and is remembered not for its accomplishments in promoting abolition, but for its projection of the "woman question" onto the international scene. This was largely owing to the fortuitous meeting of Lucretia Mott and Elizabeth Cady Stanton.

The two women's immediate liking for one another grew into mutual respect, as they spent many hours discussing the convention and its implications. Mrs. Mott found in young Elizabeth the aggressive boldness she lacked, while Elizabeth sensed in the older woman the mature leadership and steadfastness of purpose that was, as yet, wanting in her. During one of their long talks the two women concluded that something must be done to break down the prevailing prejudices against women. Something must be done and they would do it — upon their return to America they would call together a convention of American women. This was, for both, a momentous decision. Although eight years would elapse before they were able to carry it out, it was, in fact, the decision which launched the international movement for woman's rights.[5]

Mrs. Stanton reported on all these matters in her letters to the Welds. Perhaps in anticipation of the work she and Lucretia Mott were planning, she tried to solicit the active support of the sisters. "Lucretia Mott . . . thinks you have both been in a state of reticency long enough and that it is not right for you to be still [any] longer; that you should either write for the public or speak out for *oppressed* woman. . . . She says a great struggle is at hand and that all the friends of freedom for woman must rally around the Garrison *standard*." As though further to encourage the sisters she reported that their names were well known among English reformers and "always mentioned with great enthusiasm." And she added with her usual spontaneous warmth: "Dear friends how much I love you!! What a trio! for me to love. You have no idea what a hold you have on my heart." [6]

Although Sarah had, at first, deplored the sending of women delegates for fear that it would be a divisive move, she changed her mind after reading Elizabeth Stanton's account. "One thing is very clear, I think . . . that the Convention had no right to reject the female delegates; as members of the Antislavery Society they were entitled to a seat unless it could be proved that they were not persons." [7]

At this point in their lives neither of the sisters could show more than theoretical interest in the events at London. The Welds had recognized for some time that Angelina's resolve to do without domestic help was impractical; now they experienced the trials and tribulations of managing a household which kept constantly getting larger and more complicated.

Soon after the birth of Theodore they had accepted Betsy Dawson's daughter and her husband as tenant farmers. Weld had, at the time, the offer of a more favorable tenancy arrangement from a white farmer, but felt it his "duty and privilege to do what he could for Betsy Dawson's family." The nurse they had hired for the baby had to leave after a few months and there followed a succession of inadequate domestics, widows with children to support, young girls who needed training.[8]

The fourth and last slave the sisters had inherited and freed, Stephen, had finally chosen to come North. The sisters felt obliged to take him in, as they had promised, although he proved to be a considerable liability. He had two fits within twenty-four hours of his arrival; "his mind was weakened" and he had to be directed in every step. He had a bad temper, poor work habits, was slovenly and inefficient and did not take well to instruction. Still, the sisters regarded it as their duty to try and rehabilitate this "broken victim of slavery." They kept him for several years and paid him wages, although his services hardly warranted it. Angelina frankly admitted that he was hard to bear and that "the Lord was trying our principles pretty closely." After a number of years, they had the satisfaction of seeing him recover in body and spirit. He rented, then purchased, a little farm of his own and in his old age became a much respected member of his community.[9]

During the summer of 1841 Weld was in such serious financial trouble that he twice had to borrow money from Lewis Tappan. He hoped, by stringent economy measures and hard work, to put his farm in better shape and make the necessary repairs himself. He was also hopeful that he would be able to lecture again. His voice had improved so greatly that he was able to give several brief public speeches without ill effect and he looked forward to occasional lecturing, when all his plans were suddenly changed by an urgent call to Washington in the antislavery cause.[10]

The determination of Southern Congressmen to close the floor of Congress to the discussion of the slavery question had been met by staunch resistance from John Quincy Adams, who for years had carried on a lonely, seemingly hopeless fight against the annual gag rules. Recently, he had been reinforced by a small group of abolitionist Whig Congressmen, who were as determined as he to keep the question alive before the nation. Whig party leadership, although unsympathetic, tolerated the rhetorical forays of this little band in the hopes of embarrassing the Democrats. But in 1841 the gag rule had been made a standing rule of the House. Unless they wanted to concede that they had, indeed, been effectively gagged, the antislavery men would have to use new and bolder means of agitating the question. If petitions could be barred, Congressmen were still free to speak on whatever topic they chose. The little band decided to take the offensive by delivering a series of frontal attacks on slavery, not merely limiting themselves to defending the right of petition. These speeches they hoped to distribute widely under their franking privileges and by utilizing newspaper reprints. But they were overburdened with practical work and had no time for research and careful preparation. It was for this reason that they approached Theodore Weld.[11]

The leadership of this group was in the hands of Joshua Reed Giddings of Ohio, a persistent fighter, who had been introduced into the antislavery movement by Weld himself. Next in importance and devotion to abolition were William Slade of Vermont and Seth Gates of New York. Supporting them were John Mattocks of Vermont, Sherlock Andrews of Ohio, Nathaniel Borden of Massachusetts and Francis James of Pennsylvania. These eight men, including Adams, had been working closely with Joshua Leavitt, editor of *The Emancipator,* long a close co-worker of Weld's. It was Leavitt's suggestion to set up a sort of antislavery research bureau and put Weld in charge of it. Weld perceived the potential value of the move at once. "Those men are in a position to do for the Anti-Slavery cause by a single speech more than our best lecturers can do in a year." The impact on the general public would be great; it might even serve to convince third-party abolitionists of the tactical error they were committing. The country was not ready for the Liberty Party, but it would have to listen to the abolitionist Whigs. "I dare not assume the responsibility of refusing to comply with such a request," Weld quickly concluded.[12]

As often before and after, practical considerations were swept aside. Economy measures on the farm would have to wait, meanwhile help would have to be hired to do the jobs Weld had planned to do over the winter. The Congressmen had offered to supply him with money for travel, upkeep and expenses while in Washington, but he would draw no salary for his labors. For the first time in his life, and not without inner struggle, Weld asked Lewis Tappan for an outright gift to defray his expenses at home. He received the forty dollars he had asked for promptly. He hired a carpenter to make the most essential repairs and, leaving the women to manage for themselves, Weld departed.[13]

Angelina cooperatively accepted his departure and the separation, because she was glad to know that he was doing the work that suited him best. Although Weld constantly preached the blessings of farm work, Angelina always considered it a waste of his talents. At first her letters to her husband were cheerful and newsy. She and sister were managing quite well, she had even done a little writing. She and Sarah had been circulating a temperance petition from house to house. Their current houseguest, a missionary awaiting his assignment, had decided to stay the winter, although they had told him they could not afford to give him a fire in his room. C. S. Renshaw repaid them for their hospitality by instructive theological and philosophical discussions. "You see we are using our minds a little," Angelina reported. Despite his absorption with the work he was doing, Weld chafed under the enforced absence from his family. He had innumerable questions about domestic details and the progress of the children, which Angelina tried to answer fully. In her turn, she queried her husband with eager interest about the political events in which he was participating and tried to inform herself by carefully reading and clipping the newspapers. Their correspondence had something of the affectionate tenderness and that mixture of personal and political concerns which had characterized the correspondence of their courtship days. Yet in Angelina's letters there was a recurrent theme of weariness and every indication that she was leaning heavily on Sarah for support.[14]

Weld had much news of interest to report. On his first visit to John Quincy Adams the old patriarch had particularly inquired after Angelina, to whom he claimed to be related through his grandmother. Weld was delighted with this information, for it proved that he and Nina were sixth cousins, Weld's father and Adams being second cousins. He had also several times heard Angelina's cousin, Robert Barnwell Rhett, speak in Congress, but had no desire to meet this inveterate apologist for slavery.[15]

Weld worked at the Library of Congress most of the day and in his room at Mrs. Spriggs' boardinghouse until late at night. Some of his time was taken up with the case of the *Creole,* a slave ship whose cargo had revolted. But most of Weld's attention was focused on the brilliant, if somewhat eccentric campaign of "Old Man Eloquent," the self-appointed gadfly of the House on the petition question. Adams used every parliamentary trick at his command to break the gag rule, including the introduction of pro-slavery petitions asking for his removal as chairman of the Foreign Affairs Committee. He had finally enraged the Southerners to the point where they used a technicality to bring a motion of censure against him. But it was a technicality Adams had carefully laid in their path; faced with censure, he demanded the right to defend himself, which had to be granted. Adams' "defense" lasted over a week, during which time the old ex-President managed to bring every aspect of the slavery question before the attention of the nation — the very thing the gag resolutions had been designed to prevent. Adams paid his enemies back blow for blow; in the end he won their grudging personal admiration — the motion to censure him was tabled forever. Coolly exploiting this amazing triumph, Adams proceeded to bring up nearly two hundred petitions before the House adjourned. "Slave holding, slave trading and slave breeding absolutely quailed and howled under the dissecting knife," Weld reported. "The triumph of Mr. Adams is complete. This is the first victory over the slaveholders in a body ever yet achieved since the foundation of the government, and from this time their downfall takes its date." [16]

Joshua Giddings agreed with this over-optimistic statement. "I am confident that the charm of the slavepower *is now broken,*" he wrote.[17] But Weld was more precise in his second judgment. "That slavery has *begun* its fall is plain, but . . . its fall will be resisted by those who cling to it. . . . The end will be slow. Woe to abolitionists, if they dream that their work is well nigh done." [18] A few weeks later, presenting his resolutions in connection with the *Creole* case, Giddings was met with a motion of censure against him, which carried. The Whig regulars repudiated him; he resigned his seat and returned to Ohio to place his case before the voters. Giddings' re-election was another antislavery victory, which signaled the inability of the Whig party to silence its antislavery dissenters. The gag, designed to keep the lid on the troublesome issue, had only resulted in raising a lot of steam. As Weld had sensed, the second session of the 27th Congress, to which he had made his modest and silent contribution, proved to be a milestone in the antislavery struggle.

By April, Weld returned to the farm. He worked with a fury, instituted new economy measures and had the pleasure of giving weekly lectures in New Jersey. Lewis Tappan tried to convince him to take over a church, but Weld was no longer interested in the ministry. He returned to Washington for the 1842 winter session of Congress, leaving his farm only slightly improved, his finances as disordered as ever and his wife expecting their third child.

Angelina tried bravely to face the separation. "You could not have been called from home at a more favorable time for me," she wrote assuringly, "for I have entirely got over the miserable feelings I had some weeks ago. I do not need your help now as much as I shall do two months hence. . . . But, Beloved, I miss you more than I can express. I can't think of you or talk of you without my heart and eye filling." In letter after letter she discussed her problems and difficulties with Weld, always seeking his counsel as though he were the embodiment of wisdom. Soon, in a year or so, it would be up to her to instruct and teach her children, yet she was ignorant herself. "My mind has run down for some years, it is only this winter that I have read." How could she give instruction, unless she progressed herself? Had she done right in devoting her spare time to reading and study or should she make an effort to spend more time with the children? She felt guilty about burdening Sarah with their care, but she seemed to have only enough energy to mind them for a few hours at a time. She could not bear her physical weakness with any degree of patience.[19]

As it happened, Weld was not able to be with his wife when she needed him most. While he was in Washington, Angelina became quite ill. In February 1843 she had a miscarriage. Weld returned home a few weeks later, anxious to resume charge of his family. His farm was badly neglected and he worked feverishly, setting out hundreds of fruit trees, planting his fields and repairing the buildings.[20]

A few months later, Angelina, barely recovered, was expecting again. This time, although her husband was home and she was relieved of most responsibilities, she was anxious and despondent. In this mood she was receptive to a religious fanaticism from which, in a more active period of her life, her common-sense particality would have recoiled.

Starting in the 1830's the "burned-over" districts of upper New York, western Vermont and Massachusetts had been swept by a succession of revivals and utopian religious movements. The harsh struggle for existence, aggravated by the economic upheavals created by the opening of the Erie Canal and the ensuing competition with Western agriculture, had driven the younger farmers to migration. The remnant found solace in radical religious movements, of which Millerism was the latest manifestation. William Miller, a self-

appointed prophet, fixed the date of the second coming of
Christ with precision for October 12, 1843, at three A.M. That
night passed disappointingly, with the almost one million followers of Miller in a state of high tension, many of them having abandoned their families and businesses to await the day
of judgment on rooftops, clothed only in shrouds. Rapid re-
calculation convinced Miller and his charismatic disciple,
the Rev. Joshua V. Himes, that the date was actually sometime in March 1844 or possibly the following October, depending on how certain Biblical passages were interpreted.
But without doubt, the final day of judgment was near.[21]

A young friend of Angelina's had recently died in child-
birth. This fact, her own miscarriage and the prophecies of
imminent disaster and holocaust, timed for the period when
her baby was due, filled Angelina with morbid forebodings.
But the second day of the Millerite prophecy passed as un-
eventfully as had the first.

On March 22, 1844, without complications or difficulty,
Angelina was delivered of a healthy daughter, who was
named Sarah Grimké Weld. Angelina regained her physical
strength rapidly; it took her considerably longer to come to
some adjustment with her disappointed belief. She gave
considerable time and thought to finding an explanation for
the failure of Miller's prophecy. In a long letter to her sister
Sarah, about a year later, she revealed that she had passed
through a deep personal and spiritual crisis and had arrived
at a new faith. "Although I was deeply interested in Miller's
views yet my soul could never anchor on them." The mistake
of the Millerites had been in expecting the second coming of
Christ to reveal Him in human form. This was an error, for

it is not necessary that Christ should be *visible* to our
fleshly eyes in order that he should reign in the world.

. . . I fully believe in the downfall of every earthly
throne, the overthrow of every political government, the
annihilation of every Ecclesiastical Establishment and
the dissolution of every sect and party under the sun. I
feel the rocking of that great earthquake which is to
shake down and whelm forever all organizations, institutions, and every social framework of human device;
but I am calm, hopeful, happy, for I see arising out of
their ruins the Everlasting Kingdom of God.[22]

Such chiliastic rhetoric Angelina had hitherto confined to
prophecies regarding the downfall of slavery. But her involvement with Millerism and utopian religion was short-
lived and did not recur. It should be regarded not so much
as an ideological aberration, but as an emotional response to
a profound crisis in Angelina's life.

A curious reference in the correspondence of Lucy Stone
suggests that this crisis may also have affected Angelina's
views of marriage. Lucy Stone, in a letter to her brother,
which has not been preserved, apparently cited Angelina
Weld as an example and authority for the view that bearing
children at too frequent intervals was injurious to the health
of women; therefore couples should practice sexual inter-
course only for the propagation of children, for which purpose three-year intervals were advisable. "Were all to follow
the example of Mrs. Weld and the advice of yourself, when
think you would the wilderness and the solitary place in the
natural world, bud and blossom as the rose?" Frank Stone
asked his sister and continued: "I suppose individuals do not
cohabit for the sake of children only, but because they want
to. . . . I will just say here that my wife is as well now I
presume as Mrs. W. is after she has gone three years and

then had one." [23] The letter was written three years and three months after the birth of Angelina's last child. If the reference were to Angelina's expressed views and not just to Lucy Stone's opinion inferred from Angelina's example, it would indicate that the frequent episodes of childbearing and subsequent illness had led Angelina to the conclusion that woman's health and well-being could best be protected by the practice of birth control. Utopian religious reformers, such as John Humphrey Noyes, had advocated similarly drastic birth control methods, while some of the female reformers voluntarily abstained from marriage rather than face its risks. This latter view was held by Lucy Stone at this period. Since there is no other reference to such ideas to be found in Angelina's writings, and since Lucy Stone, at that time, had not yet had any personal contact with her, one may assume that this reference represents Lucy Stone's ideas rather than Angelina Weld's.

The time in any young mother's life when all the children are small and the repetitious routine of household tasks is unending, is a period of difficult adjustments. The more so in the case of an intellectually and politically active young woman like Angelina. Elizabeth Cady Stanton faced the same kind of crisis several years later. At that time, she was the mother of four children, the mistress of a large household, blessed with a reformer husband who had become a budding politician and who usually managed to be out of town during periods of domestic crisis. Elizabeth Stanton expressed, in her usual forceful way, what this period meant in her life: "The general discontent I felt with woman's portion as wife, mother, housekeeper, physician and spiritual guide, the chaotic condition into which everything fell without her constant supervision, and the wearied, anxious look of the majority of women, impressed me with the strong feeling that some active measures should be taken to remedy the wrongs of society in general and of women in particular." [24]

Mrs. Stanton was a young and unusually healthy and energetic woman. When she discovered with a shock how the majority of women lived most of their lives, she did not resign herself to her fate nor did she turn to religion. Carrying out the plan made in London, she joined with Lucretia Mott and three other young women, organized the Seneca Falls convention and, later, the woman's rights movement.

Perhaps if Angelina had been forced to assume the care of her children despite her ill health, she might have gained the psychological strength similarly to fight her situation But she, who had been a fighter all her life, was now caught between the self-sacrificing, smothering love of Sarah and her husband's prodigious energies. At the very moment when she needed all her inner resources to fashion for herself a new place in life, Sarah was there to take over. Helping out in order to "protect" Angelina's frail health, Sarah assumed the care of the children to a point where she became, functionally, their mother. Angelina accepted this help first gladly, then with an increasing sense of displacement. It was comfortable to have someone to lean on when she was tired and weak, but the pity of it was that it could become a habit. What began as a temporary expedient became a fixed pattern of family life. For the first time in their history, the sisters' roles were reversed. Sarah was now the active, indispensable head of the family, while Angelina was gradually relegated to the somewhat peripheral role of invalid, advisor and perennial student.

The complex of family responsibilities changed the pattern and style of the sisters' lives; it equally affected Theodore

Weld. For a brief period after his return from Washington Weld had resumed his work as an antislavery and temperance lecturer. But a speech at the Brooklyn Lyceum in February 1844 proved to be his last for eighteen years. His voice was not able to bear the strain of extended speech-making, although he tried rest, water cures, exercises and every quack remedy known to his contemporaries.

"Why stand ye here all the day idle?" Lewis Tappan asked with the professional reformer's usual bluntness.[25] There were pamphlets to be written, committees to serve on, organizations to be formed, meetings to attend. But Weld refused. He was too hard pressed financially to consider another absence from his farm. Organizing and writing had become luxuries he no longer could afford.

His dependents were forever increasing. Weld had to provide a home for his ailing parents, care for an invalid nephew and, at various periods, for his sister Cornelia, who later became mentally ill. For a time he also supported a ninety-six-year-old uncle and his eighty-year-old aunt and assisted his brother as well as Angelina's sister and niece, who all lived nearby. Weld always was a tower of strength to those around him and was over-generous with counsel, loans and service to all who needed him.[26]

Yet, in a sense, this personal social service was intensified only because Weld was no longer active in the antislavery movement. The reasons for this were complex. Skepticism about politics had followed upon disillusionment with the organizational aspects of moral reform to strengthen Weld in his decision to keep away from activities for a time. After his experience in Washington, Weld considered "nearly the whole of the democratic delegation in Congress and a majority of the Whigs" abject slaves, who of their own free will crawled before public sentiment as at their master's feet, "wriggling for the privilege of licking his spittle as it falls." [27] This unfavorable view of politicians was not improved by the sectional politics of the 1844 Presidential campaign. The Mexican War and the Compromise of 1850 seemed only further confirmation of the moral bankruptcy at Washington and of the ineffectiveness of antislavery resistance. Weld could not raise much enthusiasm for political abolitionism, although he endorsed its doctrines. "My heart was never in the Liberty Party movement," he wrote to Gerrit Smith in 1852. "As a programme of *operations,* with the machinery involved, it is *not mine* and I cannot make it so." [28] Yet his friendship with Gerrit Smith and James Birney was unaffected by these differences of opinion. Weld approved of Birney's acceptance of the Liberty Party nomination for President, although he had little hopes for the party's success. He had become convinced that armed conflict between the North and the South was inevitable:

Nothing short of miracles, constant miracles, and such as the world has never seen can keep at bay the two great antagonist forces. . . . They must drive against each other till *one* of them goes to the bottom. . . . Where half the government live by their own work and pay as they go and the other half, by other's work and by the longest possible credit, and where these halves are made by *Climate* — a mighty pecuniary convulsion *must* . . . hurl these two systems of labor and living into mortal conflict, and *that must* demolish the basis of all existing parties. . . .

The greater cause now at work producing this, may, in its progress encounter obstacles (the third party I think is one), but it cannot be *arrested*. *The end must come.*[29]

Weld expressed this conviction as early as 1842 and held to it, unaffected by the politics of compromise and the tactics of the different factions of reformers. Garrison's advocacy of immediate, peaceful separation from the South seemed as illusory to him as did the third party movement.

Weld was the kind of man who could only act from the deepest conviction. Doctrinal disputes and sectarian squabbles repelled him. Unlike Garrison, he was unimpressed by rhetoric; intellectual skirmishes left him cold. His talent lay in directly translating moral principles into organization. A man such as he could function best in the early, most militant stages of antislavery organization and again, in wartime, when the moral issues were clear. When the conflict he had foreseen became a bloody reality, Weld would return to antislavery harness, despite old age, ill health and family obligations. But the decades of compromise had no place for his talents. It was not so much that he had left the movement, as some of the abolitionists sometimes charged; it was that the movement, for a time, had passed him by.

This was not something he could easily explain to his former co-workers or to the new generation of abolitionists. On a visit to Belleville young Henry Blackwell, who was then courting the dedicated abolitionist and feminist Lucy Stone, asked Weld why he had retired from activity. Weld explained that he no longer quite believed in his former methods of reforming others.

He had been laboring to destroy evil in the same spirit as his antagonists. He suddenly felt that fighting was

not the best way to annihilate error. . . . All his old
opinions and principles began to loosen and scale off. He
threw aside books, newspapers, everything, and for ten
years found there was nothing on earth for him to do
but dig ditches and work upon his farm. . . .

Since then he has thought and worked and taught his
children. I tried to argue the duty of fighting error so
long as it existed, but both he and his wife simply say,
"There is a fighting era in everyone's life. While you
feel it so, fight on; it is your duty, and the best thing you
can possibly do. But when your work in that line is
done, you will reach another and higher view." [30]

Young Henry Blackwell concluded that marriage was not
to blame for this decision, but that it came from a combination of other causes. He thought that if ever there was a
perfect marriage it was that of the Welds. "Both preserve
their individuality perfectly, and on many points differ heartily, with the utmost good will." [31]

Despite Henry Blackwell's rosy view, Angelina was troubled by her husband's situation. She did not feel he was doing work that was adequate to his talents and calling and
could not bear to see him depressed and resigned. "It seems
to me dearest One," she once wrote to him, "the days of your
preparation must be over — the time must have come for
you to give up your drudging. You greatly *mistake me* if you
think it pleased me to see *you* working as you do on the farm
— in such a state of mind — because you feel constantly
that you are not in your right place." [32]

The solution to this problem was not easy to find; the
Welds arrived at it in a series of gradual steps. Always concerned over their children's education, both Angelina and

her husband spent several hours each day teaching them the rudimentary skills. In their constant need for money, they decided in 1848 to take in two other students as boarders and increased the number to four a little later.[33] Weld had always enjoyed teaching; now, after the long years of farming, he found it particularly rewarding. Friends who heard about this new activity and remembered Weld's pedagogical talents began to ask that their own children be admitted. Henry and Elizabeth Stanton sent two of their boys, Gerrit Smith and James Birney each sent their sons. From Charleston came the son of Henry Grimké, the sisters' nephew Thomas, who stayed for several years. By October 1851 the extended household had become a regular boarding school with twenty pupils. Sarah and Angelina did all the cooking, washing, cleaning and mending for the students and helped out with their instruction, Angelina teaching history and Sarah, French. For them, it was hard work, often plain drudgery, with the challenges and rewards few and far between. But Theodore Weld, as Principal of Belleville School, had at last found his second, true vocation.[34]

CHAPTER
EIGHTEEN

The most perfect social system can only be attained
where the laws which govern the sexes are based on jus-
tice and equality.

Sarah Grimké,
Notebook, undated.

THE LAST YEARS at Belleville had been burdensome and difficult. Angelina had passed through several periods of illness, with her old complaints so disabling that she sought help at a water cure establishment in Brooklyn which treated every sort of sickness by means of *sitzbaths* and cold compresses.[1] Sarah had several times been ill with pneumonia or some other sort of "fever." Weld, too, had had several seasons of ill health. "We have all worked too hard," Sarah summed it up, "although necessity compelled us to it."[2]

Despite all their hard work, the Belleville School did not pay its way. To make matters worse, they had to spend several hundred dollars on repairs and improvements for the schoolhouse in the winter of 1852. Although the work itself was satisfying, it was evident that they needed better facilities and more students if they wanted to improve their earnings.

At last, the opportunity they had been waiting for seemed at hand. Early in 1853 the Welds were invited to join Raritan Bay Union, a newly formed cooperative community.

Weld was offered the job of Director of the community's school. Like most utopian cooperatives this one, too, promised to be more than just a place to live. It was designed to provide work, companionship and a way of life which would make it possible to "strengthen all ties . . . and [to create] that loving communion, which is the only true law of life in God's kingdom, alike on earth as in heaven."[3] Raritan Bay Union was, in short, a utopian haven, designed to solve individual and family problems and serve as a model for all of society.

It was, indirectly, an offspring of the North American Phalanx at Red Bank, New Jersey, a cooperative which was the testing ground for the social theories of Fourier in America. Under Albert Brisbane's leadership it lasted eleven years, longer than any other Fourierist Phalanx in this country. Although fairly prosperous, the community was rent by dissension, which erupted at the first sign of financial reverses. In 1852 thirty dissidents, who happened to be among the leading members of the North American Phalanx, left in order to found their own community, which would have a more strongly religious and educational orientation.[4]

The founders of Raritan Bay Union offered Weld a free hand in the running of the school and Marcus Spring offered to invest $20,000 to get it started. Marcus Spring, a wealthy and philanthropic commission merchant who was married to one of the daughters of the Quaker abolitionist, Arnold Buffum, was the moving spirit of the group. Mr. and Mrs. Spring's sisters and their husbands were part of the nucleus of former associationists. George Arnold, Mrs. Rebecca Spring's brother-in-law, had for several years been President of the North American Phalanx. By January 1853 the founding group had formed a stockholding company, purchased

270 acres of fertile land at Eagleswood, New Jersey, and sent out a prospectus to attract additional subscribers. The community, in addition to its higher philosophical aims, promised to provide attractive living facilities, a school, a farm, a wharf, studios for artists, shops and workshops. It was hoped to attract to the community farmers, florists, mechanics, artits and businessmen, all who were "seeking for a freer, larger, more harmonious form of human existence." The cooperative was to be capitalized at $500,000 divided modestly into $25 shares. It would commence business when $50,000 had been subscribed, of which $15,000 had been actually paid.[5]

With high hopes for the future of the community and their school, the Welds and Sarah each invested in $1000 worth of shares of Raritan Bay Union stock, although Weld and Angelina had to borrow money from Sarah to do so.

The decision to join the association brought to a head a serious crisis in the relationship of the two sisters. As one might suspect, the dominant role Sarah had assumed in the family was not something Nina found easy to accept. During periods of her illness, her pride had suffered and she had resolved, as soon as possible, to change her role in the family and assume her rightful place. But this was not done so easily, nor could it be done without hurting Sarah's feelings. Increasingly, Nina also suffered from her family's partial dependence on Sarah's money. This must have developed quite gradually, with little gifts or loans on Sarah's part, whenever she noticed a need in the household. Angelina had, apparently, repeatedly discussed this question with Sarah. Thus she could write to her sister Mary that she hoped, after the sale of the farm, to pay Sarah her portion of the investment — something she had long been anxious to do. "We have too long been the sole recipient of her bounty — this obligation has long been *painfully heavy on my heart* — and she knows it full well." [6]

One wonders whether Sarah did not exaggerate all along, in her letters to friends, the pecuniary insolvency of the Weld family and the sad status of their school in order to justify her continuous "helping out." The more so, since Angelina flatly stated: "I depart wholly from her idea that our school does not support us." She pointed out that the school at Belleville, while not allowing them to accumulate cash savings, had provided them with a comfortable livelihood and that most of their money had been sunk into endless improvements of the farm.[7] Ultimately Angelina expressed herself quite sharply, when she wrote of the necessity of separating hers and Sarah's pecuniary interests. The situation as it existed had caused her "14 years of intensive suffering" and she felt "decisive action on this point was imperative." She was amazed that Sarah should wish to continue "a relation which has produced and ever must produce so much friction between us." [8]

Sarah met this rather practical suggestion in an emotional way. She chose to regard it as a rebuff, not only of her money, but of herself. Since she had little faith in the merits of Raritan Bay Union and did not feel qualified as a teacher, she decided this would be a good time for her to separate from the family altogether and begin an independent life. This suggestion originated with her, and perhaps she counted on abandoning it in the face of the family's protest, but Nina seized on it. "I often mourn to see her [Sarah's] mind so trammeled as it has been and must be as long as she is a member of our family, when, if she were in a different position she might stand up in the dignity of her womanhood and be a blessing to her generation." [9]

Suddenly faced with the necessity of acting on her decision, Sarah did not know which way to turn. All was in darkness. "There is plenty of work to be done, but I see nothing in the wide world that I can do. . . ."

I have for so long been cooking, sweeping and teaching the abc of French and the angles and curves of drawing that I seem to have lost the mental activity I once had. Besides the powers of my mind have never been allowed expansion; in childhood they were repressed by the false idea that a girl need not have the education I coveted. In early youth by wrong views of God and religion, then I was fairly ground to powder in the Quaker Society and have been ever since I left it . . . [suffering from] the overwhelming superiority of those with whom I have been in contact. Now, after all, what can I expect in old age? [10]

This pathetic complaint which was, in a sense, quite an accurate estimate of her situation, did not make the impending "freedom" look very inviting to Sarah Grimké.

She was now sixty years old. After the long years in the busy Weld household, a lonely, retired life was not something she could accept with equanimity. She tried to make practical plans. She might rewrite her *Letters on the Equality of the Sexes* or help develop the ideology of the woman's rights movement by writing articles and pamphlets. From this period in her life date fragments of manuscripts on the subjects of marriage, divorce, the role of women and their history. Unfortunately there are no completed manuscripts in existence, and it is unlikely that Sarah went any further than the planning stage. For she soon conceived of another project that seemed to fill a definite need. She would compile the laws pertaining to women in the different states in order to expose their unfairness and arouse the conscience of the nation. She went about it quite systematically and with considerable energy, corresponding with the lawyers of her acquaintance and traveling to Boston and Washington in order to work in the public libraries there. In Washington her interest in legislation regarding children was aroused and she spent the winter of 1853–1854 there, hoping to train herself to become a spokesman for the rights of children. She started reading anatomy and physiology, in order to understand their physical development better. These preoccupations led her to consider seriously getting a professional education, and she inquired about the possibility of studying the law, her old love, or medicine. The replies were discouraging; the study of law was still completely out of the question for women, while that of medicine, which had just begun to open up to a handful of pioneers, was not really feasible for a woman her age.[11]

In these months, Sarah derived much support and encouragement from her friendship with one of the most dramatic personalities in the early woman's rights movement. Harriot Kezia Hunt of Boston was a *cause célèbre* for being the first female medical practitioner in the United States. A small, lively woman of considerable charm, she had been privately trained by a British practitioner and had, in 1835, opened an office in Boston, where she practiced a highly unorthodox system of medicine, homeopathy and psychological consultation. In her work with women she relied heavily on what today would be considered psychotherapy combined with a conservative use of drugs. She tried to channel the energies of her patients into benevolent activities and social involvement, advocated a healthy diet, sensible exercise and mental health. After successfully practicing in this manner for twelve years, she applied in 1847 to Harvard Medical College and was refused. Three years later, encouraged by the admission of Elizabeth Blackwell to medical training in Europe, she applied again and was admitted provisionally. She was told she could attend lectures and courses, but take no degree. Even this limited privilege was withdrawn, however, after the medical students came near rioting over the news of her admission. In 1853, the newly organized Philadelphia Female Medical College gave her an honorary degree. Dr. Harriot Hunt was an ardent feminist and initiated the practice of dramatizing her demand for suffrage for women by annually paying her taxes under protest. This practice was later adopted by other supporters of woman's rights.[12]

Harriot Hunt was Sarah's closet confidante, to whom she revealed her innermost feelings in a correspondence extending over many years. Dr. Hunt expressed her deep appreciation of Sarah's friendship by dedicating her autobiography to Sarah, whom she saluted as a teacher and a "rare and true woman."[13] The position attained by Dr. Hunt must have seemed, to Sarah, an inspiring example of what was possible for a woman of determination and courage. Similarly, there was the example of her friend Sarah Douglass, who, although unhappily married to a widower with grown children, had retained her financial and personal independence by continuing her work as a schoolteacher. Recently she had been appointed to the Philadelphia public school system, one of the few Negro teachers to gain that recognition. The possibility of emulating these women or, in the case of Dr. Hunt, of going to live with her friend must have occurred to Sarah during her period of indecision. She was, thus, neither quite helpless nor devoid of choices.

That winter in Washington, during her long absence from home, Sarah finally came face to face with her deepest personal problem.

At 60 I look back on a life of deep disappointments, of withered hopes, of unlooked for suffering, of severe discipline. Yet I have sometimes tasted exquisite joy and have found solace for many a woe in the innocence and earnest love of Theodore's children. But for this my life would have little to record of mundane pleasures.[14]

"Theodore's children . . ." The phrase is telling. It occurs a few times in Sarah's correspondence. Sometimes it is simply "the children" or "my darling children," but seldom "Nina's children." To have someone to care for, someone who was absolutely dependent on her, this was the deepest need of Sarah's life. "Theodore's children" had come to fill that need and Angelina's infirmities had made the usurpation legitimate, even endowing it with the aura of heroism. Sarah Grimké, sacrificing her own rich potential to her sister and her sister's family — it was very touching. Nineteenth-century biographies are filled with similar records of sacrificing spinster sisters, to the point where that role has almost become a stereotype. The trouble was that it was only partly true. That winter, during their separation, Angelina found the strength and clarity needed to make Sarah see it.

Even after a few weeks' absence from Belleville, Sarah was homesick. Typically, her offer to return was masked by generosity — she would be so pleased to take care of the house and the children so that Nina might go away somewhere and rest. But Angelina, for once, brusquely refused. During an earlier separation she had written to Sarah: "Sister, you know how I suffer when you nurse my children. It is better

that one of us be with them at a time." [15] Now she bluntly
told Sarah to stay the winter in Washington and pointed out
that she found housekeeping easier than Sarah did and that
Sarah had taken ill each time she had taken charge of the
household in her absence.[16]

Finally, in a long and searching letter, Angelina exposed
and discussed the full scope of their problem. She confessed
to deep-rooted feelings, which she thought Sarah did not suspect, but which should be faced.

There are times I feel humbled in the dust, because I
never have been willing to share my blessings with you
equally. Often, very often, when I look at all the sorrow
and disappointment you have met with in life and all
that you have done for me I feel ashamed and con-
founded at my ingratitude and selfishness. Then again
it seems unnatural that a wife and Mother should ever
thus be willing to share of the affection of her dearest
ones with any human being and my heart refuses its as-
sent and struggles on in darkness and death for I know
these feelings wither and blight and keep me from
growth and yet it seems impossible for me to overcome
them. . . .

I often feel weary of a conflict which has lasted 15
years and wonder when and what will be the end of
it. . . .

You never meant to do me any wrong. You have only
lived out your own (in many respects) beautiful nature.
I would not, I could not blame you, altho' . . . the
conflicts thro' which I have passed have been terrible.[17]

Yet the outcome of this frank revelation was not separation, but Nina's insistence, in the same letter, that Sarah must

continue to live with them. "We all want you with us," was
the conclusion she reached.

And Sarah accepted. Not, one may assume, swayed by her
sister's arguments, but motivated by the one and only force
that could move her: her need for the children. "Separation
from these darling children, who have brightened a few
years of my lonely and sorrowful life, overwhelmed me. . . .
I turned from it in deep anguish. . . . They seemed to be
the link that bound me to life . . . without them existence
would have no charm." [18] This, making due allowance for
her sentimental rhetoric, summed up Sarah's feelings.

They were the feelings of a woman born and bred in the
late eighteenth century, whose very character had been
deeply and irrevocably molded in the culture of her time.
Nina, in early childhood, had been able, largely owing to
Sarah's influence, to grow into a different mold. She became
the pioneering spirit who lifted and pulled Sarah along at
crucial moments in their lives. Their collaboration, their
sharing of lives, freed them for their activities. But this sym-
biosis of their lives which was the blessing of their active
days, became the blight of their middle years. It could not
be otherwise at the time in which they lived. The ostracism
of their contemporaries, the attacks and censure they were
subjected to, made any other solution impossible. It was the
significance of the early woman's rights movement that it
freed individuals from this terrible burden. After Seneca
Falls, the lonely pioneers could and did gain strength from
the knowledge that there were others like them, scattered
here and there, but at least gathered annually for guidance
and inspiration at their conventions. The Stantons, Antho-
nys, Blackwells, Stones were truly the new generation standing on the shoulders of the old. The age difference which

separated Sarah and Angelina was not nearly so decisive as the twenty-year span separating them from the new generation of women leaders. The problems posed by the multiple roles of woman have defied solution even by emancipated women of twentieth-century America. They were made infinitely easier and more possible of solution by technological and social changes, by institutional sanctions and by legal approval, which the woman's rights movement won over a difficult span of seventy-five years of organized struggle. But the Grimké sisters stood at the very threshold of that struggle, one foot still in the eighteenth century, another in their own time. The worst, insoluble, part of their personal dilemma was that their minds and concepts reached way ahead into a future time. Thus the personal entanglement, the problems and conflicts of their middle years, were the price they paid for their pioneering role.

It was this that made Sarah unable to choose, for the second and last time in her life, a position of independence. It was this that made her prepare to accept life at Raritan Bay Union and find her place, irrevocably, in her sister's family. From this time on her life fitted into a pattern of resignation and more and more she was drawn to spiritualism, dream interpretation and communication with the spirits of the dead, in which she firmly believed. This is not to say that Sarah's later life was not active, rational and eminently useful. It was, but with her decision to stay with the Weld family, Sarah had finally stifled her own rebellious spirit which had made her so special a person earlier in life. The "free spirits" of women could soar only so far in the middle of the nineteenth century.

The sharp clash of tempers and personalities which Angelina had defined in her letter to Sarah never again came to the surface. Nina, too, had come to accept the limitations of her life and had learned to conquer her feelings. In a peculiar way she had finally come to accept that her own relative freedom had always been bought at the price of Sarah's submission and that, in taking over the mother's place in her family, Sarah was simply, belatedly, taking what was her due. One wonders where Weld stood in this conflict, whether it was he who ultimately determined the decision of the two women or whether, as seems more likely, the reformer's perpetual absorption with the problems of all the world made him oblivious to the problems within his own family. There is no record of his role or position in this family crisis. Thus, "the strange trio" continued in Victorian harmony, tantalizing the biographer and historian with a host of unanswered questions.

By the summer of 1853 the Raritan Bay Union had secured the necessary capital and building and settlement could begin. There were long delays, which were particularly irksome to the Welds, since they had to continue their Belleville school for another year. But at last the cooperative was ready for occupancy in the summer of 1854.

"Our location here is enchanting," Sarah wrote to Harriot Hunt. "Far far superior to our Belleville home." They were situated on Raritan Bay, twenty-five miles from New York, near Perth Amboy, New Jersey. "We have a fine expanse of water in front, have a view of the Neversink Hills and away up the bay toward the South East. . . . Our House is very pleasant, we have a suite of six rooms, an entry running between them . . . the surrounding woods are just near enough to form a delightful amphitheater." [19] Eagleswood House, the main building here described by Sarah, was a huge stone structure topped by a turret. One end was di-

vided into apartments for a number of families, the other
wing served as a school building. The center held the community dining hall and kitchen, laundry and sitting rooms
and facilities for guests. Associationists who wished to do so
and could afford it, were provided with land to build their
own houses. The Springs had an elegant separate house, as
did Arnold Buffum and his wife. James Birney and his family joined the association in 1853 and built their own house.
There the old Liberty Party Presidential candidate lived out
his remaining years, seriously crippled by a paralytic stroke.
Another well-known member was Nathaniel Peabody,
whose daughter Elizabeth taught at the Weld school for a
short time. His sons-in-law, Horace Mann and Nathaniel
Hawthorne, took a warm interest in Raritan Bay Union and
frequently lectured there.[20]

Weld had assembled a superior teaching staff for Eagleswood School. Margaret Corliss and William Channing had
been successful teachers at Belleville. Elizabeth Peabody
had taught at Bronson Alcott's famous school and had become interested in early childhood education through having
been exposed to the Froebel kindergarten system in Europe,
which she would later introduce in the United States. Edward Livingston Youmans, who was the author of a standard
text then in use, taught chemistry and arranged chemical lectures in the village school. Young Miss Shepard, who taught
Greek, Latin and mathematics was universally beloved by
students and staff. Weld taught Shakespeare and presumably it was he who personally directed the annual student
play, which was given a public performance. As before, he
was the director in charge of staff and student problems. Angelina taught history, for which she was very well qualified,
and handled first aid, medical care and a good deal of the

vast correspondence connected with the running of a large boarding school. "Aunt Sai" was housemother and taught French. It was she to whom the children came when they were troubled and needed affectionate indulgences, since Angelina had the reputation of being somewhat of a disciplinarian.[21]

The school was run on the manual labor principle. Woodwork, agriculture, household skills and bookkeeping were added to the usual academic curriculum. Drawing, art, singing and instrumental music were a regular part of the students' activities. This was, for the period, an unusually rich curriculum, considered by many daring and experimental. Even more unusual was the coeducational and interracial aspect of the school. A contemporary observer noted: "It was a pioneer institution in many ways — the first in which young women were found educating their limbs in the gymnasium, rowing in boats, and making 'records' in swimming and high diving." [22]

Weld's educational principles called for close integration of school and life, by making work and participation in the wider community part of the natural school experience of each child. Thus in addition to their well-balanced curriculum students at Eagleswood had special treats: picnics, steamboat excursions, trips to New York City and attendance at fairs and lectures in the neighboring towns. The community was drawn into the school's activities by Sunday gatherings and lyceum lectures, open to all, which were a regular and prized feature of Eagleswood life. "This is a queer place," Henry David Thoreau reported. "The central fact here is evidently Mr. Weld's school, recently established, around which various other things revolve." Thoreau had been hired by Marcus Spring to survey some of his property at Eagleswood, had stayed for several weeks, surveyed property for James Birney as well, and had drawn a handsome map of Raritan Bay Union. He had participated in a Quaker meeting and one of the Saturday dances, to which everyone, children, parents, teachers and guests turned out. It struck him as a strange sight to see Weld with his long, white beard gaily romping and dancing with the children and to see gray-haired ladies, like Mrs. Weld and her sister, wearing the Bloomer costume. Thoreau, who had become known as a lyceum lecturer, read his essay "Walking" to the special delight of the young people.[23] Bronson Alcott, Octavius B. Frothingham, William Cullen Bryant, and Horace Greeley were among the many intellectuals and reformers who visited and spoke at Eagleswood. Emerson, who several times lectured there, even reduced his customary speaking fee from $50 to $30. Unitarians, Quakers, Abolitionists, spiritualists, Grahamites, phrenologists, advocates of woman's rights, temperance, dress reform and Hungarian freedom — all were welcome and found an atmosphere of free inquiry and benevolence at Raritan Bay Union, which reminded many of the best of Brook Farm. Unlike Brook Farm, however, the "association spirit" was neither militant nor extreme at Eagleswood.

In the early months the Welds had shared in the hopeful enthusiasm of the associationists; Angelina especially had indulged in the utopian fantasies which made communal ventures so attractive to the most idealistic of her generation. Like millennialism, the founding of utopian models of the good life was a by-product of frustration. Reform urges which had been thwarted in the field of politics turned inward. Abolitionists, who in the early thirties had hoped by courage and martyrdom to accomplish the revolutionary aim of abolishing the slave system, now — more modestly — hoped to build the good life for themselves and their children on a few hundred acres and to lead, if at all, by quiet example. That the earlier goal of their efforts was in fact a good deal more realistic than the latter, was not immediately apparent to most. Sarah, for reasons of her own, never had any illusions about the advantages of cooperative life. Except for the scenery, she found little to merit her approval. The butter was poor and the bread was hard. Dining in the community hall was unpleasant and could not compare with the pleasures of a private family meal. For the most part she did not like the members of the association. Marcus Spring, in particular, proved disappointing. He had promised to take charge of community affairs, but he spent much time away from Eagleswood, turning the management over to careless and inefficient substitutes. As a result, not only did most of the ambitious projects remain unrealized, but the barest necessities of daily comfort were wanting. The promised gas lights were not installed; the heating system was faulty and the water supply so poor that they had to conserve every drop. "If there are any blessings in Unitary Life I have thus far failed to realize them," Sarah concluded quickly.[24]

We had indulged the delightful hope that Theodore would have no cares outside of the schoolroom, and Angelina would have leisure to pursue her studies and aid in the cause of woman. Her heart is in it, and her talents qualify her for enlarged usefulness. She was no more designed to serve tables than Theodore to dig potatoes. . . . We have jumped out of the frying-pan into the fire in point of leisure, for there are innumerable

sponges here to suck up every spare moment; but dear
Nina is a miracle of hope, faith, and endurance.[25]

This was Sarah's view of cooperative life, certainly highly
colored by the spirit with which she had entered upon the
venture. But, quite objectively, the school at Eagleswood
was not profitable. Weld still had to carry a daily teaching
load, which was particularly burdensome since he had been
ill for months with fever and had become quite emaciated.
By the end of the first year the Welds were ready to give up
both school and association. But the directors persuaded
them to stay another year. By the end of that year, the cooperative itself was dead. "Dead and buried," wrote Sarah, "to
my infinite satisfaction, for it worked evil, nothing but evil
and that continually." [26]

Some of the disillusioned associationists left and the community turned its assets over to Marcus Spring, who continued Raritan Bay Union as a private concern. Friends and
relatives of the remaining members purchased property and
built homes of their own on the land, gradually forming a
more congenial group of neighbors. A few years later even
Sarah had to admit that they now had a charming circle of
friends.

During all these years the sisters never gave up their interest and participation in the growing movement for woman's
rights, which in the decade before the Civil War found its
chief expression in the holding of annual conventions. The
1850 woman's rights convention in Worcester, Massachusetts, brought new leadership to the fore: socially prominent
Paulina Wright Davis; the young Oberlin graduate and fiery
speaker, Lucy Stone; the brilliant Polish immigrant, Ernestine Rose; Antoinette Brown, who would become the first fe-

male ordained minister; and Sojourner Truth, the dynamic ex-slave and lay preacher. Angelina, in recognition of her work, was elected a member of the Central Committee, although she was unable to attend in person. She was present, however, at the 1851 Rochester convention, where she participated actively. Both sisters contributed by letter to the 1852 convention at Syracuse, New York. Sarah discussed woman's role in general, and Angelina addressed herself to the major topic before the convention — the future organizational structure of the movement. She urged the women to avoid rigid organization and to keep the present informal structure. "The tendency of organization is to kill out the spirit which gave it birth. Organizations do not protect the sacredness of the individual; their tendency is to sink the individual in the mass, to sacrifice his rights, and to immolate him on the altar of some fancied good." Such artificial forms were burdens. American women were "bound together by the natural ties of spiritual affinity," they had no need of "artificial organizations," which had historically been used as engines of oppression.[27] Angelina's bitter personal experience with the sectarianism of the abolition movement found expression in this letter. It provoked a spirited discussion, which ended in the adoption of its recommendation. The loose steering committee was continued and Angelina was again elected to it. During the Civil War women would learn a different approach to organizational problems, but the informal, flexible structure advocated by Angelina was well suited to this early period.

American feminists developed the skills needed to build a mass movement at these early conventions, and it was there that they gradually developed a program. They were agreed on the need to win legal equality, especially in regard to property and custody rights over their children. The need for every woman to "own her purse" was frequently expressed; it emerged more importantly when the difficulty of raising funds in support of the movement dramatically revealed that the majority of women lived, in fact, without any money of their own. Susan B. Anthony effectively coupled the demand for opening all trades and professions to women with an attack on wage discrimination. The prevailing practice was to pay women a fourth to a third of man's wages for equal services rendered. The demand to raise women's wages to 50 or 60 percent of those of men seemed very radical at the time. Equal educational opportunities were another demand unanimously agreed upon by feminists, but there were a number of highly controversial questions which the early movement found it difficult to resolve. Among these were divorce, the problems posed by the double standard and prostitution and the issue of female suffrage, which Elizabeth Stanton had practically forced on the Seneca Falls convention. This issue would continue for many decades to be the most controversial.

Although Sarah tended to be conservative in her thinking on moral questions and never quite could make up her mind to come out in favor of divorce, she took a very strong and forthright position on suffrage. "Since the legislative body is the medium of communication between the government and the various classes of society it would seem but justice that women, who form one half of every class should be participating in it." Granting the vote to women would be as great a blessing to society, she thought, as was the granting of the franchise to foreign-born immigrants.[28]

Sarah also had a lifelong interest in the fate of working women. She deplored their low wages and pitiful working conditions and did not share the snobbism of some of the wealthier feminists. "There are in the poorer classes many strong, honest hearts weary of being slaves and tools who are worthy of freedom and who will use it worthily." She also believed that the change in the condition of women would be mainly promoted by those of the lower classes, since the wealthy seldom advanced "revolutionary causes — their wealth sheltering them from feeling oppression." [29]

Both sisters manifested their continuing interest in the cause of women by subscribing to the early feminist papers: *The Una*, edited by Paulina W. Davis, and Amelia Bloomer's, *The Lily*, a temperance paper with a strongly feminist editorial bias. They also adopted, sometime in 1852, the Bloomer costume. The first person to wear the costume publicly had been Elizabeth Miller, the daughter of Gerrit Smith. Amelia Bloomer, the editor, merely adopted it and publicized it in her paper. Her name stuck to it, as the word "bloomers" stuck to the feminists — an epithet designed to ridicule them. The scandalous costume, consisting of a tunic, short skirt and pantaloons fastened at the ankles, was designed to liberate women from the fantastically uncomfortable and unhealthy garments demanded by fashion. Especially was it to do away with tight stays, bustles and layers upon layers of petticoats. The costume naturally appealed to reformers whose philosophy inclined them toward simplicity in dress and diet. It soon became a symbol of revolt against all the senseless restrictions imposed on women and was worn with grim persistence in the face of ridicule, abuse and public censure.

The sisters never went so far as did Gerrit Smith, who regarded dress reform as the first and basic reform women needed. Both sisters wore the garb for a time, but they soon saw, as did Elizabeth Stanton, that as a reform it was not the main issue and not worth the cost. "We put the dress on for greater freedom, but what is physical freedom compared with mental bondage?" Mrs. Stanton exclaimed, when she was about ready to give up the bloomers. "It is not wise . . . to use up so much energy and feeling that way." [30] The sisters agreed with this estimate. Sarah gave the costume up gladly, for she had worn it only from conviction; Angelina did so with the understanding that in time a better and more attractive dress for women would be developed and accepted.[31]

In 1856, after the demise of the cooperative colony, there was still a long list of students waiting to be admitted to Eagleswood School. The new proprietors of the building offered Weld a somewhat more favorable lease and, at long last, made the needed repairs. Weld decided to continue the school as a private venture. In the fall, with "improved accommodations and increased facilities," which included a gymnasium and lecture rooms, the school reopened, operating along the same principles as before.

Two years later Angelina appealed to the directors to reduce the rent and the exorbitant fees charged the school for laundry and water, in view of the fact that the school was "the procuring cause of almost all the prosperity which now attends Eagleswood." For five years, she wrote, the Welds had sacrificed financially, borrowed money to meet the monthly payments, and taken a loss by not collecting any interest on their original investment. Now that the organization was successful, they felt entitled to a reduction in all the fees and rents charged them.[32] Whether or not the directors responded favorably is not known, but it would have made no difference. There was something inherent in the Weld-Grimké character which made it impossible for them to profit financially from all their devoted effort.

But in their relations with people they were highly successful. The fifty-odd students who annually attended Eagleswood School came from all over the country, some from as far away as Kansas and California. Judging from the letters and signs of love and affection which came to Weld from his students long after they had grown up, he was eminently successful as a teacher. At his school each child was treated as an individual. Weld's records take careful note of the wishes of the parents in regard to their child, and list special problems or special aptitudes. In an age when schools still relied heavily on rote learning, with threats of punishment the main inducement for performance, Weld's approach was humane and modern.

Ellie Wright, a niece of Lucretia Mott and later the wife of William Lloyd Garrison's son, spent several years at the school, as did two of her brothers. In her letters to her family she gave a vivid account of school life. To her, Eagleswood seemed a happy and busy place which managed to combine serious study with a lot of good fun for the youngsters. The way problems were handled is interesting. Frank Wright, Ellie's brother, had caused much trouble by his wild behavior and indifference to his studies. Weld's pedagogical system, grounded as it was in long years of revival and reform activity, called for huge doses of love, patience and positive example. Weld's expectation was always that each child and each human being was essentially good and would see the right way sooner or later. When signs of "conversion" were noted in Frank, the weekly staff conference decided to encourage him by offering him special accelerated work in Latin. This would enable him to catch up with his fellow students who were preparing for college. This individualized treatment paid off — in Frank's case as well as in many others. A brief student walkout, caused by homesickness and the students' longing "for fried chicken and roastbeef," items not likely to be found at the Weld's Grahamite table, was ended by persuading the dissenters of their obligation to the community as a whole. Similarly, an incident caused by a student objecting to dining with a Negro boy was treated by a combination of reasoning and firmness and ended with the objector becoming converted to Eagleswood abolitionism.[33]

For Raritan Bay Union, by its very composition, was profoundly antislavery in sentiment. While there is nothing in the record to show that the colony was a haven for fugitive slaves, the sympathies of the associationists were with the fugitives. After the repeal of the Missouri Compromise through the Kansas-Nebraska Act of 1854 the struggle in Kansas was a constant source of concern at Eagleswood. One of the students, Sarah Wattles, was the daughter of Augustus Wattles, Weld's friend of Lane days and now editor of the antislavery *Herald of Freedom* in Lawrence, Kansas. Through her the fate of the free-soil Kansas settlers became a live issue in the community, and questions of the propriety of the use of arms by antislavery men were widely discussed. Sarah Grimké was in constant correspondence with Augustus and Susan Wattles and had occasion to revise her nonviolent principles in the light of the changed political situation. She could not justify abolitionists who defended their loved ones with arms when attacked, but she hoped fervently this would not be necessary in Kansas. A committee to aid Kansas formed in Perth Amboy and the children of the school did their bit by soliciting funds in the community and holding a fund-raising fair to aid the free-soil settlers.[34]

The John Brown tragedy came very close to the Welds.

The sisters regarded Brown's action as the heroic martyr-dom of a man of deep convictions. "The John Huss of the United States now stands ready . . . to seal his testimony with his life's blood," Sarah wrote. "Last night I went in spirit to the martyr. It was my privilege to enter into sympathy with him; to go down, according to my measure, into the depths where he has travailed and feel his past exercises, his present sublime position." The Welds' friend, Gerrit Smith, had been so closely connected with John Brown that fear for the consequences of the conspiracy drove him into temporary insanity. And Rebecca Spring, who had for some time corresponded with John Brown, felt impelled to travel to Charles Town, Virginia, to visit the doomed man in jail. She promised to bring the bodies of two of the executed men, Aaron Stevens and Albert Hazlett, to Eagleswood for honorable burial. The fulfillment of this promise almost caused a riot, when Perth Amboy residents heard of the plan and threatened to throw the coffins overboard on arrival. But Eagleswood men and boys formed a determined guard and the burial proceeded quietly.[35]

Despite the increasing threat of disunion and war, the years at Raritan Bay Union were rich and fulfilling. Even Sarah had become reconciled to being a teacher and had made great efforts to increase her skills. Despite difficulties and a bad start, the experiment in living had proved successful. The young people surrounding them kept them young and busy, and to all three Eagleswood School became a source of satisfaction and pride.

CHAPTER NINETEEN

I want to be identified with the negro; until he gets his rights, we shall never have ours.

Angelina Grimké Weld,
May 14, 1863.

T HE OUTBREAK of the Civil War was an event which Weld and the sisters had, for some time, considered inevitable. Weld had spoken of it as early as 1842; Sarah said in 1854 that she no longer believed slavery could be peacefully abolished in the United States.[1] For a while she tried to convince herself of the feasibility of disunion without war, the "solution" for Northern consciences which Garrison and Wendell Phillips were then preaching. Of the Dred Scott decision she said: "It has brought a sword into our country and it cannot be sheathed until Liberty waves her banner over the Free States. It seems to me that it must end in disunion."[2]

But by 1860 the issue was joined. Angelina faced the situation realistically: "The South are dissolving the Union in order to prevent the abolition of Slavery and yet they are too blind to see that this dissolution will only hasten instead of prevent its overthrow. Things look very dark and gloomy and as I have given up all hope of its abolition except thro' blood and insurrection I feel willing it should come in my day, for the longer it is put off the worse it will be."[3]

As lifelong pacifists, the Welds and Sarah could endorse the Civil War only by seeing it as the final stand against the hated slavery system. "I profoundly believe in the righteousness of such a war as this is on its antislavery side," Weld wrote in 1862. "[We exult] in this mighty Northern uprising, notwithstanding its mixtures of motives and base alloys and half truth and whole lies. . . . The elements of a vast moral revolution are all aglow in the surging mass. A national religious revival better deserving the name, than anything that has preceded it. Simple right is getting such a hearing as never before on this continent. . . . But for this rebellion . . . the maelstrom would have dragged us all down." [4]

Like most abolitionists, the sisters had at first little confidence in Lincoln and criticized him for fighting the war for the union but not for abolition. "The government, with Lincoln at its head, has not a heart-throb for the slave," wrote Sarah. "I want the South to do her own work of emancipation. She would do it only from dire necessity, but the North will do it from no higher motive, and the South will feel less exasperation if she does it herself." [5] This shrewd estimate reflected Sarah's accurate understanding of political realities. Although in emotional and personal matters she might at times show confusion and sentimentality, her appraisal of political events was always sharp and lucid.

"We are dying by inches a coward's death because we will obstinately reject the means of our redemption," she wrote in November 1862. "I see disaster and defeat in Lincoln and McClellan. . . . We still scorn the colored man, we still live out that hateful and hating spirit." She felt that the greatest failure of the North was its hesitation and confusion on the issue of emancipation, which was depriving it of a central purpose. The South had rallied around a single idea, although a false one, the idea that it was fighting for freedom from oppression. But the North did not know what it was fighting for. "In great revolutions confusion in popular ideals is fatal." [6]

There was no doubt in Sarah's mind about the need for an immediate emancipation declaration. "The negro has generously come forward, in spite of his multiplied wrongs, and offered to help defend the country. . . . We have . . . denied him the right of citizenship and have virtually said, 'Stand back.' . . . I pray that victory may not crown our arms until the negro stands in his acknowledged manhood side by side in this conflict with the white man, until we have the nobility to say that this war is a war of abolition." [7]

Both sisters never hesitated to commit themselves fully to the Northern cause, despite their constant awareness of the inevitable suffering and destruction the war must bring to their homeland.

They had never severed their ties with their Charleston family. On the contrary, in the years since their mother's death they had made every effort to keep in touch with their remaining brothers and sisters. Brother Charles had died in 1857. The sisters showed continuing concern for their invalid brother John, the doctor. To the best of their ability they contributed to his support, even during the war, until he died in 1864. [8]

In 1851 Sarah had begun to correspond with their brother Judge Frederick Grimké of Chillicothe, Ohio. The correspondence is intriguing, because Sarah apparently managed to overcome the serious political differences that existed between herself and her brother. Judge Grimké was one of the foremost opponents of organized abolitionism, which he had attacked in his book, *The Nature and Tendency of Free Institutions*.[9] Sarah began to interest her brother in woman's rights. She sent him the proceedings of various conventions, her own and Angelina's writings on the subject, and asked his advice on various points of law. Judge Grimké, in voluminous and tediously dull letters, enlightened Sarah with his legal opinion and otherwise confined his discussion to the Graham diet, the only other interest he shared with his abolitionist sisters. But the correspondence led to a renewal of family ties; Judge Grimké even once visited the Welds.

There is no record available of their correspondence with brother Henry, a successful lawyer, planter and slaveholder, who lived with his wife and three children in Charleston. This was the same brother in whose spiritual welfare young Angelina had shown such great concern, when she had intervened with him on behalf of his slave. In 1851 and 1852 Henry's seventeen-year-old son, Thomas Smith, spent two years at the Belleville school as a student, which certainly indicates that there must have been continuous correspondence with the father. In 1852 the sisters were saddened by the death of this brother, whom they had always considered a good father and kind master. Sarah commented on it: "His slaves will feel his loss deeply. They haunt me day and night. Sleeplessness is my portion, thinking what will become of them." [10] Sarah and Angelina also kept up contact with their Charleston sisters, Mary and Eliza, who all during the war remained convinced defenders of slavery.

In the circle of the Welds' friends, one by one the men and young boys left for war service. Sons, grandsons or sons-in-law of the Tappan brothers, Gerrit Smith, Joshua Leavitt, Samuel May and many other abolitionist friends of the Welds, saw Union service. Two of James Birney's sons became major-generals, one of them, William, commanding colored troops. Two other Birney sons died of war injuries, and a grandson was a captain of cavalry.[11] Former Lane and Oberlin students and their sons were in the ranks and many of Weld's students served the war effort.

To Angelina and Weld the war brought twofold sorrow in regard to their sons. Charles Stuart, twenty-one years old at the outbreak of the war, had been attending Harvard College. He took the position of a conscientious objector and refused either to serve in the Army or to pay for a substitute. He strongly objected to his father's offer to pay for a substitute and expressed his willingness to be arrested rather than subject himself or another man to the draft in what he considered "an unjust cause." A purely pacifist objection to the war would have been easier for the parents to take than Charles' insistence that the war was "wrong." [12] A few years later Charles announced he would go to France. "It seems a strange mission for one whose parents are devoted to helping the cause of Humanity here," Sarah commented, "and whose country offers, as we abolitionists think, the most glorious field for moral and intellectual labor and progress in the world." [13] Somewhat later he planned to go to Mexico, to fight in the war on behalf of Maximilian of Hapsburg's claim to the Mexican crown, which was supported by the French. This cause seemed to him much more just than that of the Union. Nothing came of either of these plans. Charles Stuart Weld apparently suffered a reaction rather common to the children of reformers — he was thoroughly sick of the causes his parents espoused all during his childhood. It took him a long time to find himself; he finally became a writer and teacher. His specialty was French and Rumanian history; a book he published in 1897, *The Eastern Question,* was a vindication of the policies of Napoleon III and enjoyed some critical success. Charles' predilection for things French might well have been instilled in him by his Aunt Sarah. He was always extraordinarily close to her, "everything that a son . . . could be," as Angelina noted. It may be psychologically significant that he did not marry until the age of forty-one, after the death of both Sarah and his mother. He had one daughter. Weld lived out his old age in Charles' home. One can safely conclude that whatever differences of opinion might have existed between father and son did not decisively affect their relationship.[14]

Much more tragic for the parents was the incurable illness of "Sody," the Welds' beloved younger son Theodore. The illness, which may have been developing for some time, had become very apparent by 1859. The climax of the family's ordeal coincided with the outbreak of the war.

Sody had been much babied by Sarah in his early childhood, but had grown to be a sturdy intelligent youngster who participated in all the activities appropriate to his age. Except for several episodes of "fever" and one accident, caused by a chemical explosion which he survived with a number of cuts and no after-effects, Sody had been a normal youngster.[15] He did, however, stutter, for which a variety of medical and folk remedies were employed unsuccessfully. At the age of eighteen he lost interest in his studies and left home for a year to work. He returned, physically exhausted and visibly weakened, displaying a strange and alarming apathy. From the highly subjective accounts in various letters, one can gather that he was either suffering from some debilitating, degenerative disease, which affected his psychological condition, or that his physical symptoms were of a psychosomatic nature. His family was deeply concerned over his listlessness. He would neither work nor study and often sat motionless for hours. As is usually the case in situations of this kind, there followed a round of futile consultations with experts — doctors, teachers, spiritualists, faith-healers — who came up with a bewildering variety of opinions.

Mr. Cutler from Rome, New York, with whom Sody spent several months in 1860, discovered that he was under the influence of a dangerous philosophy, "a fatalistic period of speculation," the doctrine that in a state of perfect calm a higher spiritual insight is possible. Sody believed that in such a state people might be enabled to read one another's thoughts and retain the contents of an unopened book in a few minutes. It was of the essence, thought Mr. Cutler, to drive these absurd notions out of his mind.[16] A Mr. Jordan from New York thought he found a hopeful clue of a different sort. After Sody's departure from his home, he had discovered that the boy suffered from nightly "loss of seminal fluid" and he now assumed that this was the cause of all the boy's troubles. Accordingly, a New York physician was consulted, who had the boy's urine analyzed and confirmed the presence of seminal fluid. This utterly alarming diagnosis was hastily imparted to the parents; the young man needed urgent treatment or the conditions would "lead to insanity or idiocy." But Sody refused to follow this doctor's advice, the nature of which is unfortunately not noted in the letters. His alarmed parents now tried various other expedients. Sody was sent to Boston to take Dr. Dio Lewis' gymnastic exercises and cure for stuttering. When this failed, farm work was prescribed for him. This was an old cure-all Weld believed in firmly, but Sody's "mental and bodily torpor" continued.[17] Now a spiritual healer and medium was consulted. Her diagnosis and suggestions for a cure, while not medically enlightening, are certainly highly original.

Mrs. Coleman, a matron of considerable reputation as a therapist, offered to see the patient "clairvoyantly" and, to show her disinterested benevolence, suggested as an alternative the "mental magnetism" treatment of a Mr. Benjamin Ware. She was of the opinion that Sody's illness was not of an organic nature. "In this sexual age of lymphatic tendencies" sexual frustrations, which the lady genteelly described in flowery circumlocutions, had apparently become "an actual drainage upon his general system." It was abolutely necessary to "rouse into action a desire for the healthful love of woman" in order to free his brain from the fullness of "the leaden mass" created by secretion of the "elements of love." This foreign substance on the brain had been acting upon his muscles, making them "starved and flabby." Sody must change his mode of life. Instead of a "student of books" he must become a "student of the finer mechanism called woman. . . . Through the hands of woman, properly taught and properly cultured . . . an action can and must be produced, ere he can be the truly healthful man." Offering to care for him as though he were her own son, the lady admitted that she found this letter to the parents distasteful to write, but asserted that she "must speak the truth or let the young man die." [18]

The bewildered parents, who had earlier suggested to Sody that he take up some "manly pursuit" such as participation in a prospecting expedition on Lake Superior, a proposal the boy had at once rejected, now transmitted this astonishing proposal to him. Would he prefer treatment by Mrs. Coleman or Mr. Ware?

Apparently Sody's answer was not forthcoming promptly enough, for Mrs. Coleman next turned her attention to Sarah, who, she must have felt, would have the deciding voice in the matter. Considering Sarah's primness and the nature of

Mrs. Coleman's treatment, the image of Sarah considering this letter staggers the imagination.

Mrs. Coleman expressed concern that Sarah and her sister had not fully understood what action was necessary to help the "darling child." She hastened to elaborate:

> It is only necessary to lay upon the small of the back the hand often, and at other times, it is simply necessary for the hand to be placed upon the ovarium. In this manner can the brain be affected to such a degree that the love element immediately commences passing down into the testicles, filling them, when again the brain acts upon the interior organs, and they transmute to the basilar portion a liquid which forms the proper fluid by which the whole system is cleared from the otherwise thickened mass of secretions.

She declared herself "entirely willing to be used in cases of this kind, where the mind is sufficiently refined," and expressed confidence that the sisters' spiritual development would allow them to properly appreciate the purely spiritual nature of her gifts.[19]

Apparently, the sisters' spiritual development was inadequate to the occasion, for there is no evidence of any further correspondence with Mrs. Coleman. Sarah continued to consult various other "media," who with singular unanimity predicted a certain cure, provided everything were left to nature and their peculiar ministrations. One can only conclude that quackery was preying as successfully on the victims of incurable illness in nineteenth-century America as it does in our day.

Unfortunately, the medical experts offered even less hope.

A certain Dr. Bell declared after thorough study of the case, that the brain was affected and that all efforts on behalf of the patient were useless. "With a heart overflowing with love," Sarah cried out: "What can I say — I am blind and know not how to help you. . . . If your brain is really injured by the disease . . . would you like to consult some eminent physician in one of our insane asylums?" [20]

The heartbroken parents had to resign themselves to the hopeless outlook projected by the specialists they consulted. For several years Sody stayed at home, an apathetic figure in a wheelchair, tenderly cared for by his aging aunt and mother. It was on his account that the family decided, early in 1862, to give up the school and move to a private home in Perth Amboy, but the hoped-for recovery did not come. In 1862 he was sent to a farm in upstate New York, run by one of Weld's former students, Pliny Sexton. Here the invalid received custodial care and, when there was physical improvement, did light farm work. He seems to have been alert and interested in the family, who regularly visited him, took him on outings and kept him supplied with letters. His condition fluctuated; at one time he was able to live in the city for a few years, and even attempted working, but could not keep it up. The unusual ending to this unsatisfactory case history is that Sody lived to a ripe old age, surviving his parents and elder brother, although he apparently was in an institution of some kind.[21]

Of all the Weld children the least troublesome and the most normal was Sarah Grimké Weld, known as "Sissie." One can gather that "Aunt Sai" was less attached to her than she was to the nephews, for references to her are rare in her aunt's correspondence. She went away to school for a year, then spent a year learning domestic skills by managing the parental household. She contributed to the cause of woman's rights by working for some time as "an efficient aid" in the offices of the *Woman's Journal*.[22] In 1870 she married the Rev. William Hamilton, pastor of the local Unitarian church. She had four children, of whom two died in infancy.[23]

After he was relieved of the responsibilities of a school principal, Weld considered how he might best serve the war effort. He approached his old friend, Henry Bellows, who was working to organize the U. S. Sanitary Commission, for a position. Although Bellows recommended him for a post as inspector, Weld was turned down because he lacked the required medical knowledge. In September 1862, President Lincoln issued the preliminary proclamation of emancipation. A few days later, Garrison, who had been organizing pressure on the President for immediate emancipation, invited Weld to speak in Boston's Music Hall. Uncertain whether his voice would sustain him after the long years of absence from the public rostrum, Weld accepted with some hesitation. His family encouraged him to make the try and hoped it would lead to a resumption of his speaking career. "If Theodore finds that he can use his voice as a lecturer," Sarah wrote to a friend, "and any field of usefulness opens to him Nina and myself will joyfully and gratefully resign him. . . . The people need Truth more than armies." [24] Weld spoke on November 9, 1862, on the theme, "The Conspirators — their False Issues and Lying Pretenses." His speech was very well received and his voice gave him no trouble. He therefore decided to undertake an extended tour through New England, in which he was joined by Parker Pillsbury, another antislavery veteran.

It was a vastly different experience from that of the early

days, when mobs and brickbats had greeted the speakers. Now they were respectfully, often sympathetically received, and had no difficulty in getting meeting halls and audiences. Angelina was delighted with her husband's work. "He is doing the very thing my heart wants him to do," she wrote to Gerrit Smith. "Now is the accepted time and the day of Salvation from Slavery." She was praying for the President to stand firm and issue an emancipation declaration. "You see how warlike I have become. O, yes — war is better than Slavery." This, coming from an old believer in non-resistance, was indeed a change.[25]

Weld extended his tour to participate on behalf of the Republican candidate in the hotly contested New Hampshire Congressional elections of March 1863. Angelina rejoiced at his "resurrection." It must feel good to him, she thought, to experience the warm response of the people. She hoped he would keep on lecturing until peace was won. "I pray God that *you*, dearest, may one day have a mission in my native state and my birth city."[26] Weld continued on an extended Western tour, which brought him to Pennsylvania, Cleveland and Oberlin, where he revived the old tradition by speaking five times in four days to audiences to whom he represented a sort of prophet vindicated. After eighteen weeks of speaking he started on his return trip, his voice again somewhat troublesome, and lectured in Ohio and New York state. He ended the tour with one of his rare appearances at a convention. On May 12, 1863, he sat on the platform at the annual meeting of the American Anti-Slavery Society next to Garrison, Wendell Phillips, Frederick Douglass and Samuel May, and gave a stirring speech.[27]

Meanwhile, Sarah and Angelina had not been idle. In March 1863 an "Appeal to the Women of the Republic" ap-

peared in the New York *Tribune* over the signatures of Elizabeth Cady Stanton and Susan B. Anthony. It urged American women to rally to the cause of the Union and to gather in
a national convention in order to discuss how Northern
women might best serve the war effort. The "Appeal" had
been issued on behalf of the Woman's Central Committee,
the body which served as the steering committee of the
woman's rights movement between conventions. Listed
among the vice-presidents was Angelina Grimké Weld of
New Jersey.[28] Angelina attended the national convention
which met at Dr. Cheever's Church of the Puritans on May
14, 1863. Response to the appeal had come from all over the
Northern states, both by letters and delegates. It is obvious
that the introduction of Angelina Grimké Weld by the president of the convention, Lucy Stone, was regarded as something of special importance, for it and Angelina's speech
were reprinted in full in the proceedings, which had only
summarized Mrs. Stanton's opening address.

Once again, in full awareness of her unique position, Angelina spoke as the representative of South Carolina. "My
country is bleeding, my people are perishing around me," she
said. "But I feel as a South Carolinian, I am bound to tell the
North, go on! go on! Never falter, never abandon the principles which you have adopted." She developed her favorite
theme, that ending slavery would mean fulfilling the promise
of the Declaration of Independence. She ended by recalling
the position her brother Thomas had taken during the Nullification crisis of 1832, when he had stood up in the State Sen-
ate and declared that South Carolina had no right of secession. "If you persist," he had prophetically stated, "you will
be like a girdled tree, which must perish and die. You cannot
stand."

The convention proceeded to a spirited discussion of the Conscription Act, which was heartily endorsed, and to a more controversial discussion of emancipation. The delegates generally approved the President's Emancipation Proclamation, although they considered it insufficient and wanted to see an act of Congress freeing every slave everywhere in the nation. Controversy was aroused by a proposed resolution which stated: "There can never be a true peace in this Republic until the civil and political rights of all citizens of African descent and all women are practically established." The objections to this resolution were mainly that by thus linking the Negro and woman's rights, many potential supporters of the war effort might be alienated. Angelina replied to this objection: "I rejoice exceedingly that that resolution whould combine us with the negro. I feel that we have been with him. . . . True, we have not felt the slaveholder's lash; true, we have not had our hands manacled, but our *hearts* have been crushed. . . . I want to be identified with the negro; until he gets his rights, we shall never have ours." [29]

Angelina had in her own person represented the close link between woman's rights and Negro rights in 1838, when she had stood alone against the churches and the men of the abolition movement in asserting this unity of interest. She had not wavered from this position in the intervening years. In this she was much ahead of even the reformers of her time, as can be seen from the defeat of her resolution at the convention. A few years later, bitter factional strife would split the woman's rights movement over the question of endorsing the fourteenth amendment to the Constitution, which guaranteed voting rights to Negroes, while specifically denying them to women. This rift seriously weakened the movement for woman's rights and contributed to that lack of concern for Negro rights which characterized middle-class reform movements for the next thirty years.

The convention ended by forming a Woman's Loyal National League, which set itself a single goal — to collect one million signatures on a petition to Congress on behalf of an amendment to the Constitution ending slavery in the United States. At the final session Angelina Grimké Weld read a stirring "Address to the Soldiers of our Second Revolution" which she had written.

This remarkable document calls upon the Union soldiers to welcome colored soldiers as brothers in arms, to abandon race prejudice and to re-enlist once their terms of service had expired. It presents, with the vigor and passion characteristic of Angelina's style, a radical summation of the nature and purposes of the war.

This war is not, as the South falsely pretends, a war of races, nor of sections, nor of political parties, but a war of *Principles;* a war upon the working classes, whether white or black; a war against *Man,* the world over. In this war, the black man was the first victim, the workingman of whatever color the next; and now *all* who contend for the rights of labor, for free speech, free schools, free suffrage, and a free government . . . are driven to do battle in defense of these or to fall with them, victims of the same violence that for two centuries has held the black man a prisoner of war. While the South has waged this war against human rights, the North has stood by holding the garments of those who were stoning liberty to death. . . .

The nation is in a death-struggle. It must either be-

come one vast slaveocracy of petty tyrants, or wholly
the land of the free. . . .

Soldiers of this revolution, to your hands is committed
the sacred duty of carrying out in these latter days the
ideal of our fathers, which was to secure to ALL "life,
liberty and the pursuit of happiness." [30]

The convention, unlike other woman's rights meetings of
the past, received warm praise in the press. The mammoth
petition campaign was organized efficiently. Sarah and Angelina participated in it in their own community and reported an excellent response. Although the highly ambitious
goal of one million signatures in six months was not reached,
the Loyal League turned over a very impressive first install-
ment of the petition, bearing 100,000 signatures, to Senator
Charles Sumner, who in February 1864 offered it to Congress. By May of that year, Mrs. Stanton could report to the
anniversary meeting of the organization that two thousand
canvassers in twenty-three states had secured a total of 200,-
000 signatures, an impressive expression of public support
for the future thirteenth amendment.

During the war years Angelina also wrote and published *A
Declaration of War on Slavery*. This work, "one of the most
powerful things she ever wrote," according to her friend and
biographer Catherine Birney, has not survived.[31] Also scattered and unavailable are the contributions, perhaps anony-
mous, which Sarah sent during the war years to the New
York *Tribune*, *The Independent* and, later, *The Woman's
Journal*. Both sisters applauded Lincoln's second election
and watched the exploits of the colored regiments with
excitement. "The arming of the negro goes on gloriously,"
Sarah exulted. "They must be our Saviours, they our men of

sorrow are acquainted with grief." [32] They followed the news of the siege of Charleston with mixed feelings and with much anxiety. When at long last victory came and on April 14, 1865, the stars and stripes were hoisted over Fort Sumter, Weld was not among the speakers celebrating the end of the war in Charleston, as Angelina had hoped he might be. But William Lloyd Garrison was the guest of honor and the sisters must have shared in the symbolism of the celebration. The man who had led them to the abolition movement now stood in the citadel of slavery, which had given them birth. And Weld had the pleasure of speaking before thousands at a grand reunion of Lane rebels and veterans of the antislavery struggle at the 1865 Oberlin commencement exercises. This was a time of triumph for all abolitionists; the sisters especially, as white Southerners, could feel that their course, their life work, their decisions had been vindicated. But they were not the kind to indulge long in such emotions; their main concern was the frightful toll the struggle had taken.

They began at once to work for the freedmen, collecting money and clothing and supporting legislation for their rehabilitation. Angelina spoke at a small meeting on behalf of the freedmen and their former masters. "There was a refinement and dignity about her," reported a participant, "an atmosphere of gentleness and sweetness and strength, which won the way to the heart." [33]

From the Charleston sisters came a letter telling of the privations they had suffered. Having lost their property and slaves, they had for some time been subsisting on hominy and water. Yet, in the same letter Eliza and Mary insisted they would still be willing "to die for slavery and the Confederacy." [34] Sarah and Angelina sent food and money and invited their sisters to come North. Mary died shortly after this exchange of letters, but Eliza came North. For a few years, as a member of the Weld household, she recovered her strength and peace of mind and learned to appreciate that boundless supply of warmth and generous love the sisters lavished on the victims of misfortune. Eliza and her other sister, Anna Frost, later returned to Charleston.

The Welds, after leaving Raritan Bay Union, had first moved briefly to Perth Amboy, then to West Newton, Massachusetts. There they had boarded out for a few months, until Weld purchased a home in Fairmount, near Boston, soon after to become known as Hyde Park, where they spent the rest of their days. The move did not bring rest and retirement, for soon all three returned to teaching. This was prompted by a very favorable offer from Dr. Dio Lewis, the homeopathic and hydropathic practitioner, at whose institution Sody had sought a cure. Dr. Lewis, an energetic man of many interests, who was later to be instrumental in launching the Women's Christian Temperance Union, had since 1861 run the Boston Normal Institute for Physical Education. He now invited Weld to join the staff of his newly opened boarding school for young ladies at Lexington, offering him an attractive salary for teaching courses on Shakespeare and Moral Training. Since the distance involved required Weld to be absent from Hyde Park all week, the sisters decided to join him.

Angelina taught modern history, with special emphasis on the history of slavery and antislavery. She now enjoyed her work and did not mind the inconvenience of traveling to Lexington twice a week, although it was physically strenuous. "I am not satisfied to teach only what is in the text books," she wrote to a friend. "I read a great deal in larger works, so as to be a *live* teacher and lift the pupils' minds above the glitter and pomp of war and conquest."[35] Sarah, too, took pride in her teaching. When, for a period of a year, the Welds once again took in thirteen girl students as boarders, Sarah commented that having young life around her was a pleasure, since it filled the house with vitality and joyousness. Her renewed interest in her work is indicated by her completion, in 1867, of a book-length translation of Lamartine's *Joan of Arc,* which, to her great pleasure, was privately published in a small edition.[36] The same year marked an end to the sisters' teaching career, when Dr. Lewis' seminary burned down and he decided to close the school rather than rebuild it.

Weld continued for a number of years keeping school in a rented room and lecturing in and around Boston. He was active in Hyde Park community affairs, helped to organize the Free Public Library and was chairman of its board for nine years. He was also a member of the local school committee and an officer of the town. During these later years the Welds and Sarah enjoyed a close circle of friends, among whom they most frequently saw the Garrisons, Philbricks, Smiths and a host of former students. Weld, to the end of his life, continued a close friendship with Whittier, Elizur Wright and Henry Wadsworth Longfellow.[37]

The three were getting on in years: Weld and Angelina well in their sixties, Sarah seventy-five years old. But they were far from done.

One evening in February 1868 Angelina read a notice in the *Anti-Slavery Standard* concerning a meeting at Lincoln University in Pennsylvania, an institution for colored men, at which a young man named Grimké had delivered a fine address. Angelina wrote a friendly but formal note to "Mr. Grimké," introducing herself as the sister of Dr. John Grimké

of Charleston, South Carolina and inquiring whether he
might be the former slave of one of her brothers. She asked
him to tell her about himself and his family and briefly informed him of her own and her sister's and husband's anti-
slavery past.[38]

The answer came quickly. "Dear Madam." He was pleased
and surprised to hear "from Miss Angelina Grimké of Anti
Slavery celebrity" and would give her a simple sketch of his
life, as she had requested.

> I am the son of Henry Grimké a brother of Dr. John
> Grimké and [who is] therefore your brother. Of course
> you know more about my father than I do, suffice it to
> say he was a lawyer and was married to a Miss Simons
> . . . and she died leaving three children viz. Henrietta,
> Montague, and Thomas. After her death he took my
> mother, who was his slave and his children's nurse; her
> name is Nancy Weston. I dont think you know her, but
> your sister Miss Ann Grimké knows her, I heard her
> speak of you ladies often, especially Miss Ann. By my
> mother he had three children also, viz. Archibald which
> is my name, and Francis and John. He died about fif-
> teen years ago, leaving my mother, with two children
> and in a pregnant state, for John was born two mos.
> after he died, in the care of his son, Mr. E. M. Grimké
> [Montague] in his own words, as I heard, "I leave
> Nancy and her two children to be treated as members of
> the family."

Henry Grimké had made this provision, after careful consideration, because he felt Nancy Weston would thus be best
protected.

I am the eldest of the bros., was born 17th Aug. 1849. Therefore, my poor mother a defenceless woman, crippled in one arm, with no one to care for her in the world, for Mr. G. did not do as his father commanded, and three small children to provide for, was thrown upon the uncharitable world. . . .

She struggled hard and barely managed to support herself and the children. In 1860, Montague Grimké got married and wanted a servant.

He informed my mother that he wanted me and that she should send me to his house. His mandate was irresistible; it was a severe shock to my mother. . . . But this was only the beginning of her sorrows, thus he kept on until she was rendered childless.

The mother, when she protested, was briefly jailed. Archibald ran away, Frank attempted to escape and was retaken and sold, and the youngest, John, was enslaved as well. The war's end reunited the little family. The public schools of Charleston were opened to Negroes and the boys enrolled. Through the help of a Mrs. Pillsbury, the sister-in-law of Parker Pillsbury, who was then Principal of one of the Charleston public schools, Frank and Archie were sent North to be educated and finally sent to Lincoln University. Their tuition was being paid by a church committee, but there was no money provided for their books and clothing. Their brother John was still at home with his mother. "I hope dear Madam you will excuse this badly written epistle. . . . Perhaps you would like to see our pictures, they are enclosed. I shall hope to hear from you soon. Most respectfully yours, Archibald Henry Grimké." [39]

Dear young friends, [replied Angelina.] I cannot express the mingled emotions with which I perused your deeply interesting and touching letter. The facts disclosed were *no* surprise to me. Indeed had I not suspected that you might be my nephews, I should probably not have addressed you. . . . I will not dwell on the past — let that all go — it cannot be altered — our work is in the present. I am glad you have taken the name of Grimké — it was *once,* one of the noblest names of Carolina — a purer patriot never lived than my brother Thomas S. Grimké.

She hoped they would one day be able to read his views on Nullification, secession and education. She had no doubt that Thomas Grimké, had he lived longer, would have become an abolitionist. She had been deeply aggrieved that during the last war no one of the name of Grimké had been found on the side of freedom. "You my young friends now bear this *once* honored name — I charge you most solemnly by your upright conduct, and your life-long devotion to the eternal principles of justice and humanity and religion to lift *this name* out of the dust, where it now lies, and set it once more among the princes of our land." Angelina went on to ask a great many questions about the young men and announced her intention to visit them. The letter is signed, "truly your friend." [40]

Thus began an extended relationship, which is certainly remarkable and probably unique among the complexities of race relations in this country. The discovery of these young colored men was the acid test of the sisters' convictions. Many a good abolitionist would, in a similar situation, have been satisfied to engage in a friendly exchange of letters and let the matter rest at that. From Archibald Grimké's first letter it is evident that he expected just about that kind of reception. But Sarah and Angelina accepted these newly discovered nephews as members of the family and offered more than dutiful recognition and support — they offered their love. The long reference in Angelina's letter to her brother Thomas seems, at first reading, puzzling, especially when coupled with the studied lack of reference to the boys' father, Henry Grimké. But it makes sense when it is interpreted from Angelina's viewpoint. Deeply ashamed before these young men, as though she, somehow, bore part of the burden of race guilt for what they had suffered, she offered them the best the Grimké family had to offer — the heritage of their uncle Thomas. It would be hard to find a more subtle way of putting the relationship from the outset on a dignified and equal footing.

Further letters were exchanged. Frank now told his story. At the outbreak of the Civil War he had fled from his half-brother and master and had entered the Confederate Army as the valet of an officer. After two years of service he happened to be stationed in Charleston. He was recognized, arrested and sent to the workhouse for several months, where he became seriously ill from bad treatment and overwork. He was remanded to his mother's custody until he recovered, then was sold by his half-brother to another officer and again went into the Army, where he remained until the end of the war. His ordeal did not end, even after being sent North for an education. He was mistreated by the Massachusetts family with whom he was to board while going to school, and ran away again. He finally found a friendly family, who took him in and taught him shoemaking. Only through the intervention of his mentor, Mrs. Pillsbury, was he enabled to get a chance at an education.[41]

The sisters at once required of their nephews' needs and undertook to contribute regularly to their expenses. Sarah commented that from the picture they had sent it seemed Archie looked like her brother Thomas, while Frank looked like her brother, the doctor. In the early summer, Angelina, accompanied by her son Stuart, attended the commencement exercises at Lincoln University and stayed a week to become acquainted with her nephews. They impressed her very favorably and she took pride in their excellent achievements at school. She invited them to visit her home and arranged to pay for the education of their youngest brother. The visit was a great emotional strain on her and brought on a prolonged illness.[42]

With love and acceptance came good advice and the kind of fretful supervision fond parents lavish on their children. Every detail of the nephews' future was the subject of extended comment and discussion by the Welds and Sarah. The aunts offered suggestions as to where the boys should continue their education, how they should spend their vacations and whether they could afford to go South for a visit with their mother. Brother John was particularly the object of concern. He was brought to Lincoln, but he did not have an aptitude for study, nor did he like living away from Charleston. Despite all his aunts' good advice, financial help and urgings, he returned to Charleston and later lived and worked in Florida. Archie and Frank, however, took all the guidance and support with good grace. They considered the Weld home their own. As children are apt to do with their own parents, they were often neglectful in answering letters promptly or acknowledging the receipt of packages, a slight for which they were repeatedly chided by Sarah. They showed independent judgment in the shaping of their careers. Despite repeated suggestions that they attend Cornell University, they charted their own course. Both graduated from Lincoln in 1870. Francis James went on to Princeton Theological Seminary; Archibald Henry spent two more years at Lincoln, getting his MA while working part time. In 1872, he entered Harvard Law School, where he graduated with an L.L.B. in 1874.

The sisters and Weld supported the nephews throughout their years at college. At times Angelina turned all her earnings over to them, while Sarah, now retired, deprived herself of all kinds of small pleasures in order to help them. Sarah, perhaps inspired by their story, wrote a novel concerning the marriage of an octaroon to a white man. She tried to sell it, for the express purpose of using any possible return to send one or both of her nephews through law school. The book did not sell because the subject matter was considered objectionable, and Sarah abandoned this — her last — writing project.[43] One of the very last letters she wrote in her life concerned money she was raising for her "Archie-fund." Her feelings about her nephews are best expressed by herself: "Is it not remarkable that these young men should far exceed in talents any of my other Grimké nephews, even their half brothers bear no comparison with them and my brother Thomas' sons, distinguished as he was, are far inferior to them in intellectual power." [44]

Sarah spoke of the Grimké family; she might as well have spoken of the Welds. One may argue whether the Welds were successful parents and to what extent Sarah's influence on their children was a hindrance or a help. One thing is certain — none of the Weld children was in any way concerned with their parents' causes. But Archibald Henry Grimké, who became the outstanding Negro leader in the years between the death of Frederick Douglass and the ascendancy of Booker T. Washington, always credited his aunts with having made him "a liberal in religion, a radical in the woman suffrage movement, in politics and on the race question." [45] He and his brother truly carried on the work to which the Grimké sisters and Theodore Weld had dedicated their lives.

Francis James Grimké became Pastor of the 15th Street Presbyterian Church in Washington, D.C., a position he held for almost fifty years until his death. He was a trustee of Howard University, a member of the American Negro Academy and a respected national figure. Four volumes of collected speeches and articles testify to his leadership of his race. In 1878 he married Charlotte Forten, the forty-year-old daughter of James Forten of Philadelphia, a friend and co-worker of the sisters since their early days. Their only child, named Theodora, died as an infant in 1880.

Archibald Henry Grimké married Sarah Stanley and, while practicing law in Boston, lived in Hyde Park for a time. His daughter, whom he named Angelina Weld Grimké, was frequently cared for in the Weld home. In his will Theodore Weld assigned a bequest to "my nephew," Archibald Grimké, for the education of this daughter. From 1883–1885 Archibald Grimké was editor of *The Hub*, a Negro journal, and wrote many articles and pamphlets on behalf of Negro rights. He wrote biographies of Garrison and Sumner and was active in politics. In 1884 he was alternate delegate to Henry Cabot Lodge to the Republican national convention, and in 1894 was appointed United States Consul to Santo Domingo. A vice-president of the NAACP, and for over a decade President of the American Negro Academy, he won many awards and distinctions, the most

prized of which was the 1919 Spingarn medal of the NAACP
for the highest achievement of an American citizen of African descent.[46]

To the end of their long lives, the sisters were not satisfied
to be merely observers. At the age of seventy-nine, Sarah
trudged up and down the countryside, circulating and selling 150 copies of John Stuart Mill's *Subjection of Women.*
When, in January 1870, the Massachusetts Woman Suffrage
Association was founded, both sisters accepted positions on
the board of officers as vice-presidents. They continued as
officers of the organization until their deaths, as did Theodore Weld after 1878.[47] In 1870, when their old friend Lucy
Stone gave a lecture in Hyde Park, the sisters and Weld were
in the audience. Sarah participated in the discussion; all
three concurred in the sense of the meeting that more than
lectures were needed to dramatize the demand of women for
the elective suffrage. A few brave souls, both men and
women, decided that at the next election a suffrage demonstration would be organized. This was to be the first such in
Massachusetts and a forerunner of many thousands across
the nation.

A few days before the town election, a caucus meeting was
held, a slate of officers nominated and the public protest
planned. As it happened, March 7, 1870, dawned on a howl-
ing snowstorm. But the forty-two women and their male es-
corts assembled on time. It had been Weld's idea that each
gentleman present his lady with a bouquet of flowers. The
couples formed into a procession, which was headed by the
Grimké sisters and Weld. Through the driving snow they
marched to the polling place, to the jeers and cheers of the
townspeople. As they approached it, the men fell back and
each lady dropped her ballot in a special receptacle, which

the election officials had prepared for the purpose. Then the ranks reformed and the demonstrators marched back as they had come. It was no more than a small, somewhat touching gesture, but it did get fairly wide publicity. For Sarah and Angelina, who had thirty-two years earlier pioneered with the assertion of woman's equality, this was an act of faith. Women, whom they had always held to be the equals of men as rational human beings, would one day, perhaps in the far distant future, enjoy full equality before the law.[48]

Sarah died at the age of eighty-one on December 23, 1873. Angelina, paralyzed for six years by several strokes, died on October 26, 1879. Her funeral was, as Sarah's had been, an in-gathering of the veterans of abolition and reform. Eulogies were offered by Lucy Stone, Wendell Phillips, Elizur Wright and others. Garrison, who had spoken at Sarah's funeral, was himself too sick to attend. Obituaries in the very newspapers that had attacked and vilified the sisters decades ago now eulogized them as pioneers.[49]

Weld lived on until 1895, honored and respected and surrounded by friends. He edited a brief collection of the funeral speeches and statements made for his wife and Sarah, which was privately published. He always wanted to see a full biography of the sisters written and had tried to interest his son, Stuart, Garrison and others to undertake the project. He was very pleased when Catherine Birney, wife of William Birney, the elder Birney's son and a former student at Eagleswood School, undertook the writing of a biography after the sisters' death. She had resided in the Weld home and had known and loved the sisters. Her biography, published in 1885, was sympathetically written and avoided, on the whole, the sentimental distortions so often found in nineteenth-century biographies by friends. She appraised the sisters correctly as pioneers of abolition and woman's rights and succeeded in giving a sense of their personalities and character.

The Grimké sisters' lives had spanned almost a century. Now they were gone. Slavery was ended, but the black man was far from free and equal. Women, considerably freer to educate and express themselves than they had been during the sisters' early years, were many decades away from even the limited achievement of their citizenship rights. Perhaps women would not quite, as Angelina had liked to say, "turn the country upside down," but they would stand upright, and no man — guardian, father or husband — would "keep his foot upon their neck." That, according to Sarah, was what the movement was all about and the work of the sisters had been part of it.

Sarah and Angelina Grimké had lived their faith, with stubbornness, courage and dedication — a faith in the freedom and dignity of man, regardless of race, regardless of sex.

NOTES

CHAPTER ONE

1. Letter by M. W. C. (Marie Weston Chapman), *The Liberator*, March 2, 1838.
2. *Loc. cit.*
3. Guion G. Johnson, *Antebellum North Carolina* (Chapel Hill: University of North Carolina Press, 1937), pp. 221, 302.
4. Quoted in Arthur Calhoun, *A Social History of the American Family* (3 vols.; New York: Barnes & Noble, 1945), II, 84.
5. Quoted in Eleanor Flexner, *Century of Struggle: The Woman's Rights Movement in the United States* (Cambridge: Harvard University Press, 1959), p. 44.
6. Gilbert H. Barnes and Dwight L. Dumond (eds.), *Letters of Theodore Dwight Weld, Angelina Grimké Weld and Sarah Grimké, 1822–1844* (2 vols.; New York: D. Appleton-Century Co., 1934), II, 564. Hereafter referred to as *Weld-Grimké Letters*.
7. Samuel T. Pickard (ed.), *Life and Letters of John Greenleaf Whittier* (2 vols.; Boston: Houghton, Mifflin & Co., 1894), I, 239.
8. *Weld-Grimké Letters*, II, 574.
9. Elizabeth C. Stanton, "The Woman's Rights movement and its champions in the United States," *Eminent Women of the Age*, ed. James Parton (Hartford: S. M. Betts & Co., 1869), p. 363.
10. Lydia Maria Child, *Letters* (Boston: Houghton, Mifflin & Co., 1883), p. 26.
11. This and the following quotes from A. Grimké's speech: *The Liberator*, March 2, 1838.
12. Child, *loc. cit.*
13. *Weld-Grimké Letters*, II, 574.
14. Child, *loc. cit.*
15. *Weld-Grimké Letters*, II, 572–74.
16. *Ibid.*
17. All quotes concerning this meeting from *Weld-Grimké Letters*, II, 573–74. No text of Angelina Grimké's speeches at the second and third appearances is extant.
18. Boston *Gazette*, March 9, 1838.
19. Reprinted in *The Liberator*, April 29, 1838.
20. Pittsburgh *Manufacturer*, reprinted in *The Liberator*, May 11, 1838.
21. Boston *Mercantile Journal*, reprinted in *The Liberator*, April 29, 1838.
22. Reprinted in *The Liberator*, May 11, 1838.

CHAPTER TWO

1. Annie E. Miller, *Our Family Circle* (Macon, Georgia: n. p., 1931), pp. 72–95 *passim*.
2. "Genealogies of American Society: The Grimké Family of South Carolina," *Town Topics: The Journal of Society*, LXXXVI, No. 13 (Sept. 28, 1916), 18.
3. John F. Grimké, "Journal of the Campaign to the Southward," *South Carolina Historical and Genealogical Magazine*, XII, Nos. 2, 3, 4 (April, July, October, 1911), 60–69, 118–34, 190–206. "Order Book of John F. Grimké," *South Carolina Historical and Genealogical Magazine*, XIII, Nos. 1, 2, 3, 4 (January, April, July, October, 1912), 42–55, 89–103, 148–53, 205–212.
4. Allen Johnson and Dumas Malone, *Dictionary of American Biography* (22 vols.; New York: Scribner's & Sons, 1928–44), VII, 633–34.
5. Miller, *loc. cit.* For additional information about the Grimké and Smith families, the following sources were consulted: D. E. Huger Smith and A. S. Salley, Jr. (eds.), *Register of St. Philip's Parish: Charlestown or Charleston S. C.: 1754–1810* (Charleston: The South Carolina Society, Colonial Dames of America, 1927), O. Cromwell, *Directory or Guide to the Residences . . . of the City of Charleston . . . for the year . . . 1829* (Charleston: James S. Burges, 1828).
   For an interesting discussion of the Grimké family as representative Southern Mugwumps see William R. Taylor, *Cavalier and Yankee: The Old South and American National Character* (Garden City, N. Y.: Doubleday Anchor Books, 1963), pp. 32–42.
6. Entry in the Grimké Family Bible. Theodore Dwight Weld Collection, William L. Clements Library. The University of Michigan, Ann Arbor, Mich. Hereafter referred to as Weld MSS.
7. For background on Charleston social life and culture the following were consulted: Jacob N. Cardozo, *Reminiscences of Charleston* (Charleston: J. Walker, 1860); Charles Fraser, *Reminiscences of Charleston: lately published in the Charleston Courier, and now revised and enlarged by the Author . . .* (Charleston: J. Russell, 1854); Alexander Garden, *Anecdotes of the American Revolution, with sketches of characters of persons the most distinguished in the Southern states, for civil and military services . . .* (Charleston: Printed for the author by A. E. Miller, 1822); Paul H. Hayne, *Lives of Robert Young Hayne and Hugh S. Legare* (Charleston: Walker, Evans & Cogswell, 1878); William G. Simms, *The History of South Carolina . . .* (Charleston: S. Babcock & Co., 1853). Also Harriot H. Ravenel (Mrs. St. Julien). *Charleston: the Place and the People* (New York: Macmillan, 1906).
8. A list of Judge Grimké's land holdings is contained in will of John Faucheraud Grimké, October 28, 1819, recorded in Will Book F 1818–1826, Charleston, S. C., p. 121.
9. *Dictionary of American Biography, loc. cit.*
10. Frederick P. Bowes, *The Culture of Early Charleston* (Chapel Hill: University of North Carolina Press, 1942), *passim*.
11. Catherine Birney, *The Grimké Sisters: Sarah and Angelina Grimké, The First Women Advocates of Abolition and Woman's Rights* (Boston: Lee & Sheppard, 1885), p. 229.
    Catherine Birney was a personal friend of the sisters and based her biography on their diaries and letters, many of which are now to be found in the Weld MSS. Her penciled notations can still be seen in the Weld MSS. I have cross-checked them and found Birney generally accurate in her quoted and paraphrased material.
12. *Ibid.*, pp. 8–9.
13. *Ibid.*, p.10.
14. *Ibid.*, pp. 10–11.
15. John C. Hurd, *Law of Freedom and Bondage: Slave Laws of South Carolina* (2 vols.; Boston: Little, Brown & Co., 1858), I, 304.

16. *Ibid.*, p. 297.
17. Sarah Grimké diary, dated 1827, Weld MSS. There are
    two diaries by Sarah Grimké in the Weld MSS. One,
    dated 1827, and bearing no further date entries, is obvi-
    ously a recollection of childhood and the years up to 1827.
    I will hereafter refer to it as diary, dated 1827. The sec-
    ond diary was started in 1819 and shows some evidence
    of chronological sequence, although the dates are not
    always given. Where there are dates, they are in the
    Quaker phraseology; for the sake of convenience I have
    transcribed these to the conventional method of dating.
    Also, Birney, p. 12.
18. Although the diary entry only mentions a lecture and not
    who delivered it, it is most unlikely that anyone but
    Judge Grimké would have done so. Mrs. Grimké was
    indulgent and lenient toward her children and, as her
    later correspondence reveals, was temperamentally unfit
    for self-righteous lecturing.
19. Birney, pp. 12–13.

CHAPTER THREE

1. Birney, p. 13.
2. *Ibid.*, p. 14.
    On Thomas Grimké's educational ideas see *Dictionary
    of American Biography*, VII, 635–36. Also: Thomas
    Grimké, *Address on the Character and Objects of Science
    delivered before the Literary and Philosophical Society
    of South Carolina on the 9th May, 1827* (Charleston:
    A. E. Miller, 1827).
3. Birney, p. 18.
4. *Dictionary of American Biography*, VII, 635–36.
5. Sarah Grimké, "Education of Women" (essay), box 21,
    Weld MSS.
6. *Dictionary of American Biography*, VII, 635–36. Also,
    Sarah Grimké's diary, dated 1827, Weld MSS.
7. Ravenel, *passim*.
8. D. E. H. Smith, *A Charlestonian's Recollections*
    (Charleston: Carolina Art Association, 1950), *passim*.
    Also: Linda Rhea, *Hugh Swinton Legaré* (Chapel Hill:
    University of North Carolina Press, 1934), p. 53.
9. Thomas S. Grimké, *Oration Delivered in St. Philip's
    Church on the 4th of July, 1809 by the appointment of
    the South Carolina State Society of the Cincinnati
    by Thomas Smith Grimke, Member of the Cincinnati*
    (Charleston: n. n., 1809).
10. *Ibid.*
11. Miller, p. 72.
12. Birney, p. 19.
13. Harriet Martineau, *Society in America* (2 vols.; New
    York: Saunders & Otley, 1837), II, 112, 118.
14. Mary Boykin Chesnut, *A Diary from Dixie*, ed. Ben. A.
    Williams (Boston: Houghton Mifflin Co., 1961), pp.
    21–22.
15. Sarah Grimké's diary, dated 1827, Weld MSS. Also,
    Birney, pp. 18–19.
16. Both quotes: [Theodore D. Weld]. *American Slavery As
    It Is: Testimony of a Thousand Witnesses* (New York:
    American Anti-Slavery Society, 1839), Narrative and
    Testimony of Sarah Grimké.
17. "A Southern Churchwoman's View of Slavery," *Church
    Intelligencer*, Nov. 22, 1860, as quoted in Mary R. Beard
    (ed.), *America through Woman's eyes* (New York: Mac-
    millan Co., 1934), p. 145.
18. *American Slavery As It Is*, Narrative and testimony of
    Sarah M. Grimké.

19. *Ibid.* Narrative and testimony of Angelina E. Grimké.

CHAPTER FOUR

1. Sarah Grimké's diary, dated 1827, Weld MSS.
2. Sarah Grimké's diary, copied Jan. 7, 1821, Weld MSS.
3. Wm. Nelson (ed.), *The New Jersey Coast in 3 Centuries*
   (2 vols.; New York: Lewis Publishing Co., 1902), p. 51.
   Also consulted for descriptions of Long Branch:
   United States Works Progress Administration, New
   Jersey, Writers' Project, *Entertaining a Nation: The
   Career of Long Branch* (Bayonne, N. J.: The Jersey
   Printing Co., 1940); J. H. Schenck, *Descriptive Guide
   of Long Branch, N. J.* (New York: Trow & Smith Co.,
   1868).
4. Sarah Grimké's diary, copied Jan. 7, 1821, Weld MSS.
5. Description of beach scene is from Nelson, pp. 50–51, as
   quoted from *Niles' Register* (1819).
6. Sarah Grimké's diary, *loc. cit.*
7. *Ibid.*, verbatim dialogue quote.
8. Ephraim Ramsay. Judge of the Supreme Court of South
   Carolina to John F. Grimké, April 23, 1798, Gratz Collection, Pennsylvania Historical Society, Philadelphia,
   Pa.
9. G. Johnson, p. 148.

CHAPTER FIVE

1. Sarah Grimké's diary, Weld MSS.
2. Birney, p. 29. Birney does not identify the particular
   Quaker who gave Sarah the book. Sarah, in her diary,
   always refers to him by his initials or first name only. But
   there were sufficient clues in the diary and letters to
   enable me to deduce the identity of the gentleman
   in question. For material on Israel Morris and his family
   I have relied chiefly on R. C. Moon, *The Morris Family
   of Philadelphia* (5 vols.; Philadelphia: R. C. Moon, 1898-
   99).
3. Will of J. F. Grimké.
4. Sarah Grimké's diary, dated 1827, Weld MSS.
5. *Ibid.*
6. Consulted: Laura A. White, *Robert Barnwell Rhett:
   Father of Secession* (New York: Century Co., 1931).
7. Birney, p. 29.
8. John Woolman, *A Journal of the Life, Gospel Labours
   and Christian Experiences of that faithful Minister of
   Jesus Christ, John Woolman, Late of Mt. Holly in the
   Province of New Jersey, North America* (London: W.
   Phillips, 1824), pp. 19–20.
9. *Ibid.*, p. 32.
10. *American Slavery As It Is*, Narrative and testimony of
    Sarah Grimké, pp. 23–24.
11. Birney, p. 30.
12. As quoted in: Dwight L. Dumond, *Antislavery: The
    Crusade for Freedom in America* (Ann Arbor: The
    University of Michigan Press, 1961), p. 127.
13. Birney, p. 32.
14. Minutes, Monthly Meetings of Friends of Philadelphia,
    Fourth & Arch Street Meeting, 1823–31 (Arch Street
    Center, The Society of Friends, Philadelphia, Pa.).
15. Sarah Grimké's diary, dated 1827, Weld MSS.
16. *Ibid.*
17. *Ibid.*, September 1827.
18. A. Hallowell, *James and Lucretia Mott* (Boston: Hough-
    ton, Mifflin & Co., 1884), *passim*.

19. For background information on Quaker history I consulted: Thomas H. Speakman, *Divisions in the Society of Friends* (2nd ed.; Philadelphia: J. B. Lippincott Co., 1893); also, Samuel M. Janney, *History of the Religious Society of Friends from its rise to the year 1828* (4 vols.; Philadelphia: Ellwood Zell, 1867), IV, 212–36.

20. Moon, *passim*.

21. This and the following quotes: Sarah Grimké's diary, Sept. 16, 1830, Sept. 1832, and undated entry (dream), Weld MSS.

22. In the very chapter in which he undertook to explode the stereotype of the "old-maid feminist" Robert Riegel felt it necessary to attach it to Sarah Grimké, "the one quite intimidating spinster . . . practically in a class by herself." Her relationship to Israel Morris is here for the first time reconstructed from the diaries. It shows that Sarah, like Susan Anthony and Anna Dickinson, was in a position "to have made marriage easily possible if they had been interested." See Robert Riegel, *American Feminists* (Lawrence: University of Kansas Press, 1963), p. 193.

CHAPTER SIX

1. There are scattered references to this matter in several letters of sisters Eliza and Mary Grimké to Angelina G. Weld, after the death of their mother and after the publication of *American Slavery As It Is*. See also: Birney, p. 71, for reference to this by Mrs. Grimké.

2. *Ibid.*, pp. 41, 71. Also: Angelina Grimké's diary, Jan. 11, 1828, Weld MSS. Catherine Birney's version of the incident was accurately taken from the diary passage. There is another version given by Theodore Weld, *In Memory: Angelina Grimké Weld* (Boston: George Ellis, 1880), pp. 47–48. This version is a dramatized elaboration of the incident and I therefore did not use it.

Weld wrote these "Memorial Sketches" after Angelina's death from memory of oral accounts of the sisters or other relatives. He states that he made no notes of them and that he was merely trying to recall "the main thoughts and facts, scope and spirit." (Weld, *In Memory*, p. 56).

3. Birney, p. 40. Also: Weld, *In Memory*, p. 35.

4. Birney, p. 43.

5. A. Grimké to Anna Frost, March 18, 1828, Weld MSS.

6. Rev. Wm. McDowell to Rev. John A. McDowell, October 22, 1831, Gratz Collection, Pennsylvania Historical Society.

7. Weld, *In Memory*, p. 37.

8. Dumond, *Antislavery*, p. 93.

9. See p. 69.

10. Weld, *In Memory*, p. 37. Weld elaborates this incident, quoting dialogue which may not be entirely reliable. However, the incident itself fits in so well with Angelina's later behavior, especially during her appearance before the Session of the Third Presbyterian Church, that it deserves to be recorded.

11. Angelina Grimké's diary, April 20, 1828, Weld MSS.

12. Angelina's Grimké's diary, April 25, 1828, Weld MSS. Also: A. E. Grimké to Charles McIntire, May 13, 1828, Weld MSS.

13. Angelina Grimké's diary, May 7, 1828, Weld MSS. Verbatim dialogue quote.

14. Birney, pp. 60–61; also, Weld, *In Memory*, pp. 37–39.

15. Birney, p. 62.

16. Angelina Grimké's diary, Feb. 10, 1828, Weld MSS.; also Birney, p. 58.

17. Birney, p. 67.

18. Angelina Grimké's diary, April 5, 1829, Weld MSS.

19. *Ibid.*, Aug. 17, 1829.

20. Angelina Grimké's diary as quoted in Birney, pp. 70–71. Angelina frequently wrote dialogue passages in her diary. I have separated the dialogue of the different speakers for greater clarity.

21. Dumond, *Antislavery*, p. 86.

22. Angelina Grimké's diary, April 1829; also, Birney, p. 75.

23. Birney, pp. 73–75.

24. Angelina Grimké's diary, March 29, 1829, Weld MSS.; also, Birney, p. 84.

25. Angelina Grimké's diary, May 12, 1829, Weld MSS.; also, Birney, pp. 87–88.

26. *American Slavery As It Is*, p. 57.

27. Angelina Grimké's diary, May 6, 1829, Weld MSS.; also, Birney, p. 87.

28. Angelina Grimké's diary, Feb. 6, 1829, Weld MSS.; also, Birney, pp. 75–77. I have separated the dialogue of the different speakers for greater clarity.

29. Angelina Grimké's diary, Feb. 7, 1829, Weld MSS.; also, Birney, pp. 77–78.

30. Birney, pp. 80–81, 82.

31. The silent prayer meetings are described in Birney, pp. 72–73. The complaint about the absence of mosquito nets for the slaves is in *American Slavery As It Is*, p. 57.

32. Rev. Wm. A. McDowell to A. E. Grimké, May 14, 1829, Weld MSS.

33. Angelina Grimké's diary, May 20, 1829 and May 23, 1829, Weld MSS.

34. Rev. Wm. A. McDowell to A. E. Grimké, May 30, 1829, Weld MSS.

35. A. E. Grimké to Rev. Wm. A. McDowell, May 31 (n.d.), Gratz Collection, Pennsylvania Historical Society.

36. Birney, p. 90.

37. Angelina Grimké's diary, Oct. 1829, Weld MSS; also, Birney, p. 93.

38. Birney, p. 92.

CHAPTER SEVEN

1. For background on Philadelphia the following were consulted: H. D. Eberlein and C. V. Hubbard, *Portrait of a Colonial City; Philadelphia, 1670–1838* (Philadelphia: Lippincott, 1939); E. Kennedy Collection, Pennsylvania Historical Society; Dr. Conrad N. Lauer, *William Penn's Philadelphia — in 1840: A Newcomen Address* (Princeton: Princeton University Press, 1940); George Morgan, *History of Philadelphia: The City of Firsts* (Philadelphia: Published by the Historical Society of Philadelphia, 1926); Thos. Sharf and Thompson Westcott, *History of Philadelphia: 1609–1884* (3 vols.; Philadelphia: L. H. Everts & Co., 1884), Vol. II.

2. Minutes, Monthly Meeting of Friends of Philadelphia, Fourth & Arch Street Meeting, 1823–1831; Minutes, Quarterly Meetings of Friends of Philadelphia, 1826–1862; Minutes, Yearly Meetings of Friends of Philadelphia, 1828–1846; Minutes, Meeting of Women Friends of Philadelphia, 1823–1833. All at Arch Street Center, The Society of Friends, Philadelphia, Pa.

3. Friends Historical Society, *The Friends' Meeting House, Fourth and Arch Street* (Philadelphia: The J. Winston Co., 1904), p. 38.

4. Janney, *Friends*, IV, 236.

   I have used the spelling "Orthodox Quakers" to speak

of the organization after 1828. Lower case spelling indicates earlier movements and trends within the still
unified Society of Friends.
5. Angelina Grimké's diary, March 1831, Weld MSS.
6. Minutes, Monthly Meeting of Women Friends of Philadelphia, 1823–1833.
7. A. Grimké to S. Grimké, Nov. 8th, 1831, Weld MSS.
8. Thomas Grimké was at the time serving as State Senator,
representing Charleston.
9. Thos. Grimké, *Letter to the Honorable John C. Calhoun,
Vice-President of the United States . . .* (title abbreviated) (Pamphlet, Philadelphia, 1832); Birney, pp.
101–02.
10. W. P. and F. J. Garrison, *William Lloyd Garrison: 1805–
1879; The Story of His Life told by His Children* (4 vols.;
New York: The Century Co., 1885–1889), I, 225.
11. *The Friend, A Religious and Literary Journal,* Vol. IV,
No. 42, July 30, 1831; Vol. IV, No. 44, Aug. 13, 1831.
12. *Ibid.,* Vol. III, No. 8, Dec. 12, 1829.
13. *Ibid.,* No. 10, Dec. 19, 1829.
14. Angelina Grimké's diary, Weld MSS. This is a small separate diary, undated, devoted only to a summary account
of her relationship to Edward Bettle.
15. *Ibid.*
16. This description based on: Forrest Wilson, *Crusader in
Crinolines* (Philadelphia: Lippincott Co., 1941); Mary
E. Harveson, *Catherine Esther Beecher, Pioneer Educator* (Philadelphia: University of Pennsylvania, 1932);
Thomas Woody, *History of Women's Education in the
United States* (2 vols.; New York: The Science Press,
1929).
17. Angelina Grimké's diary, Aug. 3, 1831, Weld MSS. Also:
Birney, pp. 108–09.
18. Angelina Grimké's diary, Aug. 3, 1831, Weld MSS.
19. *Ibid.*
20. A. Grimké to S. Grimké, Dec. 8, 1931, Weld MSS.
21. Joseph C. Robert, *The Road from Monticello: A Study
of the Virginia Slavery Debate of 1832* ("Historical
Papers of the Trinity College Historical Society," Series
XXIV; Durham: Duke University Press, 1941), p. 35.
22. A. Grimké to S. Grimké, Feb. 4, 1832, Weld MSS.
23. Angelina Grimké's diary, March 5, 1832, Weld MSS.
24. Scharf and Westcott, *Philadelphia,* I, 632.
25. Sarah Grimké's diary, July 30, 1832, Weld MSS.
26. Scharf and Westcott, *loc. cit.*
27. Angelina Grimké's diary, undated, Weld MSS.
28. Sarah Grimké's diary, 1833, Weld MSS.
29. Thomas Grimké, *Letter to Calhoun.*
30. Thomas Grimké, "Defensive War," Part 2, published
posthumously, *The Calumet, Magazine of the American
Peace Society,* Vol. II, No. 2 (March-April 1835).
31. Weld, *In Memory,* pp. 71–72. Also: Birney, pp. 117–19.
32. "A sketch of Thomas Grimké's life written by his sisters
in Philadelphia and sent to his friends in Charleston for
their approbation," *The Calumet, Magazine of the American Peace Society,* Vol. II, No. 1 (Jan.-Feb. 1835).
33. Sarah Grimké's diary, Nov. 2, 1834, Weld MSS.
34. Jonathan Dymond, *An Inquiry into the Accordancy of
War with the Principles of Christianity . . . with notes
by Thomas S. Grimké* (title abbreviated) (Philadelphia:
I. Ashmead Co., 1834).

CHAPTER EIGHT

1. Sarah Grimké diary, Nov. 1, 1834 and Feb. 10, 1835,
Weld MSS.

2. *Ibid.,* Feb. 1835.
3. Based on Dumond, *Antislavery;* Louis Filler, *The Crusade
against Slavery, 1830–1860* (New York: Harper & Row,
1960); Herbert Aptheker (ed.), *A Documentary History
of the Negro People in the United States* (New York:
The Citadel Press, 1951), pp. 117–18.
4. Dumond, *Antislavery,* p. 199.
5. Quoted in Ralph Korngold, *Two Friends of Man: The
Story of William Lloyd Garrison and Wendell Phillips
and Their Relationship to Abraham Lincoln* (Boston:
Little, Brown & Co., 1950), p. 34.
6. The foregoing and subsequent material on Weld and the
Lane debates is based on: Benjamin D. Thomas, *Theodore Weld; Crusader for Freedom* (New Brunswick,
N. J.: Rutgers University Press, 1950), Gilbert H. Barnes,
The Antislavery Impulse, 1830–1844 (New York: D. Appleton-Century Co., 1933), *Weld-Grimké Letters, passim.*
7. Sarah Grimké, Letter on the subject of prejudice against
color amongst the Society of Friends in the United States,
April 10, 1839, Weston Papers, Boston Public Library,
Boston, Mass. This is a handwritten copy; the original is
in the Weld MSS.
8. *Ibid. .*
9. Minutes of the Philadelphia Female Anti-Slavery Society,
1834–1838, Entry Feb. 12, 1835, Philadelphia Historical
Society.
10. George Thompson, *Letters and Addresses during his
Mission in the United States, From Oct. 1, 1834 to Nov.
27, 1835* (Boston: Isaac Knapp, 1837), p. 46.
11. George Thompson, *Lectures* (Boston: Knapp, 1836),
passim.
12. Minutes, Philadelphia Female Anti-Slavery Society,
1834–1838.
　　In a letter dated 1839 (see above p. 372) Sarah
describes Angelina's attendance at antislavery meetings
in the spring of 1835, but insists that due to her own
pressure Angelina promised not to attend any such meetings for one year and that she kept this promise. This
statement seems to be contradicted by the records of
the Philadelphia Female Anti-Slavery Society. One can
assume that Sarah was not quite accurate in her memory.
13. A. Oliver Johnson, *William Lloyd Garrison and His
Times* (Boston: B. B. Russell & Co., 1880), pp. 255–56.
Also: Flexner, pp. 41–42.
14. Birney, p. 124.
15. Dumond, *Antislavery,* chap. 25.
16. *The Liberator,* Aug. 15, 1835, Reprint from *The Charleston Courier.*
17. Angelina E. Grimké, *Slavery and the Boston Riot* [A
Letter to Wm. L. Garrison] (Philadelphia, 1835, Broadside).
18. A. E. Grimké to S. Grimké, Sept. 27, 1835, Weld MSS.
Also: Birney, pp. 126–28.
19. *The Liberator,* Sept. 19, 1835.
20. Angelina Grimké's diary, Sept. 1835, Weld MSS. Also:
Birney, pp. 129–31.
21. *Ibid.*

CHAPTER NINE

1. *The Liberator,* Oct. 17, 1835; *Weld-Grimké Letters,* II,
533–34.
2. *The Liberator,* Oct. 17, 1835.
3. W. and F. Garrison, *Garrison,* II, 38.
4. *The Liberator,* Nov. 26, 1835; A. E. Grimké, *Slavery and
the Boston Riot.*

5. Dumond, *Antislavery*, p. 221; Samuel J. May, *Some Recollections of our Antislavery Conflict* (Boston: Fields, Osgood & Co., 1869), p. 162.
6. W. and F. Garrison, *Garrison*, II, 67.
7. *Weld-Grimké Letters*, I, 285, 295–301.
8. Thomas, chap. 7.
9. These stores sold only the products of free labor. They were set up to further the drive of the Free Produce Society to boycott slave-made products. See below, p. 409.
10. Letter from Lydia Maria Child in "Right and Wrong in Boston," *Report of the Boston Female Anti-Slavery Society with a concise statement of events, previous and subsequent to the Annual Meeting of 1835*. (Boston: Boston Female Anti-Slavery Society, 1836), p. 92.
11. Minutes, Philadelphia Female Anti-Slavery Society, Dec. 9, 1833.
12. *Ibid.*, Sept. 1835.
13. Lydia Maria Child, *An Appeal in Favor of That Class of Americans Called Africans* (Boston: Allen & Ticknor, 1833).
14. Child, in "Right and Wrong in Boston," p. 92.
15. W. and F. Garrison, *Garrison*, II, 55.
16. *The Liberator*, Feb. 25, 1837.
17. *Ibid.*, April 14, 1837. Letter by A. E. Grimké inserted on request of Essex County Olive Branch Society, dated 7th March 14, 1836.
18. For Free Produce Movement: N. B. Jackson, "The Free Produce Attack upon Slavery," *The Pennsylvania Magazine of History and Biography*, LXVI., No. 3 (July, 1942). For participation of Grimké sisters: Birney, p. 134.
19. Birney, p. 133.
20. S. Grimké, Letter on Prejudice, pp. 7–8, 12–13.
21. *Ibid.*, pp. 9–10.
22. Birney, pp. 134–36.
23. Minutes, Philadelphia Female Anti-Slavery Society, May 10, 1838.
24. A. E. Grimké to S. M. Grimké, July 10, 1836, Weld MSS; and A. E. Grimké to S. M. Grimké, July 19, 1836, Weld MSS.
25. Birney, p. 137.
26. *Ibid.*, pp. 137–38.
27. *Ibid.*, p. 139.
28. *Ibid.*, p. 140.
29. *Ibid.*, pp. 138, 141; Weld, *In Memory*, pp. 45–46.
30. Angelina E. Grimké, *Appeal to the Christian Women of the South* (New York: nn., 1836), p. 3.
31. *Ibid.*, p. 13.
32. *Ibid.*, pp. 16–18.
33. *Ibid.*, pp. 20, 24
34. *Ibid.*, p. 26.
35. *Ibid.*, p. 36.
36. Birney, pp. 140–41, 146; also: A. Grimké to S. Grimké, Aug. 1, 1836, Weld MSS.
37. *Weld-Grimké Letters*, I, 373.
38. A. E. Grimké to S. M. Grimké, July 31, 1836, Weld MSS.
39. Birney, p. 147.
40. George Thompson, *Slavery in America: A Reprint of an Appeal to the Christian Women of the Slave States of America, by Angelina E. Grimké of Charleston, South Carolina, with Introduction, Notes and Appendix* (London, 1837). See also: *Weld-Grimké Letters*, I, 407.
41. A. Grimké to S. Grimké, Aug. 14, 1836, Weld MSS.
42. Birney, pp. 153–54.
43. A. E. Grimké to S. Grimké, July 31, 1836, Weld MSS.

44. Birney, pp. 154–55 Also: Weld, *In Memory*, pp. 54–56. Weld's version is, again, a dramatization written from memory forty years after the event and therefore unreliable in the details, although the fact of this conversation and its general content are verifiable from the sisters' letters.
45. Angelina Grimké to Jane Smith, Sept. 18, 1836. In this letter Angelina refers to Catherine Morris' unpleasant visit, her conversation with Sarah, as well as to the trip to New York.
46. Both quotes from S. Grimké, Letter on Prejudice, pp. 24–25. On Angelina's acceptance and the decision not to take any remuneration for their work, see Birney, p. 155.

CHAPTER TEN

1. *The Liberator*, Oct. 22, 1836.
2. *Ibid.*, Nov. 5, 1836.
3. Weld, *In Memory*, pp. 53–54. Corroborating reference to the burning of the sisters' pamphlets is in S. M. Grimké, *An Epistle to the Clergy of the Southern States* (New York: n. p., 1836), p. 15.
4. Birney, p. 159.
5. The number "seventy" had been chosen because it symbolized that of the Biblical apostles, but was actually never reached. Thomas, p. 117.
6. This paragraph and the following analysis of the anti-slavery movement at the time of the agents' convention is based on Dumond, *Antislavery*, chap. 21, and was corroborated by consulting: Filler, *Crusade against Slavery*; Thomas, *Weld*; and Barnes, *Antislavery Impulse*.
7. A. Grimké to Jane Smith, Feb. 4, 1837, Weld MSS.
8. Thomas, pp. 17–18.
9. A. Grimké to J. Smith, Nov. 19, 1836, Weld MSS.
10. Both quotes *ibid.*
11. A. E. Weld to her mother, July 15, 1839, Weld MSS.
12. W. and F. Garrison, II, 117.
13. A. Grimké to J. Smith, *loc. cit.*
14. Birney, p. 161.
15. W. and F. Garrison, *loc. cit.*
16. A. Grimké to J. Smith, Jan. 20, 1837, Weld MSS. This letter bears the date Jan. 20, 1836, in A. Grimké's handwriting, which is obviously an error on her part, since the event she describes did not take place until 1837.
17. Birney, pp. 162–63.
18. A. Grimké to J. Smith, Dec. 17, 1836, Weld MSS.
19. *Ibid.*
20. A. Grimké to J. Smith, Jan. 20, 1837, Weld MSS.
21. A. Grimké to J. Smith, Feb. 4, 1837, Weld MSS.
22. Birney, p. 165.
23. *Weld-Grimké Letters*, I, 348.
24. *Ibid.*, pp. 365–72.
25. *Ibid.*, p. 368.
26. *Ibid.*, p. 273.
27. A. Grimké to J. Smith, March 22, 1837, Weld MSS.
28. A. Grimké to J. Smith, April 17, 1837, Weld MSS.
29. A. Grimké to J. Smith, Feb. 1837, Weld MSS.
30. Birney, p. 171.
31. *Ibid.*, p. 170.
32. *Weld-Grimké Letters*, I, 358.
33. *Ibid.*, pp. 360–61.
34. *Ibid.*, p. 365.

35. A. S. Grimké, Letter on Prejudice, pp. 29–30.
36. Elizabeth C. Stanton, Susan B. Anthony, and Matilda J. Gage, History of Woman Suffrage (6 vols.; New York: Fowler and Wells, 1881–1922), I, 39.
37. Weld-Grimké Letters, I, 388.
38. A. E. Grimké An Appeal to the Women of the Nominally Free States: Issued by an Anti-Slavery Convention of American Women & Held by Adjournment from the 9th to the 12th of May, 1837 (1st ed.; New York: W. S. Dorr, 1837).
39. Birney, p. 173.
40. Weld-Grimké Letters, I, 374–75.

CHAPTER ELEVEN

1. A. Grimké to J. Smith, May 29, 1837, Weld MSS.
2. A. Grimké to J. Smith, June 26, 1837, Weld MSS.
3. Weld-Grimké Letters, I, 401.
4. A. Grimké to J. Smith, May 29, 1837, Weld MSS.
5. Birney, p. 178.
6. Weld MSS., loc. cit.
7. Allan Nevins (ed.), Diary of John Quincy Adams: 1794–1845 (New York: Chas. Scribner's Sons, 1951), diary entry July 9, 1836, p. 466.
8. Ibid., Diary entry April 19, 1837, p. 479. For background on petition campaign and the fight against the "gag rule" the following were consulted: Barnes, Antislavery Impulse, chaps. 12 and 13. Also, Thomas, Weld, chap. 14.
9. Weld MSS., loc. cit.
10. Weld-Grimké Letters, I, 403.
11. Samuel Flagg Bemis, John Quincy Adams and the Union (New York: Alfred A. Knopf, 1956), p. 349.
12. Weld MSS., loc. cit.
13. In January 1837 Adams presented petitions signed by 150 women of the town of Dorchester and 228 women of South Weymouth. During the year 1837–38 the American Anti-Slavery Society sent to the House of Representatives 130,200 petitions for abolition in the District of Columbia and 23,160 for abolition of the slave trade between the states. These figures indicate only the numbers of petitions, not the millions of signatures to them. Bemis, pp. 340–41.
14. Ibid.
15. A. Grimké to J. Smith, June 26, 1837, Weld MSS. Also, Weld-Grimké Letters, I, 402.
16. Weld MSS., loc. cit.
17. Ibid.
18. Ibid.
19. Ibid.
20. The Liberator, July 7, 1837.
21. Henry C. Wright, Human Life: illustrated in my individual Experience as a Child, a Youth and a Man (Boston: B. Marsh, 1849), pp. 357–58.
    For background on position of the churches the following were consulted: Barnes, Antislavery Impulse, chaps. 9 and 10, Russell B. Nye, Wm. L. Garrison and the Humanitarian Reformers (Boston: Little, Brown and Co., 1955); Dumond, Antislavery, chaps. 16, 19, 20; W. and F. Garrison, II, chap. 3.
22. W. and F. Garrison, II, 131.
    Rev. Mr. Beecher was then, technically, a Presbyterian and his friend, Rev. Mr. Bacon, had to propose the resolution, but Rev. Mr. Beecher was the moving spirit behind it. See Barnes, Antislavery Impulse, pp. 92–96.
23. W. and F. Garrison, II, 125.

24. Samuel T. Pickard (ed.), Life and Letters of John Greenleaf Whittier (2 vols.; Boston: Houghton, Mifflin & Company, 1894), pp. 206–207.
25. Unfortunately only the intriguing title of this lecture has survived.
26. A. Grimké to J. Smith, July 16, 1837, Weld MSS.
27. Weld-Grimké Letters, I, 409.
28. Ibid., pp. 410–11.
29. Birney, p. 191.
30. Ibid., pp. 180–81.
31. Weld-Grimké Letters, I, 409.
32. W. and F. Garrison, II, 145.
33. Weld-Grimké Letters, I, 373. Also: Birney, p. 192. Birney states that the "Address" was printed. Dumond contradicts this statement for which there seems to be no extant evidence. The MS. of Sarah Grimké's Letter on the Subject of Prejudice (see Chapter 15, n. 26), in the files of the Boston Public Library, may be partially based on this earlier "Address."
34. Weld-Grimké Letters, I, 407–10.
35. Wright, Human Life, p. 348.
36. Ibid., p. 403, 380. Wright's ideas on marriage and education can be found in H. C. Wright, Marriage and Parentage: on the reproductive element in man, as a means to his elevation and happiness (Boston: B. Marsh, 1866).
37. The term "manufacturers" is here used for factory workers.
38. The Liberator, July 20, 1837.
39. Ibid., July 28, 1837.
40. Ibid.
41. Ibid., Aug. 4, 1837.
42. The Boston Morning Post, July 27, 1837.
43. Dwight L. Dumond (ed.), Letters of James Gillespie Birney (2 vols.; New York: D. Appleton-Century Co., 1938), I, 418.
44. The Liberator, July 21, 1837.
45. Dumond, Birney Letters, I, 418.
46. Weld-Grimké Letters, I, 446–67.

CHAPTER TWELVE

1. Catherine Beecher, An Essay on Slavery and Abolitionism with reference to the Duty of American Females (Philadelphia: Henry Perkins, 1837).
2. Ibid., p. 101.
3. Weld-Grimké Letters, I, 391.
4. Aptheker, Documentary History, pp. 71–72, 145–46. Also R. Billington (ed.), A Free Negro in the Slave Era; Journal of Charlotte Forten (New York: Collier Books, 1961), introduction.
5. Angelina E. Grimké, Letters to Catherine E. Beecher, in Reply to an Essay on Slavery and Abolitionism, Addressed to A. E. Grimké, Revised by the Author (Boston: Isaac Knapp, 1838), pp. 35–36, 40.
6. Ibid., pp. 12–13.
7. Ibid., pp. 112–13, 119.
8. Ibid., p. 126.
9. Weld-Grimké Letters, I, 428.
10. Sarah M. Grimké, Letters on the Equality of the Sexes and the Condition of woman: Addressed to Mary S. Parker, President of the Boston Female Anti-Slavery Society (Boston: Isaac Knapp, 1838).
11. The Liberator, June 23, 1837, quoted in W. and F. Garrison, II, 150.

12. Johnson, p. 261.
13. Stanton, *et al.*, *History of Woman Suffrage*, I, 81.
14. The New England *Spectator*, Aug. 2, 1837, reprinted in *The Liberator*, Aug. 11, 1837.
15. *The Liberator*, Aug. 18, 1837.
16. *Ibid.*, Aug. 25, 1837.
17. Stanton, *et al.*, *History of Woman Suffrage*, I, 84–86.
18. *Ibid.*, pp. 82–83.
19. *Weld-Grimké Letters*, I, 419.
20. A. Grimké to J. Smith, July 25, 1837, Weld MSS.
21. S. Grimké, *Letters on Equality*, p. 10.
22. *Ibid.*, p. 19.
23. *Ibid.*, p. 116.
24. *Ibid.*, p. 120. In 1836, Lucy Stone, then sixteen and a schoolteacher, was sewing a shirt for a young man in theological seminary, when her church sewing circle was addressed by Mary Lyon, who was then trying to raise funds for Mount Holyoke Female Seminary. Lucy Stone, coming to the same conclusion as Sarah Grimké, "left the shirt unfinished and hoped that no one would ever complete it." See Alice Blackwell, *Lucy Stone: Pioneer of Woman's Rights* (Boston: Little, Brown & Co., 1930), p. 20. There is no known connection between the two incidents.
25. S. Grimké, *Letters on Equality*, p. 122.
26. A. Grimké to J. Smith, July 18, 1837, Weld MSS.
27. Birney, p. 188.
28. *Ibid.*, pp. 223–24.
29. A. Grimké to J. Smith, Oct. 6, 1837, Weld MSS.
30. *Weld-Grimké Letters*, I, 468.
31. Dumond, *Birney Letters*, I, 478–80. This is the same Rev. Leonard Bacon mentioned in Chap. XI, above.
32. *Weld-Grimké Letters*, I, 468.
33. Samuel J. May, *Recollections*, pp. 234–36.
34. *Weld-Grimké Letters*, I, 411–12.
35. *Ibid.*, pp. 416–18.
36. *Ibid.*, p. 429.
37. *Ibid.*, pp. 423–24.
38. *Ibid.*, pp. 425–27.
39. It is interesting to note that Weld charged both sisters with responsibility for the *Spectator* articles, although they bore Sarah's signature. Angelina's addressing her reply jointly to Whittier and Weld must have been intended as a rebuke to Weld, with whom the sisters up to then had engaged in an intimate and friendly correspondence. Her rather formal address strengthens this impression.
40. *Ibid.*, pp. 427–32.
41. *Ibid.*, pp. 432–36.
42. *Ibid.*, pp. 446–52. Apparently, the Boston women had also, for a time, considered issuing a woman's paper, but had changed their minds. "We . . . conclude as long as we are not shut out from the men's papers we will use them; we do not want to separate the sexes any more into different organizations if it can be avoided. When they refuse to publish for us as I expect they will, we may then find it best to have a medium of communication with the public for ourselves." *Ibid.*, p. 439.
43. Birney, pp. 224–25.

CHAPTER THIRTEEN

1. Thomas, p. 6.
2. *Weld-Grimké Letters*, II, 577–78.

3. Description of Theodore Dwight Weld by Henry Brewster Stanton. In hand of Sarah Moore Grimké. 1838, Weld MSS.
4. *Weld-Grimké Letters*, II, 593.
5. *Ibid.*, I, 60–65.
6. *Ibid.*, 287.
7. *Ibid.*, II, 597.
8. *Ibid.*, I, 286.
9. *Ibid.*, 287.
10. *Ibid.*, 496. Also: *Ibid.*, II, 559.
11. *Ibid.*, I, 458.
12. *Ibid.*, 467.
13. *Ibid.*, 478–79.
14. *Ibid.*, 485. Also: *The Liberator*, Jan. 5, 1838.
15. *Weld-Grimké Letters*, I, 491–92.
16. *Ibid.*, 500.
17. *Ibid.*, 485.
18. *Ibid.*, 494.
19. James A. Thome and Horace Kimball, *Emancipation in the West Indies: A Six Months Tour in Antigua, Barbados and Jamaica, in the Year 1837* (New York: *The Anti-Slavery Examiner* No. 7, 1838); [Theodore Dwight Weld], *The Bible against Slavery: An Inquiry into the Patriarchal and Mosaic Systems on the Subject of Human Rights* (New York: *The Anti-Slavery Examiner* No. 6, 1838).
20. *Weld-Grimké Letters*, II, 514.
21. *Ibid.*, 520–21.
22. *Ibid.*, 532–35.
23. *Ibid.*, 536–39.
24. *Ibid.*, 554–55.
25. *Ibid.*, 556–58.
26. *Ibid.*, 560.
27. *Ibid.*, 576–80, 598.
28. *Ibid.*, 566.
29. *The Liberator*, April 29, 1838. Reprint from *The Olive Branch*.
30. *Weld-Grimké Letters*, II, 554.
31. *Ibid.*, 581–83.
32. *Ibid.*, 601.

CHAPTER FOURTEEN

1. I arrived at the figures by adding up all the attendance figures given by the sisters in their letters.

In judging the accuracy of the Grimkés' reporting, the following may be of interest: The record of their tour appears mainly in their correspondence with Jane Smith and Weld. They must have considered these letters semi-official reports, since Jane Smith reported on their experiences to the Philadelphia Female Anti-Slavery Society, and Weld, in his function of chairman of the Agents' Committee, was the person to whom they felt directly responsible.

I have cross-checked their facts with those in letters they wrote to other friends, as well as with the printed accounts in *The Liberator* and other newspapers. There are also, in specific instances, eye-witness accounts which I cross-checked. In all instances, I have found the sisters' accounts to be consistent and accurate, with the single exception that accounts in *The Liberator* generally tend to exaggerate attendance figures. (Such journalistic exuberance is quite commonplace in the press of the times).

In a letter from A. Grimké to Mrs. E. Nichols (Elizabeth Pease), Dec. 18, 1937, Weston Papers, Boston Public Library, she writes that during their New England tour they held "near 90 meetings which were attended by from 300 to 400 to 1200 to 1500 persons." This checks out almost perfectly with the number of meetings recorded elsewhere . . . Her attendance figures are higher than the ones I have credited above.

2. The attendance figures at some of the meetings in the smaller communities seemed high to me and I was particularly skeptical of the total. I was able to check in one particular instance as follows: According to Angelina, 120 persons attended the meeting in North Weymouth and 150 attended another meeting in South Weymouth. In Chas. F. Adams, *J. Q. Adams*, IX, 275, I found this entry from Adams' diary: "Jan 18, 1836. . . . A petition from 366 inhabitants of Weymouth, praying for abolition of slavery and the slave trade in the District of Columbia was presented to the Congress." If 366 inhabitants of Weymouth signed antislavery petitions in 1836, it does not seem unreasonable that 270 (combining North and South Weymouth) attended the Grimké's lecture in 1837.

3. *Sixth Annual Report of the Board of Managers of the Massachusetts Anti-Slavery Society, presented Jan. 24, 1838, with an appendix* (Boston: I. Knapp, 1838).
   The list of antislavery societies with membership figures were cross-checked against the towns the sisters had visited and dates were compared.

4. A. Grimké to J. Smith, Jan. 5, 1838, Weld MSS; *The Liberator*, Jan. 12, 1838. In this article the meeting is placed at the Odeon, but A. Grimké describes it twice, in different letters, as having taken place at the Lyceum. I consider this the more reliable information.

5. A. Grimké to T. Weld, Jan. 7, 1838, Weld MSS.
6. *Weld-Grimké Letters*, II, 602.
7. A. Grimké to T. Weld, Jan. 8, 1838, Weld MSS.
8. *Weld-Grimké Letters*, II, 609.
9. S. Grimké to J. Smith, March 24, 1838, Weld MSS.
10. *Weld-Grimké Letters*, II, 616.
11. *Ibid.*, 624.
12. *Ibid.*, 633.
13. *Ibid.*, 651.
14. Weld, *In Memory*, p. 24. Robert Wallcutt gives the number of Odeon lectures, as six, but that is an error. All other accounts, including advertisements in local newspapers, show that there were only five lectures given.
15. *Ibid.*, p. 28.
16. A. G. Weld to Jane Smith, March 27, 1838, Weld MSS.
17. *Weld-Grimké Letters*, II, 610.
18. A. G. Weld to J. Smith, March 27, 1838, Weld MSS.
19. *Weld-Grimké Letters*, II, 617–18.
20. *Ibid.*, 610.
21. *Ibid.*, 626.
22. *Ibid.*, 653.
23. *Ibid.*, 647.
24. *Ibid.*, 636–39.
25. As quoted in John A. Pollard, *John Greenleaf Whittier: Friend of Man* (Boston: Houghton Mifflin Co., 1949), p. 365.
26. As quoted in *Weld-Grimké Letters*, II, 671, footnote.
27. *Ibid.*, 657.
28. *Ibid.*, 629–30.
29. *Ibid.*, 641.
30. A. Grimké to T. Weld, April 11, 1838, Weld MSS.

31. *Weld-Grimké Letters*, II, 651–52.
32. *Ibid.*, 667–68.
33. *Ibid.*, 670. Also: A. Grimké to T. Weld, April 13, 1838, Weld MSS.
34. W. and F. Garrison, II, 211–12.
35. Eliz. Grimké to A. G. Weld, May 2, 1838, and Mrs. Grimké to T. and A. Weld and S. Grimké, June 18, 1838, Weld MSS.
36. *Weld-Grimké Letters*, II, 678–79, for description of the wedding.

CHAPTER FIFTEEN

1. *Weld-Grimké Letters*, II, 609.
2. Birney, pp. 235–36; also: Dumond, *Antislavery*, p. 226.
3. Sharf and Westcott, I, 651.
4. *The Emancipator*, May 17, 1838; also: *The Liberator*, May 25, 1838.
5. Detailed description of the destruction of Pennsylvania Hall in *The Emancipator*, May 17, 1838, and *The Liberator*, May 25, 1838; also, Birney, pp. 238–42, and W. and F. Garrison, II, 215–16.
6. Angelina Grimké Weld's speech reported in full in Stanton, *et al.*, *History of Woman Suffrage*, I, 334–36.
7. W. and F. Garrison, II, 216, fn. 1.
8. Otelia Cromwell, *Lucretia Mott* (Cambridge, Mass.: Harvard University Press, 1958), p. 59.
9. Sharf and Wescott, I, 651–52. For newspaper reaction to the destruction of Pennsylvania Hall, *The Emancipator*, May 17, 1838; *The Liberator*, May 25, 1838; *The Sun* (New York), May 19, 1838.
10. Pickard, I, 234.
11. Cromwell, pp. 57–58.
12. Jos. Sturge, *A Visit to the United States in 1841* (Boston: D. S. King, 1842), p. 64. Also: Dumond, *Antislavery*, p. 227.
13. *Proceedings of the Antislavery Convention of American Women Held in Philadelphia, May 15th, 16th, 17th and 18th, 1838* (Philadelphia: Merrihew & Gunn, 1838).
14. Edward R. Turner, *The Negro in Pennsylvania; Slavery, Servitude — Freedom: 1639–1861* (Washington, D. C.: American Historical Association, 1911), pp. 184–93.
15. *Antislavery Convention of American Women*, 1838.
16. Mrs. M. Grimké to T. and A. Weld and S. Grimké, July 13, 1838, Weld MSS.
17. A. G. Weld to L. M. Child, Aug. 10, 1838, MSS Notable American Women, Gratz Collections, Pennsylvania Historical Society, Philadelphia, Pennsylvania.
18. *Weld-Grimké Letters*, II, 649.
19. A. G. Weld to Anna W. Weston, Oct. 14, 1838, Weston papers, Boston Public Library, Boston, Mass.
20. Birney, pp. 245–46.
21. A. Grimké to J. Smith, April 15, 1838, Weld MSS.
22. Isaac E. Lloyd to A. Grimké, May 14, 1838, Weld MSS. Transfer of her property to her husband is recorded on back of this letter in A. E. Grimké's handwriting, dated Nov. 18, 1838.
23. Mrs. M. Grimké to T. Weld, July 13, 1838, Weld MSS.
24. *Weld-Grimké Letters*, II, 698–700, 708.
25. *Ibid.*, II, 683–85.
26. S. Grimké, Letter on Prejudice, dated April 10, 1839. The letter by Sarah Douglass to Wm. Bassett is reprinted in *Weld-Grimké Letters*, II, 829–32.
27. Mrs. M. Grimké to Sarah Grimké, March 10, 1839 and May 28, 1839, Weld MSS.

28. Eliza Grimké to A. G. Weld, May 2, 1838; Mrs. M. Grimké to T. and A. Weld and S. Grimké, Nov. 16, 1838, both in Weld MSS.
29. The events relating to Stephen are in letters from Mrs. Grimké to T. and A. Weld and S. Grimké dated April 13, 1839, May 28, 1839, June 18, 1839, all in Weld MSS.
30. American Slavery As It Is, p. 9.
31. Both quotes Weld-Grimké Letters, II, 718.
32. S. M. Grimké, Letter on Prejudice, p. 1.
33. Birney, pp. 258–59.
34. American Slavery As It Is, p. 111.
35. Ibid., p. 55.
36. Ibid., p. 57.
37. Thomas, pp. 222–23.
38. A. Frost to A. G. Weld, July 31 and August 14, 1839, Weld MSS.
39. A. G. Weld to A. Frost, Aug. 18, 1839, Grimké-Weld Personal Papers, Library of Congress, Washington, D. C.

CHAPTER SIXTEEN

1. Barnes, pp. 134–35.
2. Aptheker, Documentary History, Parts I and II, passim.
3. For a detailed account of the petition campaigns see Barnes, chaps. 11–14; also: Dumond, Antislavery, chap. 29. For details on women's petitions see Minutes, Philadelphia Female Anti-Slavery Society, 1833–1838, passim.
4. A. Grimké, Appeal to the Christian Women of the South, p. 26.
5. Barnes, p. 143.
6. Betsy Newton to Maria W. Chapman, July 28, 1837, Weston Papers, Vol. IX.
7. Abby Kelley to Maria W. Chapman, Nov. 25, 1839, Weston Papers, Vol. IX.
8. L. M. Child, Letters, p. 31.
9. Juliana Tappan to Anne Weston, July 21, 1837, Weston Papers, Vol. IX.
10. S. Grimké to Jane Smith, Jan. 24, 1839, Weld MSS.
11. Congressional Globe, 24th Congress, p. 337.
12. For a detailed discussion of the debates and votes on the various "gag rules" see Barnes, chap. 11.
13. Dumond, Antislavery, p. 245 and n. 7, and Barnes, p. 266, n. 35.
14. Barnes, p. 266, n. 39 and n. 35; p. 145.
15. Birney, pp. 248–50.
16. Abby Kelley to Anne Weston, May 29, 1839, Weston Papers, Vol. XI.
17. A. G. Weld to Eliz. Pease, Aug. 14, 1839, Garrison MSS.
18. Weld-Grimké Letters, II, 779–80, 791.
19. A. G. Weld to Jane Smith, Jan. 20, 1840, Weld MSS.
20. Birney, pp. 260–61. Also, Stanton, Eighty Years, p. 114.
21. S. Grimké to Jane Smith, March 14, 1839, Weld MSS.
22. Weld-Grimké Letters, II, 833. For further details on financial crisis in the antislavery movement see Barnes, pp. 149–52.
23. Weld expected to prepare a pamphlet on this subject, but the project never materialized.
24. A. G. Weld to Jane Smith, Oct. 19, 1840, Weld MSS.
25. For material on the split in the antislavery movement I have drawn on Barnes, Filler, Dumond, Elkins, Garrison and manuscript sources.
26. Weld-Grimké Letters, II, 834.
27. ·Information about the birth of Theodore in S. Grimké to Jane Smith, Jan. 3, 1841, Weld MSS. Second quote from A. G. Weld to Jane Smith, Feb. 7, 1841, Weld MSS.

28. Weld, In Memory, p. 43; Birney, pp. 241, 261.
29. S. Grimké to Harriot Hunt, Dec. 20, 1854, Weld MSS.
30. Weld, In Memory, p. 50.
31. Abby Kelley to Anne Weston, May 29, 1839, Weston Papers, Vol. XI.

CHAPTER SEVENTEEN

1. Stanton, Eighty Years, pp. 31–33.
2. Stanton, et al., History of Woman Suffrage, I, 392.
3. The material on the World Anti-Slavery Convention is based on: Stanton, et al., History of Woman Suffrage, I, 53–62; W. and F. Garrison, II, 366–404; Cromwell, p. 223; Filler, Crusade, pp. 137–38; and Barnes, pp. 171–72.
4. Cromwell, pp. 84–88; W. and F. Garrison, II, 375–76, 388; Stanton, Eighty Years, pp. 85–87.
5. Stanton, Eighty Years, pp. 82–83.
6. Weld-Grimké Letters, II, 845–48.
7. S. Grimké to Eliz. Pease, Nov. 16, 1840, Garrison MSS. Vol. X, Boston Public Library.
8. A. G. Weld to Jane Smith, Feb. 7, 1841, and A. G. Weld and S. Grimké to T. Weld, Aug. 19, 1841, both Weld MSS.
9. References to Stephen occur throughout the correspondence of the years 1841–42 and are too numerous to mention here.
10. Weld-Grimké Letters, II, 861, 876–77.
11. Description of the·Washington antislavery campaign based on Thomas, chap. 14, and Weld-Grimké Letters, II, 880–938; also, J. F. Adams, J. Q. Adams Diary, XI, 72–86 passim.
12. Weld-Grimké Letters, II, 881.
13. Ibid., 872–82.
14. Letters A. G. Weld to T. Weld from Aug. 1841 to Feb. 1842, Weld MSS.
15. Weld-Grimké Letters, II, 890, 906–907.
16. Ibid., 899, 913.
17. George W. Julian, The Life of Joshua Giddings (Chicago: A. C. McClurg, 1892), p. 111.
18. Weld quote in Weld-Grimké Letters, II, 923.
19. A. G. Weld to T. Weld, Jan. 1, 1848, Weld MSS.
20. Letters in Weld MSS covering period from Jan. to March 1843.
21. Merle Curti, The Growth of American Thought (New York and London: Harper & Bros., 1943), p. 311.
22. A. G. Weld to Sarah Grimké, January 1845, Grimké-Weld Personal Papers, Library of Congress.
23. Francis Stone to Lucy Stone, June 6, 1847, and Luther Stone to Lucy Stone, June 1, 1847, Blackwell-Stone Papers, Library of Congress.
24. Stanton, Eighty Years, pp. 147–48.
25. Thomas, p. 218.
26. S. Grimké to Sarah Douglass, Oct. 25, 1848, Weld MSS; and Birney, pp. 262–63.
27. Weld-Grimké Letters, II, 999.
28. Ibid., 1005.
29. Dwight L. Dumond (ed.), Letters of James Gillespie Birney: 1831–1857 (2 vols.; New York: D. Appleton-Century Co., 1938), II, 662.
30. Blackwell, pp. 126–29.
31. Ibid., p. 129. Henry Blackwell's favorable description of the Welds' marriage was undoubtedly designed to convince Lucy Stone that marriage to him need not interfere with her reform activities. It must have been con-

vincing, for Lucy Stone became his wife and remained, all her life, an active feminist leader.
32. A. Weld to T. Weld with note to children, 1849, Weld MSS.
33. S. Grimké to Harriot Hunt, Oct. 14, 1848, Weld MSS.
34. Account Book of Theodore Weld, 1850–1860, Education Box, Manuscripts, New York Public Library.

CHAPTER EIGHTEEN

1. This is the "sanitarium" Catherine Birney genteelly has reference to and which has given rise to the belief, through the misunderstanding of later historians, that Angelina Grimké passed some time in a mental institution. She did not and perhaps this correction will belatedly serve to restore her reputation, at least in so far as her mental health is concerned.
2. S. Grimké to Augustus and Sarah Wattles, Nov. 12 [probably 1853], Weld MSS.
3. Provisional Prospectus of Raritan Bay Union, Perth Amboy, N. J., Jan. 1, 1853, Weld MSS.
4. Arthur E. Bestor, Backwoods Utopias (Philadelphia: University of Pennsylvania Press, 1950), p. 240. Also: John Humphrey Noyes, History of American Socialism (New York: Hillary House Publications, 1961, exact reprint of the 1870 edition), pp. 449–511.
5. Prospectus of Raritan Bay Union.
6. A. Weld to Mary Grimké, with note by Sarah Grimké, ca. 1853 [probably 1852], Weld MSS.
7. Ibid.
8. A. Weld to Harriot Hunt, April 10 [probably 1853], Weld Miscellaneous Papers, Library of Congress.
9. Ibid.
10. S. Grimké to Harriot Hunt, Dec. 31, 1852, Weld MSS.
11. The preceding account of Sarah's career choices is based on many references in the letters of that period in the Weld MSS. See also: S. Grimké to Ellis Gray Loring, Feb. 10, 1856, Lydia M. Child Letters, Personal Misc. Box 2, Manuscripts, New York Public Library.
12. Harriot K. Hunt, M.D., Glances and Glimpses or Fifty Years Social Including Twenty Years Professional Life (Boston: Jewett & Co., 1856), passim. On tax protest, see: Stanton, et. al., History of Woman Suffrage, I, 226ff.
13. Hunt, Glances, Dedication page.
14. S. Grimké to H. Hunt, 1850–59 [1853], Weld MSS.
15. A. Weld to S. Grimké, 1853, Weld MSS.
16. Ibid., March 26, 1854, Weld MSS.
17. A. Weld to S. Grimk, ca. 1854 [probably March], Weld MSS.
18. S. Grimké to H. Hunt, Dec. 31, 1852, Weld MSS.
19. S. Grimké to H. Hunt, Dec. 20, 1854, Weld MSS.
20. Maude Honeyman Greene, "Raritan Bay Union, Eagleswood, New Jersey," Proceedings of the New Jersey Historical Society, LXVIII, #1, Jan. 1950, 1–20.
21. Information on teachers: Account book, T. Weld, N. Y. Public Library. On E. Peabody: Ruth M. Baylor, Elizabeth Palmer Peabody: Kindergarten Pioneer (Philadelphia: University of Pennsylvania Press, 1965), p. 37. Correspondence of Ellen Wright in Garrison Collection, Sophia Smith Collection, Smith College, Northampton, Mass. On E. L. Youmans: Thomas, p. 285.
22. Moncure D. Conway, Autobiography, Memories and Experiences (2 vols.; Boston: Houghton, Mifflin & Co., 1904), I, 332.

23. Greene, "Raritan Bay Union," pp. 15–16.
24. Sarah's criticism of Raritan Bay Union occurs throughout the correspondence of the years 1853–54. The last quote is from S. Grimké to H. Hunt, Dec. 20, 1854, Weld MSS.
25. Birney, p. 274.
26. S. Grimké to A. Wattles, June 1, 1856, Weld MSS.
27. Stanton, et al., History of Woman Suffrage, I, 540.
28. S. Grimké's notebook, undated, "Condition of Woman," Weld MSS.
29. Ibid.
30. Quoted in Flexner, p. 84.
31. Birney, pp. 281–82.
32. A. Weld to Directors, Raritan Bay Union, undated [1858], Weld MSS.
33. On Frank Wright: Wright correspondence, Garrison Papers, Sophia Smith Collection. On student walkout: S. Grimké to A. Wattles, Nov. 12 [probably 1853], Weld MSS. On incident with Negro boy: S. Grimké to Theodore G. Weld, Feb. 1861, Weld MSS.
34. On Sarah's attitude toward Kansas: S. Grimké to A. Wattles, June 10, 1854, Weld MSS. On relief activity in Perth Amboy: Thomas, p. 236.
35. Birney, pp. 282–83.

CHAPTER NINETEEN

1. S. Grimké to A. Wattles, April 2, 1854, Weld MSS.
2. Thomas, p. 236.
3. A. Weld to T. G. Weld, Dec. 12, 1960, Weld MSS.
4. Theodore Weld to Mrs. Wright [copied by Mrs. Wright], March 23, 1862, Garrison Collection, Sophia Smith Collection.
5. Birney, pp. 184–85.
6. S. Grimké to . . . , Nov. 6, 1862, Weld MSS.
7. Birney, p. 185.
8. Statistical data on Grimké relatives based on Miller, Our Family Circle, pp. 21–76.
9. This work was called one of the most penetrating criticisms of abolitionist doctrine by Barnes. See Barnes, p. 270.
10. Birney, p. 289.
11. Betty Fladeland, James Gillespie Birney: Slaveholder to Abolitionist (Ithaca: Cornell University Press, 1955), p. 288.
12. Charles Weld to T. D. Weld, June 20, 1862, Weld MSS.
13. S. Grimké to Ma bien aimée, Nov. 14, 1863, Weld MSS.
14. Angelina's quote: A. Weld to Mrs. Elizabeth M. Smith, Jan. 19, 1874, Weld MSS. Information on Charles Weld's marriage: South Carolina Historical Magazine, IV, No. 4 (Jan., 1903, 50–51; also Miller, loc. cit.
15. I found no evidence to indicate, as Thomas states on p. 240, that Sody was "almost an invalid from birth."
16. E. J. C. Cutler to T. D. Weld, no date, Weld MSS.
17. E. P. Jordan to T. D. Weld, March 26, 1860; T. D. Weld to T. G. Weld, July 26, 1860; S. Grimké to T. G. Weld, April 11, 1860, all Weld MSS.
18. C. A. Coleman to Mr. and Mrs. T. D. Weld, July 4, 1860, Weld MSS.
19. C. A. Coleman to S. Grimké, July 17, 1860, Weld MSS.
20. S. Grimké to T. G. Weld, Oct. 28, 1860, Weld MSS.
21. References to Sody's illness occur throughout the years 1860–63. Reference to his later life is in William Hamilton to Anna H. Weld (Mrs. Charles Stuart Weld), Nov. 17, 1901, Weld MSS.

22. Phebe E. Hanaford, *Daughters of America or Women of the Century* (Boston: Houghton, Mifflin, & Co., 1884), p. 335.
23. *South Carolina Historical Magazine*, IV, No. 4 (Jan., 1903), 50–51; also, Miller, *loc. cit.*
24. S. Grimké to . . . , Nov. 6, 1862, Weld MSS.
25. Thomas, pp. 243–45. Angelina's quote, *ibid.*, p. 245.
26. *Ibid.*, p. 248.
27. *Ibid.*, p. 249.
28. Stanton, *et al.*, *History of Woman Suffrage*, II, 53.
29. *Ibid.*, 60–61.
30. *Ibid.*, 890.
31. Birney, p. 285.
32. S. Grimké to Dear Friend, May 28, 1863, Weld MSS.
33. Stanton, *et al.*, *History of Woman Suffrage*, I, 406.
34. Birney, p. 286.
35. A. Weld to Rebecca, 1867, Weld MSS.
36. S. Grimké to Julia Tappan, Nov. 10, 1868, Weld MSS, for Sarah's comment. S. Grimké (trans.), Alphonse M. L. de Prat de Lamartine, *Joan of Arc: A Biography* (Boston: Adams & Co., 1867).
37. Thomas, pp. 260ff.
38. A. Weld to Archibald H. Grimké, Feb. 15, 1868, Grimké Family Papers, Howard University, Washington, D. C.
39. Archibald H. Grimké to A. G. Weld, Feb. 20, 1868, Grimké Family Papers.
40. A. Weld to Archibald and Francis J. Grimké, Feb. 29, 1868, Grimké Family Papers.
41. C. G. Woodson (ed.), *Works of Francis James Grimké* (4 vols.; Washington, D. C.: Associated Publishers, 1942), I, chap. 8.

42. S. Grimké and A. Weld to A. and F. Grimké, Nov. 26, [1868], Grimké Family Papers. References to the nephews appear throughout the correspondence in the Weld MSS in the years 1868–74.
43. H. O. Houghton & Co. to S. Grimké, May 22, 1872; S. Grimké to Francis J. Garrison, Aug. 1, 1872, both in Garrison Papers, Vol. 37, Boston Public Library, Boston, Mass.
44. Reference to "Archie-fund" in S. Grimké to Ann Smith, Oct. 29, 1872, Weld MSS. Quote about nephews in S. Grimké to W. L. Garrison, Feb. 13, 1871, Garrison Papers, Boston Public Library.
45. Angelina Weld Grimké, "A Biographical Sketch of Archibald H. Grimke," *Opportunity: A Journal of Negro Life*, III (February, 1925), 45.
46. Thomas, pp. 259–60. See also: sketch on A. H. Grimké and F. J. Grimké in *Dictionary of American Biography*, VII, 632–33.
47. Stanton, *et al.*, *History of Woman Suffrage*, III, p. 268; IV, p. 702.
48. Birney, pp. 295–97. See also Stanton, *et al.*, *History of Woman Suffrage*, III, 282. Details on the voting demonstration may be found in the clippings of contemporary newspapers in the Henry A. Rich Collection, Hyde Park Historical Society, Hyde Park Branch, Boston Public Library.
49. For obituary notices see Boston *Transcript*, Oct. 28, 1879; *The Woman's Journal*, Jan. 3, 1874 and Feb. 4, 1874. A detailed description of the funerals of the sisters may be found in Weld, *In Memory*.

BIBLIOGRAPHY

Published Writings of the Grimké Sisters

Grimké, Angelina Emily. *Slavery and the Boston Riot: A Letter to Wm. L. Garrison.* Philadelphia: August 30, 1835. Broadside.

———. *Appeal to the Christian Women of the Southern States.* New York: n.n., 1836.

———. *An Appeal to the Women of the Nominally Free States; Issued by an Anti-Slavery Convention of American Women & Held by Adjournment from the 9th to the 12th of May, 1837.* 1st ed. New York: W. S. Dorr, 1837.

———. *Letters to Catherine E. Beecher, in Reply to an Essay on Slavery and Abolitionism, Addressed to A. E. Grimké.* Revised by the Author. Boston: Isaac Knapp, 1838.

———. *Letter from Angelina Grimké Weld, to the Woman's Rights Convention, held at Syracuse, September, 1852.* Syracuse: Master's print, 1852.

Grimké, Sarah Moore. *An Epistle to the Clergy of the Southern States.* New York: n.n., 1836.

———. *Letters on the Equality of the Sexes and the Condition of Woman; Addressed to Mary Parker, President of the Boston Female Anti-Slavery Society.* Boston: Isaac Knapp, 1838.

——— (trans.). Lamartine, Alphonse M. L. de Prat de. *Joan of Arc: A Biography.* Boston: Adams & Co., 1867.

[Grimké, Sarah Moore and Angelina Emily]. "A Sketch of Thomas Grimké's Life written by his Sisters in Philadelphia and sent to his Friends in Charleston for their Approbation," *The Calumet, Magazine of the American Peace Society,* II, No. 1 (Jan.-Feb., 1835).

[Grimké, Sarah Moore and Angelina Emily (eds.)]. Jonathan Dymond, *An Inquiry into the Accordancy of War with the Principles of Christianity . . . with notes by Thomas S. Grimké.* Philadelphia: I. Ashmead & Co., 1834.

Published Speeches by Angelina Emily Grimké

Speech before the Legislative Committee of the Massachusetts Legislature, Feb. 21, 1838. *The Liberator,* May 2, 1838.

Speech in Pennsylvania Hall, May 16, 1838. Stanton, Elizabeth C., Anthony, Susan B., and Gage, Matilda J. *History of Woman Suffrage.* 6 vols. New York: Fowler & Wells, 1881–1922. Vol. I, pp. 334–36.

Speech before Woman's Loyal League, May 14, 1863. Stanton, Elizabeth C., Anthony, Susan B., and Gage, Matilda J. *History of Woman Suffrage.* 6 vols. New York: Fowler & Wells, 1881–1922. Vol. II, pp. 54–56.

"Address to the Soldiers of our second Revolution." Resolution read and adopted by the Business Meeting of the Woman's Loyal National League, May 15, 1863, written by Angelina Grimké Weld. Stanton, Elizabeth C., Anthony, Susan B., and Gage, Matilda J. *History of Woman Suffrage.* 6 vols. New York: Fowler & Wells, 1881–1922. Vol. II, 890–891.

Printed Sources

Barnes, G. H., and Dumond, D. W. (eds.). *Letters of Theodore Dwight Weld. Angelina Grimké Weld and Sarah Grimké: 1822–1844.* 2 vols. New York: D. Appleton-Century Co., 1934.

Weld, Theodore Dwight. *In Memory. Angelina Grimké Weld.* Boston: G. H. Ellis, 1880.

[Weld, Theodore Dwight]. *American Slavery as it is: Testimony of a Thousand Witnesses.* New York: American Anti-Slavery Society, 1839.

Contemporary Biographies and Biographical Sketches

Birney, Catherine. *The Grimké Sisters: Sarah and Angelina Grimké: the First Women Advocates of Abolition and Woman's Rights.* Boston: Lee & Sheppard, 1885.

Austin, George Lowell. "The Grimké Sisters," *The Bay State Monthly,* III, No. 3 (August, 1885).

Stanton, Elizabeth C. "Angelina Grimké: Reminiscences," Stanton, Elizabeth C., Anthony, Susan B., and Gage, Matilda J. *History of Woman Suffrage.* 6 vols. New York: Fowler & Wells, 1881–1922. Vol. I, pp. 392–406.

Later Biographical Sources on the Sisters and on other Members of the Family

Galbraith, C. B. "Thomas Smith Grimké," *Ohio State Archaeological and Historical Quarterly,* XXXIII, No. 3 (July, 1924), 301–312.

"Genealogies of American Society: The Grimké Family of South Carolina," *Town Topics: The Journal of Society,* LXXVI, No. 13 (Sept. 28, 1916), 18.

Genealogical Tables of the Grimké and Smith Families, "Family Table, Descendants of Col. William Rhett of South Carolina," *South Carolina Historical Magazine,* III, No. 4 (January, 1903), 50–51.

Grimké, Angelina Weld. "A Biographical Sketch of Archibald H. Grimké," *Opportunity: A Journal of Negro Life,* III (February, 1925), 44–47.

Miller, A. E. *Our Family Circle.* Macon, Ga.: n.n., 1931.

Thomas, Benjamin P. *Theodore Weld: Crusader for Freedom.* New Brunswick, N. J.: Rutgers University Press, 1950.

Published Writings of Thomas Smith Grimké (selected list)

Address on the Character and Objects of Science . . . delivered . . . the 9th of May, being the Anniversary of the Literary and Philosophical Society of South Carolina. Charleston: A. E. Miller, 1827.

"Defensive War," *The Calumet: Magazine of the American Peace Society:* Part 1, Vol. II, No. 1 (Jan.-Feb., 1835); Part 2 (published posthumously), Vol. II, No. 2 (March-April, 1835).

Letter to the Honorable John C. Calhoun, Vice-President of the United States, Robert Y. Hayne, Senator of the United States, George McDuffie, of the House of Representatives of the United States and James Hamilton, Jr., Governor of the State of South Carolina. Pamphlet. Philadelphia: Thos. Kite & Co., 1832.

Oration Delivered in St. Philip's Church on the 4th of July, 1809 by the Appointment of the South Carolina State Society of the Cincinnati by Thomas Smith Grimké, Member of the Cincinnati. Charleston: n.n., 1809.

The Temperance Reformation the Cause of Christian Mor-

als: an Address delivered before the Christian Temperance Society and the Young Men's Temperance Society of Charleston on Tuesday evening, Feb. 25, 1834 in *St. Stephens's Chapel.* Pamphlet. Charleston: n.n., 1834.

Unpublished Sources

The primary manuscript source for the Grimké sisters is the Theodore Dwight Weld Collection, William L. Clements Library, The University of Michigan, Ann Arbor, Mich. Other important sources are: Garrison Papers, Boston Public Library; Weston Papers, Boston Public Library; Grimké Personal Papers and Theodore Dwight Weld Papers, Library of Congress; Garrison Papers, Sophia Smith Collection, Smith College; and Grimké Papers, New York Historical Society.

The Grimké Family Papers, Howard University, hold the correspondence concerning the sisters' nephews, Archibald and Francis Grimké. The Account Book of Theodore Weld: 1850–1860, Education Box, New York Public Library, provides information about Eagleswood School.

Letters of the sisters are also scattered in many manuscript collections. The most important of these are: Anti-Slavery Papers, Library of Congress; Lydia Maria Child Letters, New York Public Library; Gratz Collection, Pennsylvania Historical Society, Philadelphia, Pa.; Slavery Manuscripts, New York Historical Society, New York City, N. Y.; Benjamin Smith Papers, Southern Historical Collection, University of North Carolina Library, Chapel Hill, N. C.; Lewis Tappan Manuscript and Benjamin Tappan Manuscript, Library of Congress and Elizur Wright Papers, vol. 4, Library of Congress.

Other manuscript sources consulted were: The E. Kennedy Collection, Pennsylvania Historical Society; Gerrit Smith Personal Papers, Library of Congress; and Wills of John Faucheraud Grimké and Mary S. Grimké, Charleston County Free Library, Charleston, S. C.

Minutes and Proceedings

Unpublished:

Minutes, Monthly Meeting of Friends of Philadelphia, 1823–1837, Fourth and Arch Street Meeting. Arch Street Center, The Society of Friends, Philadelphia, Pa.

Minutes, Monthly Meeting of Women Friends of Philadelphia, 1823–1833, Fourth and Arch Street Meeting. Arch Street Center, The Society of Friends, Philadelphia, Pa.

Minutes, Quarterly Meetings of Philadelphia Friends, 1826–1862. Arch Street Center, The Society of Friends, Philadelphia, Pa.

Minutes, Yearly Meetings of Philadelphia Friends, 1828–1845. Arch Street Center, The Society of Friends, Philadelphia, Pa.

Minutes, Meetings of the Board of Managers, Institute for Coloured Youth. Arch Street Center, The Society of Friends, Philadelphia, Pa.

Reports of the American Anti-Slavery Society, Meetings 1–6: 1833–1839. Weston Papers, Boston Public Library.

Minutes, Executive Committee of the American Anti-Slavery Society: 1839–1841. Weston Papers, Boston Public Library.

Minutes, Committee on Agencies, American Anti-Slavery Society: 1833–1839. Weston Papers, Boston Public Library.

Minutes, Philadelphia Female Anti-Slavery Society: 1833–1839. Philadelphia Historical Society.

Published:

Proceedings, *Anti-Slavery Convention of American Women, Held by Adjournment from the 9th to the 12th of May, 1837.* New York: W. S. Dorr, 1837.

Proceedings, *Anti-Slavery Convention of American Women, Held in Philadelphia, May 15, 16, 17 and 28, 1838.* Philadelphia: Merrihew & Gunn, 1838.

"Right and Wrong in Boston." *Report of the Boston Female Anti-Slavery Society with a concise statement of events, previous and subsequent to the Annual Meeting of 1835.* Boston: Boston Female Anti-Slavery Society, 1836.

"Right and Wrong in Boston." *Annual Report of the Boston Female Anti-Slavery Society with a sketch of the obstacles thrown in the way of Emancipation by certain Clerical Abolitionists and Advocates for the subjection of woman in 1837.* Boston: Boston Female Anti-Slavery Society, 1837.

Sixth Annual Report of the Board of Managers of the Massachusetts Anti-Slavery Society, presented Jan. 24, 1838, with an appendix. Boston: Isaac Knapp, 1838.

Newspapers and Journals

The American Anti-Slavery Almanac, 1836–41. American Anti-Slavery Society.

The Anti-Slavery Examiner, 1836–45.

The Anti-Slavery Record, 1835 and 1837.

The Calumet: Magazine of the American Peace Society, 1835.

Daily Advertiser (Boston), 1828–48.

The Emancipator, 1838–40.

Evening Transcript (Boston), 1879.

The Friend; a religious and literary journal, 1829–35.

The Liberator, 1835–38.

The Liberty Bell, 1839–58.

The Lily, 1854–55.

The National Enquirer, Jan. 1837.

The National Era, 1852.

The National Intelligencer, 1835.

The Olive Branch, 1837, and scattered issues to 1856.

Henry Rich Collection, local newspaper clippings, Boston Public Library, Hyde Park Branch.

South Carolina Historical and Genealogical Magazine, 1901–1930.

For background material pertaining to the Grimké sisters' speaking tour, the following were consulted:

Boston Evening Transcript, 1837.

Boston Independent Messenger, 1837.

Boston Mercantile Journal, 1837.

Boston Morning Post, 1837–38.

Boston Recorder, 1837–39.

New York The Colored American, 1837–38.

New York Evening Post, 1837.

New York New Yorker, 1837.

New York Spectator, 1837.

New York Sun, 1837–38.

Philadelphia Gazette, 1837–38.

Springfield Gazette, 1837–38.

Biographies, Published Correspondence and Writings of Contemporaries

Adams, Charles F. (ed.). *Memoirs of John Quincy Adams: comprising portions of his diary from 1795 to 1848.* 12 vols. Philadelphia: J. B. Lippincott Co., 1876.

Alcott, William A. *The Young Woman's Guide to Excellence.* Boston: Dexter S. King, 1842.

Ball, George. *Fifty Years in Chains or, The Life of an American Slave* . . . New York: H. Dayton, 1859.

Beecher, Catherine. *An Essay on Slavery and Abolitionism with reference to the Duty of American Females.* Philadelphia: Henry Perkins, 1837.

Beecher, Catherine E., and Stowe, Harriet Beecher. *The American Woman's Home: or, Principles of Domestic Science; being a Guide to the Formation and Maintenance of economical, healthful, beautiful, and Christian Homes.* New York: J. B. Ford & Co., 1869.

Bremer, Fredrika. *Homes of the New World: Impressions of America.* New York: Harper & Bros., 1854.

Cartland, Fernando G. *Southern Heroes or The Friends in War Time.* Poughkeepsie, N. Y.: F. G. Cartland, 1897.

Child, Lydia Maria. *Isaac T. Hooper: A true Life.* Boston: J. P. Jewett, 1853.

———. *Letters.* Boston: Houghton, Mifflin & Co., 1883.

———. *Letters from New York.* 2 vols. 3rd ed. New York: C. S. Francis & Co., 1845.

———. *The Mother's Book.* 6th ed. with corrections and additions by the author. New York: C. S. Francis & Co., 1846.

Coffin, Levi. *Reminiscences.* Cincinnati: The Robert Clarke Co., 1898.

Conway, Moncure Daniel. *Autobiography, Memories and Experiences.* 2 vols. Boston: Houghton, Mifflin & Co., 1904.

[Cooper, Thomas (ed.)]. South Carolina, Statutes. *The Statutes at large of South Carolina.* 14 vols. Columbia, S. C.: 1836–73. Vols. 1–5 edited under authority of the legislature by Thomas Cooper.

Cross, Barbara M. (ed.). *The Autobiography of Lyman Beecher.* 2 vols. Cambridge: Harvard University Press, 1961.

Doggett, John, Jr. *The Great Metropolis: New York in 1845.* New York: S. W. Benedict & Co., 1845.

Dumond, Dwight L. (ed.). *Letters of James Gillespie Birney: 1831–1857.* New York: D. Appleton-Century Co., 1938.

Emerson, Sarah Hopper. *Life of Abby Hopper Gibbons.* 2 vols. New York: G. P. Putnam's Sons, 1897.

Fitzhugh, George. *A Sociology for the South: or, The Failure of Free Society.* Richmond: A. Morris, 1857.

———. *Cannibals All! or, Slaves without Masters.* Richmond: A. Morris, 1857.

Foner, Philip (ed.). *The Life and Writings of Frederick Douglass.* 4 vols. New York: International Publishers, 1950.

Foxe, John. *Book of Martyrs* . . . *now improved by important alterations and additions by Rev. Charles A. Goodrich.* Hartford, Conn.: P. Canfield, 1830.

Fraser, Charles. *Reminiscences of Charleston: lately published in the Charleston Courier, and now revised and enlarged by the author* . . . Charleston: J. Russell, 1854.

Frothingham, Octavius Brooks. *Gerrit Smith: A Biography.* New York: G. P. Putnam's Sons, 1879.

Garden, Alexander. *Anecdotes of the American Revolution, with Sketches of Characters of Persons the most Distinguished in the Southern states, for Civil and Military Services* . . . Charleston: Printed for the author by A. E. Miller, 1822.

Garrison, Wendell P. and Francis J. *William Lloyd Garrison: 1805–1879: The Story of His Life told by his Children.* 4 vols. New York: The Century Co., 1885–1889.

Goodell, William. *Slavery and Anti-Slavery.* New York: W. Harned, 1852.

Grimké, Archibald Henry. *The Life of Charles Sumner: the Scholar in Politics.* New York: Funk & Wagnalls, 1892.

———. *William Lloyd Garrison, the Abolitionist.* London: Funk & Wagnalls, 1891.

Hallowell, Anna Davis. *James and Lucretia Mott.* Boston: Houghton, Mifflin & Co., 1884.

Hanaford, Phebe E. *Daughters of America or Women of the Century.* Augusta, Me.: True & Co., 1882.

Hayne, Paul H. *Lives of Robert Young Hayne and Hugh S. Legaré.* Charleston: Walker, Evans & Cogswell, 1878.

Higginson, Thomas Wentworth. *Contemporaries.* Boston: Houghton, Mifflin & Co., 1898.

———. *Women and the Alphabet: A Series of Essays.* Boston: Houghton, Mifflin & Co., 1878.

Hunt, Harriot Kezia, M.D. *Glances and Glimpses or Fifty Years Social including Twenty Years Professional Life.* Boston: Jewett & Co., 1856.

Hurd, John C. *Law of Freedom and Bondage: Slave Laws of South Carolina.* 2 vols. Boston: Little, Brown & Co., 1858.

Janney, Samuel M. *History of the Religious Society of Friends from its rise to the year 1828.* 4 vols. Philadelphia: Ellwood Zell, 1867.

Johnson, Oliver. *William Lloyd Garrison and His Times.* Boston: B. B. Russell & Co., 1880.

Julian, George W. *The Life of Joshua Giddings.* Chicago: A. C. McClurg, 1892.

Livermore, Mary. *The Story of my Life or The Sunshine and Shadow of Seventy Years.* Hartford, Conn.: A. D. Worthington & Co., 1897.

Lovell, Malcom R. (ed.). *Two Quaker Sisters: From the original Diaries of Elizabeth Buffum Chace and Lucy Buffum Lovell.* New York: Liveright Publishing Co., 1937.

Martineau, Harriet. *The Martyr Age of the United States.* Boston: Weeks, Jordan & Co., 1839.

———. *Society in America.* 2 vols. New York: Saunders & Otley, 1837.

May, Samuel Joseph. *Memoir.* Boston: Robert Bros., 1873.

———. *Some Recollections of the Antislavery Conflict.* Boston: Fields, Osgood & Co., 1869.

Nevins, Allan (ed.). *The Diary of John Quincy Adams: 1794–1845.* New York: Chas. Scribner's Sons, 1951.

Noyes, John Humphrey. *History of American Socialisms.* New York: Hillary House Publ., 1869. Exact reprint of the 1870 ed.

O'Neall, J. B. *Biographical Sketches of Bench and Bar in South Carolina.* 2 vols. Charleston: S. G. Courtney & Co., 1859.

Parton, James (ed.). *Eminent Women of the Age.* Hartford: S. M. Betts & Co., 1869.

Pickard, Samuel T. (ed.). *Life and Letters of John Greenleaf Whittier.* 2 vols. Boston: Houghton, Mifflin & Co., 1894.

Pillsbury, Parker. *Acts of the Anti-Slavery Apostles.* Concord, N. H.: Clague, Wegman, Schlict & Co., 1883.

Randolph, Jacob, M.D. *A Memoir on the life and character of Phillip Syng Physick, M.D.* Philadelphia: T. K. & P. G. Collins, 1839.

Sanborn, F. B. *Recollections of seventy years.* 2 vols. Boston: Richard F. Badger, 1909.

Schenck, J. H. *Descriptive Guide of Long Branch, N. J.* New York: Trow & Smith Co., 1868.

Scott, John A. (ed.). *Frances Anne Kemble: Journal of a*

Residence on a Georgian Plantation in 1838–1839. New York: Alfred A. Knopf, 1961.

Sharf, Thos., and Westcott, Thompson. *History of Philadelphia; 1609–1884*. 3 vols. Philadelphia: L. H. Everts & Co., 1884.

Simms, William G. *The History of South Carolina, from its first European Discovery to its Erection into a Republic* . . . Charleston: S. Babcock & Co., 1840.

Smith, D. E. Huger. *A Charlestonian's Recollections: 1846–1913*. Charleston: Carolina Art Association, 1950.

Southwick, Sarah H. *Reminiscences of Early Anti-Slavery Days*. Cambridge, Mass.: Privately printed, 1893. Only 150 copies.

Stanton, Elizabeth C., Anthony. Susan B., and Gage, Matilda J. *History of Woman Suffrage*. 6 vols. New York: Fowler & Wells, 1881–1922.

Stanton, Elizabeth Cady. *Eighty Years and More*. London: T. Fisher Unwin, 1898.

Still, William. *The Underground Railroad*. Philadelphia: People's Publ. Co., 1879.

Stowe, Harriet Beecher. *A Key to Uncle Tom's Cabin: presenting the original facts and documents upon which the story is founded* . . . Boston: J. P. Jewett & Co., 1853.

Sturge, Joseph. *A Visit to the United States in 1841*. Boston: D. S. King, 1842.

Tappan, Lewis. *The Life of Arthur Tappan*. New York: Hurd & Houghton, 1870.

Thompson, George. *Lectures of George Thompson* . . . Boston: Isaac Knapp, 1836.

———. *Letters and Addresses by George Thompson; During his Mission in the United States from Oct. 1, 1834 to Nov. 27, 1835*. Boston: Isaac Knapp, 1837.

Tiffany, Nina M. *Samuel E. Sewall: A Memoir*. Boston: Houghton, Mifflin & Co., 1898.

Williams, Ben Ames (ed.). *Mary Boykin Chesnut: A Diary from Dixie*. Boston: Houghton Mifflin Co., 1961.

Woolman, John. *A Journal of the Life, Gospel Labours and Christian Experiences of that faithful Minister of Jesus Christ, John Woolman, Late of Mt. Holly in the Province of New Jersey, North America*. London: W. Phillips, 1824.

[Wright, Frances or D'Arusmont, Frances]. *Views of Society and Manners in America: in a series of letters from that country to a friend in England during the years 1818, 1819, and 1820 by an Englishwoman*. New York: E. Bliss and E. White, 1821.

Wright, Henry C. *Human Life: illustrated in my individual Experience as a Child, a Youth and a Man*. Boston: B. Marsh, 1849.

———. *Marriage and Parentage: on the reproductive element in man, as a means to his elevation and happiness*. Boston: B. Marsh, 1866.

Books (Selected list)

Aptheker, Herbert (ed.). *A Documentary History of the Negro People in the United States*. New York: The Citadel Press, 1951.

Barnes, Gilbert H. *The Antislavery Impulse: 1830–1844*. New York: D. Appleton-Century Co., 1933.

Bartlett, Irving H. *Wendell Phillips: Brahmin Radical*. Boston: Beacon Press, 1961.

Baylor, Ruth M. *Elizabeth Palmer Peabody: Kindergarten Pioneer*. Philadelphia: University of Pennsylvania Press, 1965.

Beard, Mary (ed.). *America through Woman's Eyes*. New York: The Macmillan Co., 1934.

Bemis, Samuel Flagg. *John Quincy Adams and the Union*. New York: Alfred A. Knopf, 1956.

Bestor, Arthur E. *Backwoods Utopias*. Philadelphia: University of Pennsylvania Press, 1950.

Birney, William. *James G. Birney and His Times*. New York: D. Appleton & Co., 1890.

Blackwell, Alice. *Lucy Stone: Pioneer of Woman's Rights*. Boston: Little, Brown & Co., 1930.

Bowes, Frederick P. *The Culture of Early Charleston*. Chapel Hill: University of North Carolina Press, 1942.

Brodie, Fawn M. *Thaddeus Stevens: Scourge of the South*. New York: W. W. Norton & Co., 1959.

Calhoun, Arthur W. *A Social History of the American Family*. 3 vols. Cleveland: The Arthur H. Clark Co., 1918.

Cardozo, Jacob Newton. *Reminiscences of Charleston*. Charleston: J. Walker, 1860.

Chadwick, John White. *Theodore Parker: preacher and reformer*. Boston: Houghton, Mifflin & Co., 1900.

Cromwell, Otelia. *Lucretia Mott*. Cambridge: Harvard University Press, 1958.

Curti, Merle. *The Growth of American Thought*. New York: Harper & Bros., 1943.

Curtis, John G. *History of the Town of Brookline*. Boston: Houghton Mifflin & Co., 1933.

Donald, David. *Lincoln Reconsidered*. New York: Alfred A. Knopf, 1956.

Drake, Thomas E. *Quakers and Slavery in America*. New Haven: Yale University Press, 1950.

Dumond, Dwight D. *Antislavery Origins of the Civil War in the United States*. Ann Arbor: The University of Michigan Press, 1939.

———. *Antislavery: The Crusade for Freedom in America*. Ann Arbor: The University of Michigan Press, 1961.

Eberlein, H. D., and Hubbard, C. V. *Portrait of a Colonial City: Philadelphia, 1670–1838*. Philadelphia: J. B. Lippincott Co., 1939.

Elkins, Stanley M. *Slavery: A Problem in American Institutional and Intellectual Life*. 2nd ed. New York: Grosset & Dunlap, 1963.

Filler, Louis. *The Crusade against Slavery: 1830–1860*. New York: Harper & Bros., 1960.

Fladeland, Betty. *James Gillespie Birney: Slaveholder to Abolitionist*. Ithaca: Cornell University Press, 1955.

Flexner, Eleanor. *Century of Struggle: The Woman's Rights Movement in the United States*. Cambridge: Harvard University Press, 1959.

Friends Historical Society. *The Friends' Meeting House: Fourth and Arch Street*. Philadelphia: The J. Winston Co., 1904.

Harlow, Ralph Volney. *Gerrit Smith: Philanthropist and Reformer*. New York: H. Holt & Co., 1939.

Hart, A. B. *Slavery and Abolition: 1831–1841*. New York: Harper & Bros., 1906.

Harveson, Mary E. *Catherine Esther Beecher, Pioneer Educator*. Philadelphia: University of Pennsylvania Press, 1932.

Hays, Elinor R. *Morningstar: A Biography of Lucy Stone, 1818–1893*. New York: Harcourt, Brace & World, Inc., 1961.

Hofstadter, Richard. *The American Political Tradition and the Men who made it*. New York: Alfred A. Knopf, 1948.

Johnson, Guion G. *Antebellum North Carolina*. Chapel Hill: University of North Carolina Press, 1937.

Korngold, Ralph. *Two Friends of Man: William Lloyd Garrison and Wendell Phillips and their Relationship to Abraham Lincoln.* Boston: Little, Brown & Co., 1950.

Lauer, Dr. Conrad N. *William Penn's Philadelphia — in 1840: A Newcomen Address.* Princeton: Princeton University Press, 1940.

Leiding, Harriet K. *Charleston, historic and romantic.* Philadelphia: J. B. Lippincott Co., 1931.

Litwack, Leon F. *North of Slavery: The Negro in the free States, 1790–1860.* Chicago: The University of Chicago Press, 1961.

Macy, Jesse. *The Antislavery Crusade.* New Haven: Yale University Press, 1919.

McKitrick, Eric L. (ed.). *Slavery Defended: the Views of the Old South.* Englewood Cliffs, N. J.: Prentice-Hall Inc., 1963.

McPherson, James. *The Struggle for Equality: Abolitionists and the Negro in the Civil War and Reconstruction.* Princeton: Princeton University Press, 1964.

Mead, Frank S. *Handbook of Denominations in the United States.* New York: Abingdon Press, 1956.

Merrill, Walter M. *Against Wind and Tide: A Biography of William Lloyd Garrison.* Cambridge: Harvard University Press, 1963.

Molloy, Robert. *Charleston: A Gracious Heritage.* Charleston: Appleton-Century Co., 1947.

Moon, Robert Charles. *The Morris Family of Philadelphia, descendants of Anthony Morris . . . 5 vols.* Philadelphia: R. C. Moon, 1898–1909.

Morgan, George. *History of Philadelphia: The City of Firsts.* Philadelphia: Published by the Historical Society in Philadelphia, 1926.

Muelder, Herman R. *Fighters for Freedom: The History of the Anti-Slavery Activities of Men and Women associated with Knox College.* New York: Columbia University Press, 1959.

Nelson, Wm. (ed.). *The New Jersey Coast in 3 Centuries.* 2 vols. New York: Lewis Publishing Co., 1902.

Nye, Russell B. *Wm. Lloyd Garrison and the Humanitarian Reformers.* Boston: Little, Brown & Co., 1955.

O'Connor, Lillian. *Pioneer Women Orators.* New York: Columbia University Press, 1954.

Pickard, Samuel T. *Whittier-Land.* Boston: Houghton, Mifflin & Co., 1904.

Pollard, John A. *John Greenleaf Whittier: Friend of Man.* Boston: Houghton Mifflin Co., 1949.

Ravenel, Harriott H. [Mrs. St. Julien]. *Charleston: the Place and the People.* New York: The Macmillan Co., 1906.

Rhea, Linda. *Hugh Swinton Legaré.* Durham: University of North Carolina Press, 1934.

Riegel, Robert. *American Feminists.* Lawrence: University of Kansas Press, 1963.

Robert, Joseph C. *The Road from Monticello: A Study of the Virginia Slavery Debate of 1832.* "Historical Papers of the Trinity College Historical Society," Series XXIV. Durham: Duke University Press, 1941.

Ruchames, Louis (ed.). *The Abolitionists.* New York: G. P. Putnam's Sons, 1963.

Russell, Elbert. *History of Quakerism.* New York: The Macmillan Co., 1942.

Savage, W. S. *The Controversy over the Distribution of Abolitionist Literature.* Washington, D. C.: Association for the Study of Negro Life & History, 1938.

Schlesinger, Arthur M. *New Viewpoints in American History.* New York: The Macmillan Co., 1928.

Schlesinger, Arthur M., Jr. *The Age of Jackson.* Boston: Little, Brown & Co., 1945.

Seldes, Gilbert V. *The Stammering Century.* New York: The John Day Co., 1928.

Sinclair, Andrew. *The Better Half: The Emancipation of the American Woman.* New York: Harper & Row, 1965.

Smith, William Henry. *A Political History of Slavery.* 2 vols. New York: G. P. Putnam's Sons, 1903.

Speakman, Thomas H. *Divisions in the Society of Friends.* 2d ed. Philadelphia: J. B. Lippincott Co., 1893.

Suhl, Yuri. *Ernestine L. Rose and the Battle for Human Rights.* New York: Reynal & Co., 1959.

Sweet, William W. *The Story of Religions in America.* New York: Harper & Bros., 1939.

Symes, Lillian, and Travers, Clement. *Rebel America: The Story of Social Revolt in the United States.* New York: Harper & Bros., 1934.

Tannenbaum, Frank. *Slave and Citizen.* New York: Alfred A. Knopf, 1947.

Taylor, William R. *Cavalier and Yankee: The Old South and American National Character.* Garden City, N. Y.: Doubleday & Co., Anchor Books, 1963.

Thomas, John L. *The Liberator: William Lloyd Garrison: A Biography.* Boston: Little, Brown & Co., 1963.

Thorp, Margaret F. *Female Persuasion: Six strong-minded Women.* New Haven: Yale University Press, 1949.

Turner, Edward R. *The Negro in Pennsylvania: Slavery, Servitude, Freedom: 1639–1861.* Washington, D. C.: American Historical Assoc., 1911.

Tyler, Alice Felt. *Freedom's Ferment: Phases of American Social History to 1860.* Minneapolis: University of Minnesota Press, 1944.

United States Works Progress Administration, New Jersey, Writers' Project. *Entertaining a Nation: The Career of Long Branch.* Bayonne, N. J.: The Jersey Printing Co., 1940.

Weisberger, Bernard. *They gathered at the River: The Story of the Great Revivalists and their Impact upon Religion in America.* Boston: Little, Brown & Co., 1958.

White, Laura A. *Robert Barnwell Rhett: Father of Secession.* New York: Century Co., 1931.

Wilson, Forrest. *Crusader in Crinolines.* Philadelphia: J. B. Lippincott Co., 1941.

Wolf, Hazel. *On Freedom's Altar: The Martyr Complex in the Abolition Movement.* Madison: The University of Wisconsin Press, 1952.

Woodson, Carter G. *Negro Orators and their Orations.* Washington, D. C.: The Associated Publishers, 1925.

———. *The Education of the Negro, prior to 1861: A History of the Education of the Colored People of the United States from the Beginning of Slavery to the Civil War.* New York: G. P. Putnam's Sons, 1915.

Woody, Thomas. *History of Women's Education in the United States.* 2 vols. New York: The Science Press, 1929.

Articles

Cadbury, Henry J. "Negro Membership in the Society of Friends," *Journal of Negro History,* XXI, No. 2 (April, 1936), 151–213.

Charvat, Wm. "American Romanticism and the Depression of 1837," *Science and Society,* II (Winter, 1937), 67–82.

Curti, Merle. "Non-Resistance in New England," *The New England Quarterly Review*, II, No. 1 (January, 1929), 34–57.

Dillon, Merton L. "The Failure of American Abolitionists," *Journal of Southern History*, XXV, No. 2 (May, 1959), 159–77.

Greene, Maud Honeyman. "Raritan Bay Union, Eagleswood, New Jersey," *Proceedings of the New Jersey Historical Society*, LXVIII, No. 1 (January, 1950), 1–20.

Jackson, Norman B. "The Free Produce Attack upon Slavery," *The Pennsylvania Magazine of History and Biography*, LXVI, No. 3 (July, 1942), 294–313.

Quarles, Benjamin. "Sources of Abolitionist Income," *Mississippi Valley Historical Review*, XXXII, No. 3 (July, 1945), 63–76.

Ruchames, Louis. "Race, Marriage, Abolition in Massachusetts," *Journal of Negro History*, XL, No. 3 (July, 1955), 250–73.

Shanks, Carolina. "The Biblical Anti-Slavery Argument," *Journal of Negro History*, XVI, No. 2 (April, 1931), 132–57.

Shryock, Richard H. "Sylvester Graham and the Popular Health Movement, 1830–1870," *Mississippi Valley Historical Review*, XVIII, No. 2 (September, 1931), 172–80.

Thompson, R. "The Liberty Bell and other anti-slavery Gift Books," *The New England Quarterly Review*, VII, No. 1 (January, 1934), 154–62.

Zorn, Roman J. "The New England Anti-Slavery Society: Pioneer Abolition Organization," *Journal of Negro History*, XLIII (July, 1957), 157–76.

INDEX

abolitionists, 165, 194, 227; at Eagleswood School, 330–331; Judge Grimké's opposition to, 342; sectarianism among, 333; nominating convention at Albany, 285; "triumph" of, 356; *see also* American Anti-Slavery Society; anti-slavery movement

Adams, John Quincy, visited by Garrison and Grimké sisters, 166–168; at dedication of Pennsylvania Hall, 244; opposes gag rule, 274; on petitions to Congress, 275; mentioned, 301, 303–304

Adams, Rev. Nehemiah, 189

Address to Free Colored Americans (Sarah Grimké), 162

Africa colonization proposal, 57

Albany, N.Y., abolitionist nominating convention at, 285

Alcott, Abba, 129

Alcott, Bronson, 129, 328, 330

Allegheny Democrat, 95

American and Foreign Anti-Slavery Society, 286

American Anti-Slavery Society, 181, 208, 234, 351; Agents' Convention, 148–152; Boston lectures for, 163; convention in New York, 239; effect of, 269; female delegates to, 299; financial difficulties, 281; formation of, 109, 113, 150; Garrisonians' reorganization of, 286; "immediatism" of, on slavery question, 114–115; invitation to Angelina G. to speak, 137; Negro participation in, 115; New York Executive Committee, 148, 181, 197–198, 212, 283; petitions to Congress, 271–272, 275; Philadelphia convention, 121; publication of Angelina's *Appeal to the Christian Women*, 141–142; refutes arguments against abolition, 261; Theodore Weld as director of, 220; on woman's rights, 199; *see also* Female Anti-Slavery Society

American Colonization Society, 56–57, 170, 184–185

American Negro Academy, 365

American Peace Society, 108, 118

American Revolution, 53, 108

American Slavery As It Is (Weld), 99, 263, 266, 270, 275

American Sunday School Society, 176

Amesbury, Mass., slavery debates in, 178–180

Amesbury *Morning Courier*, 179–180

Andover, Mass., abolition society in, 227

Andover College, 174, 176

Andover Female Anti-Slavery Society, 190

Andover Theological Seminary, 190

Andrews, Sherlock, 302

Anthony, Susan B., 12, 334, 352